W9-ALJ-534

BOOM TOWN

SAM ANDERSON

BOOM TOWN

THE FANTASTICAL SAGA OF

OKLAHOMA CITY, ITS CHAOTIC FOUNDING,

ITS APOCALYPTIC WEATHER,

ITS PURLOINED BASKETBALL TEAM,

AND THE DREAM OF BECOMING A

WORLD-CLASS METROPOLIS

CROWN
NEW YORK

Be Free, A Way
Always There . . . In Our Hearts
Look . . . The Sun Is Rising
Try To Explain
Words and Music by Wayne Coyne and Steven Drozd
Copyright © 2013 Lovely Sorts Of Death
All Rights Administered by BMG Rights Management (US) LLC
All Rights Reserved Used by Permission
Reprinted by Permission of Hal Leonard LLC

Library of Congress Cataloging-in-Publication Data
Name: Anderson, Sam, 1977– author.
Title: Boom town : the fantastical saga of Oklahoma City, its chaotic
    founding . . . its purloined basketball team, and the dream of becoming
    a world-class metropolis / Sam Anderson.
Description: New York : Crown, 2018.
Identifiers: LCCN 2017054583 (print) | LCCN 2018011488 (ebook) |
    ISBN 9780804137324 (ebook) | ISBN 9780804137317 (hardback) |
    ISBN 9780804137331 (trade paperback)
Subjects: LCSH: Oklahoma City (Okla.)—History. | Oklahoma City (Okla.)—
    Social life and customs. | BISAC: SOCIAL SCIENCE / Sociology / Urban. |
    HISTORY / United States / State & Local / Southwest (AZ, NM, OK, TX). |
    SPORTS & RECREATION / Basketball.
Classification: LCC F704.O41 (ebook) | LCC F704.O41 A53 2018 (print) |
    DDC 976.6/38—dc23
LC record available at https://lccn.loc.gov/2017054583

ISBN 978-0-8041-3731-7
Ebook ISBN 978-0-8041-3732-4

Printed in the United States of America

Jacket design by Michael Morris
Jacket images: (skyline) Katherine Welles/Shutterstock; (cowboys) Oklahoma
Land Rush, 1889, oil on canvas, by H. Charles McBarron Jr./Peter Newark
American Pictures/Bridgeman Images; (stamp) astudio/Shutterstock;
(basketball) Lightspring/Shutterstock; (hoop) MilkBottle/Shutterstock;
(tornado) ArtMari/Shutterstock

10 9 8 7 6 5 4 3 2 1

First Edition

To Sarah

from math class

and

our two good-for-nothing children

It seems unnecessary to define an explosion, for
everyone knows what it is—a loud noise and the
sudden going away of things from the place
where they have been.

—TENNEY L. DAVIS, *The Chemistry of Powder & Explosives*

Some things are simultaneously too boring and
too exciting to write about.

—JOHN ASHBERY, "Valentine"

CONTENTS

KILLER OF THE KILLER

Red Kelley was the man who killed the man who killed Jesse James. That is: in 1892, ten years after Jesse James was shot in the back while dusting off a picture frame, Red Kelley hunted down his killer, Bob Ford, and shot him in the throat with a double-barreled shotgun. This did not happen in Oklahoma City—the famous events, the front-page news items, rarely ever do. It happened in Creede, a silver-mining boomtown in Colorado. Ford was running a saloon in a tent. Kelley walked in, said, "Hello, Bob," and shot Ford as soon as he turned around. He expected to be celebrated as a national hero for this—Jesse James, after all, was a legend whose righteousness had only grown and grown in the years since his death, and Bob Ford was (as the folk song says) a "dirty little coward."

Instead, Red Kelley was sentenced to ninety-nine years in prison. He did not get the star treatment he felt he deserved. Kelley was not a first-tier outlaw—one of those infamous, larger-than-life antiheroes who robbed the robber barons and blurred the boundaries between good and evil. He was not Billy the Kid or John Wesley Hardin or Ned Kelly or Smokin' Royce Young. He was not Butch or Sundance or—obviously—Jesse James. Red Kelley was a D-list outlaw, very far down the folk-hero food chain. He was a vigilante vigilante, the backup to the backup.

Kelley ended up serving ten years of his sentence before he managed to get himself released. He left Colorado and headed down to Oklahoma City, where the outlaw action was rumored to be hot. It was 1904 by then, the start of a new century, and the Wild West was shrinking. Some vestige of it had survived, however, in Oklahoma. Oklahoma City was only fifteen years old and, after a brief lull, booming again. For a criminal, its red-light district was a safe haven of arson, murder, gambling, drunkenness, bribery, and prostitution. Shoot-outs could be enjoyed indoors or out. Around the time of Red Kelley's arrival, a man called the Armless Wonder, whose arms were reportedly five and seven inches long, cocked his gun with his chin and shot a man who owed him money. There were riots so wild that whole buildings were left permanently infused with bullets. In a popular saloon, someone poured alcohol into a man's boots and lit them on fire, burning his feet so badly they had to be amputated.

Red Kelley fit right in. He was angry, petty, and violent. He had big ears and about three mustaches' worth of mustache. He skulked around Oklahoma City's trouble spots wearing a long overcoat, even in hot weather, with a revolver in each of his front pockets. The tips of his mustache were so long and pointy they almost looked prehensile, like they might reach out and take things off store shelves. One day, in the course of his skulking, Kelley was stopped and questioned by the Oklahoma City police. They weren't arresting him—they made no accusations, filed no charges, and allowed him to go freely on his way. But the questioning alone was enough to offend Red Kelley. He had been a lawman once, a deputy marshal in Colorado, not to mention the man who killed the man who killed motherfucking Jesse James, and he believed that he deserved more respect. This injustice would not stand. Kelley promised his underworld friends that he would take revenge, as soon as he possibly could, on the Oklahoma City police.

His opportunity came on the very next day, January 13, 1904. Officer Joe Burnett was patrolling a notorious strip of saloons and brothels when he happened to pass Kelley in the street. "Hi, Red," Burnett said. This—a friendly greeting from a passing policeman, in broad daylight—was more than Kelley was willing to endure. He drew his gun. The fight that ensued was both ridiculous and deadly, a rare combination. Officer Burnett grabbed Kelley's wrist and managed to hit him twice on the head with his club. Kelley fired wildly into the air. The two men wrestled to a stalemate. For fifteen minutes,

they dragged each other down the street. It was a slow-motion death struggle. Kelley tried to yank his wrist free while Burnett hung on, literally, for his life. At some point, one of Kelley's friends came out of a saloon and shot at Burnett, but he missed and ran away. Kelley, in his desperation, started biting Burnett's ears. As he bit, he fired his gun so many times, so close to Burnett, that its explosions lit the policeman's clothes on fire. People gathered in the street to watch. Things were getting terrible. Kelley was biting actual chunks out of Burnett's ears. Burnett kept asking bystanders for help, shouting that he was a policeman. They just answered: How do we know for sure?

You didn't really know such things, in 1904, in Oklahoma City.

The fight scraped on through the center of town. It ended up a full seventy-five feet from where it had started, in an empty lot. Burnett was smoldering and bleeding. Kelley was shooting and biting. They were a perfect balance of control and chaos. Uninterrupted, they might have fought each other until both died of natural causes. But then suddenly, by chance, the scales tipped. Across the street, the front door of a warehouse opened. A man stepped out. It happened to be one of Officer Burnett's friends. He sprinted over and grabbed Red Kelley by the wrist. "Is his gun empty?" he shouted. Kelley, defiant to the end, fired again and said, "Does it sound like it's empty?" Now that someone else had taken over the interminable duty of clinging to Red Kelley's murderous wrist, Burnett was finally able to draw his own gun. He fired. *Boom.* Kelley died in a gigantic pool of blood just off of First Street. This incident—along with many others more or less like it—titillated local newspaper readers for weeks. Oklahoma City police officer Joe Burnett was now the killer of the killer of the killer of Jesse James.

This book is a history of Oklahoma City. That may strike you as unnecessary, or unfortunate. If so, I would understand. In the larger economy of American attention, Oklahoma City's main job has always been to be ignored. When non-Oklahomans need to think about the place, we tend to fall back on clichés: tepees, wagon trains, the Dust Bowl, country music, college football, methamphetamine, radical anti-government politics. There is always, of course, the Broadway musical *Oklahoma!,* with its soaring anthems of Manifest Destiny. Every five or ten or twenty years, the world is forced to pay serious attention to Oklahoma because something terrible has happened there: a tornado or a bombing or an economic collapse. But then we go back to ignoring it. This is natural. We can't pay attention to everything. You have to know how to look past a place. And Oklahoma City, in the grand scheme of things, is a very easy place to look past.

This changed for me, very suddenly, in the summer of 2012, when I was sent to Oklahoma City on a magazine assignment: to write about the city's improbable new pro basketball team, the Thunder, which had evolved, with almost unbelievable speed, from a morally tainted laughingstock to one of the most powerful collections of talent in sports. That narrow assignment widened very fast. As soon as I got near Oklahoma City, I felt a mysterious inner needle beginning to vibrate—a needle that, in all of my journalistic wanderings, I had never noticed before. I wasn't sure what it measured, or if it measured anything at all. But there it was, moving.

For the next several years, I followed the vibrations of that needle wherever they happened to lead. That turned out to be all over Oklahoma City: to rock concerts, house parties, a megachurch, an abandoned skyscraper, locker rooms full of semi-naked men, the opening of a time capsule, the 2016 NBA Western Conference Finals, and a TV news station weather center in the middle of a deadly storm. I walked under some of the most beautiful skies I've ever seen—wide, blueberry cream–regions of stretching alien vastness—and under some of the most horrifying. I was lied to, cheerfully, dozens of times, often by people I came to consider friends. I got severe sunburns and blisters. For the first time in my life, I began to take seriously the occult power of the number 13. I sat shotgun, for days and days, while different Oklahomans drove me around the city saying wildly divergent things about exactly the same territory. I committed vandalism. I found myself formulating, over the course of many months, a question that seemed to be, on multiple levels, the key to the entire place: Is it possible to control an explosion?

The result is this book. From a distance, Oklahoma City looked like almost nothing. Up close, it turned out to be about almost everything. It became obvious immediately that the new basketball team was deeply entangled in every other aspect of the place—its politics, its history, its economics, its weather—and that this nexus of Oklahoma things was further inextricable from an even larger nexus: certain fundamental tensions in the DNA of democracy itself. Oklahoma City was like a laboratory for unavoidable American problems. What does an individual gain, and what do they lose, when they become assimilated into a group? How does something as messy as a mass of people ever organize itself into a functional system? Or is it always ultimately destined to fail?

I have come to believe, after my time there, that Oklahoma City is one of the great weirdo cities of the world—as strange, in its way, as Venice or Dubai or Versailles or Pyongyang. It is worth paying attention to, on its own terms, independent of any news cycle, strictly for the improbability of what exists there, all the time, every day. It is a place where a golden geodesic dome sits down the street from a tiny building with a giant milk bottle on its roof, where a thin-shell concrete retro-futuristic church is known affectionately, to certain locals, as the City Titty. It is a place where a blacksmith once died of the hiccups. I'm not going to argue that Oklahoma City is an ideal city—not many people, outside of certain boosterish sections of the city itself, would be willing to go that far. But it's the kind of city that, in its excesses, its imbalances, its illusions, its overcorrections, its lunges of pride and insecurity, its tragedies, and its improbable achievements, says something deeper about the nature of cities, about human togetherness, than a more well-rounded or traditional city ever could. It is an unlikely, unreasonable, and arbitrary place, a city that came into being outside of the normal run of history— and so, in a sense, a *pure* city. For the purposes of this book, and with apologies to Charleston, Austin, the Portlands, Fort Worth, Indianapolis, Chattanooga, Charlotte, Memphis, San Antonio, and of course Seattle (always special apologies to Seattle), Oklahoma City is the great minor city of America.

The main story of this book spans roughly one year in the life of Oklahoma City, from perhaps the most controversial trade in NBA history to the widest tornado ever recorded. Nesting inside that story are innumerable other stories, both famous (Ralph Ellison, Kevin Durant) and less so (civil rights leader Clara Luper, civic booster Stanley Draper, NBA bench player Daniel Orton). Because every Oklahoma City moment tends to be connected to every other, the narrative drops into and out of history. The city has existed for only a little over a single human life span—not yet 130 years—but in that time it has lived the life of many cities. From its very first moment, OKC has always wanted to hurry up—to exist, somehow, in its own glorious future. It has never been able to do so, of course. The future it hurls itself into is never the future it was fantasizing about. And so it hurls itself again. This makes the present feel like history. OKC is a place where time does not work properly: it crawls, then lurches forward, then piles up on itself, then pauses, then slides backward, then repeats itself, then freezes, then stumbles forward again. On the city's very first afternoon, in 1889, its population exploded from zero to ten thousand. ("To leave a familiar locality for a few hours," one settler wrote, "was to never find it again, so rapidly did the face of the young city change.") In the twentieth century, the skyline froze for thirty years, then was largely destroyed—intentionally—in less than a decade. ("You can't operate in 1964 with buildings designed for 1925," the mayor told his people.) The city decided it needed to be bigger, so—for absolutely no good reason—it annexed enough land to make itself the largest city, by land area, in the entire world. Several years ago, a skyscraper rose up out of an old parking lot to dominate Oklahoma City seemingly overnight. What I'm telling you, what I will continue to tell you, is that time does not make sense here. Just outside city hall, a nine-foot-tall statue of a dead civic leader bears this inscription: LOOK AROUND YOU! WHAT YOU SEE TODAY WAS HIS TOMORROW . . . YESTERDAY.

If Red Kelley and Officer Burnett were to have their fight in Oklahoma City today, 114 years later, it would happen right in the heart of a very different downtown. The zone of sin and degeneracy in which Kelley first attacked Burnett was later cleared to build grand municipal buildings. Kelley and Burnett would have dragged each other, biting and fighting, along the back side of the Devon Tower, an 850-foot glass skyscraper that is the most literal possible monument to the city's grandiose self-image. They would have seen—on passing cars and plate-glass windows and the T-shirts of passersby—infinite logos of the Oklahoma City Thunder, the basketball team that has become the international face of the city. Bystanders to the modern brawl would not be cowboys and ruffians but city workers in suits and ties heading back from lunch meetings at which they had enjoyed scarlet quinoa with roasted carrots and local honey; joining them would be self-employed hipsters who'd spent the morning in the nearby coffee shops plotting political action and designing websites for one another, plus homeless people heading toward the bus station, plus possibly even tourists coming to see the bombing memorial before getting slightly drunk at the chain restaurants in Bricktown. Today, Kelley and Burnett would have wrestled over nice pavement instead of dust. They would have scraped their way past a large rack of bicycles, part of a municipal bike-rental program called Spokies. Their fight would have ended not in an empty lot but right in the middle of the new public library—a clean white curving building with an elaborately choreographed fountain outside. Instead of a warehouse, Officer Burnett's rescuer would have come running out of the county courthouse, a stately New Deal monolith with civic quotes carved onto its limestone face. (HE WHO HAS MOST ZEAL AND ABILITY TO PROMOTE PUBLIC FELICITY, LET HIM BE THE SERVANT OF THE PUBLIC.) Red Kelley's gigantic pool of blood would have gushed out of him and—as his eyes glazed over, as he considered for the last time the cruel injustices of justice—soaked into the public library's carpet, creating a nightmare for the cleaning staff.

Red Kelley's name, it turns out, was not even actually Red Kelley. It was Edward O'Kelley. People called him Red because of his Irish hair. After the fight, his body was buried in an unmarked grave far uptown, in what would eventually become Fairlawn Cemetery, the final resting place of many of OKC's most revered city fathers. Officer Joe Burnett, it was said, never fully recovered from his injuries. He died thirteen years later and was buried in the same cemetery. Today, this cemetery is not far uptown at all; it's a short, easy drive from the scene of the crime and is now adjacent to the fashionable Paseo Arts District, where you can go on art walks the first Friday of every month and patronize funky shops with decorative knight's armor and patchouli incense and earrings made out of glass-encased cicada wings, where you can stand in an art gallery eating cheese cubes, in an atmosphere of provincial cosmopolitanism, while admiring expressive paintings with titles like *Life in the Harmonious Balance of Things Without Fear of Death,* all while young people with dreadlocks dance in drum circles on the street outside, oblivious to your very existence, a closed society that involves only the drummers and the sacred all-encompassing universe itself, not any of the actual boring people around them, *boom boom,* transcendence, *boom boom,* patchouli, *boom.* Return with me, if you will, to Oklahoma City at the end of the summer of 2012, right around the moment everything was—once again, again—about to change.

PART ONE

TIME

We cannot think of a time that is oceanless.

—T. S. ELIOT, "The Dry Salvages"

Thunder results from the superheating of the air around the lightning bolt to about five times the temperature of the sun, all within a few millionths of a second.

—GARY ENGLAND, *Those Terrible Twisters*

I just don't have time to worry about it now. I'll put it in file number 13.

—CLARA LUPER, *Behold the Walls*

A VISITOR'S GUIDE TO
OKLAHOMA CITY

Welcome to Oklahoma City. It's been a long day. You've taken two flights to get here, possibly three. You've eaten unfortunate foods. You fell asleep at the Memphis airport, somehow, with your head leaning hard against the wall—you slept so deeply that the woman working at the gate had to actually come shake you awake just before the plane took off. Don't be embarrassed. It's all part of the long, unglamorous process of getting yourself to a minor airport out in the middle of the country. But now you've made it. Welcome. Come along. Stretch your legs. The OKC airport is small, so you'll have no trouble finding your way around.

First, get yourself a car. You won't be able to survive here without one. Go to the rental desk. The clerk will be curious to know why you are here, all the way from wherever you have come; tell him. If the conversation lulls, you can talk about the Thunder. (He will be a fan.) He might ask you about the James Harden crisis. Will Harden stay or will he go? Tell him that no one knows for sure, obviously, but that if you had to bet, you'd bet he'll stay. The young man will encourage you to pay an extra $10 per day to upgrade to a Mustang—a special deal, he'll tell you—but do your best to resist the temptation, because when you get out to the parking garage, you'll suddenly remember what a Mustang looks like: like a shark, with a fat snout, bullet-nosed and swaggering. Politely refuse, and collect the keys to some kind of nondescript sedan.

Walk out of the terminal. On your way out you'll see a statue: Will Rogers, the folksy sage of the Great Plains, cast in bronze, wearing a bronze cowboy hat, riding a bronze horse, with a bronze lasso frozen in the air beside him. The whole airport is named after him: Will Rogers World Airport. "World" is meaningless here because there are actually no international flights. It's just another example of one of Oklahoma City's defining behaviors: trying to make itself seem bigger than it is. The city conducts itself, whenever possible, like a hiker threatened by a bear in the woods, hysterically exaggerating its size. Before you move on, take a moment to stop and look at the statue. (Now is perhaps not the time to think about the fact that Will Rogers died in a plane crash.) Here is another peculiarity of arriving in Oklahoma City: the statue will always be the same, but the sky over it will always be different. Most places have one sky; Oklahoma City has about twelve. There seem to be many different vectors up there, completely unrelated to one another, happening all at once. Sometimes you'll see silent lightning blinking, very high, in one region, while smooth white clouds slide around low behind you. Will Rogers's lasso, if you look through it, might be holding the sun, might be holding some ragged cirrus clouds, might be holding a volcanic piece of dusk.

Once you've come to grips with the sky, move on from the statue, walk into the parking garage, pick up your rental car, steer it out onto the streets.

Congratulations: you are now driving in Oklahoma City, an activity as characteristic as poling a gondola around Venice or weaving a moped through the crowds of central Marrakech. You have driven cars elsewhere, but it will never have felt exactly like this. Oklahoma City is the natural habitat of cars. In normal cities, cars feel slightly out of place, like zoo animals, pacing narrow roads between mobs of pedestrians. Here in Oklahoma City, cars can stretch, roar, and run free. Many of the city's neighborhoods lack sidewalks, intentionally, as a symbol of status, because walking was considered to be outmoded, primitive, impoverished, a little sad, an activity that might even distract the cars, or offend them. You will hear, while you are here, two basic axioms about driving in OKC, each of which seems to violate the laws of space-time, but each of which is true:

1. Even traffic jams move the speed limit.
2. Everywhere is only fifteen minutes away.

Drive. The airport roads are nice and new. They take you out under the wide skies. You are moving like a smooth cloud. You will notice, out your windows, that Oklahoma City has no topography to speak of: everything is flat in every direction. This is because it was once the bottom of an ancient ocean. Keep looking around. Before you've even left the airport, you will see oil pumps working along the side of the road. Oklahoma is completely devoted to sucking fossil fuels up out of the ground, and unembarrassed about its devotion. How else would it be possible to enable all of this wonderful driving? You will pass billboards for drilling equipment, and when you get into town you will see active oil pumps in people's backyards. The state capitol building had a working oil derrick in front of it for many decades before it even had a dome.

Keep driving. Leave the airport, merge onto the freeway, head toward the city center. There are signs, but you won't need them: you can navigate by the skyscraper—skyscraper, singular, because there is, by modern standards, only the one, and it is so completely out of scale to the rest of the city that you can see it from everywhere else. It is nearly twice as tall as any other structure for one hundred miles in every direction. It dominates downtown, glittering like an open blade. This is the Devon Tower, headquarters of one of OKC's biggest energy companies, a glass-and-steel monument to the miracle of hydraulic fracturing, a.k.a. "fracking," the lucrative but controversial practice of destroying underground rock formations with a slurry of wet chemicals in order to release huge quantities of natural gas. But don't worry about the source of the wealth. You are here to enjoy Oklahoma City, the newly shiny center of which you are rapidly approaching. The skyscraper was meant to make the city seem big, but mostly it makes everything around it look small: thick, stocky, ancient, heavy, extremely midwestern.

It is perfect, however, for navigation. Ignore your GPS. It can't help you now. Keep your eye on the skyscraper. OKC is in the midst of a downtown renaissance, a growth whose improbability—after decades of busts and self-inflicted disappointments and unspeakable tragedies—has made the place almost legendary among contemporary American cities, and one result of this renaissance is constant construction. Streets are being rerouted, public art installed, medians expensively landscaped. Competing energy companies are building themselves increasingly grand headquarters. The old elevated highway that has loomed, for nearly fifty years, over the center of the city is now in the midst of being torn down. Its on-ramps and off-ramps end, eerily, in midair—entrances and exits to a ghost road that your GPS will keep trying to make you drive on. Ignore it. Drive on the actual roads. You'll cross over the Oklahoma River, healthy and full, although it is not, technically, a river anymore, because it has been corralled in a concrete trough that is fed and drained by dams at either end, which makes it more like a canal, really, or an inland lake. But at least now it is full of water, more dependable than the natural river, and as such it has become the anchor of a whole new area of town: the Boathouse District, which draws competitive rowers from all over the world, and which is getting ready to host an episode of *American Idol.* As you drive over the water, you might see Olympic kayakers training.

Keep driving. Now that you're in Oklahoma City, it won't take you long to get to know the basic landmarks. You'll see signs for the tourist destinations: Bricktown, Stockyards City, Myriad Botanical Gardens, Chesapeake Energy Arena, the National Memorial. Everything is more or less right on top of everything else. Neighborhoods that sound like whole separate regions (Automobile Alley, Midtown, SoSA) are really just a few blocks apart. You could walk it all easily, if that's how things were done here. The Plaza District, one of the city's much-touted hip new neighborhoods, is basically two blocks of Sixteenth Street. Oklahoma City is tiny and huge at the same time, sprawling and compressed. Residents often refer to it as "the biggest small town in America," and that might be literally true. Although its population ranks only twenty-ninth in the contiguous United States, it is an absolute juggernaut in square mileage—bigger, by far, than Los Angeles or New York or Chicago. Drive for fifteen minutes in any direction and the city will begin to blend with the country. You'll think you've left town, but you haven't. Not even close. It will take many more miles of driving, much more open country, before you'll see a sign that says, out of nowhere, LEAVING OKLAHOMA CITY.

But let's not do that. Why would we do that? This is Oklahoma City. Settle in. We'll be here for a while.

BEARD

James Harden, 2012.

The first time I saw James Harden up close, I was hypnotized by his beard. It was dense and black and shockingly large—a whole second head, practically, hanging under Harden's regular head: a shadow head. I stared and stared. This was October 2012, during Thunder training camp—a hinge moment, although we didn't know it yet, on which the future of Oklahoma City was right about to turn. Harden was talking (there was a hole in the middle of his beard for his mouth), but I could hardly pay attention to what he was saying because the beard, up close, was overwhelming, a real ninety-ninth-percentile super-mammalian face bush. A slow-motion testosterone explosion. I had seen it many times before, of course, on screens. Harden was one of the NBA's rising young stars, and the Thunder was one of the great stories in all of professional sports, and so his beard had become, over the previous months, not only a local folk hero and symbol of the OKC renaissance but a full-on international brand, one of America's most famous hair things. (There was a new Foot Locker commercial in which Harden's teammate Russell Westbrook squirted mustard on it, only for Harden to rip the beard off to reveal, underneath, another equally lush backup beard.) In person, however, the beard was something else entirely, more urgent and commanding and strange. It was wet from practice, and as Harden spoke, it shifted and glistened, scattering tiny sparkles in every direction.

Harden was, at that moment, one of the youngest members of one of the youngest basketball teams in NBA history, a team that had improved so much, so quickly, over the previous few seasons that it seemed destined soon to devour the league. The question, in those days, was not if the Thunder would win a championship, only of how many times. The previous season had been almost impossibly glorious: a 16–3 start, two players (the angelic Kevin Durant, the devilish Russell Westbrook) honored with selection to All-NBA Teams, a Sixth Man of the Year Award for Harden, and all of it capped off by an underdog run to the NBA Finals. In July, all three of the Thunder's young stars were chosen to represent the United States in the Olympics, making OKC the first franchise in NBA history to send three players to the U.S. national team. There was no reason, going forward, for anything other than wild optimism. Unless, of course— unless. Unless James Harden.

Harden and his beard were standing, on that afternoon, in the Thunder's new and extremely shiny $19 million practice facility. I was part of a large crowd of reporters, local and national, who had assembled to ask him questions. We were hoping to extract some new shred of intel, however small, about what was beginning to be thought of, in OKC and beyond, as the Harden crisis. Would James Harden stay with the Thunder, everyone was asking, or would he go find his own team somewhere else? This threat had become, slowly, the story of the summer—it had begun to overshadow even the euphoric afterglow of that magical trip to the Finals. The citizens of OKC were terrified, suddenly, that Harden was going to leave them. "I wouldn't take anyone in the league over the Beard," wrote a fan on the discussion board OKCTalk. "I will trade in all of my Thunder gear and wipe my memory of Thunder games if that happens."

What we knew, so far, was only this: James Harden was an unorthodox and magnetic young player, far better than anyone had reasonably expected, and his sudden rise toward stardom had elevated the Thunder from a very good team to a potentially great one. But it had also complicated things. Harden came off the bench behind the exotic Swiss defensive specialist Thabo Sefolosha. The problem was that Harden was clearly too good to be a backup. He was a precious node of order among the chaos of an NBA game. You could give him the ball and get out of the way and trust him, almost every time, to do something dangerous with it. But the Thunder already had two ball-dominating stars in Westbrook and Durant. Was there really room for a third?

Harden's rookie contract was set to expire at the end of the coming season, in the summer of 2013, but everyone expected him to solve things much sooner than that, like any second now, in the offseason of 2012, to keep the Thunder's momentum rolling. Early signs were good. "This team is like a family," Harden said, right after the Finals ended. "We're really brothers. We hang out most of the time every single day. You won't find any other team like this. I love it here." And yet the weeks passed, and the Thunder took care of all kinds of other business—the draft, a contract extension for their head coach—and still Harden's new deal did not get signed. The team picked up the seven-foot-three Hasheem Thabeet, the tallest man in the NBA, as their backup center. They extended the contract of their power forward, Serge Ibaka, and filled front-office positions. But they could not pin down James Harden.

As the summer churned on, people in OKC remained optimistic. In July, at Team USA training camp, *Sports Illustrated* asked Harden about his plans. "I'm pretty—a hundred percent—I'm pretty sure that I'm going to be in Oklahoma City," he said. This was meant to be reassuring, but there was a large difference between "pretty sure" and "a hundred percent," and much of OKC's basketball future now hung in that zone. A Thunder blog, *Welcome to Loud City*, ran a poll about Harden's future, and 80 percent of respondents predicted that he would stay—that he either "remains 6th man and keeps the Thunder as the most balanced team in the NBA" or "moves to the starting SG position and continues his ascent." The two pessimistic options, that Harden would refuse to sign or that OKC would trade him, sank right to the bottom, tied with only thirteen votes apiece.

August, then. The contract would get done in August. Harden would come home from the Olympics in London and sit down with the Thunder's management and they would all focus hard and hash everything out. "If it's a max deal, or even close to it," wrote Royce Young at *Daily Thunder*, "Harden is likely to sign on without thinking much about it." At the end of August, however, there was no contract. Harden turned twenty-three, and photos emerged of his birthday party, and he did not look overly worried: he sat shirtless on a yacht, wearing a thick gold chain and a tiger-print cowboy hat, clutching an open wine bottle, thoroughly entangled with a large crowd of women dressed in tight white clothes. The *Oklahoman* turned moralistic. "Oklahoma City," it wrote, "can save Harden from himself."

September.

Something, somewhere, seemed to be going wrong. Harden's services were worth a lot of money, of course, and so the team was offering a lot of money, but it was not offering the absolute maximum salary the NBA allowed, and this, for Harden, seemed to be a problem. He was refusing to sign. Whether it was a fatal and permanent error or just a temporary glitch, no one could say, but the whole thing was dragging on worryingly long. As a player, Harden's greatest strength was his unpredictability: it was impossible to know, at any given moment, whether he would zig here or zag there—he was, at all times, a herky-jerky mystery. Now this same quality was torturing OKC. The city was paralyzed. Toward the end of September, as the crisis rose toward its climax, several citizens joked to me that they would be perfectly willing to vote for a temporary sales tax if the money would help convince Harden to stay. As soon as I laughed at this, it became clear that the citizens were not actually joking. I mentioned the hypothetical tax to the mayor, who agreed. Keeping Harden was not just a matter of basketball excellence but of civic health; losing him would be like pulling one of the downtown buildings out of the skyline. In the grand scheme of things, Harden was only the third-best basketball player in the twenty-ninth-largest city in America. At that moment, however, he seemed to be right at the center of everything.

So there we stood, in October, at the Thunder's practice facility, TV cameras rolling, voice recorders shoved toward James Harden's face, waiting for him to give us some kind of hint about whatever he might be thinking. I continued to stare into his beard.

"There's a battle at point guard," one of the local reporters said. "But really you've kind of taken control of the second team."

This seemed like an innocuous bit of sports jargon but it was actually, in code, an attempt to get at something crucial. The standoff between Harden and the Thunder was, at root, a question of control. Was there enough space, in OKC, for Harden to turn himself into the superstar he suspected he might be good enough to become? Were the Thunder's two bigger stars willing to yield some space to make room for him to do so? Were the team's fiscally conservative owners willing to pay Harden a superstar salary, thereby triggering the odious luxury tax, which would restrict the team's control over future decisions? And what did Harden really want, anyway? Did he want to win as part of the group in Oklahoma City, or did he want his very own spotlight somewhere else in a bigger city?

All of this was implied, very subtly, in the local reporter's question.

Harden, however, was a master of control, and he refused to tip his hand.

"We have three very good point guards on the team," he said, with an incredible lack of inflection, "three tremendous point guards who can all play that role, and who are playing very well. They run the team. I'm just trying to fit in where I can."

This was a blatant falsehood, on several levels, and everyone standing there knew it, but we let the statement pass. Sports interviews are a special category of non-conversation, and this was particularly true in Oklahoma City, where a typical Thunder media session was a call-and-response of non-questions and non-answers so relentlessly empty that it became almost profound, like the chanting of

Buddhist monks. The culture of the organization, in those early days, was buttoned-up, icy, strict, severe—a zone of bulletproof message control. Reporters traded whispered stories like dissidents in an authoritarian state. Every time anyone interviewed a player, a Thunder PR man would lurk in a nearby doorway, eavesdropping while faux-casually pretending to look at his phone, like a bad CIA agent.

This, I came to believe, was one of the essential functions of Harden's enormous beard: to give people something to stare at while the man himself said nothing, at great length, into all the microphones he was professionally obligated to speak into almost every day of his famous young life. Harden rattled off his clichés with all the enthusiasm of a third grader reciting the Gettysburg Address. I held my voice recorder out at arm's length, toward Harden's mouth hole, like all of the other reporters, but I had no questions for him, no comments, no insights, no language. All I could do was stare into his beard. I had been sucked, like the rest of OKC, into the secret dimension of hairspace.

"Guys are doing a great job," Harden said.

The beard looked like a wilderness on the edge of civilization.

"Our main focus is defensively," he said.

It seemed to contain, somehow, something important: an essence, a promise.

"It's about maturity and taking care of your body," Harden said.

No one asked James Harden, at least explicitly, the only thing everyone really wanted to know, which was whether or not he was going to stay.

After several minutes of staring, I was able to break out of my hypnotic beard trance and look closely at James Harden's actual face. What I saw was disorienting. On TV, from a distance, Harden's beard gave him an air of wisdom, maturity, depth, mystique. Up close, however, there were things that didn't show up on screens: human things, the micromovements of eyes and mouth. It became clear to me, suddenly and viscerally, that James Harden was actually an extremely young man. He was a multimillionaire, an Olympic gold medalist, a burgeoning international celebrity—but he was also just barely not a teenager, a kid who happened to be wearing an incongruously giant beard. In person, up close, the beard looked like a disguise. It may as well have been rubber-banded to his face. It was real, of course, but it implied things that weren't real. Most of all, it implied age. The beard was a big curly pile of time. And time was the one thing James Harden and the Thunder no longer had.

MIDDLENESS

Oklahoma City sits near the geographical center of the contiguous United States. But it is not even quite that. The real center is a little north, in Kansas. This gives OKC's middleness a "not quite" quality—it is less America's belly button than the disturbing mole a few inches away. It's unclear, in fact, what part of the country Oklahoma actually belongs to. It is spoken of, variously, as part of the Southwest, Midwest, Bible Belt, and Heartland. It's easier to say what it is not: it's not the arid West or the frigid North or the humid South or the old-world East. Instead, it is precisely where all of those things meet.

Oklahoma is, inarguably, a flyover state. Planes fly over it all the time, and if you look out the window of one you will see barrenness, crop geometry, vivid red dirt—all the markers of the Great Plains, the vast strip of flatness that runs right down the center of North America, of which Oklahoma is most certainly a part. The state is profoundly landlocked, as landlocked as a place can be: the Gulf of Mexico is four hundred miles away, the Pacific and Atlantic Oceans more than a thousand. Oceanlessness has defined the place for millennia. In American popular culture, Oklahoma exists most powerfully as the epicenter of the Dust Bowl, a dryness so deep that it allowed the state's perpetual wind to lift up the entire surface of the land, trillions of grains at a time, and whip it away, at very high speeds, clear across the continent. Oklahoma's dust went so far, so fast, that the people of New York City had to turn their lights on in the middle of the day, and sailors had to sweep their decks three hundred miles out to sea. Thousands of Okies were forced to flee the blasted landscape, as dramatized, canonically—to the dismay of the state's boosters—in John Steinbeck's *The Grapes of Wrath*.

Oklahoma, however, was not always dry. For a long time, in fact, it was defined by its wetness. Before there was a United States, before there was even a North America, the land that would become Oklahoma sat right on the paleoequator, in the middle of the supercontinent Pangaea. For five hundred million years, off and on, Oklahoma City would have been at the bottom of an ancient sea. The sea filled up, then receded, then filled up, then receded, then filled up again. Its water was salty and warm. City residents would have included sharks and ancient clammy things called blastoids and brachiopods. Even during its relative dry spells, Oklahoma would have been wet and oozy. For roughly twenty million years, it was overrun by dimetrodons: lizards with giant sails on their backs that preceded the dinosaurs. None of this seems possible, but the fossil record is clear. Slowly, as the world's plates drifted and clashed, chains of mountains as tall as the Himalayas rose up around Oklahoma City—the Rockies to the west, the Wichita and Ouachita and Arbuckle down south, the Ozarks to the northeast—and all of these dumped their mountain trash (mud, gravel, sand, clay) into Oklahoma, which was still not a state, of course, but only a flat trough between all of those dramatic peaks. The flotsam piled up and dried. Oklahoma was overrun, at various times, by dinosaurs, mammoths, rhinos, horses, and camels, all running wild, eating and mating, owning the land outright. Again, to someone who knows only modern Oklahoma City, to someone who has watched a tennis shoe float down the Bricktown Canal past Toby Keith's I ♥ This Bar & Grill, none of this will seem possible. But it happened. For a while, the Gulf of Mexico came right up to Oklahoma's southern border. When the Rockies rose to their full height, they tilted the entire state like a table with a broken leg, pouring the ancient sea right off it. Glaciers formed and crawled around on the mountaintops, and when they finally melted, their water came gushing down across Oklahoma, forming its modern rivers.

And that was basically that. What was left, after all this geological action, was a sunbaked sheet of primordial ooze sloping very gently from Colorado to Arkansas. It was a perfect place for grass to grow—such a nice place, in fact, that the grass and the soil became almost indistinguishable: a block of soil, in Oklahoma, was also a block of grass. Beneath that living surface, prairie dogs built their underground colonies, thousands and thousands of tunnels, some with false bottoms to fool predators, some leading to rough bedrooms and storerooms and bathrooms, all of them invisibly interconnected and meticulously organized into distinct neighborhoods. The largest prairie dog colonies covered hundreds of square miles, and above them buffalo grazed by the millions. It was a teeming abundance of life, operating almost without restriction, farther than the eye could see.

In other words, in American terms, Oklahoma was a wasteland. For many centuries, Europeans looking for value in the region had trouble finding any. In the sixteenth century, the Spanish explorer Francisco Vázquez de Coronado y Luján searched the wilderness of northern Mexico, which included Oklahoma, on his quest for the Cities of Gold. He didn't find them, and in his disgust he wrote a letter back to Spain with the most damning indictment of the place he could think of: "There is not any gold or any other metal . . . nothing but villages."

But this, in fact, was the region's wealth: its villages, all of those humans congregating and moving to live in concert with these vast spreads of land. Mammoth hunters evolved into foragers, who eventually became farmers living together in grass huts. Out east were the Mound Builders, a civilization organized enough to construct elaborate ceremonial mountains of dirt. Hundreds of years later, when archaeologists finally excavated the mounds, they found copper from the Great Lakes, shells from Florida, pottery from Nebraska, and obsidian from Mexico. Oklahoma had apparently been the hub of a huge network of trade—a central market for prehistoric North America.

Here, then, was the secret genius of Oklahoma, the advantage of being stranded so far away from everything else: middleness. Oklahoma was where the mountains touched the plains, and where the plains turned into the tall-grass prairie and the tall-grass prairie turned into the short-grass prairie, and these contact zones created incredible richness, not only of flora and fauna but of human cultures. Migrating herds intersected with rivers, which attracted tribes, which attracted trade routes, which attracted new explorers and their rivals and the people they had enslaved, some of whom stayed behind and made new lives in the spreading wasteland. Oklahoma was a hadron supercollider of a place. People and creatures were thrown together, from distant points and at unpredictable angles, again and again and again and again. Despite its relative material poverty, its lack of obvious treasure, Oklahoma always had this unusual talent for improvised community.

Besides, in the end, the conquistadors were wrong. Oklahoma's treasure had been there all along, just at a depth and in a form that they weren't equipped to exploit: huge underground lakes of oil, dead black and untapped. This was yet another secret reward of middleness. By the time humans arrived, many eons of life had already thrived and died way out there in the center of the world, and now it sat hidden as a secret rich ooze, waiting to be discovered. When it finally was, it would make Oklahoma one of the wealthiest places on earth. But all of that would come in time.

IN THE BEGINNING

To understand all of the civic anxiety clustering around the Harden crisis—the media frenzy and message-board screeds, the wild speculation in grocery store lines, the back-room strategizing among politicians in city hall—you first have to understand the wretched origins of basketball in Oklahoma City.

In the beginning, things were very, very bad.

I'm talking about October 2008. The Thunder was a brand-new team, the newest in the NBA, and it was a laughingstock. Its players looked like clowns. Their uniforms were blue and orange—not the classic, valiant deep blue and orange of the New York Mets or Knicks but lighter shades somehow reminiscent of a coupon for an off-brand smoothie chain. And the logo. Design blogs were tripping all over themselves to make fun of the Thunder's logo. ("I don't understand what is happening here," wrote one. "This isn't a fucking contemporary living room. . . . Is that a clip-art basketball?") Everything about the team seemed to confirm, to the casual NBA fan, the worst stereotypes about its new home. Oklahoma was provincial, amateur, terminally uncool. It could not be trusted to handle a piece of culture as sophisticated as a big-league American sports team. Even the name: "Thunder." What was that? The team had been named after sky noise? Sportswriters hated the word because you couldn't tell if it was a collective or an individual noun. Were you supposed to write, "The Thunder *is* on an interminable losing streak" or "The Thunder *are* on an interminable losing streak"?

Sometimes it was hard to tell whether the team itself—the actual assemblage of humans that took the floor together to play the sport—was a collective or an individual noun. The players didn't exactly congeal. The Thunder had one potential superstar in Kevin Durant, the universally beloved second pick in the 2007 draft, but Durant was still only twenty, and he was skinny, inefficient, and often overmatched. He had such long arms that sportswriters, trying to describe them, reached for inhuman metaphors: pterodactyl wings, capellini. Durant spent much of his early career peeling himself off the floor, being bullied by cynical grown-up defenders. He was joined in his misadventures by Jeff Green, a young potential sort-of-maybe star who projected, eventually, to be a nice wingman for Durant but who replicated many of Durant's skills and therefore fit with him about as well as the fonts in the Thunder's logo. The rest of the roster was made up of castoffs and role players and lost-looking rookies. The Thunder were (was?) not anything close to a winning team.

And so the Thunder did not win. It did not win and did not win and did not win and did not win. Of the team's first thirty-two games, the Thunder managed to win three. This was not just bad, it was one of the worst starts in the history of sports. Talking heads debated, very seriously, whether or not OKC's clown-colored team was the most overmatched collection of basketball talent in league history. To make things worse, almost everyone outside Oklahoma was basking in the Thunder's failure, giddy with schadenfreude. If any sports team deserved to be humiliatingly bad, people said, it was Oklahoma City's. This was because, like Oklahoma itself—like America, for that matter, and actually like all of mankind, if you sub-scribe to the Christian theology that dominates OKC—the Thunder was cursed by the stain of its shameful origin. The Thunder, from the very beginning, had quite a lot to answer for.

EWING

In 1880, Oklahoma still did not exist. This was light-years into the American experiment, more than a century after the Declaration of Independence, fifteen years after the end of the Civil War. By then, all the states around it existed: Arkansas, Missouri, Kansas, Texas, Colorado. But not Oklahoma. Certain people were getting tired of waiting. The land was there, of course—it was the same flat, grassy expanse that had been brewing and growing and oozing since the time of Pangaea. What we know today, however, as the state of Oklahoma—the pot-shaped chunk of map between Texas and Kansas—was back then something else entirely. It was known, simply, as "Indian Territory." For decades, the U.S. government had been using Oklahoma as a storage area for its dispossessed indigenous peoples. As European settlers systematically invaded every last pocket of the continent, the tribes were forced out of their ancestral homes and into the sprawling wasteland. Oklahoma was the endpoint of all the many Trails of Tears. The Choctaw, the Cherokee, the Chickasaw, and dozens of others—sea people, swamp people, forest dwellers, nomads—were marched off to the (almost) center of the center of the Great Plains and told to stay put, to civilize, to praise Jesus in English and farm as the white men farmed, and, above all, to be grateful for what they had. In the flood of injustice surging over the continent, Indian Territory was meant to be a small island of relief. The survivors of genocide could live there, unharassed and sovereign, "as long as"—to quote the famous treaty—"grass shall grow and water run."

By 1880, however, even this modest promise was under assault. It started right at the center of Indian Territory, on nearly two million acres of land that had belonged, for thirty years, to the Creek and Seminole Indians—a consolation prize for losing their ancestral homelands in Georgia and Florida. But then, for complex reasons, the tribes chose to side with the South during the Civil War. It was a losing gamble. As punishment, after the war, the United States government seized the land and gave it to nobody.

It came to be known as the Unassigned Lands: a vacuum, nearly half the size of Connecticut, right near the center of America.

Vacuums, by nature, tend to get themselves filled, often with sudden violence. People in the neighboring states—Kansas, Texas— noticed the emptiness of the Unassigned Lands. They became obsessed with the place. They wanted to fill it. They lusted after it. They gave it a name: Oklahoma, Choctaw for "red people." Some managed to convince themselves that Oklahoma was their destiny, that they were somehow entitled to it.

Imagine their excitement. America's great promise, in its early days, was that it was the anti-Europe: an endless virgin wilderness that you could explore and claim without getting snaggled in millennia of geopolitical barbed wire. By the 1880s, however, that fantasy had been exhausted. America, like everywhere else, was thoroughly settled. The good land had all been claimed. The Gold Rushes had been rushed. The New World was old.

Then, suddenly: Oklahoma.

The potential settlers pressured Congress to give them the Unassigned Lands. They propagandized in newspapers. The railroads got behind them. (Oklahoma was a market waiting to be supplied.) The surrounding tribes, of course, vehemently objected. The Civil War had blown a hole in the center of Indian Territory, but the rest of it was still guaranteed forever. Allowing white settlers to pour into the Unassigned Lands would threaten the integrity of everything that surrounded it. Who could say what chaos might follow?

Congress deliberated. White settlers lobbied. For years, everyone waited.

Finally, someone decided to take action. This was David Payne, a rabble-rousing frontiersman from Kansas. Payne was a heavy drinker, a freeloader, a veteran of Custer's wars against the natives, a distant relative of Davy Crockett's, a charming opportunist who'd managed to live, for decades, off other people's money. If the government couldn't figure out what to do with Oklahoma, Payne decided, he would show them: he would gather a force, invade the land, settle it, and build a great American city in the wilderness that would so thoroughly blow the authorities' minds they'd be forced to open the Unassigned Lands.

Payne specialized in such fantastical gestures. He was Oklahoma's first master of PR—the first to realize that public-

David Payne, dapper propagandist.

ity was, in this blank territory, very nearly the entire game: almost the same thing as reality. He was six foot four, the same height as Abraham Lincoln—the same height, in fact, as James Harden without shoes—and he used his size to deliver electrifying speeches from wagons about the plight of the landless poor. Payne was a propagandist. He started a newspaper called the *Oklahoma War Chief*. He raised an army of land seekers, a cult of ruined Americans—people for whom Oklahoma represented the very last best chance. Payne and his followers called themselves the Boomers. They exaggerated their size and power whenever they could, making themselves sound like an army of one hundred thousand that was going to turn the country inside out. The only thing that could stop them, the Boomers said, was the immediate opening of Oklahoma, the New World Holy Land, the site of their destiny, the final real scrap of untaken America.

Somehow, the federal government was unmoved. Oklahoma was not forthcoming. One day, on behalf of all the Boomers, real and imagined, Payne decided to go out and take it.

It was nighttime, actually. Under a full moon, on the evening of April 24, 1880, Payne slipped out of Wichita, Kansas. He slept in a haystack, met up with a small party of Boomers near the border, and then they all headed south toward Oklahoma. Soldiers were patrolling the territory for invaders, but the prairie was wide and wild, and the Boomers managed to find a way through. Payne and his miniature army traveled for a week, right in the middle of the Oklahoma springtime, the death season, when the wide sky reaches down, over and over, and tries to kill you. (Things happen year-round in Oklahoma, but the really high drama, meteorological and otherwise, tends to pool in the spring.) The Boomers crossed flooded rivers, suffered through terrible storms, and endured threats from the Nez Perce Indians. As they rode, they scooped up buffalo skulls, bleached ultra-white by decades and centuries of sun, and dropped them in a line behind them to mark their trail. Finally, exhausted, Payne and his men arrived at a bend of the North Canadian River. This piece of land is the site, today, of downtown Oklahoma City: the basketball arena, the skyscraper, the botanical garden, the bombing memorial. At that time, however, it was blank prairie in every direction: flowers, stands of cottonwood trees, bluestem grass as tall as a man. There were little rises here and there, and Payne and his men rode off to one, a panoramic hill a couple miles south, from the top of which they admired the full glorious sweep of the Oklahoma country. This hill, Payne declared, would be the site of his great city, a city that would change the very shape and texture of America—a showpiece of the power of civilization over savagery. Payne and his men settled down, in the wilderness, and got to work.

Thirteen days later, when federal troops came to evict the Boomers from their hill, Payne greeted them warmly. He welcomed them to his magnificent city. He offered them food and gave them a tour. What they saw must have confused them. It was, indeed, a great city, insofar as it could be said to be anything at all. Mostly, though, it was an absence, a strategic lack of vegetation meant to evoke future urban potential. The Boomers had chopped down the wild grass and the bushes. They had mowed a large central square and, radiating out from it, stately spacious roads: 150-foot-wide boulevards connected by 80-foot-wide streets. There were gardens and the beginnings of cabins. They had chopped down all the trees and used them to build a protective wall. Every city has to start somewhere, and this one—despite its lack of real buildings, despite its population of twenty-one—must still have been weirdly impressive. Payne and his men, in their backcountry way, had built a scale-model Philadelphia, Paris, Boston, or Vienna—an orderly old-world metropolis. It was almost nothing, and yet that nothing hinted at something grand, a city far grander than any city that had ever existed in the American West. It was a propaganda city, a city of pure publicity.

The troops arrested all of the Boomers and took them back to Kansas.

Payne called his imaginary city "Ewing." Ewing was the beginning, a first draft of Oklahoma City. The real Oklahoma City would not come into being until after another nine years of fantasizing and raiding—in the middle of which time Payne would die, suddenly, over breakfast, on the day after Thanksgiving, after he had made one of the greatest speeches of his life. Upon his death, the Boomer torch would be passed to Payne's lieutenant, William Couch. Couch's job was to keep the Boomers booming. Fourteen days after his fallen leader's death, he paid Payne the ultimate tribute: he led a raid of two hundred people, in the bitterness of December, back toward Ewing. Unfortunately, they never made it—these raiders, too, were forced out by federal troops, and Ewing remained permanently unpopulated, an idea with no reality. Gradually, the prairie reclaimed it, choking the streets with grass and trees. When Oklahoma City did finally arrive, nine years later, in 1889, it was in a slightly different spot: on the bending river where Payne had originally stopped, not the hill where he'd tried to settle. And it turned out that Payne's trial version of the city—the thoroughly planned metropolis of pure wilderness landscaping—was a lot more orderly than the real place would ever manage to be. Oklahoma City was never more coherent than when it was nothing. But it couldn't stay nothing forever.

OPERATION BONGO

The Thunder, like almost everything else in Oklahoma City, was not native to the region. Its transplant was sudden, violent, scandalous, messy, and—for everyone involved—transformative. For decades, the team that would eventually belong to OKC belonged, happily, to Seattle, a real city fifteen hundred miles away, with a metro area of more than three million people and an iconic skyline and world-conquering brands (Microsoft, Starbucks, UPS, Nirvana). Despite its position in the extreme northwest corner of America, despite a climate that seemed specifically designed to nurture mossy tree bark, Seattle had managed to get itself settled nearly forty years before Oklahoma City. By the time OKC got around to existing, Seattle was already a thriving port with an elaborate streetcar system and labor riots. It had the Pacific Ocean and the Cascade Mountains. It was a place, in other words, that made sense, that fulfilled the classical requirements of a city, that existed meaningfully in relation to other metropolises, that held a distinct place in the national imagination. Seattle *mattered,* in America and in the world, in a way that Oklahoma City very much did not.

It was only proper, then, that Seattle had professional sports teams. Real cities did. By the late twentieth century, Seattle was practically overrun with them. In football, Seattle had the Seahawks, a once sad-sack franchise that (pumped up on Microsoft money) would become twenty-first-century Super Bowl champions. In baseball, Seattle had the Mariners, another sad-sack franchise that nevertheless incubated superstars (Ken Griffey Jr., Randy Johnson, Alex Rodriguez) for more illustrious teams.

But Seattle's oldest and proudest team, the most Seattle of all the city's franchises, played basketball: the Seattle SuperSonics. The team was created in 1966, back when the Space Needle was still new, when the city was actively rebranding itself from a loggy old frontier town into a shiny technotopia of glass and light. Basketball, at that time, was a sport of the future. The NBA was less than twenty years old, and it was in the process of expanding from nine to fourteen teams, with an emphasis on colonizing the untapped West—Seattle, Phoenix, San Diego. This was, at the time, a gamble. No one could have known just how explosively successful the league would turn out to be. Sports TV was in its infancy; Michael Jordan was only three years old. But Seattle was one of the cities willing to take that bet. It paid the NBA $1.75 million for the privilege.

Seattle's brand-new basketball team, obviously, would need a futuristic name. Fortunately, the city had one near at hand. One of the great tech fantasies rippling through Cold War America was supersonic flight—the idea that commercial jets would soon be carrying passengers around the world faster than the speed of sound. The French and English were already working on such a plane, and the Russians were rumored to be doing so, too, which meant, of course, that America had to leap in, as quickly as possible, to prove its superiority. The company charged with working out the details was Boeing. Boeing happened to be based in Seattle. In a grand show of civic-corporate synergy, Seattle named its new basketball team after Boeing's big new project: the Supersonics. (The name didn't acquire its second capital S until 1969.)

What no one knew, at the time, was that supersonic flight was doomed, and the Seattle Supersonics were also doomed, and it was largely, in both cases, because of Oklahoma City.

Which brings us to Operation Bongo.

Among the many problems with supersonic flight—vast expense, nearly impossible engineering puzzles, fuel inefficiency, danger—perhaps the most serious was the noise. When a large object exceeds the speed of sound, it essentially crushes the air molecules it moves through. When that air manages, very suddenly, to uncrush itself, to decompress, it creates a violent, explosive rumble that we know as a

sonic boom. It is more or less the same mechanism as thunder; a supersonic jet, in effect, carries its own perpetual thunderstorm. This is
often confusing, and terrifying, to people on the ground.

Sonic booms were a potential PR disaster—serious enough, perhaps, to endanger the whole program. How would regular American
citizens react to spontaneous explosions concussing their cities many
times a day? What would happen when houses shook, pets ran off,
children woke up screaming from naps? Would everyone eventually
adapt or would the country be driven slowly insane?

The only way to find out, the U.S. government decided, was to
test it: to unleash sonic booms at regular intervals, for an extended
period of time, on an actual American city.

But what city on earth would agree to subject itself to this kind of
torture? It would have to be a very special kind of place: not too big,
not too small, somewhere outside the national mainstream but not
so far outside that it was completely irrelevant. It would have to be a
place desperate to improve its standing in the world, a place whose
power brokers had enough control to bypass the traditional govern-
mental strictures that would normally slow things down. A place
where the media had been trained to play along, where residents had
been conditioned to suffer for the common good. It would have to
be a place where people had grown accustomed, over the course of
generations, to sudden violence erupting from the sky.

What American city could this possibly be?

The American city, of course, was the City of Oklahoma City.

The OKC chamber of commerce, a sort of corporate shadow government led by a hyperaggressive booster named Stanley Draper,
lobbied hard for the privilege of allowing the Federal Aviation Administration to rain down artificial thunder on its citizens. Just
as David Payne and his Boomers, eighty years before, had tried to
wrench Oklahoma into existence out of nothing, Draper and his
business allies were obsessed with taking that something and flinging it forward—launching the city, no matter the cost, out of the rank
of second- or third-tier American places and into the metropolitan
big leagues. The city would benefit immensely, the chamber of commerce believed, for agreeing to endure six months of sonic booms.

Among other incentives, the federal government was promising nearly $1 million to build an extra-long runway at Will Rogers World Airport, which would position OKC to become the nation's first supersonic flight hub. A temporary period of mild aural discomfort seemed like a small price to pay for pole position in the race to the future. In 1964, when Oklahoma City was chosen to host the sonic boom experiment, the chamber of commerce actually threw a party to celebrate.

Operation Bongo II, as it was officially called, began on February 3, 1964, a Monday. At 10:05 a.m., an F-104 jet—a sharp silver military dart—lifted off from Tinker Air Force Base and pierced the infinite Great Plains sky, ripping toward Oklahoma City at 1,210 miles per hour. The plane left, in its wake, what scientists call a "boom carpet"—two cones of shocked air that formed a path of noise, miles wide, on the ground. Residents experienced this as two incongruous claps of thunder. Houses shook. Dishes clattered in cabinets. People leaped from their beds. Windows cracked. Plaster fell from ceilings. The allegedly mild aural discomfort the chamber of commerce had promised turned out to be rather severe. The following day brought two more booms, the next day three. Thursday and Friday saw four and five. By the weekend, jets were hitting OKC with seven sonic booms a day, on a schedule beginning at 7:00 a.m. and lasting until evening. This would eventually increase to eight. The plan was to keep up the booms, on a regular schedule, for six whole months. The people of OKC were making history, enduring the first sustained programmatic unleashing of sonic booms anywhere in the world.

Researchers noticed, right away, something peculiar about the citizens of Oklahoma City: a "general reluctance to complain about local problems," as they would put it in their official report, perhaps due to a "general feeling of futility." Oklahomans were a stoic people, predisposed to toughing things out. This made it all the more remarkable that, during the very first week of Operation Bongo, the citizens filed 655 official complaints. By the end of three weeks, such a clamor had been raised against the relentless booming that the Oklahoma City Council voted, unanimously, to ask the FAA to stop the experiment.

This should have been the end of it, and in a normal city it would have been, but before the city council could alert the FAA, Stanley Draper's chamber of commerce stepped out of the shadows to tell the council members, in very strong terms, that such insubordination would likely cost the city its future. Annoyed residents, the chamber argued, did not realize what was at stake. Someday, in the supersonic future, they would thank the city's leaders for staying the course. Technically, the city council held the power in this standoff, but everyone knew that the businessmen really controlled the town. So the city council capitulated and reversed its vote. Operation Bongo boomed on.

Later that week, the head of the FAA personally visited OKC to raise the beleaguered citizens' spirits. He received multiple death threats and had to be escorted around town by police officers. The U.S. government, he assured the city, cared deeply about the people's "ears and nerves," but OKC's suffering would allow the country to build the best supersonic plane in the world—a vehicle that would, he promised, be a "gee-whiz aircraft." "However," he added, "if the people here do not want the tests, we will revise or discontinue them."

This, however, was false. Despite the constant complaints, despite everyone's houses rattling many times every day, the sonic booms continued. In fact, the intensity of the booms escalated. The FAA wanted to study everything: underpressure, overpressure, pounds per square foot, boom signature, superbooms. ("Double reflections by two intersecting surfaces," a report read, "can quadruple the boom pressure.") It wanted to push people's tolerance to the limit. Word got out nationwide, and reporters came from around the country to gawk at the poor citizens of OKC. The *Saturday Review* published a partial list of residents' complaints that sounded like an incoherent nightmare: "a schoolroom ceiling lamp had dropped and knocked a boy out of class for an hour . . . plaster from a bedroom ceiling had cut a three-inch gash in a sleeping woman's head . . . flocks of chickens had been crazed into erratic flight with considerable loss of egg yield and some loss of life." Even readers in London and Berlin marveled at the crazy experiment going on in America's Great Plains.

Despite local outrage and global bad press, however, the sonic booms boomed down on the people of Oklahoma City for six months, all the way until the end of July. The only scheduled day off was Easter Sunday. In the end, the city suffered 1,253 booms—a number that added up, the government calculated, to 642 million "boom-person exposures."

The following year, the National Opinion Research Center published its official report, vivisecting OKC's misery from every possible statistical angle. ("The four types of complaint activity shown in Table 15 can be combined into a Guttman scale of intensity of complaint feelings.") After thousands of interviews and hundreds of pages of charts, after adjusting for bias and sample size, the report reached a grand conclusion. "Annoyance," it announced, "increased steadily over the six month period." Residents of American cities, it turned out, even the long-suffering residents of cities in Tornado Alley, did not enjoy having their days punctuated by the explosive sound of other people, high overhead, leaving the region as fast as was physically possible.

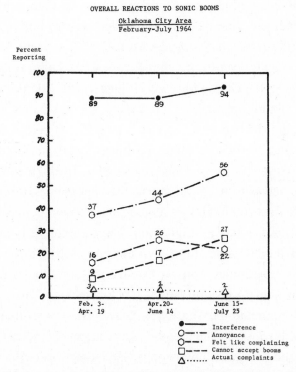

An official graph of Oklahomans' displeasure with Operation Bongo.

Not long after the end of Operation Bongo, the U.S. supersonic program went bust. Boeing's jets, it was determined, were too costly, and the outcry against sonic booms was too loud. The program was scrapped before the prototypes could even be built. In 1973, supersonic flight over the United States was legally banned. The people of Oklahoma City, for the benefit of a company in Seattle, had endured the downside of an age of supersonics that would never actually arrive.

Seattle's basketball team, meanwhile, continued to play on, its name now orphaned from its inspiration. "Seattle SuperSonics" was suddenly as nonsensical as "Los Angeles Lakers" or "Utah Jazz." The Sonics were very bad; then for a few years they were good—they won a fairy-tale championship in 1979, thirteen years after the team's inception—but then they were bad again. In the 1980s, when the NBA really took off in American pop culture, the Sonics were thoroughly mediocre. They had no transcendent star, no Bird or Magic or Jordan, and so they were second-class basketball citizens.

In the 1990s, everything changed. Seattle's cultural stock rose dramatically. The city's reigning tech juggernaut, Microsoft, led the global revolution in personal computing; its rock bands swept the nation under the banner of "grunge"; its gourmet coffee culture, as approximated by the local chain Starbucks, began to colonize every available corner of every other metropolis. Through some magic symbiosis between civics and sports, the SuperSonics, too, began to dominate. The team finally got its superstars: Shawn Kemp, the most ferocious dunker in the league, and Gary Payton, a big-mouthed point guard who could shut down any other city's best player. In 1996, the SuperSonics won an astonishing sixty-four games and plowed through the play-offs all the way to the Finals, where they met Michael Jordan and the Chicago Bulls and, like every other team in that situation, lost. Seattle became one of many second-tier U.S. cities (Portland, Orlando, Indianapolis, Salt Lake) whose athletic glory, and the civic glory that would have come along with it, got stomped out by Jordan and Chicago in the 1990s. It's interesting to speculate about what might have happened if those Chicago Bulls had never existed, how much revenue and esteem would have been spread around the other cities of the United States—cities that had invested so much into exactly that possibility. If the SuperSonics had won a championship, the team's stars would almost certainly have returned and, with the frenzied support of the whole city behind them, challenged for more championships. The 1990s would have been, even more than they already were, Seattle's decade, and it would probably have been impossible for any other city, no matter how determined, to pry the Sonics away a mere ten years later.

But the SuperSonics lost, and they never made it back to the Finals, and the stars on their roster slowly dispersed, and the team fell back into mediocrity, and then into something worse. Its stars were old, and the whole franchise smacked of desperation, resignation, faded glory, irrelevance. Entire civic histories can turn like this, on a game or two. The low point probably came in 2000, only four years after that Finals run, when the SuperSonics acquired the former New York Knicks superstar Patrick Ewing, nearly forty now and with balky knees. Seattle had become, once again, a second-tier city, picking up castoffs from more glorious places. Ewing was the end. The city's attention turned to baseball and football, more dependable roads to glory and civic self-esteem.

Meanwhile, Oklahoma City seemed to be on exactly the opposite trajectory. In the 1990s, when Seattle's stock was high, OKC's was bottoming out. Downtown was abandoned; young people and major industries were fleeing. It would have been hard to imagine a less culturally relevant place. When Seattle was hip, Oklahoma City was tragic, famous mainly for the 1995 bombing of the Alfred P. Murrah Federal Building, the deadliest attack on American soil since Pearl Harbor.

Around the turn of the millennium, however, when the Sonics were beginning to sink deeper into desperation, Oklahoma City was beginning to rise. Downtown was being tentatively rebuilt. The city had managed to talk its citizens into approving a temporary sales tax that would renew the center of the city. What would push that renaissance over the top, the city believed, was a pro sports team. City leaders fantasized openly about the National Hockey League—the least glamorous of the four major sports, more Canadian than American, but the best, everyone believed, that a city as small and drab as OKC could reasonably hope for. In its DNA, Oklahoma was a football state, with everyone's allegiance divided fiercely between the two major college teams—the Sooners and the Cowboys—but the place was far too small to attract an NFL team. Even the NHL was the longest of long shots.

City voters agreed to fund a sports arena. It would not be fancy; it would be cheap and utilitarian, without any of the amenities of a modern big-league sports arena. But it would be paid for up front, leaving Oklahoma City debt-free—important for a fiscally conservative place. The hope was that it would be just enough to lure the NHL. In 1997, two years before groundbreaking on the arena, OKC was announced as one of six contenders for four new hockey expansion teams—excellent odds. Unfortunately, the NHL crossed OKC off its list in the very first round of cuts. Arena or no arena, the league decided, Oklahoma City's TV market was too small to support a team.

Oklahoma City built its arena anyway, just in case, on the site of an abandoned Wonder Bread factory, in a section of downtown that had been known, previously, for prostitution. The new stadium hosted concerts, circuses, minor minor league hockey games, and a short-lived Arena Football team called the Oklahoma City Yard Dawgz. None of this was anywhere near the glory the city had been dreaming of, but it was something instead of nothing, and in the end, Oklahoma City believed, that was all you really needed to get yourself into the game: something.

MICROWAVE POPCORN

When does a city begin?

In most cases, we have no idea. We are forced to invent origin stories: wolves raising twins, eagles carrying snakes. The volcano god belches: civilization. We want the birth of a city to make sense, to be grand. We want it to lend its citizens meaning. But the reality is almost always far less dramatic. Cities creep into existence, like algae. (Lewis Mumford: "The city is a fact in nature, like a cave, a run of mackerel or an ant-heap.") It's silly to talk about beginnings. No one is standing there firing a starting gun. There is no primordial boom. It happens in slow motion, over generations, by accident. Travelers stop by a river to rest, they have babies, they attract and seduce enemies, they trade with rivals, they congregate, and then one century there are enough of them—the babies of the babies of the babies of the babies of the babies of the babies of the babies—to call citizens. Celts and Romans and Anglo-Saxons and Normans cross a muddy river until, after a few millennia, they congeal into London. Cavemen and Genghis Khan simmer into Beijing. The details are almost entirely lost to us. Later we can do the science (potsherds, clam shells, bone spoons, inscriptions on ruined temples), and if we're lucky we can pinpoint a century or a decade or even a year in which the city began. But we'll never know what most cities were like during their very first hour, minute, second. It doesn't even really make sense to ask. Cities are not microwave popcorn.

Unless you are talking, as we are, about Oklahoma City.

Oklahoma City is microwave popcorn. It was born all at once. It has a birthday: April 22, 1889. Noon. Precisely at that moment, history flipped a switch. Before, there was prairie. After, there was a city.

Oklahoma City was born in an event called, with extreme dramatic understatement, the Land Run. The Land Run should be called something like "Chaos Explosion Apocalypse Town" or "Reckoning of the DoomSettlers: Clusterfuck on the Prairie." It should be one of the major events in American history—dramatizations of it should be projected onto IMAX screens with 3-D explosions, in endless loops, forever. Because the Land Run was, even by the standards of America, absurd. It was a very bad idea, executed very badly. It would be hard to think of a worse way to start a city. *Harper's Weekly,* which had a reporter on the ground, called it "one of the most bizarre and chaotic episodes of town founding in world history." A century later, the scholar John William Reps reviewed the evidence and concurred. The founding of Oklahoma City, he wrote, was "the most disorderly episode of urban settlement this country, and perhaps the world, has ever witnessed."

It's hard, today, to imagine the scale of it. The idea of so many people, wanting so desperately, to move to Oklahoma. But it happened. Four years after David Payne died over his breakfast, after his relentless lieutenant William Couch stepped up to keep the Boomers booming, Congress finally succumbed to the combined pressure of the Boomers and the railroads. It agreed to open Oklahoma—the Unassigned Lands at the center of Indian Territory—for settlement. There was no orderly procedure for doing so, no process. The authorities would simply fling the land open and let everyone go at it. The rules were minimal and extremely hard to enforce. You could claim 160 acres out in the country or a small lot on a townsite. All you had to do was get yourself there, hammer in your stakes, and fight off competitors. Oklahoma would be, more or less, a free-for-all.

When President Harrison signed the document announcing the date of the Land Run—April 22, 1889—his signature sent a bat signal out over the end of the nineteenth century. Oklahoma was a gift: a free chunk of America for anyone who needed it. But it was also an emergency: it was free only to those who could get there first. The hysteria spread worldwide. People rushed from everywhere. European ports, from Liverpool to Hamburg, teemed with sudden (as they were sometimes called) Oklahomaists. There were Scots and Swedes, bands of Mormons from Utah. Classified ads appeared in the newspapers of Chicago and New York calling for meetings of potential settlers. Many of the invaders were businessmen, legal and illegal, looking to exploit the coming boom market. Others were destitute: traumatized Civil War veterans, farmers ruined by drought, beggars.

Into the middle of that tumult stepped a mild-looking lawyer named Angelo Scott. He was thirty-one years old, narrow-shouldered and clean-shaven, carefully dressed in a suit and tie. Scott had devoted his life largely to education, his own and others'. He was valedictorian of the University of Kansas, class of '77, a Shakespeare enthusiast and a European traveler, armed with enough academic degrees to scatter the acronyms freely over everyone lining up around him for the Run—AB, AM, LLB, LLM, LittD. With his gentle, intelligent face, Scott looked completely unequipped for the violence of the prairie. And yet here he was, right on its brink. The settlers around him could have had no way of knowing, before all the madness began, how central Scott would be to the survival of Oklahoma City—how much all of their lives would come to depend on the sound of his voice. He was a civilizing force; he believed in democracy, order, the larger good. For now he stood quietly, watching, one of the gathering crowd, a small node of order in the midst of all that chaos.

All around Angelo Scott, in southern Kansas, the villages near the border of Indian Territory, the buffer zone, exploded into temporary boomtowns. Suburbs of tents spread in every direction: tent casinos, tent brothels, tent churches, tent hotels, tent restaurants, tent newspapers. Swindlers arrived to siphon off the settlers' money. Dreams of new lives went up in smoke. Sham real estate agents tricked people into buying property in Oklahoma City, Texas. Some settlers ran out of money before the Run even started and had to go begging in the shantytown streets. Others just gave up and went home, not only ruined, as they had been when they'd arrived, but now double- or triple-ruined. Something like one hundred thousand settlers showed up to wait for the starting gun—roughly the entire population, at the time, of Indianapolis. It was far too many people for the amount of good land available, but from the very start, Oklahoma was an idea that far exceeded its reality.

The border of Oklahoma, this magic threshold to which settlers flocked from all over the world, was as tenuous as a border could be. It was more than three hundred miles long and in many places unmarked; where it was marked, it was often only with barbed wire or a creek or a pile of stones. It was impossible to fully patrol. Rumors circulated about nefarious schemes. Cheaters, it was said, planned to sneak in early and burn the railroad bridges so no one could follow. A French hot air balloonist planned to hover just over Oklahoma until noon, then descend onto his favorite spot before anyone else had a chance.

The only thing everyone knew for sure was that they needed to get to Oklahoma first. Time started to twist into itself. "Every man wanted to be 15 minutes ahead of everybody," one observer wrote, "and not 15 minutes behind anybody."

The day before the Land Run—April 21, 1889—was Easter Sunday. U.S. troops escorted the settlers through Indian Territory to the temporary camps near the vacancy of the Unassigned Lands. This journey, in itself, was a process. In retrospect, the Land Run seems spontaneous and wild, and it was, but nothing about it was easy. Thousands of people and thousands of animals had to be chaperoned across flooded rivers. Oklahoma's treacherous spring weather did not pause for the big event. People had to balance on rickety railroad bridges. Whole families drowned. The settlers who survived carried civilization with them in tiny pieces, like ants, in order to collectively reassemble those pieces in Oklahoma. They brought all they could afford: shovels, forks, saws, underwear, crackers, bologna, bacon, canteens, dairy cows, heavy machinery, libraries. All day on Easter, streams of wagons arrived at the border. Some settlers came alone, others as part of strategically assembled teams. Angelo Scott traveled with his brother W. W. Scott—they planned to start a newspaper together. Everyone in those roiling crowds was exhausted but giddy. The normal rules of life seemed to have been suspended. Men marched around the temporary camps hooting and firing guns. They wrestled, raced horses, played baseball, sang hymns, and shot recreationally at prairie dogs.

When the settlers woke up the next morning—at least those who had managed to sleep—it was suddenly the day itself: April 22, Land Run Day. The Oklahoma skies were a perfect blue. Throughout the morning, troops led the pioneers from the temporary overnight camps to the territorial line itself, the three-hundred-mile membrane inside of which a new civilization was waiting to be born. Everyone stood and waited. All around the Unassigned Lands, the mass thickened and thickened: humans, horses, wagons, buggies, oxen, and mules—the future population of a future American place, waiting to race into the middle of cities that didn't yet exist but that would in the next couple of hours.

Oklahoma was about to happen.

All around the border, time collapsed into a single moment—noon.

SONICSGATE

In 2005, downtown Oklahoma City was rebuilding but still sad. Streets were vacant at night. Restaurants closed at 9:00 p.m. The city could not, for the life of it, acquire a major-league sports team. It could not make itself relevant on the larger American scene. Then, as so often happened, a terrible force burst out of the sky—not, this time, over OKC but six hundred miles to the south. Hurricane Katrina wrecked New Orleans, surging over the city and devastating its infrastructure, wrenching an entire population out of its home, killing more than eighteen hundred people. It was unthinkable. Somewhere down near the bottom of the city's logistical problems was what to do with its professional basketball team, the largely unsuccessful and unloved Hornets, which New Orleans had imported from Charlotte only three years before, and which now had no practical place to play its games. The hurricane had hit in August, not long before the start of the NBA season. The team would need a temporary home.

With real grace and compassion, and also some degree of opportunism, Oklahoma City stepped forward to help. It offered itself as a host city for the Hornets, just until New Orleans could recover. After all, OKC's arena was already ready to go. The city had struck out on NHL hockey, but it was perfectly suited to this. It would be a chance to test out the arena and the fan base, to prove that it could support a real sports team, to audition for a shot at a team of its own. The NBA approved the arrangement. And so it was that, against all the odds, outside all the usual channels, and only temporarily, Oklahoma City had itself a professional sports team—and not only a team but an NBA team, one of the premier leagues in the world.

The team was called, awkwardly, the New Orleans/Oklahoma City Hornets. For Oklahomans, however, awkwardness be damned, this team was a miraculous gift. A pro basketball franchise, even a secondhand one, meant national news stories and TV broadcasts and thirty-five nights of action downtown. It meant that some of the most famous humans on earth—Kobe Bryant, Shaquille O'Neal, Kevin Garnett, LeBron James—would literally be coming to Oklahoma City, staying in its vacant hotels, eating at its merely functional restaurants. Thousands of less famous humans would naturally follow. It was not only an economic boon, it was validation: an outside chance to become a real place.

The people of Oklahoma City went crazy for their borrowed team. The Hornets were losers, but now they were Oklahoma City losers: young and plucky and wearing jerseys (at least for special games in OKC) that said OKLAHOMA CITY right on the front. Local ecstasy went far beyond any reasonable response to the basketball on display. The Hornets lost roughly half of their games and missed the play-offs, but OKC's arena was almost always sold out, and it became instantly notorious as one of the loudest places in the league. This was not run-of-the-mill sports fandom. It was an eruption of emotion from a deep primal well.

Oklahoma City fell so deeply in love with the Hornets, in fact, that it eventually decided it wanted to keep them forever. This, as you might imagine, involved some rather delicate PR maneuvering. The people of OKC did not want to be perceived as stealing another city's team in the wake of a serious tragedy, especially only ten years after Oklahoma City's own defining tragedy. But they did want to take the team. Complicating things further was the fact that the Hornets organization, at least in part, reciprocated this feeling. Attendance in Oklahoma City was far higher than it had ever been in New Orleans. Revenue was exploding. Oklahomans turned out to be insane for pro basketball, even for a team that was not fully theirs. It was the kind of fan base every franchise dreams of.

Oklahoma City made respectful overtures. A team of business-men, led by the local power Clay Bennett and the flamboyant oilman Aubrey McClendon, made an offer to buy the franchise. The Hor-nets considered this offer with interest. In the end, however, a deal never emerged. The Hornets played in Oklahoma City for two years, and then—like so many others in the city's history—they left. OKC's arena, and the downtown that surrounded it, was empty once again. That little taste of big-league glory had fled as quickly as it had come.

It was not, however, for nothing. The NBA noticed the bizarre instant passion of the people of Oklahoma City. It noticed, too, the city leadership's ability to deliver on complex logistics, responsibly, in almost no time at all. The league liked this odd mix of frenzy and level-headedness. If hosting the Hornets had been an audition, OKC had surprised everyone by nailing it. The city had launched itself, from out of nowhere, onto the top of the NBA's list of cities for pos-sible relocation. The next time a franchise was considering a move, OKC—of all the godforsaken small-time places—would be right there in the mix.

But that was a little like being next in line for inclusion on Mount Rushmore. NBA teams relocated in only the most extreme circum-stances. It took just the right string of failures at precisely the right moment: a chronically unsupportive fan base, a decaying arena, inept ownership. OKC could not afford to wait around. It knew that the momentum it had gained from the Hornets interlude wouldn't last forever. It was going to have to go out and engineer some extreme circumstances on its own.

The next NBA team to move, it turned out, was the Seattle SuperSon-ics, and the Sonics moved from Seattle largely because Oklahoma City made them move.

More specifically, it was that same collection of OKC power brokers—the corporate booster Clay Bennett, the wildcatter Aubrey McClendon—who had tried but failed to buy the New Orleans Hornets. After the Hornets refused Oklahoma City's invitations to stay, Bennett and his group surveyed the rest of the NBA landscape for vulnerable teams. They found the SuperSonics, the once-proud franchise now languishing in mediocrity, stuck in a subpar arena, ticket sales fading. Seattle loved the Sonics, sure, but it had plenty of other distractions: football, baseball, restaurants, music, theater—all that bounty of cultural relevance.

OKC, at this point, had only one focus: an NBA team of its very own, to have and to hold forever. This desire was not so much an open secret in NBA circles as a naked fact, right out there for everyone to see. "The bottom line is, we want a team for this market," Bennett said. It's hard, in retrospect, to map all the currents and crosscurrents of delusion, collusion, deception, self-deception, naïveté, false consciousness, and magical thinking that must have allowed what happened next to happen. It's hard to believe that businessmen at this level could have failed to think through the most obvious ramifications of a deal. And yet: the owners of the Seattle SuperSonics, led by Starbucks CEO Howard Schultz, sold the team to the Oklahoma City ownership group because Bennett said, however laughable this may seem today, that they were "willing to give it a shot in Seattle." "It is our desire to have the Sonics and Storm"—Seattle's WNBA team—"continue their existence in the Greater Seattle Area," Bennett wrote, "and it is not our intention to move or relocate the teams so long, of course, as we are able to negotiate an attractive successor venue and lease arrangement."

Despite much controversy and skepticism, the sale went through. This created a highly unstable situation: businessmen from Oklahoma City—men who were obsessed with maximizing their hometown's glory—now owned a pro basketball team in Seattle.

When the sale closed, Aubrey McClendon e-mailed Clay Bennett: "the OKLAHOMA CITY SONIC BOOM (or maybe SONIC BOOMERS!) baby!!!!!!!!!!"

From there, things went exactly as you would expect. Seattle declined to bankroll a new $500 million stadium for the Oklahoma ownership group. The state of Washington declined as well. It seemed presumptuous for these outsiders to expect such a lavish gift. Cool your jets, Oklahomans. Settle down. Enjoy owning our team. Don't get any big ideas.

In the face of this rejection, the Oklahoman owners e-mailed one another with the rollicking confidence of men who believed they would never be subpoenaed.

"Is there any way to move here for next season or are we doomed to have another lame duck season in Seattle?" wrote Tom Ward.

To which Bennett replied: "I am a man possessed! Will do everything we can. Thanks for hanging with me boys, the game is getting started!"

Aubrey McClendon, in his inimitable way, actually said it right out loud, to an Oklahoma City newspaper reporter: "We didn't buy the team to keep it in Seattle." For this indiscretion, the NBA fined him $250,000.

The lack of a new stadium was all it took. Clay Bennett announced that he was going to break his old Seattle stadium lease and move the SuperSonics to another, more appropriate city—a city that just happened to be the City of Oklahoma City.

This seemed like the world's most obvious bait and switch, a swindle in broad daylight, for which both sides were partly culpable. Mayhem ensued: lawsuit after lawsuit. Things got nasty. Seattle fans launched a campaign called "Save Our Sonics," as well as a Facebook group called "I Want to Kill Clay Bennett." Bennett had to surround himself, when he traveled for court appearances, with large teams of security. In aggregate, it was a PR disaster that became known, to some, as "Sonicsgate."

OKC's ownership group may have been reviled nationwide, but it got the job done. After a civil suit and some very large fines and a touch-and-go process with the NBA, after volley after volley of terrible publicity that included devastating insults from rival NBA owners (Mark Cuban: "My prejudice is against having a Dust Bowl Division"), Oklahoma City got its team—a real NBA team, no strings attached. The Seattle SuperSonics became the Oklahoma City Thunder. OKC, a city that had suffered more than any city ever should and helped other cities when they were most in need, had now acquired an NBA team through what was viewed, by many people, as a blatant act of theft. (For years, the popular sportswriter Bill Simmons referred to the Thunder insistently as "the Zombie Sonics.") Seattle was forced to yield; OKC stepped into its place. And so, nearly forty-five years after the fact, Operation Bongo found its logical conclusion in Sonicsgate.

NOONERS

What is noon?

If you think about it hard enough, like a stoner or a phenomenologist, the concept of "noon" starts to get fuzzy around the edges. Is it a clock fact—12:00—or is it an astronomical fact: when the sun is directly overhead? And who gets to decide? If it's about the sun being directly over you, then strictly speaking, in solar terms, every single place on earth—my house, your house, your left foot, your right foot—would have a subtly different noon.

On April 22, 1889, the settlers of Oklahoma thought very hard about noon. All around the Unassigned Lands, noon became a fluid concept. There was soldier noon, settler noon, bugle noon, solar noon. Wristwatches along the border were found to differ by as much as half an hour. Unsupervised settlers went with whatever version of noon seemed most advantageous. They squinted at the sun, trusted their guts, and made a run for it. In some places, there were official signals. On the western border, the military fired its howitzers—loud little snub-nosed cannons—to give people permission to run. In the south, five thousand people stood in the middle of a river, trying not to sink into the quicksand, waiting for a soldier to blow his bugle. In the north, soldiers held a rope taut across the border to keep the settlers back.

Eventually, nonsynchronously, the various noons came. The Land Run began. The people poured in. The moment the bugle touched the bugler's lips, before he'd even squeezed out a note, the settlers burst through the rope. Oklahoma was born. Rich men rode racehorses they'd bought for enormous sums only days before. Farmers rode broken-down mules. A handful of eccentrics pedaled bicycles. Poor people walked. All over Oklahoma, the people came.

Some settlers stopped just across the border, claiming the first open land they could find. Most, however, raced deeper into the territory. They wanted the good land, the prime plots near the rivers or the railroad tracks or—even better—where the rivers and the railroad tracks converged. Oklahoma City was one of those places. Another was Guthrie, thirty miles north. These hypothetical towns pulled in settlers like magnets. From every direction, people raced to grab a chunk of them.

The country was rough, and the settlers' wagons weren't designed for it; they hit dry creek beds or buffalo wallows and busted apart. The drivers flew out, got up, limped on. Before long, the prairie was covered with wrecks. Spooked horses threw their riders. At least one man fell and broke his neck. Other horses died of exhaustion. One settler fired his gun to speed up his horse but accidentally shot and killed another settler. It was absolute chaos, an explosion of humans. Actually, it was like a reverse explosion: tens of thousands of people who had been scattered across the globe, who had never had any reason to think they might be connected in any way, were suddenly thrown, in tumbling chaos, from every direction, to assemble, together at last, in a dense core in the middle of America.

THE FIRST PLAYER

James Harden was the first player ever drafted by this strange new franchise, the Oklahoma City Thunder—the first player who belonged entirely, unquestionably, to Oklahoma City, not Seattle. (The team's other young stars had all been picked when it was still just barely the SuperSonics.) Harden was the first healthy fruit of Sonicsgate and, therefore, the living embodiment of OKC's basketball dream, the beginning of a fresh, positive, native professional sports tradition. As it turned out, Harden was even more. His arrival marked the moment the switch flipped—when the Thunder began its ridiculously fast ascent from the bottom of the league to the top, from one of the worst teams in sports history to one of the most promising. He was the first player on OKC's roster to experience only success, to always win more than he lost. Harden was like a good luck charm. Actually, the beard—the beard seemed to be the good luck charm. Its arrival was when everything really finally took off.

The Thunder picked James Harden third in the 2009 draft. From the beginning, he was an unusual prospect, a twenty-year-old left-handed shooting guard with an old man's game, full of the kind of tricks you might see at your local YMCA: quick shots, misdirections, sudden shifts in speed, counterintuitive arm motions designed not necessarily to score but to bait defenders into fouls. It was hard to know how much of this would translate successfully to the NBA, and some critics thought the Thunder picked him a little high. He was not the sort of talent who was going to single-handedly lift a franchise. His destiny appeared to be more modest: to become a first-rate supporting player. In fact, this was why the Thunder wanted him. They already had their rising stars in Westbrook and Durant. Now they needed some elite backup. Harden, unusually for a young player, told the team that this was exactly what he wanted. He was more than willing to come off the bench. He wanted to be not the driver of the franchise but a cog in the machine.

During Harden's rookie season, 2009–10, the beard was modest and closely cropped, the kind of thing you could wear to a business meeting without raising eyebrows. His play was, like most rookies', promising but inconsistent. And yet the team, with Harden on board, immediately leaped several rungs up the NBA's ladder of success. By the spring of 2010, the Thunder had more than doubled their win total from the previous year and even, unaccountably, made the play-offs, during the first round of which they managed to bother the mighty world-champion Lakers. The Thunder lost, in Game 6, on a desperate last-second putback after a Kobe Bryant air ball. It was a loss, but it was also a miracle, and after the buzzer the fans remained on their feet, sending wave after wave of rapturous noise crashing down over the players. All of this suffering had been worth it: giving the Hornets back to New Orleans, the radioactive taint of Sonicsgate, the early days of losing and losing. Civics and sports were beginning to merge into glory, something that had eluded the city for its entire history. The fantasies were becoming real. So much hypothetical goodness was so obviously on its way.

In Harden's second year, he started to grow the beard out. As it grew, so did his mojo. As the shag began to hang from his face, Harden's tricks started, improbably, to work in the NBA. He played in every single game in 2010–11, and the Thunder improved again, winning fifty-five regular-season games and crushing their first-round opponent in the play-offs. This would have been plenty, all by itself, but things kept going. The Thunder won their second-round series as well, an epic bloodbath against the Memphis Grizzlies that went all seven games and included four overtimes—the kind of test that a very young team almost never ends up surviving. This meant that, less than two years after being discussed as possibly the worst team of all time, the Thunder were playing in the Western Conference Finals, one step from competing for the actual title. They didn't make

it there, not yet—the Dallas Mavericks, that year's eventual champions, knocked the Thunder out—but it was another loss that felt like
a triumph. Harden, meanwhile, had grown into exactly the player
the Thunder had hoped he would become. In the 2011 play-offs, as a
featured substitute, Harden's scoring average matched his uniform
number: 13.

The next year, 2011–12, Harden's beard grew thicker and more
unruly, and Harden himself began to exceed everyone's expectations. He became not just a good NBA player, not just a key part of
a winning team, but one of the most efficient scorers the league has
ever seen. Still coming off the bench, he averaged seventeen points a
game—not an earth-shattering number in itself, but amazing considering the way he did it. In his third year, Harden was scoring
more efficiently than LeBron James, Kobe Bryant, Michael Jordan,
Wilt Chamberlain, or any of the other all-time greats you'd care to
name. His game had matured into a beautiful funkiness. He could
create offense instantly, out of nothing—hesitation dribbles followed
by explosions of speed, huge wandering steps that made everyone
think he was committing traveling violations when, in fact, somehow
he wasn't. Harden was beginning to innovate, exploring the outer
boundaries of basketball in a way that only special players do. All of
this made him an absurdly powerful weapon off the bench. He won
Sixth Man of the Year the way Freddie Mercury would have won a
small-town dive bar's Wednesday night karaoke contest.

When the Thunder entered the 2012 play-offs, expectations were
basically infinite. All of the team's bets on young prospects had, impossibly, paid off: Durant was a full-on superstar, Westbrook was
heading in that direction, Serge Ibaka led the league in blocked shots,
and Harden was unlike anyone else on the planet, present or past. In
the most crucial moments of the most crucial games, he was often
given control of the Thunder's offense. If you needed an improbable
basket, Harden would find a way. The Thunder blew through the
first round, fought through the second, and even, this time, made it
through the third. After all the controversy and the shame and the
losing, Oklahoma City became the youngest team in thirty-five years
to reach the NBA Finals.

By this time, Harden's beard was ragged and long, a full-on Rip Van Winkle. The people of Oklahoma City had embraced it as a kind of spiritual mascot. During the play-offs, a local building hung a giant Harden beard from its facade. A local supermarket made a James Harden cake, with a huge mess of black icing extending off its sheet-cake chin. The Internet swarmed with memes. Someone posted a photo of a Harden fruit salad: pineapple head, blackberry beard. A superfan got a large tattoo of James Harden's hairy face on his arm. In the official Thunder retail store at the OKC arena, the best-selling item was a Harden-style fake black beard, which fans at home games would rubber-band to their faces. Harden's beard was one of the great PR victories of modern Oklahoma City: an image of hip, young, urban blackness—excessive and silly and joyful—representing a place previously known for none of those things. It was a busy vector of national media attention, ubiquitous on ABC and TNT and ESPN, joked about by broadcasting crews. Every single time the beard flashed on the screen, Oklahoma City's brand shifted slightly; it was nudged a little further toward cool and young and quirky and relevant. The beard was undoing many decades of history. The Finals couldn't come quickly enough.

When they arrived, the glory-starved fans of Oklahoma City packed themselves into the middle of their overwhelmingly underwhelming downtown, onto a block that used to smell like baking bread, into their budget sports arena that had been built in a failed attempt to lure a hockey team. And—blessings upon blessings—the Thunder actually won the game. The Oklahoma City Thunder, a team that had not existed five years before, held a 1–0 lead in the NBA Finals. This was against the Miami Heat, the most famous superteam in the world, led by multiple imported all-stars, including the omnipotent LeBron James. OKC was winning, at last, on so many levels at once.

Game 2 came down to the final seconds, as did Games 3 and 4. Unfortunately, somehow, none of them went Oklahoma City's way. In the end, the magic of that obscenely young team ran out. It was only a shot here and a whistle there, but the Miami Heat pulled away. It seemed like a classic case of a rising team being not quite ready for the biggest moments. LeBron James won his first championship, and all of Oklahoma City went home to vibrate, uncontrollably, in anticipation of the following year. No one held this loss against the Thunder, and no one doubted that they'd be back. After the series was over, the Thunder players landed at Will Rogers World Airport to discover a great loving mob of Oklahomans waiting for them, screaming their gratitude into the clear prairie air. It was mass hysteria, Great Plains Beatlemania. The Thunder's failure in the Finals didn't matter, and not only because a return trip seemed more or less guaranteed. The team's failure didn't matter because even failure, at such a rarefied level, was so much more than Oklahoma City had ever dared to dream it might have.

It would have been hard to find anyone, in the summer of 2012, who didn't think of the Thunder as future champions. NBA narrative law basically required it. People were beginning, cautiously, to use the word "dynasty." At that moment, both the city and the team—the least likely NBA city in America and its unlikely juggernaut—were quivering right on the edge of ultimate victory. All they had to do was let time catch up with them.

IN PRESTI WE TRUST

One day I happened to be standing in the Thunder's practice facility, an hour or two after a team workout, when I saw a man suddenly step out onto the empty gym floor. He was not a player. He was slim, bespectacled, and clean-shaven, with neatly trimmed red hair. He wore slacks and a button-up shirt. The man emerged from a corner office, walking fast, with focused purpose, on an errand that sent him cutting across the floor—until, as if he had heard a sharp noise behind him, he stopped. He pivoted, turned back, and walked straight to the nearest ball rack, where he bent over, reached down, and took one of the basketballs between his fingertips. Very slightly, the man rotated the ball. Then he stood up and scrutinized his work.

This, I thought, was interesting.

The Thunder's practice facility—formally, the INTEGRIS Health Thunder Development Center—sits some distance north of downtown, on a stretch of service roads where the city begins to show signs of reverting to prairie. Inside, the building is a world unto itself, a shimmering kingdom of order and precision. Everything is new and state of the art. There are hydrotherapy pools and a theater-style film room with leather seats. There are private chefs who cook the players special-order omelets and whatever else they might want. The building seems to contain its own weather.

The true signature of the practice facility, however, the thing that all visitors will eventually notice, is the straightness of its balls. There are racks built into every wall, all the way around the gym—three-by-three grids of official leather Spaldings—and every ball, at every moment, has its label out and its letters horizontal, as if a crew of surveyors has just rolled through with calipers and laser levels. The perfection is uncanny, unrealistic. I often stood and marveled. It looks like the balls have never been used, and yet everyone could see them being used every day. In spare moments, I found myself scanning them, one by one, looking for a glitch in the matrix. But I never found one. Occasionally you would see an assistant coach or an equipment manager stoop down to straighten a ball, but mostly they were just there already, straight. A player once told me that he sometimes hesitated to grab one to shoot with because he didn't want to ruin the symmetry.

Now, out on the gym floor, I watched the red-haired man continue to straighten the balls. He adjusted one, then another, then another. He worked with remarkable pace and precision, like an action hero defusing a bomb. What intrigued me was that this man was not an equipment manager or an assistant coach or a trainer. He was, outside of Kevin Durant, the most important person in the building: Sam Presti, the Thunder's executive vice president and general manager. Presti was the architect of OKC's basketball success. He had drafted all of the Thunder's young stars, negotiated their contracts, hired their coach, surrounded them with veterans, and even helped to design the practice facility itself. It was his job, ultimately, to find a way to resolve the Harden crisis. He was the man on whom the future of Oklahoma City basketball depended. And now here he was, alone in the gym, straightening the balls.

I watched Presti work on the rack until every discernible imperfection, however minor, had apparently been fixed. Then he stood and turned and walked away, back to his original errand, striding across the gym—until, after only a couple of steps, he stopped again. He turned around, walked back to the rack, bent down, and made one final adjustment. The balls, now, were straight beyond straightness. Presti turned and walked away, this time with all of his original focus, crossing the gym and eventually disappearing through a door in the distance. On the other side of that door, no doubt, some other problem was waiting to be straightened out.

———

In most professional sports organizations, James Harden would have had everything he wanted immediately—max contract, larger role in the offense, ubiquitous billboards, whatever. If this had cost extra money, if it had complicated the team's chemistry, well, that was the cost of a dynasty. A talent boom like the Thunder was riding was worth every risk. If the citizens of Oklahoma City had been in charge, the situation would have been taken care of long before— Harden might have become the first basketball player ever to live in his own publicly funded skyscraper. So how was it possible that we were in the middle of October, right on the brink of the new season, and Harden's contract was still unresolved?

This was in large part because the other major player in the Harden crisis was Sam Presti, who approached every situation with exactly the rigor he applied to the straightening of the balls.

Like the owners of the team, like the citizens who filled the arena, Presti wanted Oklahoma City to enjoy every ounce of its potential glory. But he had a distinct vision of what that glory was, and of how the city would get there. True success, Presti believed, was sustainable—not a narrow spike but a long, high line. Every detail and decision, however small, had to be coordinated with a larger plan. If that ruled out instant gratification or risky stabs at short-term value, Presti was perfectly willing to give those things up. He was methodical, logical, patient, and precise; he abhorred shortcuts and half measures. This was, of course, an admirable approach for someone running an organization as complex as an NBA franchise. And yet it could not have contrasted more sharply with the presiding spirit of Oklahoma City.

Oklahoma City had chaos in its DNA. It was a boomtown, past and present. The Thunder's arena was named after Chesapeake Energy, one of the most aggressive energy companies in the world. Its notorious co-founder Aubrey McClendon was like a figure straight out of the Wild West, a human avatar of the spirit of Boom—infamous not only for his brazen public statement about stealing the Sonics from Seattle but for his never-ending pursuit of risky deals of sometimes dubious legal status. McClendon was simultaneously filthy rich and dirt-poor, with an $8 million wine collection but also enough loans to sink him many times over. Boom thrived on exactly this kind of risk, recklessness, confidence, and opportunism. It looked for unexploited pockets of value that normal people were too cautious to seize—whether land, oil, loans, or layups—and it lunged for them. If there were obvious downsides to that lunging, well, Boom would deal with that someday in the future—not now, not when the booming was good. Boom believed that it could surf on booms, beating the odds forever. When a bust eventually came, all of those previous booms would have been worth it, and the next one, surely, would make up for the loss. Boom believed that the only crime was not to go for it.

In this world, Presti's approach was alien, confusing, sometimes upsetting. He was like a column of soldiers marching, in tight formation, through the middle of a bison stampede. Presti's process was unglamorous and incremental, risk-averse and disciplined. "Process," in fact, was exactly the word he used most often to describe it. "You have to believe in the process," he would say, almost constantly, with such quiet conviction that it became a sort of incantation hovering outside of everyday language: the Process. "Process" might sound like nothing—generic bureaucratese—but the more time you spent around the Thunder organization, the more you felt its power. The Process involved thinking not three months but three years ahead; it involved understanding every rule, however minor, of the NBA's Collective Bargaining Agreement; it involved knowing the salary and contract status of every player in the entire league; it involved ending every practice with extra free throws. (The Thunder had led the league in free-throw percentage two years in a row.) It meant sending your PR team to listen in on every interview. The spirit of the Process was beginning to catch on in NBA front offices across the league, but Presti was one of the earliest and most extreme practitioners. The Process was like a spell that could turn every other virtuous abstraction—culture, community, stability, winning—into reality. "You have to believe in the Process," people around Presti would say. "The Process will take as long as it takes."

I once asked Kevin Durant to tell me about his first years in the NBA—the losing and losing and losing.

"It was terrible," he said. "In Seattle, my rookie year, we didn't win. My second year, in OKC, we were working hard but we weren't winning. I remember we lost three or four games right at the buzzer. I was like, Why is that happening to us? We worked so hard, we're out here outplaying teams, and at the end they just beat us. That pisses you off. I'll put it like that. It does. But I learned that you can't get bored with the Process."

I stopped him.

The Process, I said—that's a Sam Presti thing.

"Yeah," he said. "That's what I learned from him."

You have to believe in the Process.

Sam Presti was essential to Oklahoma City, but he wasn't an Oklahoman. He grew up about as far from the place as you could get, both geographically and spiritually: Concord, Massachusetts, home of the Puritans and Transcendentalists, birthplace of the Revolutionary War. Presti was Concordian, in a deep sense: puritanical and transcendental, flinty and idealistic—a revolution of one. He was determined to leave every organization radically better than it had been when he joined it. As the captain of his college basketball team, Presti required teammates to sign a code of conduct in which they promised to quit if they didn't work hard enough. He once personally took six charges in a single game, an almost mythical feat of self-sacrifice.

Presti was the first major hire of the Oklahoman businessmen who seized control of the Seattle SuperSonics. He was only twenty-nine years old and working for the San Antonio Spurs, where he had established himself, in no time at all, as a front-office prodigy, rising from making smoothies at the practice facility to designing a scouting database so sophisticated it was adopted across the NBA. As a scout, Presti discovered, and then convinced the Spurs to draft, an unheralded French teenage point guard named Tony Parker, who would go on to lead San Antonio to four championships. One year before their move to Oklahoma City, the SuperSonics hired Presti and put him in charge of overhauling the entire organization. He was, by far, the youngest GM in the league.

"We want to initiate a process," Presti said in his first official press conference.

In Seattle, Presti looked at the Sonics roster and saw perpetual mediocrity. So he intentionally blew it up. He traded the team's established stars—Ray Allen, Rashard Lewis—and started to build again from scratch, this time according to a rational plan. This would require, he knew, some immediate short-term trauma, perhaps even some losing seasons, but the losing would result in high draft picks, which would yield future stars, which would eventually lead to sustainable excellence. It was the only way. At the time, critics referred to this, disdainfully, as "the Presti method." For Presti, it was simply the first necessary step of the Process.

Presti governed not only traditional basketball decisions (scouting, drafting, trading) but absolutely everything. No detail was too small. He gave the practice facility new carpeting and brighter lights. He had distracting decorations removed: photos of old Sonics all-stars, a big mural of the NBA championship trophy. What good was nostalgia about past glory days or aimless fantasies about future titles? Parking lot attendants were told to learn the names of everyone who used the arena's private lot. Promotional images of players were strictly regulated. With the second pick of the 2007 draft, Presti chose Kevin Durant, one of the most heralded basketball teenagers since LeBron James, and then prohibited the Sonics marketing people, against all of their instincts, from anointing him the next Michael Jordan and the savior of the franchise. Media access to players was severely restricted—a policy that, predictably, did not play well with the media. "The buttoning up of the organization," the *Seattle Times* reported, "comes across as militant to some."

Militant or not, Presti's control paid off. In 2008, when the franchise moved to Oklahoma City, Presti oversaw the design of the team's uniforms, its practice facility, its locker rooms, its ticket stubs. Faster than anyone could have imagined, the Process produced real-world success. The Thunder improved, dramatically, every year of its existence, both in terms of regular-season winning percentage (28, 61, 67, 71) and play-off advancement (no play-offs, first round, Conference Finals, Finals). By 2012, when confetti was raining down on the people and players of Oklahoma City, it seemed like there must have been some kind of hiccup in the space-time continuum. Entire generations of basketball progress had been compressed into four short years. Rookies had bloomed into instant stars. No one important ever got injured. ESPN ranked the Thunder the No. 1 franchise in all of sports. The Thunder's luck was so good that it seemed to transcend luck. It seemed like magic. The fans began to invest their fanaticism not only in the players on the team but in the reclusive red-haired man at the top. A popular motto started to circulate in Oklahoma City; Thunder fans repeated it to one another the same way that Trekkies said, "Live long and prosper." The motto was "In Presti we trust."

It was all thrilling. And yet the euphoria was at least partly based on a deep misundertanding. Many people in Oklahoma City worshipped Presti not because they bought into the Process but because the Process had been, in this case, so explosively successful that it looked exactly like a boom. For all his meticulousness, Presti looked like a gambler with a scorchingly hot hand. Surely this misunderstanding would be revealed in time. And what would happen when it was? The culture clash would be fundamental. The Process is for people who trust time. Boom is for people who don't.

I was granted an official meeting with Sam Presti in the fall of 2012, while the city was still paralyzed by the Harden crisis. Presti asked me to meet him at Oklahoma City's most sacred spot: the National Memorial, site of the 1995 bombing of the Alfred P. Murrah Federal Building. Many OKC residents saw the Thunder and the bombing as opposite ends of the same civic spectrum—a public triumph that helped heal a public tragedy. Civic leaders tended to be season ticket holders. This included the National Memorial's director, who encouraged her staff to wear Thunder blue on game days. Presti was a member of the memorial's board, and he was careful to incorporate the memory of the bombing into the identity of the team. Every new player was required to take a tour, before he ever set foot on the court, so he could better understand the community he would be representing.

Presti met me in the museum's lobby. He was only thirty-five and looked even younger, with an absence of beard every bit as powerful and expressive as James Harden's presence of beard. He wore designer glasses and hip sneakers, and he gave the impression of a man with a recurring haircut appointment on his calendar. He was, as an interview subject, unusually quiet. As the museum's director gave us a tour, Presti ceded the floor almost entirely to her. When he did speak, it was with obvious caution, each word weighed and reweighed, and he often stopped himself, in mid-sentence, to rephrase.

The most revealing thing Presti said to me came after our museum tour, when we walked together around the memorial's grounds, past the reflecting pool that marked the spot where the bomb was detonated, past the 168 bronze chairs that represented each of the dead. Oklahoma's summer had been unusually hot, and the city's lawns were on life support, and Presti pointed out the health of the memorial's grass. It was so thick and lush that it looked almost fake, and it had been mowed into precise circles around the trunks of manicured trees. Presti pointed out how much work it takes to keep everything looking like that—how much deliberate organization, how much vigilance.

Basketball's defining challenge, once you get past the physical stuff, is social. More than any other American sport, it is a game of civics. Every player, on every play, has to find the proper balance between self-interest and self-sacrifice—a threshold that moves with just about every bounce of the ball. The game is fluid, with everyone shifting roles and responsibilities more or less constantly. The calculus of selfishness versus self-sacrifice can be crushingly complex. A

properly balanced team can make that calc
unbalanced team can make it hopeless.

The Harden crisis, for the Thunder, wa
ics. The team's offense featured three pla
been an entire offense unto himself—a vo
best case. There is only one ball and onl
The pairing of Durant and Westbrook
own—two opposite temperaments and t
The sudden emergence of Harden threat
disaster. When the Thunder's offense wa
run to the Finals, it looked like organiz
as it had been at crucial points during
stagnation, isolation, wild shots. The o
component parts, none of which was p

Presti's decision was tricky on sev
clearly too good for the role he had be
creative, too effective, too much in c
was scandalously overqualified. And
quite good enough for the new role h
yet, as Westbrook or Durant, and no
NBA history was littered with pro
spotlight, flopped. In Oklahoma Ci
be the absolute center of everything
as his boosters said, even if the Thu
on the floor to utilize all his goodr
trouble affording him. As the end
he was asking for the maximum
for four years, the same kind of m
But the Thunder was already righ
and if they blew past it they wou
something OKC's conservative ow
ing. A salary cap penalty would a
flexibility—a restriction that wa
required absolute control. Blowi
ting someone walk into the gym
balls before practice.

To
tions,
out its
the pe
sat ou
bench
It wen
scoring
game
context
game, a
months
his tale
ers, tha
der beat
to see w
unit Ha
Houston
his game
for Hard
This
pride. Th
one wee
entirely—
year that
promised
$50 milli
signature.

ward the end of October, in the midst of the Harden negotia-
the Thunder conducted a small test. The team was finishing
preseason—a formality for a title contender such as OKC. But
nultimate game held special interest. Durant and Westbrook
. Harden played. The spotlight was his. It was a chance for the
player to show everyone what he could do as a No. 1 option.
t horribly. Harden took seventeen shots and made only two,
his 13 points almost entirely on free throws. One preseason
as the smallest possible sample size, of course, but given the
, it took on extra weight. Critics argued that Harden's poor
long with his underwhelming performance in the Finals a few
before, was proof that he didn't deserve superstar money, that
t was too dependent on being surrounded by superior play-
he should never leave the team. As the *Oklahoman*'s Thun-
writer, Darnell Mayberry, wrote after the game: "Harden got
hat life is sometimes like for a max player. That's the type of
rden will be expected to carry if he inks a max deal in, say,
or Charlotte or Phoenix. I think we can all agree that's not
. . . . This game could (and maybe even should) be a red flag
en signaling what life is like on your own."

was how the preseason ended: a warning against excessive
ere was now only one week left until the real games started,
before the Harden crisis morphed into something else
-a dark cloud hanging low over the actual season, over a
was supposed to have been a sun-drenched march to the
land. Every day, the pressure built. The offers increased:
n, $52 million. Still Harden did not sign. $54 million. No
$55 million. Nothing.

PRAIRIE CHICKENS

Oklahoma City two hours before the Land Run.

In the moments just before the Land Run, in the grassy open space that was about to become Oklahoma City, a wonderful calm, for the last time, reigned. Wind wove itself through blades of grass. Water burbled in the river. Troops talked quietly. They were stationed here, on this looping portion of the North Canadian River, to oversee a patent absurdity: the birth, in a single day, of a city. The man in charge was Captain Daniel Stiles, formerly a federal marshal in the frontier town of Waco, Texas. He wore the deep blue uniform of federal power under a perfect light blue sky. It was cloudless, for once, threatening nothing—deferring, perhaps, to the chaos of humans brewing on the ground. Oklahoma Station was out in the middle of the Unassigned Lands, where the Santa Fe railroad tracks crossed the North Canadian River—a promising site for a brand-new city.

At that moment, the teeming crowds of pioneers were still lined up at the border, very far away. But Captain Stiles knew that they would be coming, and his job was to make sure they behaved themselves when they did.

At noon, or something like it, Captain Stiles signaled his bugler. The bugler bugled: the quick, peppy notes of a military camp song hopped out over the empty prairie. This was mostly symbolic, because the only residents currently within earshot were frogs, prairie dogs, ducks, turkeys, deer, quail, and huge flapping flocks of weird birds called prairie chickens. Male prairie chickens have inflatable orange throats and what looks like a second set of wings—pure black—on their necks. At that time of year, they would have been busy with a ritual called "booming": puffing their orange throat sacs, flapping their neck wings, leaping around, squawking for mates. It's possible that the infantry captain and his bugler were watching the prairie chickens boom. It's possible that they were not. History does not record this fact. Other than that, the place was empty. Once upon a time, there would have been bison here, vast shaggy multitudes of them, but they had all been wiped out in the great bison holocaust of the previous decades. The Indians, too, were gone; they'd been evacuated from the Unassigned Lands, for spurious reasons, twenty years before. Oklahoma City was now a purely American blank slate: a strip of railroad tracks, a few ramshackle buildings for the railroad workers, and—to the horizon in every direction—inhuman gobs of open land, blooming and blowing and sprouting in the spring. It was April 22, 1889—the magic day, moment zero. The wildflowers, everyone reported, were infinite. Dogwoods were in bloom. Bits of grass would have been drifting around from south to north, visual tracers of the constant Oklahoma wind.

As the bugle sounded, Captain Stiles prepared himself to wait. Chaos, he knew, was on its way, but it would take a while to get there. The border was fifteen miles off in every direction, in some places much farther, and he calculated that even a man riding a racehorse at reckless speeds from the nearest point would take an hour to arrive. The waves upon waves of less fortunate settlers—the families stuffed, with all of their possessions, into canvas-covered wagons, the dirty men flogging starving mules, the buggies clattering over dry creek beds, the passengers leaping through the broken windows of overloaded train cars, the riderless horses, the last lonely men staggering in on foot—these would all take much longer. By nightfall there would be thousands of citizens here, an instant society. But first, Captain Stiles could have reasonably expected one last hour of silence.

He would have been wrong. Oklahoma City happened immediately. The bugle notes had yet to fade when, like some kind of ancient creation myth, the empty landscape sprouted people. It was an ambush of settlers. "Almost like the rush of jack rabbits from cover," the historian Stan Hoig describes it, "men suddenly appeared out of the long grass around the depot area, bounding here and there. They dropped from the leafy branches of trees; they crawled out of and from under freight cars; they sprang from gullies and bushes; they poured from the few buildings at the station; and they suddenly came galloping up on horseback from nowhere." These were, in the lingo of the times, Sooners, or Moonlighters. We would call them cheaters. They had been waiting for this moment for years. Some of them had been part of David Payne's original Boomer army, nearly a decade before, so they felt specially entitled to the land. Some had been hiding out in the wilderness around the station, illegally, for weeks or months, living in holes or bushes or improvised huts, dreaming of the glory of Oklahoma City. Some had leaped off moving trains just the night before, thumping and rolling over the prairie at high speed, breaking various bones—a physical tax on early entry that they were perfectly willing to pay.

At the sound of the bugle, all of the cheaters came running. The land was free, they knew, only for those who got there first. There weren't nearly enough troops to stop them all, and there was too much chaos to even know whom to stop. An entire crew of surveyors popped out of the wilderness, complete with their equipment—chains, poles—and started organizing the prairie on the run, marking off lots and blocks on a completely theoretical Main Street. Twenty minutes after the bugle sounded, there were already forty tents set up. By 12:45, fifteen minutes before Captain Stiles had expected to see his very first settler, the city's best spots had all been taken. By the end of the day, tents would stretch to the horizon—it looked, according to *Harper's Weekly,* like "a handful of white dice thrown out across the prairie." The wildflowers were crushed, the soil torn up. The frogs and ducks and prairie chickens had scattered. In a matter of hours, Angelo Scott wrote, "the natural beauty of the scene was completely obliterated, beyond recognition or hope of repair."

Settlers race for plots during the Land Run, April 22, 1889.

This was the beginning of Oklahoma City. Captain Stiles did his best, but he didn't have much help. As an officer, he was trained to recognize chains of authority, and in Oklahoma the chains of authority were twisted, broken, stolen, melted down. The city had an instant population of ten thousand with no organization whatsoever—no government, no official limits, no laws, no framework for making laws, no legal entity on behalf of which to even build a framework on which to eventually make laws. There was no state of Oklahoma. There was no historical precedent. It was pirate civics. The men who were supposed to be helping Captain Stiles, the U.S. marshal and his deputies, were busy instead grabbing the best land for themselves. (Most of the deputies had signed on only for this purpose, and they took the bugle call as a signal of their resignation.) Technically, government officials were not allowed to claim land, but practically it was a free-for-all. The railroad station's postmaster left his post office—a converted dirt-floored chicken house—and claimed 160 acres right on the edge of town. One military man who'd been stationed just outside Oklahoma City to guard against cheaters spent the weeks leading up to the Land Run building a house on rollers so that he could move it, at noon, to his favorite site in the area. People claimed land not only for themselves but for distant relatives who never intended to come to Oklahoma and for fictional characters they invented on the spot. The settlers of Oklahoma City explored the nearly infinite gradations between cheating and non-cheating. One man who'd sneaked onto the townsite early soaped up his horse to make it look foamy, as if he'd just galloped a long way. Another shaved off his beard and dyed his mustache black so no one would recognize him.

The first legal settler of Oklahoma City, by most accounts, was a rancher named William McClure, one of the major landowners in the territory east of the Unassigned Lands. He came riding into town just before 1:00 p.m.—an inhumanly fast trip. It turned out that McClure had paid some of his cowboys to go into the territory ahead of time and leave a relay of fresh horses along the trail. When McClure's horse got tired, he jumped onto a new one. When that horse got tired, he switched again. He had found a way, without technically cheating, to outrace time.

Just after 2:00 p.m., in the middle of all that chaos, the first train of settlers pulled into Oklahoma Station. It was twenty-four cars long. Settlers were hanging off the sides and clinging to the roof; heads and arms were sticking through the broken windows. Eyewitnesses said it looked like a giant centipede wriggling toward the city. As the train began to slow down, passengers came spilling out from all sides. They hit the ground, rolled, and went sprinting for lots. According to one settler, "The whole country where the city now stands was black with a surging, crowding, running, yelling mass of humanity." "It seemed," Angelo Scott would remember, "as if some thousands of human beings had gone mad." The townsite had only one well, and an enterprising settler cornered it immediately, standing on top of it, guns drawn. He set up a lucrative business charging five cents per drink, an exorbitant price that the people, their throats clogged with prairie dust, had no choice but to pay. Eventually, Captain Stiles's soldiers seized the well and returned it to the public.

Who was in charge? Nobody. People claimed every available scrap of land, without regard for how the city might eventually need to function. "Every stake driven represented a gamble," Scott wrote. "It might prove to be on a lot, when lots should be established, and with almost equal chance it might prove to be on a street or an alley." One woman staked her claim in the middle of the railroad right-of-way. It took the soldiers some time to convince her that, if she chose to build there, her property would be rumbled to the brink of destruction, over and over, on a regular schedule, for the rest of her natural life.

The first night in Oklahoma City must have been profoundly disorienting—some combination of sleepover, refugee camp, Super Bowl tailgate party, sit-in, and Visigoth raid of imperial Rome. At dusk, as if by agreement, the settlers of the new city all stopped working. They laid down their hammers and rifles, took a break from jockeying for plots. They made campfires. It was the end of what would have been, without exception, the strangest day of everyone's life. These former strangers had become, in no time at all, a single town.

Oklahoma City, from that point on, would grow in fast forward, a parody of a normal city. Within days there would be wooden houses, slapped together quickly out of preassembled frames; within months, brick warehouses and shops; within years, grand stone mansions; within decades, skyscrapers, convention centers, sports arenas—all the precursors of the twenty-first-century renaissance.

That first night, however, it was only dirt. Dirt on the ground, dirt in the air. The soil, having lost the anchor of its plants, blew around freely in the wind. The day had been hot, but the night was uncomfortably cold. Fortunate settlers had tents. Those who didn't just lay on the ground—strangers, side by side, packed together for warmth. Centipedes swarmed all over the place, wondering what the fuck was going on. Men walked together through the night, talking. New residents continued to arrive in the dark.

As Oklahoma City struggled to settle down to its first night of sleep, something strange happened, an incident that everyone present would remember for the rest of their lives. Between 10:00 p.m. and midnight—accounts vary—a man's voice suddenly penetrated the silence. It was deep, slow, and loud enough to carry all the way across the new city, over the tents, the railroad tracks, the cotton-woods, the river, to every one of the ten thousand. The message it carried was clear but mysterious. "Oh, Joe!" the voice called out. "Here's your mule!" This phrase hung in the air, not explaining itself, until suddenly another resident echoed it, every bit as loud: "Oh, Joe—here's your mule!" The voices crossed, and then other settlers started joining in. "Oh, Joe!" they called. "Here's your mule!" It turned into a kind of game. Soon the landscape filled with voices shouting the nonsensical mantra, louder and louder: "OH, JOE—HERE'S YOUR MULE!" On a hill a mile from town, Captain Stiles and his troops heard the call, and they joined in, too. It was coming now from everywhere, out of sync, overlapping. The words didn't matter anymore; the particular man and his mule, if they even existed, didn't matter—as far as most people knew, there was no Joe, there was no mule. The words were a closed loop, an incantation through which Oklahoma City was going to chant itself into existence. This was an experiment in civilization. The place was so new and precarious, so strange, that its residents had to shock themselves into community using whatever method they could find—the way a human body, freezing to death, tries to generate its own heat by shivering. Perhaps that crazy late-night shouting could create just enough of a bond to allow Oklahoma City to withstand the turbulence of the next several days, years, decades. It was later reported that "Oh, Joe—here's your mule!" spread that night across the entire Unassigned Lands, across Indian Territory, more than one hundred miles, all the way back up to Kansas.

NO BEARD

At 11:58 p.m., eastern time, on October 27, 2012, three days before the start of the NBA season, Kevin Durant tweeted the word "Wow."

Over the next ten minutes, that word was retweeted more than ten thousand times. An unbelievable thing had just happened. Sam Presti, against all expectations, against conventional wisdom, against narrative law, against everything that was true and good and right in the world, had solved the James Harden problem. He had done so at a time, and in a way, that no one had expected, and that many people would struggle to accept for many years to come.

Sam Presti had traded James Harden.

Everyone was shocked. News this big usually leaks before it happens, or it is so obvious that it doesn't need a leak, but there were no leaks in the Thunder organization, and no one had seen this coming. Sam Presti had traded James Harden. He had sent the beard out of town. He had done so ruthlessly, in cold blood, at the least likely possible moment, directly before the first game of the season—a time when teams are typically tightening screws and doing everything possible to avoid drama or change of any kind. It was as if someone had flung an open bucket of paint into a restaurant's kitchen ten minutes before it opened. The decision seemed rash, desperate, impulsive, self-destructive. But it came from Sam Presti, so it couldn't have been any of those things. It must have been the Process in action.

Harden's beard, the hairy encapsulation of the Oklahoma City renaissance, was suddenly gone. It now belonged to, of all places, Houston. The odious braggadocious Texans were going to enjoy OKC's first-chosen young star. The particulars of the trade were secondary to the shock, but soon they became part of the shock. Harden was arguably the best young shooting guard in the league, and yet the Thunder had received no equivalent star in return. What they got back looked like a drawer of spare parts: a few middling draft picks, a dubiously promising rookie, and a veteran shooting guard named Kevin Martin. It was almost nothing, in the aggregate, with the slight potential to someday become sort of something. It seemed like the kind of trade that a team agreed to only under extreme duress, not the situation the Thunder found itself in: an ostensibly happy player, part of a rising young core, still under contract for another year, was asking for a few more million than management was offering. Even if Harden had refused to sign a new contract extension, most people had expected the Thunder to hold on to him for the season, ride his blooming talent back to the Finals, and hope that success might change things—either soften Harden's negotiating stance or send enough money pouring into the organization that the owners would throw caution to the wind. That was the conventional wisdom. Presti, however, had blown the conventional wisdom up. He was straining the very outer limits of "In Presti we trust."

What on earth had happened?

The basic facts were simple: Harden had asked for the max, $60 million over four years. The Thunder had refused to give it to him.

They had offered, in the end, $55.5 million, but they'd refused to go all the way to $60 million.

There were, of course, different explanations for this.

One was a victim narrative. The Thunder was part of the NBA's persecuted underclass: a small-market team. With its paltry Dust Bowl revenue streams, it simply couldn't afford to stockpile stars, an advantage, for the most part, limited to the big-city franchises: the Lakers, Bulls, Knicks, Nets. (OKC's TV revenue, for instance, was thirty times smaller than Los Angeles'.) By the summer of 2012, when Presti was negotiating with Harden, the disparity between rich and poor in the NBA was worse than it had ever been. A new Collective Bargaining Agreement had imposed a draconian luxury tax, which turned out to be especially punitive for the Thunder. The team could no longer afford to pay for all the young stars it had drafted so well. Presti was a victim of his own success. The league itself had stepped in to derail the Process.

That was the victim narrative.

But there was also a villain narrative. This was the argument that the Thunder was actually raking in profits, was, in fact, one of the wealthiest teams in the entire league, and could therefore easily have afforded to pay Harden. The only problem was that the owners were cheap. What would they care if Durant and Westbrook, two of the most exciting young stars in the NBA, never won a title? What did they care that a championship in Oklahoma City would have transcended basketball and become a larger civic good—a way to redefine the place forever, to purge historical demons and radically expand the possibilities of the future? What kind of monsters would go to all that trouble to steal the team from Seattle, devastating its friendly rain-soaked people, and then whip poor Oklahomans into a frenzy of hope and expectation—only to suddenly close their wallets when the city needed them most? Who would do such a thing? Clay Bennett, Aubrey McClendon, et al. were perpetrating a fraud, basically, on the people of Oklahoma City—all so they could save what amounted, for them, to pocket change.

That was the villain narrative.

The truth, of course, was trickier. Neither narrative, victim or villain, fully explained the facts.

The Thunder's final offer to Harden had been less than the max, yes, but barely: $55.5 million instead of $60 million. And here is something curious. Contrary to popular belief, that $4.5 million gap would not have kept Oklahoma City out of the luxury tax. If Harden had signed the offer on the table, an offer that Sam Presti presumably wanted him to sign, the Thunder's payroll would have busted right through the salary cap, incurring all kinds of penalties.

This raised a rather large question. If Presti and the owners had been willing to go into the luxury tax to keep Harden, why didn't they just go all in and offer him the max? Surely $4.5 million dollars, spread over the life of a four-year contract, could not have been the deal breaker. The answer had to be something other than money.

It was, of course, the Process. That $4.5 million gap was symbolic: a test of Harden's civic commitment to the Thunder. Earlier in the summer, Serge Ibaka had accepted less than a max extension, when everyone knew he could have waited to get more on the open market the following year. Even Westbrook, in accepting his max offer the previous year, had agreed to waive certain standard incentives. Only Durant—the golden child, the one who would be there forever—made no concessions in his contract. To remain a part of the team, Harden would need to prove that he was willing to sacrifice. If he wasn't willing to give up that fraction of a maximum salary, he probably wouldn't be willing, later, to sacrifice more important things: playing time, shots, individual glory. Such trade-offs were at the heart of Sam Presti's vision of long-term success.

But Harden, it seemed, was tired of being overshadowed. He was intrigued by the possibility of leading his own team. During the Olympics, that summer, he had been pumped full of confidence by Kobe Bryant and Chris Paul, who'd told him—perhaps sincerely, perhaps strategically in hopes of breaking up a rival team, probably both—that he was too good to be coming off the bench, too good to defer to anyone else, that he needed to get out of Oklahoma City.

At the end of October, when the Thunder tendered its final offer to Harden, Presti made it clear that it was now or never. Rejecting the offer would be the equivalent of a trade demand. To which Harden responded, flatly, "Do what you have to do."

The Process dictated what to do next. Presti reacted immediately, coldly, on principle. There was no point in keeping Harden around for the rest of the season, compromising the integrity of the team, possibly ruining its chemistry, only to eventually lose him for nothing the next summer. To take that approach—hoping, irrationally, that things would get better—would have been to embrace the spirit of Boom.

This was an extreme test-case for Presti. If there had ever been an excuse to ditch the Process and go all in on a Boom, 2012 Harden was it. The talent he was beginning to show overflowed any spreadsheet cell. You couldn't find it on an actuarial table. This was as close as Boom and Process could ever come to touching each other, to trading places. Boom, in this very rare instance, might actually have been safer than the Process.

If Sam Presti was going to gamble, however, he was going to gamble on the sanctity of the Process. If that meant risking an immediate championship, being skewered on ESPN, alienating sections of the fan base, he was perfectly willing to take it. He would surrender one risky shot at glory now for five sounder shots down the road. What good was one championship, however great it felt in the moment, if the conditions that made it possible immediately disappeared, forcing everything to start all over again? How long could a people take comfort in a single trophy sitting alone on a shelf, gathering dust? The Process had spoken. Harden was gone. Oklahoma City would move on without him.

This left many people in OKC deeply confused. They had heard Presti talk about the Process, of course, and they approved of it in the abstract, but that had been in a very different context, in the middle of an unprecedented boom of talent and success. Presti's approach, they were about to learn, also inevitably involved real pain. In the wake of the Harden trade, the citizens regarded the bespectacled architect of their basketball success in a slightly new light. The difference between Boom and Process was only now being properly seen. Sam Presti's solution to the Harden crisis was about to be put to the test, in real time, in front of the entire world. The season was about to begin.

PART TWO

SIZE

Plato limited the size of his ideal city to the number of
citizens who might be addressed by a single voice.
—LEWIS MUMFORD, *The City in History*

Oklahoma City is too big to go back now, but there was a
time when she was not too big to go back. The great boom
had not come, and say what you will, it is booms that make cities.
—ANGELO C. SCOTT, *The Story of Oklahoma City*

You can't teach size.
—TRADITIONAL BASKETBALL WISDOM

OUR HOLY CHIEF METEOROLOGIST
AND SEVERE WEATHER SAVIOR

Gary England in the early 1970s.

No propaganda, perhaps, has ever been more transparently false than this account of Oklahoma City's weather, published in 1890 by one of the town's first settlers:

> There is something in the very air that brings an actual sense of rest. It is a mature glory; one of nature's poems, and while lulling and soothing tired men and jaded women, it does not enervate like the climate of the tropics, but fires the blood, puts

light behind the eyes and polishes the intellect. . . . The valley of the North Canadian is a veritable garden of Eden. Natural splendors glisten upon every hand. The soil will produce every plant, fruit and cereal known in the United States. There are no drouths [*sic*], no cyclones, no grasshoppers, no floods, no devestating [*sic*] rains or storms. It is the happy average of every joy and rest known to the world. It is the mundane "home of the soul." Come, live and be happy.

The writer of this alternate-reality meteorological fantasy was not a sci-fi novelist but a journalist who published under the pen name "Bunky," and of course he knew perfectly well that what he wrote was absurd. The wind was probably whipping at his hair and blowing dirt into his face even as he scribbled on the page. The settlers of 1889 arrived to find all kinds of trouble brewing in the sky: terrifying thunderstorms, stultifying heat, and, above all, a needling, relentless wind that blew sand into their tents and pants and sandwiches.

Oklahoma, it became clear almost immediately, was not in fact an earthly paradise but a place cursed with all of the things Bunky insisted it wasn't: droughts, cyclones, grasshoppers, floods, and (especially) devastating rains and storms. Indeed, it was cursed with even more: dust storms, leftover hurricanes from the Gulf, and hail so outrageous that people have come to describe it by analogy to sports equipment—Ping-Pong balls, golf balls, baseballs, softballs. The only constant in Oklahoma's atmosphere is inconstancy. If you don't like the weather, locals always say, wait five minutes. Systems pass through the sky like moods: blue, black, gray, steady, misty, gusty, placid, vicious, freezing, scorching, wet. What Bunky chose to interpret as a golden mean—"the happy average" of every other type of climate—was actually its opposite: a hundred-car pileup, both spectacular and deadly, of every possible kind of American weather.

What were Oklahomans to do? Well, endure. All they could ever do was endure. There was no way to know when a storm might come or what would be left when it passed. The tribes of the plains had sacred rituals through which their holy men could speak with the sky; a tornado would tell them, in a voice that sounded like fire, how big it would be and where it was heading and what it wanted to achieve. The pioneers had only folk wisdom. You knew a tornado was coming because the horses were acting crazy or the birds had stopped singing or the air was suddenly turning green. Then you braced yourself and hoped to survive.

Modern Oklahoma City, fortunately, had developed better defenses than folk wisdom. It had built up, in its relatively short life span, a lavish arsenal of weather prediction technology—a whole meteorological-industrial complex. At any given moment, hundreds of forecasters sat staring at thousands of screens, across which slid data-rich psychedelic blobs that represented the earth's atmosphere in miniature: its moistures and pressures, flows and counterflows, lightning strikes and hailstones. Across the state, radars stood silhouetted against the flat horizon, harvesting information out of the Great Plains air. Just south of OKC sat one of the greatest hubs of weather knowledge in the world: the National Weather Service's Storm Prediction Center, at which federally funded scientists huddled under fluorescent lights, studying detailed statistical breakdowns of every solitary hiccup in the sky. In times of looming crisis, OKC residents' smartphones blared with push alerts—Severe Thunderstorm Warning, Dangerous Hail, Tornado Warning, Tornado Watch—and bizarre vehicles rolled out onto the wet roads: SUVs loaded with dashboard cameras and stabilization spikes and wind gauges and probes to be launched into the heart of the funnels themselves.

Among all of this drama and hubbub, in the popular imagination, one figure rose above the rest: Gary England. He was the chief meteorologist at Channel 9, and had been for forty years, and in this time he had established himself as the most powerful weatherman in all of the Great Plains—a far grander position than that might, at first, seem. TV weathermen, with their goofy neckties and catchphrases, are by nature slightly comical figures. Under the predatory skies of Oklahoma, however, the job was about much more than slapping suns and rain clouds up onto giant maps. It was often literally a matter of life and death. In the worst tornadoes, despite all the advanced technology, despite the storm shelters and sirens, dozens of people would still inevitably die. In such times, England's job was not only to warn the areas most in danger, but also to help manage people's emotions: their sorrow, relief, confusion, and awe. Multiple times every spring, England would guide Oklahomans through experiences so intense they bordered on religion. He was a small man, two or three heads shorter than the basketball stars who were making the city famous, but in times of high meteorological stress, his voice filled the entire state. He was able to interpret, for the masses on the ground, the mysterious forces descending from the sky.

OKC's most popular blog, a satirical outlet called the *Lost Ogle*, tracked the city's meteorologists as if they were pro athletes, and over the years it had elevated England to a position all his own, referring to him, only half-jokingly, as "our holy chief meteorologist and severe weather savior." It supplied him with a whole elaborate mythological backstory. ("At the Carnegie State Fair in 1971, Gary fought off a large squall line with only a sword and shield.") On October 3, 2012, in celebration of England's seventy-third birthday, the site's proprietor declared an official Gary England Day, for which he took a pilgrimage to the weatherman's tiny hometown of Seiling, one hundred miles northwest of OKC, and made an offering of old hailstones at the tornado siren. For the people of Oklahoma, England had become a kind of cult figure—some combination of Obi-Wan Kenobi, Foghorn Leghorn, Uncle Jesse from *The Dukes of Hazzard*, and Zeus.

My personal introduction to Gary England only reinforced this legend. One afternoon, under agitated skies, I drove up to the Channel 9 Weather Center, which sat in the middle of a wide, flat field just down the road from the Thunder's practice facility. I found England standing there, in the center of the studio, inside of his command module—a horseshoe of seemingly infinite screens lit up with vivid colors. He wore a dark suit; studio makeup made his skin slightly orange. Although England was seventy-three, he was blond and baby-faced and looked, somehow, perpetually nine years old. He leaned over his screens, studying the atmosphere, describing what he saw for the people of Oklahoma City.

After a while, England took a short break, and the news moved on to something else. He relaxed his posture and stretched. I walked over to introduce myself. Just as I approached his command module, however, England glanced at one of his screens—and suddenly he started running. He burst right past me, through the studio, past further banks of screens, and the station's younger meteorologists stood up one by one to follow him, and soon there was a chain of people streaming toward the exit. England finally stopped at the back of the building, where a big metal door sealed the weather center off from the actual weather outside. He leaned against it, easing it open. A burst of moist air flooded into the studio. England leaned outside and looked up. The rest of us crowded behind him, craning our necks, looking for whatever Gary England had come all this way to see.

Outside was only the parking lot. The weather floating over it looked exactly as it had when I arrived a short time before: a hunched gray sky pouring steady rain, clouds sucked forward by a wind that would have been obscene anywhere else but in Oklahoma was just a stiff spring breeze. The trees seemed to be rolling their shoulders, loosening up for some vigorous activity to come.

England pointed to a red-and-white metal broadcast tower on the building's back lawn.

"Watch the tower," he said.

We all watched the tower.

A few seconds later he added, with the rhythmic precision of an orchestra conductor calling in the kettledrums, "It should be coming—right . . . now."

And then it came. The clouds accelerated, whipping past the tower as if fleeing something terrible. The rain went from a steady pour to dense, hectic, laser-targeted swarms coming in at us sideways. The trees churned with new urgency.

England, having apparently seen all he needed to see, turned and left us at the door. It was unclear whether we had just witnessed a weather forecast or a feat of shamanism—if England had been predicting or controlling the storm.

———

Gary England became the chief meteorologist at Channel 9 in 1972, when he was thirty-three years old. There was no reason to believe, at the time, that he was on his way to becoming anything special. He was a country boy of no great distinction, born in a wooden shack, by the light of a kerosene lamp, into the hands of a doctor who, according to family lore, was paid in chickens. The England family moved frequently throughout his childhood, once living in an old bank vault. For years, Gary dreamed of being a pig farmer. When he finally left home, as a teenager, he spent weeks sleeping in his car on the outskirts of Oklahoma City.

Through all of this, England had one passion: the sky. He grew up in a world in which tornadoes were deadly mysteries. There were no radar warnings; if you were lucky, a policeman would be stationed at the edge of town to watch the sky for funnels. Growing up, England listened to stories about the killer tornadoes of the old days and saw grainy photos of their aftermath: dead bodies piled in wagons or stacked in saloons. At nine years old, he lay awake all night listening to emergency vehicles screaming past his house on their way to the town of Woodward, which had just been hit by a historic storm. A funnel had ripped across the ground for a hundred miles, swelling at times to nearly two miles wide, killing or maiming more than one thousand people. It was April 9, 1947—the first entry in a long list of notorious dates that would come to dominate England's life. He and his father once had to take shelter from a sudden storm in a chicken coop. "Good Lord!" his father shouted over the noise. "Will we ever know when these darn things are going to hit us?"

England's life mission became figuring out when those darn things were going to hit us. He studied meteorology when it was barely even a recognized field. In the navy, he got access to his first actual radar, and when he touched it, he shook with excitement. Back in Oklahoma City, he started forecasting the weather for a small radio station, working in the attic of a tiny house downtown, with an old radar repurposed from the nose of an airplane. Eventually he made the leap to TV, where traditional journalists shunned him in the halls, and producers sometimes asked him to wear a wizard hat on the air. A weatherman was still a novelty, an informational clown.

And yet England's appeal transcended those narrow constraints. He brought to the job just the right combination of showmanship, ambition, devotion, and folksy charm. He spoke in a deep-country Oklahoma accent, a mild blend of drawls and twangs. He pronounced the word "precautions" "per-cautions." He invented a creature called the Thunder Lizard, a 1,200-pound beast that changed color with the weather. Viewers would call in to report sightings. People smiled at his corny catchphrases: "Jump back, Loretta!" "It's Friday night in the Big Town!" At the end of late-night storm sessions, England would turn to the camera and ask his wife, Mary, to put a pot of coffee on for him.

The sky, in those days, had an overwhelming advantage. Forecasting tools were still low-tech: chalkboards, magnets, hand-drawn maps. In the early 1970s, England used to drive out to Tinker Air Force Base, in the middle of the night, to scavenge first-rate meteorological maps from garbage cans. The standard warning time for a tornado was roughly sixty seconds, which meant that, in the interval it took to make a piece of toast, the clouds could reach down out of nowhere and thrash your house to splinters, flinging your furniture all the way to the middle of Missouri, destroying your entire life.

England was obsessed with improving this state of affairs. Somehow, he convinced the owner of Channel 9 to invest $50,000 in a new, purpose-built radar system. This allowed him to extend warning times so significantly that he was able to issue a public warning before the National Weather Service did—a scandalous violation, back in the day, of the meteorological hierarchy. Ratings rose. Eventually, England talked the station into further investments: its own satellite, color radar technology. In 1980, he persuaded the station to spend $250,000—an astronomical sum—on a new system that no one was even sure would work. Doppler radar promised not only to show where storms were but to look *inside* them, to reveal their inner motions. It worked, spectacularly, improving tornado warning times from one minute to more than twenty. In 1982, England used his Doppler to warn the city of Ada one full hour before a tornado arrived.

As the technology improved, England's popularity grew. When

the skies turned dark, everyone in the region huddled around their TVs, mainlining the coverage—the helicopter footage and radar images and projected storm paths and screaming storm chasers— and England blended all of those inputs like an orchestra conductor. He elevated the science of meteorology to a kind of public art. Channel 9's ratings exploded. In the 1980s, England became the first media figure in Tornado Alley to sign a million-dollar contract. He made barnstorming tours across the region, lecturing crowds of thousands about the subtle violences of the ocean of air that churned and teemed and flowed over them. He helped to make people fluent in the language of supercells, wall clouds, dry lines, wind shear. In 1996, England appeared as himself in the movie *Twister*. By then, he had inspired his own traditions of folk wisdom. You knew a storm was going to be bad, Oklahomans would say, when Gary England took off his jacket.

As a tornado chewed through town after town, intersection by intersection, England was focused and practical—less a news anchor than a sort of televised first responder. He told people exactly what to do, reminding viewers constantly of the essential precautions: if you can't get underground, get to the center of your house; put on protective layers; climb into the bathtub; cover yourself with a mattress. When England's storm chasers took unnecessary risks out on the roads to get spectacular shots, he reprimanded them on the air. He often turned to the camera and spoke directly to any children who might be trapped at home alone. It was almost like Gary England was right there in the house with you, except he was also in everyone else's house, and somehow he was up in the sky, too, feeling it out firsthand.

After decades of this, Gary England inspired a public love and gratitude that went far beyond anything that could be measured in ratings. A former governor of Oklahoma described him as "omnipresent, like the clouds and the sun." Survivors of the strongest tornado in recorded history—May 3, 1999—painted GOD BLESS GARY ENGLAND and THANKS GARY ENGLAND FOR GETTING US OUT ALIVE!! on the wreckage of their houses.

In the final days of the James Harden crisis, toward the end of October 2012, Channel 9 threw Gary England a party. It was his fortieth anniversary as the station's chief meteorologist. There were corny taped testimonials from the on-air talent—"Lookin' good, big guy," said the anchor Robin Marsh—as well as tributes from prominent community figures. Tom Ward, head of the local energy giant SandRidge and one of the co-owners of the Thunder, sent bland regards from his beige corporate headquarters; two women holding a massive boa constrictor sent congratulations from England's "friendssss" at the zoo. The Thunder cheerleaders shook their pom-poms. A local gun-range owner, tipping a shotgun over his shoulder, said, "Gary, you've been the real big shot in Oklahoma for over forty years."

The milestone, however, was bittersweet, because it also meant that England's career was coming to an end. He was as revered a public figure as Oklahoma City had—a stability to counter the instability of the sky—but he could not stay on the air forever. The thought of clicking over to Channel 9 during a tornado outbreak to find someone else standing there, someone with different rhythms and judgment and lingo, was enough to send jitters of distress through certain segments of the civic nervous system. "Being a weatherman in OKC is a big deal," wrote the Lost Ogle, "but being the Chief Meteorologist at Channel 9 is something special."

"The day Gary England retires will be a monumental changing of the guard," wrote a commenter at OKCTalk.

At the end of its fortieth anniversary tribute, Channel 9 announced that it had managed to accomplish what Sam Presti and the Thunder could not: it had signed its star, Gary England, to a new "lifetime contract." But this was largely symbolic. The next day, word leaked out that the station had already hired England's successor—and their choice was surprising, on several levels. To fill the most august weather slot in all of Tornado Alley, Channel 9 had poached a storm chaser from its rival, Channel 4. David Payne (no relation to the other David Payne, long-dead leader of the Boomers) was, in many ways, the opposite of Gary England: loud and excitable, a showman, famous for pushing the boundaries of danger and driving recklessly close to tornadoes. *Lost Ogle* commenters referred to him mockingly as "Doomsday Payne." As one reader put it after the announcement was made: "He isnt a stormCHASER!! He is a supervisor of CHAOS!!!"

England's new lifetime contract contained an escape clause. He could go off the air, at any point, and still be paid as if he were on the air. As 2012 dragged toward its close, England thought about this option constantly. Sanity called him toward it. The job was exhausting. During the worst storms, he could be on his feet for twelve hours without a break. His eyes stung; his legs ached. It was a terrible pressure to know that people were inevitably going to die, and that his smallest decisions could make that number lower or higher. England still worked constantly, poring over data, planning coverage, sparring with news directors, researching new technology. There was tension behind the scenes at the network; England had accrued huge power over the years, and corporate leadership was looking forward to moving on to someone with less of it. No one England had started his career with was still around. His replacement was already on the staff, waiting to go.

But Gary England was not done yet. He did not enjoy the job anymore—it wasn't that. He felt no thrill, these days, at the arrival of a major storm. A tornado was an arm of pure terror reaching down to destroy lives on the ground, and he felt a civic responsibility to stay and fight it off for as long as he could. He believed that TV meteorology was not just a vehicle for selling advertising but a serious public good. He did not like the networks' trend toward sensationalism— the hyperventilating wall-to-wall coverage of every blip, designed not to inform people but to scare them into watching. In recent years, the storm seasons had been relatively quiet, but England knew the sky was bound to wake up soon, and he was going to hang on as long as he could so he would be there when it did. The sky was not done with the people of Oklahoma City, which meant that Gary England was not done with the sky.

THE SCARS OF A BLOODLESS CONFLICT

Oklahoma City's first day was total chaos: the sudden injection of ten thousand people into a formerly empty patch of the plains.

What came after the chaos?

More chaos. When the sun came up on Tuesday, April 23, 1889, the morning after the Land Run, it was clear that the settlers had created a mess. You could not, with a straight face, have called this place a city. A first come, first served wilderness adventure turned out not to be a successful urban planning policy. Among many other things, a functional city needs negative space: streets, alleys, parks, plazas—room for people to move. Oklahoma City had none of these. It was wall-to-wall private property. The settlers' claims were packed so tightly that the narrowest alley couldn't have squeezed between them. There was no room for actual streets, let alone the grand boulevards David Payne had imagined and mowed in Ewing nine years before. Some individual lots had been claimed by three or four or five rival settlers simultaneously, none of whom was willing to yield.

Angelo Scott, wedged into that mess, recognized the problem right away. Somehow, for the city to survive, it was going to have to be organized. This was a polite way, Scott knew, of saying that some residents were going to have to give up their land. And this, of course, was no casual thing. Land was the only possession of real value that many settlers owned in the world, the very thing that they had just raced and half-starved and frozen themselves to procure. Now they were going to be asked to surrender it, and for what? Not for money—some plots would probably already have been worth thousands of dollars on the open market—but for an abstraction: the benefit of the future of the town. The public good. Even under ideal circumstances, this would have been a very hard sell.

And circumstances were far from ideal. No one was in charge to negotiate such delicate transactions. There was no way to hit the Pause button on the city's ridiculous growth. Oklahoma City just kept going. Minute by minute, the settlers became more entrenched on their claims. The tents already stretched, practically flap to flap, across the city, and now some of them were being replaced by hasty wooden shacks, hammered together out of lumber waiting at the train station. Oklahoma City's disorder was beginning to solidify.

The city's most viable chance for order came, ironically, from its most shameless cheaters. These included William Couch, the leader of the Boomers. After the death of David Payne in 1884, Couch had spent years agitating politicians, recruiting new followers, cultivating ties with the railroads, and leading his illegal raids into the Unassigned Lands. Once the date of the opening was announced, he did not waste any time. He helped found the Seminole Town and Improvement Company, a group of profiteers from Kansas who, in the absence of legal organization, decided to organize Oklahoma City illegally. (The Seminoles were not actually Seminole Indians, of course—having stolen tribal land, white businessmen were now stealing tribal names.) Couch and the STIC knew that, in the middle of so much entropy, order meant profit. Months before the Land Run, they had signed on as railroad workers and deputy marshals, not in order to actually work but to gain access to the territory. They entered the Unassigned Lands, over and over, to scout and scheme about the best way to lay out the still-hypothetical town. Standing knee-deep in the scrubby grass, they mapped out streets, intersections, and lots. On the morning of the Land Run itself, while most settlers stood waiting anxiously on the border for noon, the gentlemen of the STIC chugged right past them on a special early train direct to Oklahoma Station. The waiting settlers booed, sensing some evil that they were powerless to stop. On that train, the Seminoles carried secret maps on which Oklahoma City had already been laid out, in great detail, to their exact specifications. When Captain Stiles's bugle sounded, it was Couch and the Seminole surveyors who immediately came crashing out of the bushes. They marked off the town, one historian writes, "with military precision." By the time most settlers arrived, eager to grab a patch of virgin prairie, the Seminole Town and Improvement Company was waiting to greet them, offering to sell $25 certificates of ownership for pieces of prime real estate in the already-laid-out town.

"It was really a brazen attempt to steal the townsite and sell it to the people," Scott wrote. "To this day I stand astounded at the audacity of these men. Were there not thousands of men watching every movement? Could they possibly have believed that in all that multitude there was no one intelligent enough to know that their scheme was utterly fraudulent and unlawful?"

Scott called the Seminoles "the evil genius of the founding of Oklahoma City." And yet he was also forced to acknowledge a bitter paradox: any order, even a corrupt order, was better than total chaos. "Oklahoma City would have been spared her birth-pain agonies," Scott wrote, "if those first-day citizens had tamely accepted the Seminole survey in full and paid the modest price demanded. Thus would Oklahoma City have been founded in absolute peace upon the basis of absolute fraud!"

But there was not absolute peace. Nor was there absolute fraud. Everything was thoroughly intermixed. The Seminoles, in fact, were not the only aspiring organizers of Oklahoma City. A rival group from Kansas, the Oklahoma Town Company, also planned to control the settling of the city, but its members didn't arrive until 1:15 p.m.—far too late. (Never mind that this would have been a record trip in a buggy without the benefit of roads and, therefore, probably evidence of cheating on their part, too; they hadn't cheated well enough.) The OTC arrived to find that the STIC had already laid out the heart of the city, so in a panic they rushed to the other side of the tracks and started organizing there, until they realized that federal troops were already using that land, so they rushed south in even more of a panic and started organizing there. Two rival and incompatible plans for Oklahoma City began to emerge. The OTC's plan, on the south side, was laid out according to the points of the compass. The STIC's, up north, was aligned with the railroad tracks, which ran at an angle. It soon became obvious that the widths and directions of their streets would not match up. Neither company was willing to yield. Meanwhile, unaffiliated citizens were racing around grabbing every scrap of land they could find, ignoring any suggestion of order.

A crisis seemed inevitable. Everyone was armed. Everyone was desperate. No one was truly in charge. It is a miracle that, in the midst of all this chaos, Oklahoma City didn't explode into violence.

A good portion of that miracle came down to Angelo Scott. He was, as another settler put it, "one of the wonders of the frontier . . . the only man in town who could come out of a tent in the midst of an Oklahoma dust storm immaculate in white collar, white tie, Prince Albert coat and a plug hat." On the morning of the second day, surveying the chaos in his finery, Scott decided to act. He called over three boys, handed them bells, and sent them riding off on ponies, ringing and shouting, announcing a town meeting later that day on the corner of what the cheaters had already marked off as Main and Broadway.

Citizens thronged there by the thousands. A wooden box was turned over and set down in the dust. Onto that box stepped Angelo Scott. A human voice, at that time, was still strong enough to carry across the entire city, and Scott's boomed out, oratorically, to describe everything that was at stake: the group of men attempting, illegally, to control the town; the time to stop them running out. The settlers listened intently. The citizenry, Scott said, would need to work together, immediately, to stop William Couch and the Seminoles' coup. He proposed a democratic solution: a planning committee, popularly elected, that would shape Oklahoma City purely for the public good.

The crowd agreed. One by one, candidates stepped up onto a box next to Scott, and the crowd shouted out questions—name, origin, occupation. Based on their answers and their looks, candidates were either booed or cheered. Much booing and cheering led, eventually, to the election of a committee of six. This committee was charged with trying to reconcile the two competing town companies, either convincing one to yield or the two of them to blend.

The town companies, however, refused to hear it.

Another, even larger mass meeting was convened. Men stood on wagons and shouted out speeches. Some of the loudest voices advocated violence. The people had already tried diplomacy, they argued, and it had failed. The cheaters were flagrantly cheating, and soon it would be too late to reverse the damage. It was still only twenty-seven hours into the existence of Oklahoma City, and somehow the entire future of everything seemed to be at stake. This meeting went on for three tumultuous hours. Men shouted threats, offered arguments and refutations. The town teetered toward, and then away from, civil war. Whenever he could, Scott counseled order and restraint. He was a small man, but he had authority, and the people listened to him.

In the end, under Scott's enlightened influence, the mob chose nonviolence. With the ballots of their boos and cheers, they elected a committee of fourteen and a subcommittee of five. These men were charged with rooting out the disorder hardening at the center of the city. Their mission was to override the clashing town companies and

Part of the citizens' committee to organize the town.
Angelo Scott, clean-shaven proponent of order, stands at the far right.

supervise an entirely new survey, one made in the spirit of long-term civic health, not for the immediate profit of a privileged few. Oklahoma City, on the second day of its existence, was determined to pull civilization out of the chaos.

And so the committee of fourteen—with Angelo Scott as its leader—and the subcommittee of five—of which Scott was also a member—marched out, in a spirit of civilian justice, to organize the town. They went systematically from lot to lot, telling settlers, in the name of fairness and reason, who would be allowed to stay and who would need to go. A huge crowd followed them, critiquing or approving each ruling. In some cases, the subcommittee had to listen to the evidence of five rival settlers on a single lot, then decide, right there, which of them was telling the truth. It was grueling, ugly, complicated, unsatisfying work, and yet it had to be done. It was the Process. Scott and the men worked all day, and then, by torchlight, deep into the night. They started again at dawn.

Eventually, the crowd following the committee and subcommittee grew so large and rowdy, cheering and jeering every decision, that Angelo Scott and his officials had to walk inside a portable riot fence: a triangular frame of three long boards, nailed hastily together, that they carried with them wherever they went. Captain Stiles sent soldiers with bayonets to help keep the peace. For two days, the committee and subcommittee worked inside their triangle of justice, grinding their way north toward Main Street, leaving a rational town in their wake: streets, blocks, one claimant per lot. Their rulings left plenty of people unhappy, but also an emerging sense of order.

Finally, on Friday, the real trouble began. The committee of fourteen and subcommittee of five were approaching Main Street, which marked the southern edge of the Seminole Town and Improvement Company's control. The settlers who lived there had paid for the privilege of doing so, and the STIC was prepared to guarantee that investment. No one seemed likely to move.

At this point, Angelo Scott paused to consider his options. He sent a telegram to the United States secretary of the interior in Washington, D.C., to confirm, officially, federally, before any of the trouble started, what he already believed to be true: that William Couch and his cabal of private businessmen had no legal authority to organize Oklahoma City for their own profit, at the expense of every other citizen.

The secretary of the interior confirmed it. Scott led the committee of fourteen and the subcommittee of five ahead, into enemy territory, to mark out new lines for the town.

They put down stakes on Main Street.

The settlers there pulled them up.

They put down more stakes.

The settlers pulled them up again.

This went on for a while, until finally a group of men with rifles arrived to suggest that everyone would be better off if Scott and his organizing citizens would simply leave this part of town alone.

Faced with the direct threat of violence, the committee did what committees do best: they retreated, conferred, and decided to call another meeting.

Once again, thousands of settlers converged on the corner of Broadway and Main. Men climbed back up onto the wagons and shouted themselves hoarse. Justice was clearly on the side of the citizens, but—just as clearly—actual violence would be required to impose it. The temptation to be justly violent must have been extremely strong—the urge to take up arms and march, in formation, south against north, waging actual battle, blood soaking into the mud that had been so recently prairie.

This was the closest Oklahoma City would ever come to a full-on civil war.

Instead, the citizens swallowed their anger and found it in themselves to compromise. They agreed to elect another committee, this one an unpleasant hybrid: five citizens, five Seminole cheaters. Angelo Scott, naturally, was one of the five citizens. After some deliberation among the ten, it was clear that Couch and his cronies were not going to back down. They would not even consider changing the layout of their side of town. So the hybrid committee was forced to come up with an awkward solution that pleased no one. Where the two incompatible surveys met—the citizens' survey and the STIC's— the planners stitched them together with "jogs": funky mismatched blocks, in the middle of downtown, all along Grand Avenue. Suddenly, to keep going straight on any of the city's north–south streets, you had to turn ten feet out of your way. It was an affront to urban geometry and a nightmare for traffic, but it prevented a war, so it had to be done. Settlers in this transitional zone, who had only very recently survived the arbitration of the citizens' committee, were now forced to give up their land to make way for the jogs. A newspaper said that Grand Avenue should be called "Stolen Avenue" in honor of everyone who lost their lots because of the realignment. Angelo Scott called the jogs "very literally the scars of a bloodless conflict." They remain in Oklahoma City to this day—reminders, across the generations, of the messy necessity of occasionally joining incompatible things.

An intersection in Oklahoma City's first days.

Kevin Durant and Russell Westbrook, 2012.

In terms of pure talent, Kevin Durant and Russell Westbrook formed as powerful a duo as you were ever likely to see in sports. It was absurd, really, that one team had both. Durant was seven feet tall, slim and smooth, with a skill set no one his size had ever come close to showing. Watching him play was like watching the Eiffel Tower breakdance. Westbrook was only six foot three but so ripped with muscles that a teammate once described him as "a He-Man doll," and he attacked opponents with an eye-popping headstrong fury that made him look, at times, actually insane.

In playing style and mojo, the two stars were as different as twenty-four-year-old professional athletes could be. Durant had soft, thoughtful eyes, and when he spoke to you he really *looked* at you, checking in, gauging your reactions to his words. Westbrook's eyes were so intense it seemed like they might actually hurt what they looked at, and so it was probably a blessing that he rarely made direct eye contact. During media sessions, he spoke as if he were being interviewed by the inanimate objects around him—fielding urgent questions from the locker-room door, with follow-ups from the carpet and the ceiling tiles.

Durant and Westbrook were a mighty but imperfect fit. They clashed and blended, amplified and diminished each other, in ways that were hard to parse. KD was civilization; Russ was chaos. KD was the metronome; Russ was the thrashing guitar solo. KD was the scenic cliff, Russ the waterfall raging primally over the top of it. It was tempting to call them a yin and a yang, but in a yin-yang, the oppositions are perfectly balanced. KD and Russ were more like a yorn-yarng, or a bling-blornk-blarnxtttthhh: some kind of oblong, asymmetrical shape in which clashing colors bleed into one another and you can never figure out which way is supposed to be up. Together, they were the embodiment of life's ineluctable disharmony. True equilibrium seemed impossible.

The irony was that the Thunder had drafted Russell Westbrook, back in 2008, to serve as the perfect complement to Kevin Durant. Unlike Durant, Westbrook had been an unheralded teenage prospect; only a late high school growth spurt had won him a scholarship to UCLA, where he managed to establish himself as a hyperaggressive defensive specialist. He seemed to thrive without the ball, which made him, theoretically, the ideal sidekick to Durant. OKC's once-in-a-generation scorer would be free to control the offense and shoot whenever he wanted. Westbrook would hustle around and fill in all the gaps.

Instead, Westbrook took over the team. His mind did not distinguish between gaps and non-gaps. This was part of his power. Westbrook filled everything, everywhere, all the time. Although Durant was clearly the better player—he lived naturally at a height of talent that Westbrook could reach only sporadically, through inhuman spasms of will—Westbrook had more force. His intensity took up far more space, in the locker room and on the court, than Durant's mildness. In the early days, Westbrook had few of the skills that defined a traditional point guard—vision, ball handling, outside shooting. Nevertheless, he was the team's point guard, so he initiated the action on the floor. Which meant that the action on the floor was wild. Durant was often the one left to fill in the gaps.

As the Thunder rose closer and closer to glory, as Durant and Westbrook both improved, the relationship between the two stars was analyzed and argued over with an intensity usually reserved for celebrity affairs. Although in public the teammates always spoke supportively of each other, if you watched the games closely, there were incidents—scowls, harsh words, arms thrown in frustration. In the 2011 play-offs, during a time-out, TV cameras caught Durant and Westbrook in a heated argument over shot selection. (Westbrook shot thirty times that game, Durant eighteen, and the still up-and-coming James Harden only five.) During a time-out the following season, the cameras zoomed in on the two stars yelling at each other again, this time with so much heat that they had to be separated by teammates. (Westbrook shot zero for thirteen that night, including a short jumper that missed so badly it went off the top of the backboard.) At the end of that altercation, the cameras captured KD putting a peacemaking hand on Westbrook's head. This reinforced the dominant narrative: Westbrook was a selfish, irrational hothead, but KD was so profoundly good that he made up for it. Wildness versus mildness—that was the simplest way to understand the relationship. But, of course, the simplest stories are rarely entirely accurate.

Were Durant and Westbrook better off together or apart? On the cable sports shows, the talking heads screamed themselves bright red. Many insisted that the success of one detracted from the success of the other—that as long as both were together, neither could be whole.

There were calls to trade Westbrook, to allow KD to play with a non-crazy point guard who would subordinate himself appropriately. It was easy to imagine Westbrook outgrowing Oklahoma City eventually anyway, moving to some megalopolis where he could hang out with designers and work the late-night talk-show circuit. He was flashy, a peacock, a prankster hero of the fashion world. Before and after games, Westbrook wore skintight iridescent bodysuits, ragged denim vests, dashing hats with feathers in them, $10,000 T-shirts, and oversized red eyeglasses with no lenses. In the waning days of 2011, just after KD and Westbrook had publicly feuded on the bench during a time-out, a *Daily Thunder* commenter offered this somewhat reasonable prediction: "Russ will leave in free agency. Nets seem like a possible destination. Harden will be the sidekick, and OKC will still win a couple titles. Honestly, I think that's what's going to happen." But, obviously, that is not what happened at all. Two weeks after that altercation, in the midst of a horrific Westbrook shooting slump, the Thunder doubled down on its stormy point guard, signing him to a five-year, $80 million contract extension. OKC would not run from the chaos of Russell Westbrook. It would embrace it.

In the Thunder locker room, Durant and Westbrook sat almost, but not quite, directly next to each other. There was one locker in between: James Harden's. Now that locker belonged to no one, and it would sit empty for the rest of the year. Durant and Westbrook were suddenly in direct contact, like the closed switch of an electrical circuit, or like the bones in an old man's knee. The Thunder would rely on the pair of them almost completely, which meant that the city's civic health would rely heavily on them, too. In trading Harden, Presti had bet everything that the connection between Westbrook and Durant would be complementary, not conflicting—electric, not grinding.

THE DEATH OF MAYOR COUCH

Oklahoma City's first week was so frantic with crisis—the race for land, the battle over the shape of the town—that the settlers had hardly a moment of peace to think about what they'd done. This was probably for the best. Once everything finally began to quiet down, there must have been an oddly sinking feeling. After so much drama, all anyone had actually won was the chance to continue to fight to survive in this blasted alien outpost. The wind still blew sand in everyone's faces. Food was scarce. Prairie chickens were not going to last forever. Wild dog packs roamed the outskirts of town, menacing settlers riding in and out. (These were thought to be the feral descendants of the Indian tribes' old pets.) The cottonwood planks people used to build their houses quickly started to warp, leaving holes in the walls big enough (as one settler put it) to throw a cat through. At the end of every day, a film of red dirt covered everyone's pillows and dishes.

Even then, in the shifting ground of that precarious boomtown, Angelo Scott worked to plant the seedlings of culture. He and his brother published their newspaper, the *Oklahoma Times*. "Don't confound this paper with *The Oklahoma City Times*," the first issue read, in May. "That paper is not yet on the ground. Keep this paper—it is the first paper ever published in Oklahoma City." Scott helped organize the YMCA, the philharmonic, a local singing group, and the First Presbyterian Church. He set up a small law office and hotel. In a city of brawls and shoot-outs and power grabs, Scott remained almost universally well-liked. He was level-headed and high-minded; he rallied people to noble causes. Scott clearly wanted what was best for the town, not only what was best for himself. In times of civic stress, the people of Oklahoma City listened for his voice. He classed the place up.

"Naturally," Scott would remember later, "in this short time the town had not caught up with its people. It was undeniably crude, and I suppose sprawling and ugly. But in our eyes it was not so. We idealized it, and we were dazzled with the vision of what it would be. And so in our social affairs we looked our best and dressed our best for the honor of Oklahoma City."

William Couch, on the other hand—well, William Couch was a living legend. He was the hero of the opening of the Unassigned Lands, the man who, through sheer relentless force of will, had made Oklahoma happen. He had led the raids when things looked hopeless and lobbied Congress until it cracked. People actually called him "Oklahoma Moses." Although Angelo Scott was a useful citizen, William Couch was the whole reason Oklahoma City existed. Everyone in the territory was living inside his impossible Boomer dream.

During the Land Run, as we have seen, Couch and his associates arrived early. He therefore had his pick of the lots, and of course he

William Couch and an associate, the month before the Land Run, surveying the future site of Oklahoma City.

chose his claim strategically. He avoided the chaotic center of town, where he must have known that, despite the Seminoles' head start, property would be subject to disputes and realignments. Instead, he chose to hammer his stakes out on the periphery, directly west of the townsite's official limits. Out there he could make a bigger claim—a country lot instead of a city lot—and he knew that the value of the land would explode if Oklahoma City survived and grew to include it. Couch's choice was a bet: he put everything he had into the future expansion of the city.

While Couch staked his claim out in the country, his Seminole associates made sure everything was going according to plan back in the city center. In general, things were. Settlers were buying Seminole lots. Despite objections here and there, no one had mounted a serious challenge to their power. There was, however, one major problem: the question of mayor. The rival town company asserting control on the south side of OKC had pulled a gambit so reckless and brash that it surprised even the Seminoles. Instantly, on the first afternoon of the very first day, they announced an election. The Seminoles could only watch in horror as hundreds of settlers filed into a tent and elected, as the new leader of America's youngest and weirdest city, a preacher named James Murray, who had already managed to found his own church.

Couch and the Seminoles mustered all of their power to delegitimize this election. Be reasonable, they said. It's far too early to make such major decisions. Besides, the Seminoles insisted, the Oklahoma Town Company had no proper authority to hold an election for mayor. A *legal* election should take place later, once everyone had had a chance to settle in and get to know the business of the town.

But of course, the Seminoles argued, the city could not have no leader. It would need someone to temporarily take command. Not the man who had just been elected. Someone else. To this end, the Seminoles hijacked one of Angelo Scott's mass meetings and offered up, for public service, the legend himself: William Couch—Oklahoma Moses, old Ox Heart, the Prince of the Boomers. The crowd roared. The previous election was voided. Couch was successfully installed as the acting mayor of the town.

Temporary Mayor Couch announced that the first official mayoral election—the one that would give everyone plenty of time to learn the ins and outs of Oklahoma City—would take place the following week. The Seminoles organized the election themselves. To no one's surprise, the result was a Seminole sweep. William Couch was installed as the first real mayor of the town.

From that point forward, the Seminoles were ascendant. They used their new power to consolidate their old power. Under the guise of keeping order, they passed a series of ordinances that made it illegal to challenge Seminole control. Their land certificates—arbitrary pieces of paper just days before—became the official proof of property ownership in Oklahoma City. The Seminoles' town survey, so heavily contested from the start, now reigned supreme.

Resistance sprang up. An opposition party came to be called the Kickapoos, because it kicked so relentlessly against the Seminole order. (Again, white men who had taken over Indian Territory were now fighting, shamelessly, under the banner of tribal names.) Over the next six months, through OKC's first summer, the Seminoles and Kickapoos waged an epic war for the soul of the town. For a bunch of men trying not to starve to death while squabbling over patches of mud, they clung to surprisingly high-minded ideas. They cited the Constitution and the Magna Carta and the Founding Fathers. They quoted Latin. "There has never been any tribute to England's form of government like the opening and settlement of Oklahoma is to that of the United States," wrote the propagandist Bunky. "There is nothing in the history of any country or government that can be compared to the peaceable settlement of the Oklahoma country. It was a boon of mercy to thousands of souls."

As the months passed, Oklahoma City started to settle down and resemble an actual town. Tents were replaced almost entirely by wooden buildings. Brick structures appeared. Now that the worst of the drama was over, women and children were sent for. Schools were established. Domestic order began to assert itself.

Mayor Couch, however, was a tumultuous man, and his reign was marked by conflict. In September, a city council meeting ended in a brawl after one of Couch's opponents tried to speak out against the corruption of the police force. Mayor Couch, who happened to like the police force, abruptly struck his gavel. One of the mayor's brothers called the councilman a liar, and the councilman responded by punching the mayor's brother in the face so hard that he flew into the street and landed in a mudhole. Mayor Couch attempted to hit the councilman with a chair, but one of his cronies held him back. Eventually one of Couch's other cronies clubbed the councilman over the head with a revolver—a blow that adjourned the meeting for good.

Such violence tends to snowball. Later that week the Kickapoos, bristling after five months in the minority, prepared to do something drastic. Without any authority, and against clear warnings from the federal government, they announced an election on a new city charter that, if passed, would effectively end Seminole rule. It would be a coup via democracy. The wisdom of this strategy was debated hotly in the city papers. Although Angelo Scott was no fan of the Seminoles, he cautioned that the new charter would only create a civic schism. "Are we willing to establish for ourselves the Mexican principle of setting up a new government by force every time we tire of the old one?" he asked.

But the Kickapoos ignored Angelo Scott. They announced a date and set up polling stations. The election arrived. It did not go well. When citizens ventured out to cast their ballots, they found soldiers waiting for them with bayonets. Mild wounding occurred. Once again, OKC found itself on the brink of serious violence. Once again, civility prevailed. The citizens dispersed peacefully, out of respect for federal law.

Federal law, however, had had enough of Oklahoma City. In its five months of existence, the town had proven itself to be too dysfunctional, too many times. Washington, D.C., decided that it couldn't simply stand by and watch a place try to rip itself apart. So the United States government officially stripped Oklahoma City of its right to govern itself. All local officials were relieved of their power. Federal marshals were sent to take over. As a test case of American democracy, Oklahoma City had failed spectacularly.

Amid all the tumult, William Couch stepped down as mayor. He had been planning to do so anyway, for the most OKC reason possible: to keep possession of his land. Territorial rules required a settler to occupy his claim full-time, beginning no later than six months after he staked it. Couch's property was outside of town, which meant he couldn't live there while also performing his duties as mayor. In November, Couch resigned his official position, rode back out to his lonely patch of prairie, and proceeded to set up a home. The problem was that someone else was already there. In fact, multiple rival settlers had claimed Couch's land. They already lived there, in fact, isolated on their own separate pieces of that very large spread, and they were not inclined to leave. It would have been more than enough space for everyone to share, but communal living was not really the spirit of early OKC.

On April 14, 1889, William Couch was riding out toward the property he liked to think of as his. A rival claimant saw him coming and, two hundred yards away, raised his Winchester. He fired. Just outside the city limits of Oklahoma City, on the edge of the town he had devoted so much of his life to settling, William Couch, OKC's first mayor, took a bullet to the knee.

It was a ghastly injury to suffer in a raw frontier town with no real hospital. One week later, on April 21, William Couch died.

And so it happened that, on the very first anniversary of the Land Run—April 22, 1890—Oklahoma City found itself holding a public funeral for its first mayor. The calendar itself seemed to be mocking the city. Citizens gathered by the thousands, in shock and sorrow, on the corner of Robinson and Fourth, at the First Methodist Church—the church founded by James Murray, the preacher who had been elected mayor on the city's first afternoon, before the Seminoles rushed in to displace him in favor of William Couch. OKC's first year ended the only way it logically could have: with its founder sacrificed on the altar of chaos that he himself had built.

KD IS NICE

When Kevin Durant was eleven years old, skinny as a stack of pencils, his father came back to town and taught him a lesson. This was in 1999, near Washington, D.C., at Durant's aunt's house, in the driveway. It was long before the thought of Oklahoma City would have had any reason to enter Durant's mind. The SuperSonics still played in Seattle; OKC was still lobbying, unsuccessfully, for an NHL team. But Kevin Durant wasn't thinking about any of that. His mind was fully occupied. He and his father were playing one-on-one.

This was unusual. Durant's father, Wayne Pratt, had left the family just before Kevin turned one, and his son had grown up without him. They didn't even share a last name. The only name they shared was Kevin's middle: Wayne. It was not much of a stretch to say that basketball had stepped into KD's life to fill the void his father left. As a boy, he basically lived in his town's rec center, shooting and shooting and shooting, finding solace in the game, and now that he was hitting adolescence, his body was beginning to change, to stretch out, to match exactly what basketball asked of it: height and length. Durant was playing AAU ball, getting good, blowing teams out. The KD the whole world would come to know, ten years later—the effortless stretchy shooter—was already in formation.

Meanwhile, back in the driveway, KD's father was not having it. He was destroying his son, shoving him around, backing him down—*bang, bang, bang, bang*—turning, dunking, screaming, cursing. One-on-one basketball is the atomic state of the game, a pure test of strength, speed, aggression, and violence, and against his father, eleven-year-old Kevin Durant had nowhere to hide. There were no teammates to defer to. Durant's personality didn't quite match his booming talent: he was a shy kid, quiet, passive, always worrying about what everyone around him was thinking. His coaches struggled to convince him to shoot, even when he was on fire, his skinny arms stroking in beautiful jumpers from all over the court. He didn't want to seem selfish, didn't want his teammates to be mad at him.

Now Durant's father was talking trash, swaggering, letting everyone within shouting distance know that, even though he'd been out of the picture for ten years, even though he'd left Wanda to raise the kids all by herself, he was still the man, and Kevin was only a boy. Wayne Pratt was huge, strong, and Kevin was Kevin: thin, gentle, watchful, kind. And so the father scored and scored and scored, with brutal efficiency, and the boy could get nothing. Maybe it was a lesson, an alpha thing: you have to be mean to survive. Winning was not something the world was going to just hand you. If you wanted it, you had to go out and take it.

Kevin Durant, however, could only take so much. As the blowout escalated, as his father celebrated, as his brother watched on the sideline, KD broke down. He burst into tears and ran away, into the empty house. He closed the garage behind him and locked every single door. He refused to let anyone in. For a long time, he just sat there alone, with the whole house to himself, crying.

I knew this story because Durant told it to me, out of the blue, thirteen years after it happened. We were sitting in the Thunder's luxurious practice facility, surrounded by all of Sam Presti's perfectly straight balls—an impossible distance from that East Coast driveway in 1999. Durant was telling me the story, he said, because that moment had changed him. Locked alone in the house, with tears on his face, eleven-year-old Durant had an epiphany.

"I sat back and thought about it," he said, glancing over at me with his big soft eyes. "I was like, 'What am I so mad at?'" In that moment of emotional overload, he said, he made a decision. "It's good to be passionate, it's good to hate losing. But I've got to channel it in the right way. After a while, I started to learn to leave it where it's at, get rid of it. Once you're done and you're off the court or out of the venue or whatever, go back to being you."

Every sports superstar becomes a cartoon. That's the nature of superstardom: some cellular speck of an actual human is extracted, exploded, and then reproduced, infinitely, internationally, in simple lines and primary colors, and presented as if it were the actual person. Michael Jordan was "epic noble willpower champion." Magic Johnson was "smiley sunshine party friend." The cartoon version of Kevin Durant—the greatest scorer of his (or possibly any) generation and the savior of Oklahoma City—was "nice." Just that: nice. KD is nice.

It wasn't much, but it was enough to differentiate him, in the eyes of the public, from some of his predecessors and peers. NBA superstars were not known for being nice. They got paraded through news cycles for doing bad things: punching teammates, choking coaches, berating refs, wagering small fortunes unwisely, recording terrible rap albums, keeping guns in their lockers, engaging in dogfighting, driving luxury cars at high speeds on public roads, instigating ugly contract disputes, giving long speeches about the silliness of practice, showboating after dunks, smoking illegal drugs. Perhaps you detect subtle racial overtones to that list. For the first several decades of its existence, this was one of the NBA's defining PR tensions, and one that it sometimes handled poorly. It was a multibillion-dollar business designed to sell the performances of young black multimillionaires—many of whom (like Durant) grew up poor in the nation's poorest communities—to a largely white, largely middle-class, largely suburban audience.

Such tensions were particularly fraught in the case of the Oklahoma City Thunder, a new NBA franchise in a state historically dominated by the white and rural right-wing poor—a demographic for whom hip-hop culture was not a thrilling expression of American creativity but a crisis, an invasion, a postapocalyptic nightmare vision of the very end of the nation. Oklahoma was often referred to, with either pride or loathing, as "the reddest state in the nation." It was the target audience for right-wing radio's conspiracy theories about the New World Order and, particularly in those days, Barack Obama's Kenyan birth. In 2008, the year the Thunder arrived, Oklahoma was the only state in the nation where Obama did not win a single county.

But: Kevin Durant was nice, and niceness, it turned out, did a surprising amount of ideological work. Although KD's official biography claimed that he had been raised in a suburb of Washington, D.C., he could just as easily have been dreamed up in a laboratory by the Oklahoma City chamber of commerce. He was the perfect bridge between the NBA and Oklahomans. His pregame routine involved kissing his mother, as did his postgame routine, which also involved reading the Bible. His personal motto, which he was glad to repeat at any time, for any reason, was a bit of Yoda-like egalitarianism: "Hard work beats talent when talent fails to work hard." In Durant's one year of college at the University of Texas, during what was probably the greatest freshman season in NCAA history, a reporter asked him if he realized that he had just single-handedly outscored the entire opposing team in the second half of a game. Durant answered, with what seemed like absolute sincerity, "Who, me?" That was Kevin Durant: baby-faced angel of humility.

In 2010, Durant signed a new contract to stay with the Thunder for five years, but you got the feeling he would have signed on for the rest of his life if the players' union would have allowed it. He seemed to have formed a perfect mind meld with the people of OKC. He would go to the mall by himself, with no security, just to hang out. He'd play pickup basketball with almost anyone. Neighborhood kids would come knock on the door of his house, and he'd invite them inside to play video games. He talked frequently about how he couldn't imagine ever leaving, how he wanted to live and win in Oklahoma City forever. Durant was so exactly what this city needed, on so many levels, and he seemed like a one-franchise guy all the way down to his very long bones. He would do for OKC what Tim Duncan did for San Antonio or Dirk Nowitzki did for Dallas, would bring stability, awards, championships, two decades of good times. But in this case, it would mean so much more, because Oklahoma City didn't have a tenth of what those places had.

Durant had no tattoos, zero of them, not a single tattoo anywhere on his entire body—an absence that was often cited by Oklahomans, in the early years, as evidence of his virtue. (Oklahoma was the last state in America to legalize tattoo parlors—in the year, believe it or not, 2006.) Durant was so deeply nice, it seemed, that his skin repelled tattoos. During postgame interviews, he wore a little tiny backpack, like a cheerful fourth grader who had stopped to chat, on his walk home, with a neighbor who happened to be out watering the lawn. A reporter once asked him what he kept in the backpack. He said water and his Bible.

When I asked the Thunder's head coach, Scott Brooks, if all the rumors of Durant's otherworldly niceness were true, he laughed.

"I mean, why even ask?" he said. "Whatever you say nice, you can print it out and I'll just say I said it. Because it's true."

So it was true: KD was nice.

But what kind of a force, exactly, was niceness? In Durant's five years in the league, he had become a transcendent player; there was no arguing that. The one consistent criticism of him, however, was that he was maybe a little too nice, that he wasn't aggressive enough, that too often he failed to use his nuclear skills with maximum violence, the way a meaner player (Jordan, Barkley, Iverson, Kobe) would have. Durant's basketball arsenal was unfair, but sometimes it looked like he was trying to use it in a fair way. There were times, during games, when he seemed slightly removed from the action, simultaneously present and absent. Part of this may just have been his incredible level of skill: it looked so easy for him to stroke four consecutive three-pointers, or to toss in a little running half-hook over two defenders, that it was tempting to imagine he was thinking about other things the whole time, that the real Kevin Durant was watching from a little viewing platform deep inside his own head, reading a magazine, clipping his nails, ready to engage fully again when things got suitably intense. But what if it was something more fundamental? What if Durant was just, at the core of his being, a little passive and deferential? At the Olympics, Durant was by far the best scorer on the floor, but LeBron James told reporters that he sometimes had to beg him to shoot—as if the U.S. national team were only AAU ball, and KD was trying not to hurt anyone's feelings.

During the waning days of the Harden crisis, Thunder practices frequently turned angry. Harden was pumped up on praise and beginning to explore the ever-growing borders of his talent. In scrimmages, he drove hard against Westbrook and Durant, talking trash, tweaking the established order. Sometimes, Harden's practice squad of backups and rookies actually beat the first team, which sent everybody, especially Durant and Westbrook, into ruthless competitive overdrive.

When I sat down with Durant a few minutes after one of these hostile practices, he showed no trace of negative energy. He was calm, polite, thoughtful, obliging. We sat on chairs at the edge of the gym, and he said pretty much everything you would expect him to say in exactly the way you would expect him to say it. He went out of his way to praise his teammates, singling out Westbrook as a "killer" and insisting that, despite the media's constant attempts to create controversy between them, there was no tension about sharing the ball. It would be ridiculous to put Westbrook "on a leash," Durant said, "just so I can get two or three more shots up a game." He praised his teammates' unselfishness and said he had learned to play unselfishly, too. He told me that, although he'd known almost nothing about Oklahoma City before the team moved there, now he couldn't imagine playing anywhere else.

When I tried to compliment Durant on the way he'd handled his contract extension in 2010—announcing it quietly in a tweet as opposed to LeBron James's public showboating—he, characteristically, wouldn't accept it. In fact, Durant seemed mildly offended by the attempt to praise him at someone else's expense. He defended LeBron, pointing out that their situations were completely different. LeBron was in a later phase of his career; KD was just extending his rookie deal. Anybody, Durant said, would have signed the extension he did. And when the time came for his own next contract, he said, who knew what he would do?

This struck me as laughable, to imagine KD doing anything like what LeBron had done—holding the nation hostage in a high-stakes free-agency showdown, making a spectacle of himself, abandoning a small, hard-luck organization in a humble middle-American city for a glitzy superteam on the coast. It was anathema to everything Durant stood for. At that moment, KD and LeBron were at opposite ends of the NBA's moral spectrum.

I told Durant that, all over town, people kept giving me spontaneous speeches about what a nice guy he was. He was Oklahoma City Gandhi.

His response was impeccably nice.

"I'm just being me, man," he said. "I'm just enjoying this all. I wasn't raised to be a jerk to anybody, you know what I mean? My mama wouldn't like that. So that's just all I know: being nice to people and enjoying what I do."

But how is it possible, I asked, to be as competitive as he must be while also being so nice? Didn't those impulses conflict?

This was when Durant told me, out of nowhere, the story of his father destroying him in the driveway in the game of one-on-one: the trash-talking, the shoving, the humiliation, the lonely weeping locked inside the house. In the years since that incident, Durant had obviously succeeded, brilliantly, in internalizing the lesson of the day. He had learned to master his negative emotions, to present himself, publicly, as faultlessly nice.

Occasionally, however, if you watched closely, you could see Durant shuttling between worlds. He would dunk and, in his excitement, begin to stare down his opponent, showboat-style, and you'd think, "Wait a second, that's not how KD acts"—and then, inevitably, a second or so later, he would catch himself and jog back down the court to give all of the credit, nicely, to whichever of his teammates had set him up. He would get clobbered on a drive and turn to the referee with hatred in his eyes, but then he would turn away before he created an incident or got a technical foul. It was hard to tell how much of KD's niceness was real, essential to him, and how much was a projection of the image he knew people wanted to see, especially in Oklahoma. Durant was still a very young man, and I wondered if he had imprinted, in a way, on OKC and its expectations. He was not, it seemed to me, uncomplicatedly nice. Durant knew that he was being watched, and he knew the nature of that watching; he had become an expert in watching himself being watched. He had learned to modulate, with exact precision, his transitions between niceness and not-niceness. You could sometimes see the impulse and the correction—to get Freudian for a second, the id and the superego.

Eventually, toward the end of our conversation, Durant leaned over and started unlacing his shoes. I took this as a signal that he was ready to leave. He was tired, no doubt, and had other things to do. I wrapped up the interview and thanked him for his time. He popped immediately out of his seat and started walking away, in huge strides, across the gym. After a few steps, however, he caught himself. He turned around, walked back, and shook my hand. "Nice to meet you," he said.

Once you noticed the small gaps in Durant's public persona, you started to see them everywhere. One of his early signature moves, for instance, and a source of at least mild controversy, was a trick called the "rip-through." Durant would whip his long, skinny arms, on purpose, into the arms of an unwitting defender, getting himself intentionally tangled up, and—after that forced contact—would fling a fake dead duck of a shot in order to make it look like he had been fouled in the act of shooting. The defender, having done nothing wrong, would be called for a foul. This wasn't basketball; it was a swindle. The rip-through didn't violate the rules, so it wasn't exactly cheating, but it was done in the spirit of cheating. It was, if such a thing is possible, cheating *within* the rules: a paradox of nice not-niceness. Durant used the move so often that the league was forced to modify its rules in 2011.

When the *Oklahoman* asked Durant about the rip-through, his answer was the exact opposite of the Golden Rule.

"When a guy does it on me," Durant said, "I don't think it's a good basketball play. But when I do it, it is."

Not nice.

Also, it turned out, to many Oklahomans' dismay, that Kevin Durant had a lot of tattoos. A whole lot of them. In fact, Durant's entire torso—which everyone had always assumed was nice and blank, there in the secret regions under his jersey—turned out to be covered, back and front, with ink. The tattoos were, as far as tattoos go, incredibly wholesome—not a skull or a dagger or a naked lady in sight, nothing that could even begin to be interpreted negatively. They formed, in the aggregate, a heartwarming pictorial autobiography of the world's most wholesome man: a drawing of the house he grew up in, a crucifix, a Texas Longhorns logo in honor of his one-year college alma mater, two Bible verses, the names of his mother (Wanda) and his grandmother (Barbara) topped by a rose and a dove.

Still: secret tattoos. Although Durant's body art was angelic—literally angelic—it kicked off a "firestorm," one local told me, in Oklahoma. A shirtless picture of Durant circulated on the Internet, and some fans decided he had perpetrated a conspiracy, had fooled them into believing he was something he was not. He had been a Trojan horse of niceness. They had welcomed him into their city, and look what had happened—tattoos! There were passionate debates. Eventually, in most cases, Durant was forgiven, because winning does a lot, but it was a tiny grain of sand in the previously smooth public narrative of KD's niceness.

As the new season started, Kevin Durant and his business tattoos were expected not only to lead Oklahoma City back to the Finals but to win it all this time, and to do so under constant scrutiny as a paragon of pure moral virtue and noble humility, as a representative of everything Oklahoma City had always desperately dreamed that it could be: world-class, first-rate, special, stable, dominant, permanent, forever.

THE GRAND CANAL

In the fall of 1889, after the fed-up federal government stepped in to strip OKC of self-rule, the humiliated city refused to abandon its grand plans. If anything, its plans got even grander. Oklahoma City's civic powers announced the launch of a transformative new undertaking—a project so huge it promised to vault the place up the ranks of real American cities. Like Venice or Beijing, Oklahoma City was going to build itself a Grand Canal. It would harness almighty nature and put her to work. The North Canadian River was a lovely waterway, twisting in crazy loops all through the center of town, but it was also a typical prairie river, which meant that it was temperamental, drying up and flooding at seemingly random intervals. All through that first summer, the river had been overflowing its banks, turning the city's streets into a muddy, stinking mess. The city powers had, frankly, had enough of its nonsense. They wanted the river to behave more like the railroad: rational, industrious, straight. This was the era of triumphant global canals, and the city's newspapers were full of inspiring examples of hydroengineering. There were new canals in Panama, Suez, Nicaragua, the Baltic Sea; a sixteen-mile-long canal in England was entirely underground; a five-thousand-year-old Egyptian irrigation ditch still ran alongside the Nile. Oklahoma City, at six months old, could see no reason not to join this glorious tradition.

Digging equipment rolled into the city in early December, in what one newspaper described as "an almost endless procession of wagons." Through the city's first bleak winter, when jobs were scarce and supplies were low, hundreds of men worked to dig the canal. These wages almost certainly saved families from starving. Spring arrived, and the men continued to dig. They dug all through the summer. The canal began to stretch around the town. Excitement over the project grew into a collective fever. All of Oklahoma City poured its hopes into the still-dry trough. Businessmen built mills and factories and cotton gins along its length. City leaders made plans for the canal to power an extensive system of streetlights and trolleys. It was the rare project that everyone could support, Seminole and Kickapoo alike. The Grand Canal, Bunky wrote, was "the most gigantic undertaking in Oklahoma Territory or in the entire southwest"—and then he added, characteristically, as if time had collapsed and the project was already done, "It has made her the metropolis and commercial center of the Territory and in the future will be her beacon light."

In the end, the Grand Canal took one whole year to dig. It was more than six miles long, with a gradual drop of thirty-two feet. The opening ceremony was held on Christmas Eve 1890, and that festive date seemed appropriate. This was a public celebration of the birth of a whole new city. All the citizens came out to watch the water begin to flow. The engineers opened the dike. Water poured in. Fantasy gushed into reality. The natural river fed the man-made river. Useless water became useful. Oklahoma City was transformed. People threw empty barrels into the canal in celebration, just to watch them float.

But then something terrible happened: the water disappeared. One minute the Grand Canal was gushing and then, all of a sudden, it was dry. Where did the water go? The ground had swallowed it. Nobody understood why. A similar canal in Kansas, dug in similarly sandy prairie soil, had worked just fine. The engineers turned the water back on, and the canal filled back up. Once again, however, the ground swallowed it. This went on, again and again, with increasing desperation, for weeks and months. The new land was thirstier than anyone could have known. Some blamed it on gophers, others on quicksand, but "the sickening fact remained," Angelo Scott later wrote, "that our canal, the very treasure of our hearts, would not

function." It was hard not to read this failure as an ominous metaphor, a message to the settlers from the core of the earth itself. Pour
as much as you could into Oklahoma City; it would find a way to
make your investment disappear. Every hope would eventually find
its disappointment. Every boom would meet its bust.

ALWAYS TRYING

On Thunder game days, the lower bowl of Chesapeake Energy Arena filled up with civic leaders: OKC's mayor and police chief, its oil barons and city council members, its architects and historians and judges and bankers and senators. Forty-odd nights a year, for a few charmed hours, all city business ceased so the people could huddle together and cheer. The team's owners sat on the baseline, dodging errant passes. Sometimes you could even find Wayne Coyne, lead singer of OKC's most famous rock band, the Flaming Lips—he would sit courtside with his large flamboyant hair, face covered in glitter, cheering indiscriminately for both teams because he didn't really understand what was going on. "That was wicked!" Wayne would shout, and the people around him would point out, not always kindly, that the player he was complimenting was Kobe Bryant, a deeply loathed opponent, and Wayne would look around, slightly confused, and repeat, "But that was wicked."

One celebrity you would never find at the arena was Gary England. Although he was a Thunder fan, like everyone else, England was too busy forecasting the weather in the evenings to make it down to the games. This went double during the play-offs, which took place in the spring, at the height of Oklahoma's storm season. People needed England's attention on the sky, not on basketball.

Still, he found other ways to show his support. One year, during the play-offs, England surprised his producers by slipping on—just before he stepped on camera—a fake James Harden beard. Across the state, on people's TV screens, the familiar tiny blond man appeared in his usual suit and tie, talking in his usual Okie voice about cold fronts and air pressure and humidity, but now there was a huge black beard hanging off his chin. It was the perfect fusion of OKC worlds: weather and basketball, England and Harden, the sky and the ground. Now, of course, that combination would never happen again.

Once, in the early days of the Thunder, Gary England had been called upon to intervene meteorologically on behalf of the team. Scott Brooks, the team's head coach, was new to Oklahoma, and the state's constant wind was driving his family crazy. They lived north of OKC, on a golf course, and the low-level jet stream came ripping and howling and moaning around their house, and in the middle of the night it roared like Armageddon, and sometimes the Brooks family was sure that a tornado was about to destroy everything, and they would all leap out of bed and huddle in the closet in terror.

Gary England was happy to help.

Coach Brooks's wife, Sherry, made a visit to the Channel 9 Weather Center, where England talked to her, as he had talked to generations of Oklahomans, about the ceaseless nature of the region's wind.

It started blowing long before anyone alive was born, England said, and it would keep blowing long after everyone alive was gone. The state's atmosphere was perpetually unbalanced in a way that sent the air rushing, almost always, from south to north, on an invisible track from Texas to Kansas—so consistently, in fact, that if you ever happen to find yourself lost in the countryside of Oklahoma, you can just look at the trees: they lean north. Stray newspapers blow north; traffic lights bob north. The people themselves might lean slightly north. The atmosphere is always trying desperately to balance itself, and yet true equilibrium is impossible, because every flow only creates a new imbalance somewhere else. The wind is a symptom of that endless struggle. This is what was keeping the Brooks family awake at night: the ocean of air over the Great Plains trying, but failing, to bring itself to rest.

Tornadoes, however, England reassured Mrs. Brooks, are something else entirely. They do not come dropping randomly out of otherwise placid skies. They are the result of absolutely perfect conditions: huge loads of distant air—a warm, wet flow from the Gulf of Mexico, an arctic blast from Canada—crossing the continent to intersect over Oklahoma. Even then, the jet stream has to fire precisely through the heart of that mixture, twisting normal thunderstorms into deadly supercells. It wasn't something that happened casually. If a major storm was on the way, England said, the Brooks family would be warned well in advance. Modern weathermen understood tornadoes to an astonishing degree of detail. They knew that that the funnels tend to spawn in families, that they rotate counterclockwise, and that the very worst of them form at the back edge of a storm where they can feast, unopposed, on all the moisture left in the atmosphere. They knew that a tornado is often preceded by giant hail, that it usually hits the southwest corner of a house first, and that its parent storm eventually kills it off with its own cold wind. According to England you could even *smell* a tornado coming: the air, he said, smelled almost like fish. Not exactly like fish, but almost.

It was this degree of expertise that helped the Brooks family, and many others in Oklahoma, sleep at night.

Science, however, can only go so far. The weathermen could forecast all day long, but they would never change the central fact about tornadoes: the pure, primal, apocalyptic terror. Once a funnel drops out of the clouds, everyone in the region is suddenly living in a horror movie in which the sky is hunting humans. In the heat of such a crisis, even the weathermen would sometimes abandon their professional detachment, referring to tornadoes on the air as "beasts" or "monsters" or "hogs." I often found myself staring at tornado footage and wondering, over and over, the most basic questions: What *is* that thing? Why does it exist? What on earth does it want?

I once asked England these questions. He chuckled.

"Well, they're kind of like humans," he said. "They're born, and they grow and grow, and when they reach a mature size and run out of conditions, they start to die. Then they go away. They're just like humans, except they don't last very long. But I've known some humans about as mean as them."

YOU DON'T GET TO BARGAIN WITH ME

Perhaps the ultimate proof that Kevin Durant was nice, the strongest case for his sainthood, was his ability to tolerate Russell Westbrook. Any other scorer of KD's stature would, no doubt, have bristled at sharing the court with such a petulant, impulsive, cursing, scowling, unbalanced, bullheaded vortex of doom. Durant would have been well within his rights to create a crisis, divide the locker room, demand a trade. He could have forced Sam Presti's hand. But Durant was not a normal superstar, in this or in any other way. Almost always, he handled his co-star with patient grace, even when Westbrook was flying into one of his frenzies or playing keep-away from his own teammates. KD was apparently so deeply virtuous that he could absorb his point guard's negative energy on behalf of the people of Oklahoma City, allowing everyone else to focus on Westbrook's positives—which were considerable, if you could manage to see them.

Traditionally, the job of a point guard is organization: he handles the ball, calls plays, sets up teammates for easy shots, and sacrifices his own immediate glory for the long-term good of the group. He's like an orchestra conductor, balancing hundreds of inputs at once, profoundly aware of the feelings and needs of everyone else on the floor. He leads by deferring. Throughout NBA history, the archetypal point guard has been short, slight, empathetic, and altruistic.

Russell Westbrook was a living affront to this tradition. On the court, he was ferociously, maniacally, relentlessly assertive—almost certainly the least deferential human in the arena. He attacked and attacked, even when it made no sense, even when it meant ignoring wide-open teammates to force his own rash shot over multiple defenders. His signature move was the pull-up jumper: he'd charge toward the rim with reckless lunacy, sending his defender scrambling backward to try to prevent a dunk—at which point Westbrook would stop, with impossible suddenness, and launch himself straight into the air, like a fighter pilot ejecting from a cockpit, and as the defender continued to stagger helplessly backward, Westbrook would rise and rise, now surrounded by open space, and shoot, all alone. It was a risky, impulsive, individualistic move, by its very nature a gamble. But Westbrook made the shot with surprising frequency.

After big plays, Westbrook stomped and strutted all over the court, and every time he sank a three-pointer, he held his hands up in an "OK" sign—the referee's official signal for a made three—and then thrust them down violently, as if he were holstering guns, while screaming "Boom!" so loud you could hear it many rows up in the crowd.

I once happened to be reading an academic book about the history and chemistry of explosives when I stopped to scribble "Westbrook" in the margin. "It should be remembered," the author wrote, "that total energy and actual effectiveness are different matters. The effectiveness of an explosive depends in large part upon the rate at which its energy is liberated."

This was precisely the thing about Russell Westbrook. He liberated all of his energy, in every situation, all at once, over and over. No one has ever chased a loose ball with more urgency. In the third quarter of a meaningless game, Westbrook would leap after a trivial rebound like a man in a winner-takes-all dunk contest against the Devil himself. He appeared to be insulted by the very concepts of size, distance, limitations, restraint. To watch him play was to be constantly amazed that another human being could be, somehow, *like that.*

And yet the abundance of Westbrook's energy was not always effective. He could be furiously inefficient. In both of his first two seasons, he led the NBA in turnovers. Even in 2012, when the Thunder reached the Finals, Oklahoma City was dead last in the league in passes and assists—damning statistics for a point guard. During the

Finals itself, with the entire world watching and the Thunder holding a one-game lead, Westbrook fumbled and bumbled the ball so carelessly, and launched so many ill-advised shots, that Magic Johnson—Westbrook's childhood hero and an unimpeachable authority on point guardism—was moved to declare at halftime of Game 2, "That was the worst point guard in a championship finals I've ever seen."

In Westbrook's good moments, however, when the dice came up in his favor, he was incredibly good. Through sheer willpower and self-belief, he found seams in the defense that didn't exist. He dunked when it was not possible—flying screaming hammers that he threw down in the face of the entire world. Every such moment, of course, only confirmed Westbrook's radical self-belief, increasing the likelihood that he would do it again the next time down the floor. His superpower was to exist right on the line between confidence and delusion. His personal motto, which he wrote on his shoes and had printed on his underwear, was simply the question "Why Not?" (He once tweeted, apropos of nothing: "WHYNOT?!!! #whynot #whynot.") In Game 4 of the Finals, only a few days after that disastrous Game 2, Westbrook scored forty-three points on an array of shots so wild and improbable he seemed to be in a fugue state. It was all inseparable. The brilliance was the wildness. The boom was the bust.

Meeting Russell Westbrook was exactly the opposite of meeting Kevin Durant. One afternoon, at training camp, I was scheduled to speak with him directly after practice, but he kept me waiting on the edge of the gym for more than an hour. Eventually, Westbrook emerged from the back of the building, escorted by a PR man, and sauntered across the floor. The chaperone, however, was unnecessary. Westbrook shut down all of my questions with ruthless efficiency—a word, a sentence, a stare. I asked him what might surprise me, as an outsider, to learn about the team.

"Nothing," he said.

No surprises?

"No," he said. "It's self-explanatory. The way we play is the way we act."

It felt, at times, like he was performing some kind of art project about the futility of human connection. Despite my best efforts to keep the conversation going, it petered out in less than ten minutes—a good percentage of which time Westbrook spent talking on the phone, telling a friend that he was currently doing an interview but not to worry because it would be over very soon.

The PR guys had told me that Westbrook was famous for giving everyone in the organization nicknames. He called various staffers Alfalfa, Ace Ventura, and Snakes on a Plane. I asked him what nicknames he'd given his teammates.

"Those are my secrets," he said.

I asked if he could share any of his secrets.

"I don't let out secrets."

I surrendered and thanked Westbrook for his time. He stood and walked off to take care of some business in the PR office. The PR guys all seemed to genuinely love Westbrook. They defended him all the time to reporters, insisting that he was misunderstood, that he was actually wonderful behind the scenes, charismatic, funny, smart, thoughtful—nothing at all like he was with us on the record. But now I watched Westbrook stand in the PR office and complain about the amount of merchandise a company was asking him to sign. He admired a new addition to the room—a big, freestanding, color-coded season schedule—and asked if he could have it. The PR guys said no, they were using it to plan the season, but they would be happy to get another one printed out especially for him. Westbrook asked why he couldn't just take this one right now, and then they could get another schedule printed for themselves. That way he wouldn't have to wait. He was the player, he said. Shouldn't he have priority?

Even in the middle of the PR office, in other words, Westbrook was having a PR problem. Witnessing it in person, however, even immediately after my unsuccessful interview, I could see why people liked him. As I watched Westbrook act like a jerk firsthand, it became clear to me that he wasn't actually a jerk, or at least not *only* a jerk—not uncomplicatedly a jerk, in the same way that Kevin Durant was not uncomplicatedly nice. By traditional social standards, saying the kinds of things Westbrook was saying is bad form. But that's in the same way that, by traditional basketball standards, it's bad form to charge into a one-on-four fast break and pull up for a contested free-throw-line jumper—until Westbrook, as he regularly does, somehow pulls it off. He was a social gambler as well as a basketball gambler: one of those people who knows how to play on the line between charisma and rudeness, teasing and affection. He was putting on a little show, for the PR guys, for himself, and maybe even a little for me. It was fun to watch. For the first time since I'd entered his orbit, I was enjoying myself.

Westbrook sat down at one of the PR desks and picked up a stack of documents. He grabbed a pen and started signing. He held the pen in his left hand.

"Little-known fact about Russell," one of the PR guys said. "He shoots with his right hand, it says he's right-handed in the media guide, but he writes with his left."

Westbrook's head snapped up. He looked straight at me, where I was leaning against the doorframe.

"Don't put that in your article," he said.

I told him we could make a deal: I wouldn't write about it if he would tell me one of his teammates' nicknames.

"You don't get to bargain with me, motherfucker," Westbrook said, with so much venom that I laughed out loud, and he did not smile but just went back to signing papers with his left hand.

There was a surprise, however, buried deep in Russell Westbrook's character. On the court, he was a chaotic, fire-breathing hothead. Off the court, his life was defined by an obsessive commitment to order. On days when Sam Presti wasn't straightening balls at the practice facility, it seemed likely that his starting point guard was. Westbrook built his life around inflexible routines: daily calls to his parents, a designated parking spot, morning shooting on Court 3—always and only Court 3. He expected every room to be neat and clean, at work and at home. He had a revulsion to stray hairs. Before every game, Westbrook ate a peanut butter and jelly sandwich, and his requirements for it were so exact—fillings spread thin, bread cut on the diagonal—that the Thunder's team chefs had been trained in the proper technique. (On the road, Westbrook couldn't trust anyone, so he made the sandwich himself.) He was compulsively aware of the tiniest details of his shoes—color schemes, sole flexibility, insole thickness—to the point that, uniquely among the players, he had his own personal shoe rack in the back of the practice facility. He decided himself which pairs came on every road trip. On the team plane, Westbrook sometimes got so absorbed in film study that he woke his teammates up, in the middle of the night, to show them an angle they had missed on a play. At the arena, he took the floor exactly three hours before tip-off, every game, and his warm-up routine ended invariably with the same shot—a rainbow from behind the basket out of bounds—and as soon as he made it he sprinted, at full speed, directly to the locker room. Precisely one hour before tip-off, Westbrook went to chapel, and when the pregame countdown clock hit 6:17, not a second more or less, Westbrook leaped off the bench and screamed "Two lines!" to initiate the team's final layup drill. I once asked him if there was some kind of numerology behind this—a June 17 birthday, a favorite Bible verse.

"No particular reason," he said. "I just do it. Nothing special."

This was the paradox of Russell Westbrook: what looked like chaos was built on a foundation of intense self-control. He grew up in inner-city Los Angeles, where his father meticulously structured his sons' lives to keep them away from trouble. Westbrook and his father ran through endless drills at the local park, laboring over his pull-up jump shot, again and again and again and again, until that impulsive burst became automatic, algorithmic—until chaos merged with order. Control was how Russell Westbrook survived. When he looked wild on the court, it was only the flip side of his focus. His mind could reduce the entire universe to one immediate goal, outside of which everything—teammates, opponents, fans, journalists—shrank to nothing. It was control so extreme it was avant-garde—control that wrapped all the way back around to wildness. This is why Presti and Oklahoma City were so enamored of him.

Once, I asked someone in the organization if, in addition to loving Westbrook, everyone was also scared of him. There was a significant silence. "I wouldn't say *scared*," he answered, finally. "But I would say that he keeps us on edge." Westbrook's personality, the sheer intensity of his presence, seeped into every square centimeter of the Thunder organization. When he was around, everyone was aware of him, and he was never not around. Players arrived at the gym in the morning to find him already there. Sometimes they came in at night to shoot and he would be there again, in the weight room, working out. In the afternoons, he sat in the back of the practice facility writing checks, paying his bills. (Westbrook always paid his own bills.) People thought twice, and often a third and fourth time, before mentioning something they weren't sure Westbrook would like, whether it was an interview request or a meme. He created a constant low-grade tension. This struck me as perhaps a deliberate tool, a way for Westbrook to extend his own unusual focus to the people around him. His personality was like a grinding stone—he dragged blades across it, all the time, to keep them sharp. Everyone around him got dragged too, whether they felt like being sharpened or not.

FEDERAL LARCENY

Very quickly, after the opening surge of the Land Run, Oklahoma City's population began to slide backward. Once-hopeful settlers were driven away by fear, poverty, hunger, and lack of good land. There was very little decent work. New land grabs in other parts of Indian Territory drew people off to try their luck elsewhere. By the end of its first year, the instant city of ten thousand had dwindled to only four thousand. OKC was failing to thrive. The Land Run had come too late in the season to establish a viable crop, and soon food was dangerously scarce. Those who remained clung to their land, waiting for the town to mature into its promised glory, enduring the nearly constant drama: the mass meetings and failed coups, the bayonets in the streets, the shocking death of Mayor Couch, the failure of the Grand Canal. After a while, these allegedly self-sufficient settlers—men who had clamored at Congress, for so many years, to be given access to Oklahoma, who had insisted that the tribes were only wasting paradise—had to swallow their pride and ask the federal government to bail them out. Distribution of the donated goods (flour, potatoes, beans, sugar, pork) was entrusted to Angelo Scott. "Demand for it," he reported, "was very brisk."

It was at this vulnerable moment, when the pride of the town had already been so badly wounded, when its very future seemed to be in question, that the United States Congress twisted the knife. It announced that the official capital of the newly created Territory of Oklahoma would not be Oklahoma City but a rival town thirty miles to the north: Guthrie.

Guthrie, alas, was a reasonable choice. It, too, had been a major destination in the Land Run—another instant city of roughly ten thousand. It, too, offered settlers a magical combination of river and railroad. Now, in the spring of 1890, one year after the drama of the Run, Guthrie was emerging as Oklahoma City's most serious enemy: not only a competitor but an actual existential threat.

Imagine the indignity. Guthrie's population was fully a third higher than OKC's, and it had grand buildings, eight newspapers, and eleven schools. It was, by many measures, handling its business. But of course Oklahoma City was not interested in second place. It still considered itself, somehow, the superior city. Capital status was not simply a question of pride; it was about survival. The prairie was littered with ruined towns that would soon disappear from maps: Ball, Buckhead, Waterloo, Dodsworth, Thurston, Springvale, Paradise. In these places, hope had outrun reality. Once a town got weak, the railroads could hold it ransom, asking for fees in exchange for continued service. The odds of survival got worse and worse. A capital city, however, would be safe from such bullying. It would be sustained by official decrees, recognized not only around the nation but across the world. For Oklahoma City, capital status would provide the one thing the city had always, by its very nature, lacked: stability.

And so Oklahoma City leaders fought, with the mighty righteousness of undeserved pride, to steal the capital from Guthrie. In the territorial legislature, the OKC faction tried to force capital relocation votes over and over, only to be thwarted by the Guthrie faction. Once again, as in the case of the Grand Canal, all of OKC became united by an obsession. Seminoles and Kickapoos joined hands. "For days and weeks," Angelo Scott remembered, "we talked of nothing else and thought of nothing else but the capital fight." It was a bottomless pit, absorbing civic energy that should have gone to more basic issues: water, food, revenue, order. At the territory's first legislative session, one historian writes, "100 days were spent on that problem, and 10 days on other matters." There were arguments and altercations, including an episode in which a representative from OKC—falsely believed to be in possession of the relocation bill—was chased around the city by representatives from Guthrie. He escaped by hiding, for three hours, behind an icebox in a butcher shop.

Finally, using every ounce of its influence, Oklahoma City managed to force a relocation vote. It even narrowly won. But it still didn't matter. Washington, D.C., was by now so thoroughly acquainted with OKC's nonsense that it had appointed, as territorial governor, a hard military man, a veteran of Sherman's infamous march to the sea, and he immediately vetoed the bill. This was a civic catastrophe. Guthrie would hold the capital, intolerably, for another twenty years.

Oklahoma City survived. Life went on. Angelo Scott continued to pour his civilizing energy into the town. He harmonized with his choirmates, delivered lectures, wrote for the paper, and attended plays and galas. He once rescued a large crowd of people from a burning church downtown. From his office on Main Street, Scott helped the federal courts sift through all of the many property disputes left over after the Land Run. Among other things, they found that William Couch had died for no reason: the court ruled that he had not legally owned the land he was shot over, and neither, for that matter, had the man who shot him. In 1893, the governor chose Angelo Scott to represent Oklahoma Territory at the Chicago World's Fair. When he got back, he was elected president of the territorial senate, a position he used to fight against the death penalty and the barbaric sport of prizefighting. Everyone urged him to run for governor, but Scott declined. Politics was not his passion. His true purpose was to make sure Oklahoma City flourished, spiritually as well as materially.

In 1894, five years after the Land Run, when the town had begun to stabilize somewhat, Angelo Scott increased its population by one. He married, and then somehow induced to come to the frontier, a musician named Lola May Smeltzer. They had grown up together in Kansas, back in Scott's previous life, long before all of this Oklahoma madness began. Lola and Angelo seemed like a perfect match. She had studied at a conservatory in Boston and was an avid reader of poetry and novels and plays. In Oklahoma City, the two were an instant cultural power couple. Lola wrote regular letters to the territorial legislature, arguing for better treatment of juvenile offenders.

She became president of Oklahoma's Federation of Women's Clubs, a network of cultured ladies who gathered in the town's fancier houses to discuss such lofty topics as *Hamlet,* Homer, Saki, Maeterlinck, and the Irish mystic AE.

Not long after Lola's arrival, Oklahoma City's luck finally shifted. In 1898, after many years of suffocating drought, the sky erupted. The flat earth was ecstatically wet. As a result, Oklahoma City experienced something it had been waiting for since the Land Run: a new boom. The Great Plains exploded into agricultural life, and all of the wealth of the farms came pouring from the countryside into the city, where it was stacked and sorted and traded and sold and shipped out on the railroads. Wooden buildings turned to brick; brick buildings turned to stone. The city spasmed and expanded. New residents flooded in. By 1900, Oklahoma City was, once again, a city of ten thousand. It had recovered all of the population it had lost in that first bad year. More railroads arrived. Streetcar lines began to stretch across the town, carrying residents out of the city center to increasingly far-flung clusters of houses, and even to other cities. On one of these lines, in a town called Stillwater, Angelo Scott was hired to serve as president of an agricultural and mechanical college, where farmers' children came to learn about Shakespeare and Mozart and scientific soil management techniques.

The wealth rolled in and multiplied, sloshing all over the early years of the new century. Oklahoma City hit twenty thousand residents, then thirty thousand, then fifty thousand. New neighborhoods bloomed. Developers bought up land in formerly desolate mudflats and began to fill them with houses. The claim that William Couch had died for, way out on the edge of town, would now have been absorbed into the city, proving his gamble right. To the north of the crowded downtown, on a slight rise at the edge of the river's floodplain, a neighborhood of mansions rose up. These were huge new homes for the city's elite, the bankers and politicians and businessmen—the winners of the booms. The neighborhood boasted luxuries unknown in other parts of the city: sidewalks, ample yards, elm trees, pocket parks. "Come live with the Big Bugs," the developer's advertisements read. The architecture was grand in a way that was pure Oklahoma City: eclectic to the point of absurdity. There were mansions that looked like Greek temples, French châteaus, Spanish villas, and German gingerbread hunting lodges. There were imitation Italian Renaissance palazzos, complete with statuary and orange-tiled roofs. It was like a theme park of global fanciness. The brand-new city was attempting to replicate, in fast forward, all of the majestic European styles that had simmered into being over centuries. The men who lived in these mansions were city boosters whose names would someday adorn the streets and landmarks downtown: Colcord, Overholser, Classen, Shartel, Gaylord.

In such flush days, it seemed even more outrageous that Oklahoma City was not the capital. The city was no longer struggling to survive, no longer begging the federal government for food. It was now, by far, the grandest city in the territory. OKC's population was more than sixty thousand—three times the size of Guthrie's. It was a major railroad hub, a center for the livestock trade, and the primary engine of the territorial economy. Skyscrapers as high as eight and nine stories were beginning to rise downtown. And yet Washington, D.C., still seemed determined to spite the place.

In 1907, the stakes of the capital fight went up significantly when Oklahoma, the former wasteland, became an honest-to-God United States state: the forty-sixth in the nation. Teddy Roosevelt signed the order himself. It was the wildest fantasy of men who were now dead and buried. Oklahoma was suddenly the equal of New York, Massachusetts, and Virginia. The only bitterness was that Guthrie, not Oklahoma City, had been elevated to true capital status, on equal footing with Boston and Richmond and Atlanta. It was in the middle of Guthrie, not OKC, that thirty thousand citizens gathered for a statehood ceremony featuring a symbolic wedding between "Mr. Oklahoma" (played for the occasion by Charles "Gristmill" Jones, an OKC businessman and former mayor) and "Miss Indian Territory" (a local woman of Cherokee descent). One of the official statehood provisions was that Guthrie would hold the capital for at least six more years, until 1913. A legitimate U.S. state needed stability, and Oklahoma City, despite its recent business success, could hardly be trusted with that.

But Oklahoma City was done waiting. City leaders argued that the federal government had no right to fix a state's capital against the will of its people. In defiance of Washington, OKC decided to organize a special election. The city's secret power players began to ply their secret powers. E. K. Gaylord, owner of the *Oklahoman,* used his influence to launch a strategic PR campaign. He sent his circulation men to distribute petitions demanding a public vote for relocation, while at the same time keeping the story out of the newspapers so Guthrie couldn't counterattack. It worked. In June of 1910, a special statewide election would be held to determine, once and for all, which city deserved the glory of representing the new state of Oklahoma.

OKC's PR machine cranked as hard as it could. Billboards went up extolling the city's virtues: its centrality, its tall buildings, its ninety-four miles of paved roads. "It has the best churches and schools," the advertisements claimed. "Its hotels are best and biggest. It has the best public and private buildings. It's [*sic*] building operations are the talk of the country. It has the finest boulevard and park system in the Southwest." These claims ranged from debatable to absurd. The "boulevard and park system," for instance, didn't actually exist—it was a quixotic plan to build a racetrack circling the city, connecting four huge parks at its corners. But after almost a decade of planning, it would be abandoned, half-built. The city, however, was unable to meaningfully distinguish between its fantasies of the future and its actual present. And it would say anything, at this point, to increase its chances of stealing the capital.

On the day of the relocation vote, one historian contends that OKC resorted to election fraud, mobilizing the homeless encampment on the riverbank—the so-called Hobo Roost—to stuff the ballot box. But this would not have been necessary. In the end, the results were not even close. Oklahoma City won in a landslide, garnering more than 70 percent of the vote to vanquish—finally, after twenty years—its annoyingly persistent rival.

There was still, however, the small matter of the federal government, which had stipulated that Guthrie would be the state capital for at least another three years. But three years, for Oklahoma City, was eternity. The very night of the election, the governor of Oklahoma decided to heed the sacred will of the people. He left Guthrie, immediately, for OKC, where he set up downtown in the Huckins Hotel and wrote a formal decree, on hotel stationery, declaring that Oklahoma City was from that moment forward the official capital of the state. Meanwhile, his secretary headed back to Guthrie, in secret, to retrieve the state seal. The details of what happened that night are still in dispute—all we know is that it happened fast. Legend has it that the secretary climbed in through a window and smuggled the seal out in a basket of laundry. In any case, the coup was complete. The federal government surrendered. After two decades of trying, Oklahoma City had stolen the capital from Guthrie. It was, once again, at the very center of everything.

The capitol building, still under construction, six years after OKC
stole capital status from Guthrie.

GAME 1: THOSE WHO SIT BESIDE YOU

Every morning, in a small box at the bottom of its front page, the *Oklahoman* printed a prayer. On November 1, 2012, opening day of OKC's new NBA season, the prayer was short. "We give thanks for those who sit beside You," it read, "for they are holy and inspire us. Amen."

Kevin Durant and Russell Westbrook still sat beside one another, wearing uniforms that said OKLAHOMA CITY. James Harden, however, no longer sat between them. He was in Houston. Four days after the trade, the Rockets had signed Harden to the most lavish contract the league would allow: $80 million over five years. His new team was gambling everything that Harden was secretly a superstar. The *Oklahoman's* lead Thunder reporter, Darnell Mayberry, was skeptical. "We'll see how that works out for Houston," he wrote. "My take is it's a reach. . . . Does anyone think Harden is capable of doing for Houston what Kevin freaking Durant does for OKC? How about what Russell Westbrook does? . . . I never saw him possessing that ability, nor the desire to have that pressure on him. He was comfortable playing alongside two all-stars. It suited him and the Thunder perfectly. Now those days are long gone and he might spend the rest of his career wishing he could have them back."

Just one day after signing his questionable extension, Harden played his first game with his new team. All game, the ball was in his hands. There was no one to defer to. It was his first test. He played like an absolute superstar, shimmying through double-teams, bulldozing defenders, scoring inside and out, making his mediocre teammates better, finishing with thirty-seven points and twelve assists. It wasn't proof, of course, that the Thunder should have kept Harden, or that he was an actual real-deal long-term superstar, but it was quite an opening statement in the case. For one night, at least, Houston got a glimpse of the player it fantasized it had signed. The Thunder's entire season, Mayberry wrote, was about to become "a referendum on Harden's trade to Houston."

For OKC, that referendum began the following night in San Antonio. As an initial post-Harden test, the Spurs were perfect on many levels. It was the organization in which Sam Presti had gotten his start, and on which he had largely modeled the Thunder. It was also the team the Thunder had beaten the previous year to reach the Finals, clawing their way back from an 0–2 deficit, using every drop of talent available in all three of their young stars—a trio that included Harden, of course, who had clinched the series with a three-pointer at the end of Game 6. How would the Thunder look now in his absence? Would the minor players be able to raise their games? Would Durant and Westbrook find a balance without their old third option? Would Westbrook be able to control himself?

Back in Oklahoma City, Thunder fans sat clustered around screens, feeling fragile, turning these questions over in their minds, alert to any sign of trouble, sending their hopes and dreams out into the universe. "I hope for a win, but I don't expect it with the last minute shake-up this weekend," wrote a commenter on OKCTalk.

In the first minutes of the first quarter of the new season's first game, the collective sigh of relief emanating from the people of Oklahoma City might have been powerful enough to register on Gary England's screens. Every Thunder starter made his first shot of the year—not only Westbrook and Durant but Ibaka and Sefolosha, the deep cuts, the role players. The only one who didn't join the scoring party was Kendrick Perkins, the center, because he wasn't shooting at all, because that was the nature of Kendrick Perkins. After a summer of anticipation, after a week of agonized confusion, it was a perfect few minutes. Perhaps everything was actually going to be fine.

The game's most interesting matchup was between the point guards, Russell Westbrook and Tony Parker—the Ghost of Presti Present versus the Ghost of Presti Past. In the early 2000s, when

Presti discovered Parker in France, he had seen a player much like Westbrook was now: a gambler, fast and fearless and resilient, a small guy who made his name throwing himself recklessly into crowds of giants. Now, thirteen years later, Parker was a Spurs legend, a three-time champion and Finals MVP, and his game had mellowed to become logical and un-frantic: every possession was a puzzle to be solved, patiently. He was a kind of anti-Westbrook. You could trust him to do the right thing in just about any situation. Parker looked at defenders, when they tried to guard him, with dismissive French ennui. Even his missed shots tended to be good misses.

Westbrook, meanwhile, started the season Westbrooking as hard as he could possibly Westbrook. He kept asking the universe "Why not?" and the universe kept responding with an impressive variety of answers. Westbrook seemed determined to dominate Tony Parker, and Parker used that energy against him. Early in the game, Westbrook backed Parker down, spun wildly toward the hoop, threw the ball on a straight line clear past the rim, and then screamed at the referee about a theoretical foul—all while Parker pursed his lips and furrowed his brow like someone trying to identify the precise terroir of a particularly tricky Bordeaux. Westbrook was pressing. He was always looking for fresh chips to put on his shoulders, and it seemed, perhaps, that this Harden situation was teetering up there now. He seemed to want his own first game to be an answer to Harden's, to prove to the world that the Thunder had kept the better player. In San Antonio, against the level-headed Tony Parker, it was not working. Westbrook was forcing shots and passes all over the court, and after its hot start, the Thunder's offense completely lost its flow. What Harden brought—steady control when the bigger stars didn't have it—was exactly what the team could have used. OKC shot a meager 37 percent for the game, and Westbrook was even worse than that, making only six of twenty-one shots.

Despite all of this, however, the game remained close. Durant threw down long-armed leaning dunks. Kevin Martin, Harden's replacement, flung in deep opportunistic threes, doing his best impression of the absent man. With three minutes left, the Thunder trailed by only one. Westbrook dribbled up the court, surveyed the action, reared back, and flung a pass so wild it ricocheted off the bottom of the backboard, sending its apparent target, Kevin Durant, crashing to the floor. Somehow, in the ensuing chaos, Westbrook got the ball back—a precious extra possession, so late in a close game—only to immediately force an off-balance jump shot between two defenders. He missed.

Sixty seconds later, Westbrook took a rash three-pointer off the dribble.

He missed that too.

Over the next minute, Westbrook managed to spin and fling his way to some free throws, which he made, giving the Thunder the lead. Then he drove for a short layup that would have put the Thunder up by five, effectively sealing the game, but he missed it, and in the scramble that followed he allowed Tony Parker to get free for a wide-open three-pointer, which Parker made. Tie game.

Even by Westbrook's lofty standards, this had been a maddening sequence: a cascade of unforced errors, none of which was decisive on its own but in the aggregate added up to just enough to give the Spurs a chance. The silver lining was that this was now a perfect test. OKC found itself tied with a great opponent in the final seconds. How would Durant and Westbrook find balance without Harden? Would one defer to the other, or would they work together? Who would control the control?

Westbrook dribbled, surveying, and Durant came running out toward him, and Westbrook passed him the ball, and it did not go well—either Durant was too slow or the players weren't on the same page, because Durant's defender managed to reach out and tip the pass, and Durant fumbled the catch, and the Spurs took it away. They called a time-out. Durant walked off the floor hanging his head. Westbrook thrashed his arms in anger. Officially, the turnover was charged to Westbrook—his sixth of the game, against only five assists—but it could just as easily have been charged to the ghost of James Harden or to Sam Presti's Process or to the bling-blorng-blarnxxx, ancient symbol of life's ineluctable disharmony.

Still, the game was not over. The players returned to the floor with the game tied and less than five seconds left. At the whistle,

Tony Parker made a looping run across the court, dodging through crowds, and Westbrook, who was supposed to be guarding him, got lost. He ended up standing, for no good reason, all the way under the rim, leaving Parker open twenty feet away—where he caught the ball, took one calm dribble, and, at the buzzer, swished the game-winning jump shot.

The San Antonio crowd exploded, and the Spurs all clustered next to the scorer's table and leaped like giddy children. The Thunder went off to sit somberly in the locker room, where the mood was so low that even the reporters hesitated to break the silence. "Every few seconds," Mayberry wrote, with postgame lyricism, "a singular profanity would spring from around the corner, where running water rained down from the showers. It was all that pierced through the air."

Thunder fans were less restrained. On comment boards, deep in the middle of the night, they began to panic. This was a terrible way to start the season: 0–1, winless without James Harden, on pace to lose all eighty-two games and become the worst team, by far, in the history of the NBA. The team's flaws had been exposed, and the people of OKC pecked at them, ruthlessly, with their keyboards.

11:08 p.m.: "If Westbrook has the ball for more than 15 seconds in a possession it will end in a turnover."

11:12 p.m.: "The second team looked awful without Harden."

3:11 a.m.: "Brooks is a horrible coach. resigning him will hurt this franchise more than letting Harden go in the long run."

4:34 a.m.: "If Harden was still in town, Thunder win this game easily."

5:50 a.m.: "Please, please, please Russ . . . you are a year older . . . playing under control 75% of the time not only is acceptable but it's what elite players do."

7:09 a.m.: "KD has to demand the ball at the end. Russ must get him the ball. This is absurdly frustrating."

8:33 a.m.: "Wussell oh Wussell, still pulling that same ol' wabbit out of the hat I see, same thing for KD, nonchalant as usual . . ."

10:10 a.m.: "2 chances to go up 2 possessions and 1 chance to have game winning opportunity = 3 bad RW decisions."

10:16 a.m.: "I knew it. Fourth quarter of close games, you need James Harden. His calm, his play-making, his scoring."

But James Harden was busy elsewhere. In his second game with the Rockets, Harden was somehow even better than in the first: he made fourteen of nineteen shots and scored forty-five points, a new career high. He was now averaging forty-one points per game, first in the league by a very wide margin. It was a minuscule sample size, but for OKC the data looked bad. James Harden, a player who had been coming off of the Thunder's bench one week earlier, was now looking like a superstar among the superstars.

ETERNAL PRESENT

Lola May Smeltzer, wife of Angelo Scott and leader of
Oklahoma City's Women's Clubs.

One chilly Thursday on Fifteenth Street, in the stately home of Mrs.
I. R. McQueen, among the horse buggies and trolleys of the still-
developing town, the Modern Classics Club met to listen to Lola
Scott speak about literature—always a memorable event. The subject, that day, would have been of particular interest to the women
of Oklahoma City: the Mystery of Time. They would be discussing
the work of the English writer J. B. Priestley, whose philosophical
plays were then all the rage in London. Our conventional notions
of time, Priestley posited, were far too simplistic—the idea that we

move through life shedding moments behind us like flower petals, one by one, as we stride off into the future. Instead, Priestley argued, we live in an "Eternal Now," in which "the Past has not vanished like a pricked bubble." Lola Scott read to the ladies from, among other works, Priestley's book *Midnight on the Desert*:

> Our consciousness travels along this track as we might travel on a railway journey. Then the Past is the station we have just left, and the Future is the station we are approaching. The Past has not been destroyed any more than the last station was destroyed when the train left it. Just as the station is still there, with its porters and ticket inspectors and bookstalls and its noise and bustle, so the Past still exists, not as a dim memory, but in all its colour and hum. Somewhere back along that fourth dimensional track of the world, the dinosaurs are still roving, the ice age is melting, men are building the Pyramids and Babylon, Caesar is being assassinated, Shakespeare is just finishing *Hamlet,* and Lincoln is making his Gettysburg speech. Nothing—not a syllable, not the wink of an eyelash—has been lost. . . . All its Past is in existence along this track, not as a ghostly memory, a shadow show, but solidly real in its own eternal Present.

Priestley even raised the radical notion, mentioned to him once by a sea captain, that "it might be possible for a number of people, working together, to change the Past."

In the years after stealing the capital, time would have been much on the minds of the citizens of Oklahoma City. The place had changed so much, so quickly. The prairie was disappearing rapidly at the edges of town. The old pioneer days were tipping hard toward an unknown future. Even prairie chickens were becoming increasingly scarce.

In 1913, in order to capture some fragment of that disappearing world, the members of the Ladies Aid Society decided to create a time capsule. They called it the Century Chest. Leading citizens of OKC paid a fee to enter objects and documents: newspapers, shoes, telephones, letters to the people of the future. The money would go toward buying a massive pipe organ for the First Lutheran Church. Angelo Scott, who was now in his mid-fifties, was conscripted to write a brief message to the citizens of the twenty-first century. His voice, reading the message, was recorded on a wax cylinder, and this too was carefully cataloged and packed alongside all of the other items. On the twenty-fourth anniversary of the Land Run, amid much pomp and circumstance, the Century Chest was buried beneath the floor of the church, on Thirteenth Street, along with strict instructions to exhume and open it exactly one hundred years later, on April 22, 2013—a date that must have seemed as unreal, at the time, as supersonic flight or pocket computers.

Two years later, in 1915, Angelo and Lola Scott settled into a home on Sixteenth Street. This was on the absolute edge of the expanding city, at the northern border of the neighborhood of mansions—all of those gaudy monuments to OKC's new money. The Scotts' house, by contrast, was spacious but understated. Angelo knew this area well from the days of the Land Run twenty-six years before, when it had been the distant countryside, full of wildflowers, and he would ride out to escape the squabbling crowds of the city. Once, Scott wrote, he had "gathered 26 varieties of flowers in less than as many minutes." From that distance, in those old days, the city would have been only a speck on the horizon.

Now, however, there were houses all the way, including his and Lola's. Sixteenth Street was an in-between place—city to the south, country to the north—and at night, with their windows open to catch Oklahoma's cooling breezes, the Scotts would have heard cows mooing. During the day, in the muddy distance to the north, they would have seen the cows grazing around the construction site of the new capitol building, which they would watch rising, slowly, over the course of several years, in the middle of absolutely nowhere. Even out there, however, developers were beginning to buy up land. Oklahoma City's nowheres were disappearing fast, and it was possible to imagine a day when they would actually be outnumbered by somewheres—people, structures, destinations, congregations. Someday, there would be no more countryside at all, no more cows, only houses. Only city.

PART THREE

COLOR

It is always possible to bind quite large numbers of people together in love, provided that others are left out as targets for aggression.

—SIGMUND FREUD, *Civilization and Its Discontents*

This puts us in a somewhat paradoxical situation, in that we claim both that common knowledge is a prerequisite for agreement and coordinated action and that it cannot be attained.

—RONALD FAGIN ET AL., *Reasoning About Knowledge*

Good and Evil
That's just people.

—JABEE, *Everything Was Beautiful and Nothing Hurt*

GOLDEN GRENADE

Wayne Coyne at a Flaming Lips concert, in his transparent bubble of joy.

Two weeks into the 2012 NBA season, on an otherwise unassuming Saturday, Wayne Coyne shut down the Oklahoma City airport. It was an innocent mistake. You know how sometimes you accidentally leave a bottle of water in your carry-on bag, or some nail scissors, and airport security finds it and goes a little crazy? Well, Wayne Coyne had a grenade. Again: it was perfectly innocent. Wayne was on his way to Los Angeles to watch rehearsals of a musical based on *Yoshimi Battles the Pink Robots,* the Flaming Lips' gold-selling 2002 space-epic quasi–concept album, and before that he'd been up all night at a house party, and at some point in the swirl of the chaos a fan had given Wayne this odd little art object: a real, metal, weapons-grade military grenade—heavy and deadly-looking—but painted all gold. Yesss!!! A golden grenade! It was inactive, of course; there was a hole in the bottom. It was not a weapon, it was a metaphor: peace and color and art are more powerful than war YESSSSS!!!!

Wayne had graciously accepted the gift, yeah yeah, because this was one of the bizarre constants in the great psychedelic journey that was the life of Wayne Coyne. People were always coming up to him, all over the world, and presenting him with unsolicited tokens of love, brotherhood, tribute—books, figurines, clothing, truly awful oil paintings of the Flaming Lips onstage in which all of the band members' faces were out of proportion and weirdly buglike. Wayne had learned that you just have to be nice and accept it, whatever it is. One time he'd tried to leave a painting in a cab, because it was ugly and a total hassle to carry around—but the cabbie had made inquiries, tracked Wayne down, and the painting found its way back to him. The golden grenade, though, that was actually cool, so he took that happily. Yeah yeah. Wayne liked things that were shiny and golden and weird, he liked explosions—video footage of mushroom clouds often flared up behind him onstage—so he threw the grenade into his duffel bag, where he throws all of the strangers' gifts that will fit, and then he totally forgot all about it and grabbed his bag and headed off to the airport to fly to L.A.

The security crew at Will Rogers World Airport found Wayne Coyne's grenade for him. On the X-ray screen of lane 2, amid the endless innocent drift of shoes and coins and laptops and jackets, an officer saw the unmistakable outline of a deadly explosive device. Alarms went off. The area was cleared. Certain nonnegotiable emergency procedures were set into motion. A bomb expert was summoned. People trying to leave Oklahoma City were suddenly stuck in an unmoving line. Flights had to be rebooked.

Wayne Coyne felt terrible. He stood there, next to the X-ray machine, in his rumpled suit, necktie hanging loose, shirt half unbuttoned, wild gray hair throbbing in bushy curls around his head, with glitter on his face and his fingernails painted in an electric spectrum of colors, and he explained to the men and women in uniform about the guy at the party, the duffel bag, the Flaming Lips, the terrible fan paintings. He was a good citizen! He had never, even once, in all his decades of international rock 'n' roll shenanigans, been in any serious trouble with the law. The Flaming Lips were dues-paying members of the OKC chamber of commerce, for God's sake! There was a picture of Wayne and the band etched into the glass at this very airport, in its mural of famous Oklahomans—GRAMMY-WINNING ALTERNATIVE PSYCHEDELIC ROCK, it said—and in that etching, Wayne was actually smiling and flashing a peace sign. The golden grenade, if you thought about it, was the *opposite* of terrorism. It was peace-orism.

In the end, security was pretty cool about the whole thing. They believed Wayne that he wasn't trying to blow up the airport, and even the official police report painted him in a sympathetic light. ("Crime: POSSESS BOMB . . . VERY COOPERATIVE AND UP FRONT . . . SAID HE SHOULD HAVE KNOWN BETTER.") Still, once the bomb squad has been summoned, you can't just call everything off. There is a process. Even if the perpetrator happens to be the city's most famous goofball clown, a one-man glitter storm, a Technicolor rock 'n' roll Willy Wonka trying to make the whole world conform to his own private epic slow-mo spirit-journey mushroom-fantasy vision—even then, you can never be too careful. The only proper antidote to an explosion is time.

Wayne Coyne was only being Wayne Coyne. He didn't mean any harm. But Wayne being Wayne intersected at a strange angle with the City of Oklahoma City being the City of Oklahoma City. The relationship between city and citizen was awkwardly charged. Wayne was famous enough that OKC basically *had* to claim him as a cultural asset, had to try to siphon out whatever quotient of hipness and glory it could from the association. It had to check its "rock star" box. But it was hardly a safe transaction. Wayne was famous in a slightly dangerous way; he was unpredictable to a degree that the conservative city did not like. This was a place whose newspaper published not only a daily prayer on its front page but near-constant caricatures of an idiotic Barack Obama on its editorial page, and where a six-foot-tall granite monument of the Ten Commandments would soon be erected next to the state capitol. Meanwhile, Wayne Coyne doused himself onstage with fake blood and reveled in public nudity, and sometimes he invited hundreds of fans to gather in parking garages, without any kind of permit, to play coordinated music from their car stereos. If you looked at Wayne's house on Google Maps, you would see him out in his front yard, apparently taking a bath. And so the city hesitated. Wayne Coyne was certainly *around*—city leaders appreciated that—but he was too full of some kind of unidentifiable sloppy energy that Oklahoma City could not safely control. Any public embrace risked turning into a civic embarrassment.

There had been attempts, recently, to achieve some tentative city-celebrity fusion. The most serious of these had come in 2007, almost exactly five years before the grenade incident, when OKC was right on the brink of seizing the Sonics from Seattle, and the fracking money was pouring in, and construction was booming, and the city was feeling strong and cocky and resurgent and up for a calculated risk. On a cool, clear Thursday in October, the Oklahoma City government invited its citizens to attend an official ceremony: the dedication of Flaming Lips Alley.

This was a bit of a joke, of course—an alley, not a street. It was a wink at the band's weirdness and underground ethos. But it was also a hedge. It contained plausible deniability.

Flaming Lips Alley stretched for four shabby blocks on the western edge of Bricktown, OKC's up-and-coming tourist district, a zone of formerly abandoned warehouses now occupied by chain restaurants and bars and one of the city's only Starbucks. The ceremony took place at the entrance to the minor league baseball stadium. A crowd of several hundred gathered near a bronze statue of Mickey Mantle, bat in hand, swinging his Okie heart out. Mantle was probably the most famous Oklahoman of all time, but his talent had been too big for the state, and so he had made his legendary career out in New York City, where he'd become a placeless everyman, winning seven World Series and appearing on the cover of *Time*. Although Mantle had a statue in Oklahoma City, he belonged to all of America.

Wayne Coyne belonged, uniquely, to Oklahoma City. In public, he liked to pretend that he was some kind of extraterrestrial born out of one of Pink Floyd's tube amps, but this was only a pose. Wayne was as pure a product of Oklahoma City as the place had ever produced. His shaggy face should probably have been featured on the city seal. Wayne had come to OKC as a baby, in the early 1960s, and unlike most of his creative peers, he never left. Even after the Flaming Lips hit it big in the early 1990s, after they signed with Warner Bros. and went into heavy rotation on MTV and appeared on an episode of *Beverly Hills 90210* and won multiple Grammys and co-headlined Lollapalooza with Prince—even at the height of all that, when the band was playing Buenos Aires and Tokyo and L.A. and Paris and Berlin and Melbourne and Toronto and New York, Wayne Coyne stayed. He bought a house in his childhood neighborhood, the unglamorous inner-city enclave known as Classen Ten Penn, where dog packs roamed through weedy lots and drug deals went down behind the empty storefronts, and he hung out at dive bars and rode his bike all over the place and photocopied flyers at the local Kinko's. The Flaming Lips reclaimed pieces of OKC's blasted landscape and folded them into their art: they conducted sonic experiments in empty parking garages, made a film inside of an old gas-station storage tank from a junkyard, and incorporated audio of one of their neighborhood dog packs into a song.

Although the dedication of Flaming Lips Alley was an official city ceremony, Wayne and the band had been allowed to take the lead in designing it, so it looked like a miniature version of one of their concerts—somewhere on the aesthetic continuum between a North Korean state function and a low-budget educational puppet show about the dangers of LSD. Wayne warmed up the stage by playing a military camp song on a toy trumpet—the quick, peppy notes hopped out over the Bricktown streets. All around him, extras in costumes filled the stage—a crowd of beardless Santas, a cluster of green-headed Martians, an anthropomorphic yellow sun that bobbed back and forth, waggling its arms. Blizzards of confetti gushed in the wind. In front of all of this colorful nonsense stood a line of men in dark suits, official representatives of the City of Oklahoma City, looking like they had somehow been pranked.

Eventually, one by one, the potentates stepped forward and spoke. "It sure is a lot cooler to have an alley than to have a street," the Oklahoma state treasurer said, and he produced a huge gilded folder, from which he read an official commendation of the Flaming Lips from the governor himself: "Oklahoma's history has been brightened through the gift of your work."

"Now, that's cool!" said the vice chairman of the Bank of Oklahoma, and he proceeded to allow some words to spill out of his mouth on the subject of the Oklahoma City chamber of commerce—"which I'm sure a lot of you think," he said, "are just a bunch of staid, old, gray-haired, hairy-legged guys that sit around thinking about how to beat up on young guys." He gave the crowd a moment to consider this image. "It's not true," he continued. "It's a very hip organization. It's committed to making this city the coolest city out there, and we've got a very hip and cool chairman president, Roy Williams!" Roy Williams—black suit, red tie—fired a zany blast of steam out of some kind of transparent tube and walked to the microphone to unveil a gift from the chamber: a large novelty snow globe, tall as a human, featuring photos of the Flaming Lips superimposed over the uninspiring OKC skyline. The snow globe wobbled visibly, suggesting inferior craftsmanship.

It was hard to imagine that any of these men had ever listened, on purpose, to a Flaming Lips album. Although the band's style was constantly changing, and although some of its songs were widely appealing—symphonic singalongs you might tap your foot to while waiting in line at Bricktown's Starbucks—the majority of the Flaming Lips catalog was noisy and experimental and almost painfully idiosyncratic. One album, *Zaireeka,* was designed to be listened to on four CDs simultaneously, via four different sound systems, and featured song titles such as "The Big Ol' Bug Is the New Baby Now" and "March of the Rotten Vegetables." The businessmen onstage probably didn't know the band's music well enough to know how thoroughly they would have disliked it.

Nevertheless, there was an alley to dedicate. Suit after suit strode to the microphone, and the aliens cheered, and confetti rained down, and a huge gray caterpillar, with crazy eyes and rosy cheeks and a golden crown, went skittering around through the crowd, and eventually Mayor Mick Cornett thrust the new street sign over his head like he had just won WrestleMania and shouted, triumphantly, "Flaming Lips Alley!"

Wayne Coyne shimmered to the front of the stage. He wore a ruffly pink dress shirt under a pin-striped suit, bow tie hanging loose under the scraggle of his short beard. He was, at that time, forty-six years old, and his hair was just beginning to gray at the temples, with a stylish white streak in the front. He looked raffish and teasing and naughty, like he was on his way home at the end of a night of wild excess. "He looks like a best man," a YouTube commenter would later put it, "the morning after a wedding where he randomly worked his way through all the bridesmaids."

But this was the funny thing about Wayne, and one of the reasons he was acceptable, barely, to the city's corporate sponsors. Despite his wild appearance, Wayne was as stable, in his way, as any of these gray-haired businessmen. He famously did not do drugs, and he worked like a dog on his music, and he had somehow managed to sustain one monogamous relationship for twenty years with an equally eccentric artist named Michelle. And of course, most important, Wayne Coyne had committed himself to Oklahoma City. This was the thing he shared, above all, with the other men onstage. Through OKC's bad decades, through its many busts and failures, none of them had abandoned the place, as so many others had, for Dallas or Austin or New York or Los Angeles. Every local newspaper article about Wayne ended with some version of this statement: "With his wife, Michelle, Coyne still lives in the neighborhood where he grew up." It was the kind of press any chamber of commerce would love.

Wayne hugged the Flaming Lips Alley sign to his chest with both arms, like a favorite niece, and began to speak to the crowd.

"As this, um, this, this—alley—has sort of been—*christened* this week," he said, "everybody has sort of asked me—um, Wayne, why do you think, um, it took so long, um, for Oklahoma City, um, to recognize you?"

This was odd. Wayne was normally an effortless speaker, in every context imaginable, whether talking to a late-night TV host or a journalist in his car or an ecstatic arena of 30,000 fans. He could go on for hours about anything, until his interlocutors begged him for mercy. And yet now he seemed overwhelmed, emotional, almost on the brink of tears. What was wrong with him? Any normal Beelzebub-fearing rock star would have regarded this goofy civic honor as laughably square—and certainly a rock star like Wayne, who would sell his fans gummy fetuses and inject the blood of collaborators into the vinyl of his albums. But here in Bricktown, Wayne was floundering. This ceremony was somehow touching him deeply. The chamber of commerce had nicked a powerful force at Wayne Coyne's core. It took him a full minute onstage before he burst out with something identifiably Wayne-like. "It's pretty fucking cool," he finally said, "to have an alley named after you."

The crowd roared, and at Wayne's side Mayor Cornett grimaced at the expletive, then hung his head and covered his face with both hands, rubbing his eyes. It was a devil's bargain, this transaction. It was like hiring an actual pirate to perform at your child's birthday party.

But it was too late for the city to back away. Flaming Lips Alley existed. Wayne and his kooky band had been legally inscribed onto the infrastructure of Oklahoma City, added to the official maps alongside all the other historic men and women (but mostly men) who had helped to make the city almost sort of great, in its way. If you started at Flaming Lips Alley, you could traverse the whole heart of downtown on nothing but famous names: Mickey Mantle Drive, Johnny Bench Drive, E. K. Gaylord Boulevard, Robert S. Kerr Avenue, Couch Drive—baseball stars, a media mogul, an oil baron and political powerhouse, and the Boomer mayor who died for his land.

"Any artist in the world," Wayne told the crowd, picking up steam, "if they felt somehow disheartened or discouraged, or wondered if anybody ever cared out there in the world, I'd say, 'Well, come to Oklahoma City and walk down Flaming Lips Alley.' And even though it has Dumpsters, and maybe some trucks unloading some beer in the back, I think it would really encourage them to know that we never demanded anybody give us anything. . . . But little by little, it was the people of Oklahoma City that believed in us. And even the people in the city government."

Here, it struck me, was the emotion roiling Wayne Coyne: he loved Oklahoma City. He actually loved it. OKC was not a major city, by any stretch, but it was exactly the right place to grow a Wayne. The city's wasted landscape was full of cracks, and those cracks were full of soil, and that soil contained precisely the right nutrients to nurture whatever outlandish micro-species of weedflower Wayne was—a spiky sort of kudzu vine with Venus flytrap heads, its tendrils eager to climb any structure that happened to be nearby, regardless of how rusty or uninspiring. No one had any idea what to do with this plant, but it was oddly fun to look at, even if it sometimes scattered stinky, oozy seedpods all over people's sidewalks and yards. Besides, it didn't matter if you liked it or not, because it was impossible to uproot.

One more time, standing next to the mayor, Wayne Coyne swore on the municipal stage. "We're on our way to becoming, I think, the fucking coolest city in America," he said, and this time the crowd lost it completely, and Mayor Cornett's face remained frozen in an official smile until he and Wayne, a short time later, went off to cut a red ribbon together with matching golden shears.

In retrospect, that awkward civic ceremony was the high point in the strained marriage of Wayne Coyne and the City of Oklahoma City. The years that followed brought a string of public embarrassments, major and minor. In 2011, it was the absolute boondoggle of the Womb, when Wayne and the Flaming Lips rented a large brick building downtown and, without asking the landlord or getting any of the necessary permits, had it painted overnight with explosive colors, complete with garish murals of robots shooting lasers and marijuana leaves stenciled on the sidewalk outside. The building's front door looked like a giant abstract vagina. Wayne announced that it was going to be an art gallery called the Womb, inside of which would be an even larger, more realistic vagina for visitors to walk through.

He told the local news that the gallery would be inaugurated with a fantastical New Year's party, to which the entire world was invited, and at which teenagers might be able to drop acid with Yoko Ono.

But this party, sadly, would never occur. Shortly after Wayne's announcement, the fire marshal showed up at the Womb, and he moved stoically through the building pointing out code violations everywhere. The giant vagina, it was determined, did not provide sufficient egress for a crowd of more than fifty people. A red sticker was affixed to the Womb's front door: ALL WORK OPERATIONS STOPPED.

There were further incidents. A citizen poll chose the Flaming Lips song "Do You Realize??" as the official state rock song of Oklahoma, but the state's conservative House of Representatives refused to approve it after the band's bassist, Michael Ivins, came to the capitol wearing a T-shirt featuring a hammer and sickle. (Another legislator cited, with disapproval, Wayne's cursing at the Flaming Lips Alley ceremony years before. "Their lips ought to be on fire," he said.) In the summer of 2012, as the Womb still languished in limbo, Wayne Coyne suffered a personal trauma: he and Michelle, the bohemian power couple of the Great Plains, suddenly divorced—a gossipy scandal that was much whispered and blogged about in OKC and beyond. Wayne's stable life began to destabilize. After decades of principled abstinence, he started to use recreational drugs: MDMA, mushrooms, cocaine. On Twitter, he posted a picture of huge powdery lines on a mirror next to a rolled-up dollar bill. He managed to get himself kicked off of Instagram, twice, for violating the site's nudity policy. He got into a feud, somehow, with Erykah Badu. Meanwhile, the Flaming Lips were in a dry spell of real commercial success. Their best-known single, the silly alt-rock anthem "She Don't Use Jelly," was by then nearly twenty years old, and their critically revered album *The Soft Bulletin* was thirteen. Recent reviews had been mixed. Wayne's singing voice—a reedy, awkward, scraping thing on its very best day—was beginning to lose its upper range.

It was in the midst of all these problems that Wayne brought his grenade to the OKC airport. The incident became international news. It was picked up by the *Guardian, Rolling Stone,* the *Huffington Post* ("Wayne Coyne Grenade Debacle"), CBS ("notoriously eccentric"),

Spin ("reputation for unusual behavior"), and numerous online gossip sites. (TMZ: "He pulled the 'nade stunt because he and his lame band are currently residing in the 'where are they now' file.") Twitter users addressed Wayne directly: "I'm less bothered by your airport grenade than I am about the fact that you are 51 and dress like a crazy asshole everyday."

In Oklahoma City, the incident rattled its way through the court of public opinion. At a Thunder game one day, a local sportswriter said to me, rather bluntly, "That guy is such a douche—bringing a grenade into the airport, on purpose, just to get attention. It's pathetic." The *Lost Ogle*, the same blog that spent much of its bandwidth mythologizing the godlike powers of Gary England, seized upon the golden grenade incident to unleash a brutal referendum on late-phase Wayne Coyne. The site interviewed a furious traveler who'd been forced to pay $1,000 to rebook a flight, and it accused Wayne of degenerating "from a fun-loving, goofy creative genius who writes and performs psychedelic pop songs into a sex-obsessed creepy old man who hunts down 21-year-old groupies in the OKC bar scene." In the city that had so recently honored him, the legend of Wayne Coyne was beginning to curdle.

And yet Wayne remained. This was his way. Oklahoma City could abandon him completely—could mock him at every turn, tear down the Flaming Lips Alley signs, flee the city en masse, allow the skyscrapers to collapse and the landscape to revert to prairie, and Wayne would not leave. He would cobble together a life, alone, out of the OKC rubble. He would pour his essence into the empty alleys and streets and parking garages and dumps and underpasses and warehouses, adapting them all to his own inscrutable ends. Wayne Coyne was Oklahoma City, and Oklahoma City was Wayne Coyne, and it would be that way until the very end, when he would die and be absorbed into the place completely, merging with it eternally.

GAME 7: MR. OKLAHOMA CITY

After the Thunder's unfortunate opening night in San Antonio, when Russell Westbrook managed to wildcat a win into a last-second loss, the team began to recover. Over the next week, Oklahoma City beat Portland and Toronto and Chicago, winning by margins that no amount of Why Not? could ruin. Still, the vibe on the court was strange. The players seemed to be haunted by their Hardenlessness. Everyone was acting weird. Serge Ibaka, the shot-blocking power forward, had begun to experiment unsuccessfully with shooting threes. Westbrook was as erratic and individualistic as ever, shooting and shooting and shooting and shooting, despite making a frankly offensive 37 percent of his shots.

Even Kevin Durant, human metronome of basketball excellence, was a little off. He seemed to be trying to compensate for Westbrook's excess shooting by hardly shooting at all. Instead, Durant was attempting to transform himself, against the natural order of things, into a passer. But he was not a passer; he was a scorer. Durant had been the reigning NBA scoring champion since the unprecedented age of twenty-one, and now he was twenty-four, and all signs pointed to him leading the league in scoring until he was thirty-one or forty-one or however long he felt like it. In the opening week of the season, however, Durant was inexplicably forcing passes all over the court, and he was turning the ball over at an alarming rate; he had twice as many turnovers as even Russell Westbrook, the NBA's poster boy for the reckless squandering of possessions.

Still, somehow, the Thunder were winning. Even at its non-best, Oklahoma City had enough talent to vanquish the rival cities of

North America. Destiny, sometimes, will agree to look the other way until the details match up with its grand plan.

During this opening stretch, if you happened to look down toward the end of the team's bench—very far down, past Westbrook and Durant and all of the role players, then past all of those players' backups, and then even farther than that, past everyone, in fact, who was wearing a Thunder uniform—you might have noticed, eventually, a very large man dressed in a very large suit. This was Daniel Orton. He was hard to miss. At nearly seven feet tall and more than 250 pounds, Orton was, even by NBA standards, unusually big and wide. And yet he sat at the end of the bench, with a gentle expressionless face, watching the game, saying nothing. Orton was the Thunder's backup backup center, trapped in the depth chart behind both the offensively challenged Kendrick Perkins and the omni-challenged Hasheem Thabeet. Although he was a marginal player, Orton represented something that neither of the other two centers ever could—he brought something to the team, in fact, that not even Durant or Westbrook could bring on their best days. Daniel Orton had a superpower: on the whole roster, in the whole history of the Thunder franchise, he was the only player who was actually from Oklahoma City.

Orton grew up, among cul-de-sacs and strip malls, in a neighborhood north of OKC's downtown core. In high school, he won three consecutive state championships and turned himself into a five-star national recruit. In college, he was a member of the legendary 2010 University of Kentucky team that started the season 19–0 and finished 35–3 and saw five of its players, including Orton, picked in the first round of the NBA draft. Orton, however, did not immediately flourish as a pro. He was drafted by Orlando, where he had to sit behind the mighty Dwight Howard, and before he could find a way to earn himself any playing time, he blew out his knee, and eventually, after two seasons of rehab and disappointment, the Magic released him—an ignominious fate for a first-round pick.

But then Orton's hometown came calling. That summer, in search of another credible big man, the Thunder invited Daniel Orton to training camp. He was still only twenty-two, still potentially a real player in the league. During scrimmages, Orton watched the drama boiling among Durant and Westbrook and Harden, and in the midst of all that he was able to show off his own game: real power, good hands, a soft touch, and flamboyant passing skills for a big man. It was all impressive—Durant later told people, privately, that he thought Orton was the best center on the roster—but apparently to the coaches it was not quite impressive enough. At the end of training camp, on the Saturday morning before the season began, Orton was the last man cut from the team. He and his agent started to talk, very seriously, about a career in China.

Later that night, Orton's phone lit up, like everyone else's, with the news that Sam Presti had traded James Harden. People were shocked, but Orton was not: he had sensed it coming. Then Orton's phone lit up again, and this time it *was* a shock. Presti wanted him back. The Harden trade had sent out more players than it brought in, which meant that the Thunder suddenly needed to fill a roster spot. Less than twenty-four hours after he'd been cut, Orton was back on the team. Just like that, he went from being jobless and desperate to having a guaranteed spot, at a salary of nearly $1 million, with the defending Western Conference champions of the entire NBA, who also happened to play in his hometown.

Orton was roughly the same age as Westbrook and Durant, and yet his career had been so derailed by injuries and lack of opportunity that hardly anyone, even in OKC, knew who he was. In terms of celebrity, he was a perfect counterbalance to his superstar teammates. In San Antonio, on opening night, Orton sat in his suit on the end of the bench and watched, stoically, anonymously, as Westbrook turned the ball over and allowed Tony Parker to hit the game-winning shot. Orton didn't play the next night, either, in the team's home opener, when Westbrook removed his feet from James Harden's empty locker-room chair long enough to score thirty-two points in a blowout win over the Trailblazers. Two days later, during a bad home loss to a weak Atlanta Hawks team, Orton watched Westbrook and Thabo Sefolosha bicker so insistently that they had to be separated. He sat on the bench during the Thunder's fourth game, watching as

Hasheem Thabeet burst out into the open court with a steal on his way toward a highlight dunk, only to trip spectacularly over his own legs and go crashing to the floor. While some of the players on the Thunder bench stood to give Thabeet a laughing ovation, Orton just sat there, watching.

This is what Orton did: he sat and watched. He didn't perform sideline theatrics, as most NBA bench players did, didn't dance after highlight dunks or launch into elaborate high-five routines. Friends told him that he looked bored during games, that he should try to be more enthusiastic. But that just wasn't him. He struggled to stay focused when he wasn't involved. Even in the locker room, he was quiet. Orton would always gather his things and sneak out before the media was allowed in—he hated the awkwardness of those locker-room interactions, reporters milling around while everyone got dressed, trying to work up the courage to ask players questions, so he vanished. Orton was the Thunder's invisible man.

Even when Orton did manage to get recognized in public, it wasn't as himself. This was one of the great ironies of his return to Oklahoma City: everyone on the street thought that he was Russell Westbrook. Their faces looked uncannily alike, and so everywhere Orton went—restaurants, gas stations, grocery stores—people would whisper and point and reach for their phones. After a while, Orton gave up on correcting them; he would just nod, smile for the photo, and move on. It was the worst of both worlds: a nondescript career attached to the face of a celebrity. He had been existentially displaced in his own hometown.

On November 11, the day after Wayne Coyne tried to board a plane with his golden grenade, Daniel Orton's opportunity finally came. It was the seventh game of the season. The Cleveland Cavaliers were in town. Thabeet was out with a sprained ankle, so Orton was put on the active list, which meant, if nothing else, that he actually got to wear his uniform while sitting on the bench. November 11 also happened to be a fateful date in the history of OKC: the anniversary of the resignation, in 1889, of William Couch, the city's first mayor, when he left office to defend his contested land outside of town, a decision that set him in motion toward his doom. (Somehow, no acknowledgment of this fact was made over the arena's PA system.) Orton sat and watched as the game turned into a blowout. Finally, with two minutes and two seconds left, Scott Brooks called his name. Orton shed his warm-ups, ambled over to the scorer's table, and checked in. It was only garbage time, but it was basketball, and Orton played well, considering. Even in the NBA, his body took up an impressive amount of space on the floor. He defended the post stubbornly and rebounded with strength. With twenty seconds left in the game, Orton had a moment: he leaped out on defense and got his fingertips on an opponent's three-point shot, blocking it, and then he raced to the other end, caught a pass on the run, and finished a fast-break layup. Two points. In the grand scheme of things, this meant nothing, but it was the first time Daniel Orton had put a ball through the hoop during an official game in Oklahoma City since the glory days of high school. It was, perhaps, the beginning of the new beginning.

One day, at the end of a practice, I sat down with Daniel Orton to ask him about his fairy-tale return to his hometown—this sudden opportunity to win a championship in front of all of his family and friends. Orton, in my mind, had become the human embodiment of the OKC renaissance, a living link between the people and the team. If everything broke properly, his personal story would be the perfect ending to the larger story of the Thunder: the native son, standing shoulder to shoulder with the stars, bringing long-deserved glory to his humble hometown. Maybe Orton's presence on the team could even help heal the wound left by the absence of Harden.

I asked Orton if he felt this way.

He did not. Not at all.

"It doesn't really matter to me," he said in a flat voice. "I mean, it's basketball. Anywhere is basketball. As long as you get to play. Any type of court I'm on, I'm home. I don't really think about it. Not really. Not really."

I was, for a moment, genuinely shocked. For months, I had been steeped in the triumphant narrative of the Oklahoma City Thunder, a fable of pure selfless solidarity in which everything got infinitely better at all times. Orton, however, expressed a deep alienation from the city, and a wariness toward the Thunder organization, that I had yet to hear from anyone else. His more famous teammates—young men from Los Angeles, D.C., Switzerland, and the Congo—seemed more attached to OKC, and more permanently settled there, than Orton did. Place and identity had slipped out of alignment. In fact, Orton told me that he had come to think of Orlando as his true home— that's where he'd been drafted, he said, where he had a house, where his girlfriend lived.

In the months that followed, I came to appreciate this about Orton: he was bluntly honest, sometimes to the point of comedy. Unlike Durant, he didn't slip into telling you what he knew you wanted to hear. Unlike Westbrook, he didn't defiantly shut you down. He just politely said what he thought, at all times. It would have been easy for Orton to play up his connection to Oklahoma City—easier, in many ways, than telling the uninspiring truth. But he never did. If Orton was, indeed, some kind of living embodiment of the place, as I had prematurely decided, it was not the chamber of commerce's version of the city, the booster brochure that was beginning to appear in national magazine stories: a community surfing to collective glory on basketball and Big Energy and visionary citizen-funded infrastructure programs. Orton represented a different place entirely. He was young, but he had already seen plenty of difficulty, both personal and civic, and he was willing to talk about it: how his mother had died of lupus when he was still a teenager, how he had struggled during his single year of college, how his knees had ruined his rookie season, how he had become estranged from his father. Orton still believed that he would become an NBA star someday, but he knew that the story would not be simple. It was too late for that. He was never going to have anything like the relationship his teammates had with OKC. They had all arrived as heroes; Orton had arrived as a baby. If he stood for anything at all, it was not the fantasy of Oklahoma City but the thing itself: the plain old muddy expanse that had once been at the bottom of an ocean, the world of spectacular dreams brought back down to earth. There were dark strains to the place, past and present—complexities, tensions, uneasinesses, outbreaks of violence, crimes excluded from the official story of progress. Oklahoma City was a place where time did not work properly, where things did not move only forward. No matter how hard the chamber of commerce worked to make them disappear, these realities were never going to go away. They were fundamental. And they were very much a part of the world Daniel Orton had just come back to.

NEGROPHOBIA

The Land Run was for white men. Not officially, in a legal sense, but in practice. The number of African Americans who made the Run is, like many things about that day, hard to pin down, but at least one historian guesses it was fewer than fifty. Others estimate two hundred, or somewhere near one thousand. In any case, it was a tiny fraction of the human tide—roughly 100,000 strong—that rushed in that day over the prairie. Given the opportunity the Land Run represented, especially for the poor and marginalized, that absence screams volumes. Oklahoma's settlers were a heavily armed white mob. Black Americans would have known to proceed with caution. Before the opening, some visionaries in the black community had argued that the Unassigned Lands should be reserved for a special purpose: America's first all-black state. But white interest in the region was too strong, and this idea never came close to happening. When the starting guns went off, it was white men who came pouring in.

The vast majority of Oklahoma's black residents arrived in the weeks and months afterward, once the metaphorical dust had settled. (The literal dust was still blowing around everywhere.) In addition to OKC's universal disadvantages—chaos, dirt, tornadoes, middleness—black settlers had to deal with special disadvantages all their own. By the time they arrived, the good land had been claimed, and most of the bad land too. Black residents were excluded from the signature dramas of the town's first days: "Oh, Joe—here's your mule," the Seminoles versus the subcommittees, the trauma of the jogs. They found themselves relegated to the least appealing pockets of remaining land, up against the railroad tracks and down by the river. One of their neighborhoods, Sandtown, flooded so often that its houses were built on stilts. Residents were frequently rescued by boats.

Still, black Americans came. It was hard to resist the promise of a blank slate, not to mention the promise of a boom. Soon they numbered in the hundreds, then the thousands. They worked mainly on the city's East Side, as laborers for the railroad and in the warehouses, delivering ice and coal and crates of vegetables, hammering together new buildings. OKC, in those early days, was a strange loose mixture of people: merchants, bankers, outlaws, gamblers, southerners and northerners, foreigners and natives. This, however, would have been the most obvious division. The wealthier center of the place was white; its muddy edges were black.

Some preached harmony. During the summer of 1890, on the sidewalk outside of his office, Angelo Scott saw a gang of white bullies harassing a black boy who was new to the town. Scott dispersed the group, and he and the boy struck up what he called "a curious friendship." Every morning, the boy swept out Scott's office, and whenever Scott came home from a trip, the boy would be there waiting for him at the train station. "I plead for kindness and consideration for these people," Scott later wrote. "I always treated them as human beings, and always hated with all my soul the poisonous attitude of so many so-called Christian people of Oklahoma against their race."

But that poisonous attitude ran deep. As Oklahoma City matured, as its rich and poor neighborhoods solidified, the lines between black and white became more pronounced. In 1907, when Oklahoma Territory was promoted to a state, it aligned itself politically with the Deep South. In his inaugural address at the constitutional convention, the political powerhouse Alfalfa Bill Murray made his white supremacist views clear. "We must provide the means for the advancement of the negro race," he told legislators, "and accept him as God gave him to us and use him for the good of society. As a rule, they are failures as lawyers, doctors, and in other professions. He must be taught in the line of his own sphere, as porters, bootblacks, and barbers." (Years later, Murray would rise all the way to governor based on his promise to battle "the three C's—corporations, carpetbaggers, and coons.") When it came time to write the state constitution, Teddy Roosevelt

had to step in and explicity forbid Murray and his allies from including segregation—an absence that they filled in, soon thereafter, at
the first meeting of the state legislature, where Jim Crow laws passed
with a huge majority.

Streetcars, schools, bathrooms, swimming pools, parks, restaurants—all of Oklahoma's public spaces became strictly divided by
race. Intermarriage was outlawed. Literacy tests were imposed on
black voters; white voters were exempted by a brazen "grandfather
clause," which excluded anyone whose grandfather had been eligible
to vote before January 1866—a date, of course, before black citizens
were allowed to vote.

Roscoe Dunjee had a word for all of this: "Negrophobia." He was
the publisher of the *Black Dispatch*, Oklahoma City's leading black
newspaper, and he did not shy away from confrontation. When Dunjee rode the streetcar, he sat up front, daring the conductor to ask
him to move. He was just light-skinned enough to give white passengers pause; he gazed out from behind round glasses with civilized
defiance. Dunjee's father had been a Baptist missionary, a benefi-
ciary of the Underground Railroad, a graduate of Oberlin College,
and a friend of Frederick Douglass. Not long after the Land Run,
he brought his family to save souls in the strange new territory of
Oklahoma. During the terrible drought of the 1890s, young Roscoe
hunted prairie chickens to help the family survive. He had no formal
education to speak of, but after his father's death he inherited the
family's private library of fifteen hundred books.

By 1914, Dunjee was publishing his ragtag East Side newspaper.
His publication had none of the advantages of a white paper like
the *Oklahoman:* a powerful owner, rich advertisers, an affluent and
growing subscriber base. The *Black Dispatch* was notorious for its
smeared ink and typos—it "often caused fellow printers to shudder,"
a rival newspaper wrote—and it was always fighting off bankruptcy.
In a note at the bottom of one front page, Dunjee attempted to inspire guilt in freeloading readers: "EVIDENTLY," he wrote, "You

do not know that it costs money to print this paper, if you do know that it costs money, you are quite obviously laboring under the delusion that we pay our bills with JAZZ or a fairy wand. Shake yourself, WAKE UP!, it costs money to print the Black Dispatch and you owe us NOW."

Despite all of its disadvantages, the *Black Dispatch* became a powerful force in Oklahoma City and beyond. The paper taught black history—a rarity at the time—and encouraged black entrepreneurs; it carried local gossip and ads for East Side businesses; it reported the major news of Oklahoma City scrubbed free of white bias; it excoriated politicians by name and always stressed the power of voting. "BALLOTS ARE BULLETS!" one front page read. "SHOOT EARLY TUESDAY." Even the name of Dunjee's paper was a provocation: "black dispatch" was slang for unreliable gossip. ("I decided to dignify a slur," he wrote.) Dunjee became the public voice of a community that was otherwise essentially voiceless. Week by week, he performed a thorough study of Oklahoma City's Negrophobia—its varieties and consequences, its most promising points of weakness. "The price we pay to exist in the state of Oklahoma," Dunjee wrote, "is too great."

Dunjee sent complimentary copies of the *Black Dispatch* to all the public figures he critiqued so bitterly, including Alfalfa Bill Murray. When he found out that the FBI had opened an investigation on him, Dunjee added its address to his mailing list too. "You remind me of a fellow walking around with a chip on his shoulder trying to get someone to knock it off," the governor once wrote to him—a critique Dunjee published as a letter to the editor.

Dunjee turned out to be much more than a publisher. He was an organizational genius. For a black newspaper, surviving a single year was an achievement. Dunjee edited the *Black Dispatch* for more than forty. He did not care that Oklahoma City wasn't a power center; he was there, so he would make it one. He rose to the top of every black organization he could find, national and local, and where there were gaps, he founded his own. "Just as our white enemies are organizing and raising money to thwart our progress," Dunjee wrote, "we must organize, raise money and be on the alert to oppose every move that tends to thwart us in the free exercise of our just rights."

Early on, Dunjee recognized the potential of a new organization based in New York City: the National Association for the Advancement of Colored People. He founded an Oklahoma City chapter, then organized chapters statewide, and very quickly Oklahoma's NAACP became, pound for pound, one of the mightiest in America. The national organization's first major victory came when the Supreme Court struck down Oklahoma's grandfather clause, calling it "repugnant" to the Fifteenth Amendment—a decision that led to an actual brawl in the state legislature, where lawmakers threw books and inkwells and paperweights at one another, leaving a prominent Republican unconscious on the floor. They rallied, of course, with a new law, requiring all unregistered voters to register during a single twelve-day period, upon penalty of being disenfranchised forever. Dunjee reported on the chicanery of the registrars, who would hide from black voters or claim they didn't have their registration books handy.

Despite such abuses, Dunjee's success against the grandfather clause set a pattern. He would instigate local action, and the NAACP would help push those cases up the legal ladder until, eventually, they reached judges who would strike down Oklahoma's most discriminatory laws. Dunjee insisted on funding these causes himself; he mortgaged his newspaper headquarters multiple times and accepted donations from readers in pennies. Through Dunjee, Oklahoma City became the wedge with which the NAACP began to move the laws of the entire nation.

"Somehow this little bandy-legged, hawk-nosed, brilliant, luminous man understood that the American covenant was not to be thrown away," wrote the author Ralph Ellison, who grew up on OKC's East Side and read the *Black Dispatch* all his life. "We had to be reminded that the way white Americans defined us was not what we were, and that the way we were described in the white press was not an adequate description of the breadth of our humanity."

Dunjee's fiercest fight in OKC was for the simple right to take up space. Following statehood, new residents came pouring into OKC's black neighborhoods; by the teens, more than 10 percent of the city's population was black. And yet the neighborhoods were not allowed to expand. Dunjee's newspaper office was in the heart of a neighborhood called Deep Deuce, where Second Street sloped down toward the river east of the railroad tracks. Its main drag was busy with drugstores and barbershops and jazz clubs, at which all the era's giants performed. (When Louis Armstrong came to Deep Deuce, even OKC's white residents crossed the tracks to see him.) The neighborhood's housing, however, was appalling—dilapidated, overcrowded, unsanitary, and starved for basic city services. When tuberculosis swept through, there was no black hospital to slow it down.

Dunjee denounced OKC's leaders as "common murderers." Like Angelo Scott in the city's first days, he called a mass meeting. He distributed ten thousand placards reading, SEGREGATION IS NOT DEMOCRACY. Black residents, Dunjee argued, deserved the right of "natural expansion" every bit as much as the white community. Deep Deuce's most practical outlet for growth was to the north, but this was forbidden because white people lived there. Every time black residents tried to inch in that direction, policemen came and evicted them, throwing their possessions into the street. Vigilantes occasionally bombed their houses.

"This civilization," Dunjee told his readers, "is going down in chaos—out of it will rise a better world."

In May 1919, with an eye toward that better world, Dunjee began to systematically test OKC's rigid neighborhood borders. One by one, he enlisted community members to buy houses on the northern edge of Deep Deuce. When these pioneers were arrested, Dunjee bailed them out and sent them back to get arrested again. A shoemaker named William Floyd managed to get arrested five times in a single day. In police court, the attorney representing Oklahoma City issued a blunt warning. "One thing certain," he said, "if these people don't stop meddling in our ordinances there is going to be a lot of dead niggers around." But meddling in ordinances was Roscoe Dunjee's sacred life mission, and history was on his side. Floyd's case climbed through the legal system until finally, in federal court, it won. Despite bomb threats, Floyd moved into a house on a street that touched the very bottom edge of a white neighborhood. And so, after many years of confinement, by the tiniest possible increment, OKC's black world began to expand.

EVERYTHING WHICH MAKES LIFE
MORE LIVABLE

Stanley Draper, 1937.

On August 19, 1919, Oklahoma City's newest resident stepped off a train and into the center of downtown. What he saw was a total mess. Traffic swarmed everywhere. The very train he had just stepped out of was now blocking the streets, creating a snarl that looked like a historical montage of the evolution of transportation: cowboys on horseback, dandies on bicycles, farmers in horse-drawn wagons, workers in delivery trucks, families crowded into Model Ts. The congestion was shocking. Every building sprouted a thousand signs. There was no greenery to speak of. The streets and sidewalks teemed with food carts, stray dogs, oxen, women hauling laundry, workmen delivering blocks of ice. Train cars clanked and boomed on the depots' side tracks, coupling and decoupling. The sky above was sliced into grids by streetcar wires, under which trolley after trolley rumbled past. The chaos of the Land Run had been extrapolating itself, at that point, for thirty years. The man's first impression was of the Wild West—that somehow he had left modern America and stepped into a dime novel.

In the midst of all that noise and motion, this new man would not have drawn much attention. He was white, average height and average build, nothing much for Oklahoma City to look at. But he was very busy looking at Oklahoma City. His eyebrows slanted hard, at nearly forty-five degrees, and as he walked he would have noticed everything: the flows and clogs, the little boys selling newspapers, the untapped resources, the missing teeth, the hints of ghosts of future buildings. Among the saloons and hotels, occasional skyscrapers rose, towering eight and nine stories tall. One was white stone and looked like a Venetian palace, with fanciful rows of pointed windows and arches and spires. In the distance, the man would have seen Henry Ford's Model T plant, cranking out future traffic, and that, at least, would have pleased him. He would have noticed that the streets didn't quite match up; the city had apparently been assembled wrong. But that was something that, given the proper approach, could be fixed.

And so Stanley Draper entered Oklahoma City. No one could have known it, that August afternoon, but it was a crucial moment of contact—something like the young Michelangelo pausing to assess, for the first time, the flawed block of marble he would one day turn into his *David*. Rarely have a city and a citizen been so perfectly matched. Draper was as obsessed with cities as OKC was obsessed with being a city. He believed, religiously, that a place wasn't just somewhere you happened to live; it was your identity, your spiritual context, the very reason for your being. As Draper walked, he began to organize Oklahoma City in his mind. It would make sense to streamline all this traffic, to move the trains out of downtown, to straighten the jogs and tame the river and find room so everyone could spread out, to ease all of this congestion. The mo-

ment he stepped off the train, the process had begun. OKC would be Draperized.

There were good reasons, of course, that Oklahoma City was such a mess. Its biggest natural advantage had always been its centrality: it was thirteen hundred miles to Los Angeles and Washington, D.C., eight hundred miles to Chicago and Atlanta, five hundred miles to St. Louis and Santa Fe. The city was not a destination but a crossroads, a hub. It grew, accordingly, on secondary industries: moving and storing and selling other people's stuff. This was lucrative, but it also created perpetual crises of organization—many interests competing over the same patches of space downtown. The city had formed spontaneously, with no central organizer, and the town was full of boom-minded people—not only those who'd been born that way but those who had been converted to the cause. Local politics was too turbulent to manage the problem. The mayor and the members of city council pulled against one another constantly, exhausting all of their power. Bootleggers and saloonkeepers and prostitutes bribed everyone in sight. Political factions still split off, as they had in the Land Run days, into committees and subcommittees, which merged with other committees and subcommittees to swallow rival committees and subcommittees and spit out new committees and subcommittees. Oklahoma City was desperately in need of a master organizer.

Draper was twenty-nine years old, almost exactly the same age as OKC itself—both had been born, by cosmic coincidence, in 1889. Unlike his existential twin, however, Draper had started not in the Great Plains but far outside, in rural North Carolina, where his family went back many generations. (One of his ancestors fought in the Revolutionary War, on the side of the British.) Like many others, Draper had come to OKC to accept a job, and a rather boring one at that. He was there to increase the membership of the city's chamber of commerce. In light of everything Draper would eventually accomplish, this was something like inviting Sherlock Holmes to a crime scene just to put up the yellow police tape. By the end of Draper's reign, OKC would be a completely different city—a place much closer to the fantasy version of itself that it had always imagined it saw in the mirror.

When Stanley Draper arrived, he didn't even know what a chamber of commerce was. This was understandable. A chamber, by nature, has influence but no formal power. It is a way for businessmen to lobby the city government for favorable business conditions, but— given its position outside of that government—its influence is necessarily limited. Much of its work is a kind of civic PR: sponsoring art contests, holiday decorations, scholarships, and ceremonial street namings.

Oklahoma City's chamber, however, was unusually vital to the town. It had been founded less than a month after the Land Run by Angelo Scott himself. Scott was a businessman, of course—he had his newspaper, his law practice, and a small hotel—and he knew that commercial success was crucial for the town to survive. What he called the "board of trade" was a merchant collective that sought to win industry to the city, and it succeeded. It managed to lure the railroads to the center of town and meatpacking plants down by the river—economic engines that helped Oklahoma City grow after the lean early years. The congestion that had bothered Draper downtown was a result of the board of trade's success.

Draper seized the baton from Angelo Scott and his pioneer colleagues and moved in directions, and at a pace, that they could never have imagined. Before long, Stanley Draper was no longer simply trying to increase the chamber's membership—he was running the whole thing himself. Draper turned out to be an organizational dynamo. He worked ninety-hour weeks, read eleven newspapers a day, and walked around with a briefcase bulging with notes. He took notes on everything: the strengths and vulnerabilities of rival cities, his garden, psychology books whose techniques might help him more efficiently exploit the people around him. ("The Draper Method," his biographer wrote, was "to use people as other men use money or power.") At football games, Draper sat in the crowd scribbling notes;

in the middle of the night, he woke up to scribble more notes. Before long, the chamber had hired two secretaries to keep up with him.

Draper's vision of the chamber of commerce extended far beyond simply attracting new businesses. He saw it as the prime organizing force of Oklahoma City. Official government, Draper believed, was too timid, too constrained, too visible; its power was dispersed across too many people, most of whom were subject to the silly popularity contests of elections. Draper's crucial insight was that the chamber's amateurishness, its very lack of official power, was in fact its great strength. The chamber could exercise its control at a much deeper level than democracy, with its checks and balances, would ever allow. It was invisible to the average citizen. It sat right in the sweet spot between public and private, corporate and community, profit and service. For Draper, the chamber of commerce was the answer to every important civic question. It was the most powerful tool anyone would ever devise to wrench Oklahoma City forward into the future.

One of Draper's first obsessions was a detail so small that no one, in thirty years, had bothered to take care of it: the name of Oklahoma City itself. From the beginning, people had referred to the place, almost universally, as "Oklahoma City," but that had never been its official title. Its actual name was a remnant from the days before the Land Run, when the place was only a tiny railroad stop on the single line of tracks that ran through the Unassigned Lands: Oklahoma Station. A city couldn't be a proper city, Draper believed, if it wasn't even willing to call itself one. So he changed it. Oklahoma Station became Oklahoma City. Such attention to detail would define his reign.

Draper worked to clean up the congestion downtown. He had the train tracks torn up and relocated down south, out of the way, at a new hub called Union Station. He sent workers out to put up mileage signs on every road within three hundred miles, answering a question that drivers otherwise never would have asked: How far is it to Oklahoma City? These signs, Draper calculated, would increase the perception, all over the region, that Oklahoma City was a hub, a place people were thinking about, a place worth going to.

Draper used Oklahoma City's business community like an ATM.

He could raise $1 million for a project in an afternoon. He spent entire days on the telephone, chain-smoking and ordering people around, never saying hello or good-bye, just talking when he was ready and hanging up when he was done, a habit that terrified everyone, including his family. OKC businessmen would greet one another by asking, "Have you been Draperized lately?" Draper stole industries from other cities and lured dozens of conferences to the streamlined downtown. City building, to Draper, was a zero-sum game, and his enemies were the other mid-tier cities of America: St. Louis, Fort Worth, Denver, Dallas, El Paso. The war was one of publicity, infrastructure, access, favors, and the allocation of federal funds. Under Draper, Oklahoma City acquired a national reputation for the ravenous snatching of everything worth having: money, publicity, projects, land.

Draper turned the chamber into a monster of coordinated power, with eighteen separate departments, all working together to siphon nutrients away from competitors. One department was devoted entirely to lobbying Washington, D.C. (Draper was so crazy for federal funds, in fact, that he moved to D.C. himself one summer to personally lobby the president.) In terms of U.S. population, Oklahoma City was barely in the top fifty cities. But it had one of the nation's five largest chambers of commerce. What once had been a very minor stop on the convention circuit was now a destination, hosting hundreds every year.

If anyone in OKC tried to resist Draper's advances, he would always invoke Tulsa. "If we don't do it," he would warn, "Tulsa will," and donors would go racing for their checkbooks. For most of its history, Tulsa had been comfortably inferior to OKC: a Podunk old Indian village a hundred miles northeast, a frontier town that hadn't even figured in the Land Run. (It had been just outside the boundaries of the Unassigned Lands.) Through dumb luck, however, Tulsa had recently raised its station dramatically. It had struck oil, first in 1901, then again in 1905, and then again and again and again and again, until Tulsa—weak little provincial ancient Tulsa—had boomed into one of the richest cities in the world. Tens of thousands of new citizens went pouring in, an influx that OKC might have captured if only its luck had broken differently, and Tulsa's population surged ahead and its downtown sprouted Art Deco showpieces that made OKC look like a pioneer mudhole. Tulsa was now threatening to become the dominant city in the state. Oklahoma City was crazy with envy. It, too, should have been sitting on huge underground lakes of oil—all the geology suggested it—but no one could find them. It made no sense. Meanwhile, Tulsa was sucking so much wealth out of the ground that there was hardly even room to store it. If the state's center of economic gravity was allowed to shift decisively to the northeast, OKC might shrivel and die, as Guthrie had after it lost the capital. Draper exploited this anxiety for all the leverage he could.

Then suddenly, finally, OKC's luck broke.

On December 4, 1928—the Feast Day of Saint Barbara, Patron Saint of Explosions—the tip of a drill working near the south edge of OKC nicked the glorious future: it hit a reservoir of oil. Oklahoma City had been sitting, innocently, for its entire existence, on top of the second-largest lake of oil in the world—and now they had found it. Immediately, the city exploded. Dense forests of derricks sprouted all over the south, then spread to every other part of town, into residential neighborhoods, along street medians, even directly in front of the capitol building itself. On the East Side, the black community's only public park—a place Roscoe Dunjee had lobbied hard for in the *Black Dispatch*—was discovered to be sitting on top of oil, and so the city took it back and pumped the land for all it was worth. Thousands of new residents poured in to seek fortunes. The rush was so intense that, even when the entire American economy crashed in 1929, Oklahoma City continued to surge. New residential developments (whites only) were poured into the empty spaces far beyond downtown, past even the cow pastures where the capitol had been built, and they were given names like "Crestwood," and developers such as John James Harden, scion of the ubiquitous Western Paving Company, made a fortune not only on the sales of homes but on all the roads it took to get to them. Vast new stretches of prairie were paved. New skyscrapers sprang up downtown. Two of them raced side by side, floor by floor, to become the tallest in the city, and the eventual winner—built in only nine months—was the First National

Bank headquarters: thirty-three stories, nearly five hundred feet tall, a miniature copy of the Empire State Building, with aluminum embroidery copied from King Tut's tomb. It would house the grandest banking lobby in the state—a huge marble sanctuary complete with busts of Roman emperors and a mural of the Land Run—as well as the Beacon Club, where Stanley Draper and OKC's other power brokers would sit in cigar smoke and plan the city's future.

Draper's great patron and partner was the reclusive E. K. Gaylord, owner of the *Oklahoman,* the most powerful man in the city. (To this day, people refer to him as "the Mr. Burns" of OKC.) When oil was struck, Gaylord happened to be traveling in London, and he wired home, instructing his associates to immediately buy the radio station, WKY, in order to increase his media empire. Gaylord and Draper believed that the Great Depression was largely a consequence of negative thinking. Hopped up on Oklahoma City's booming success, they launched something called the "Let's Go!" program, a citywide initiative of positive thinking, which consisted largely of the local newspapers writing glowing stories—hundreds of them—about the work of the chamber of commerce. (Draper was allowed to personally revise stories about himself before they were published.)

It was only ten years since Draper had first stepped off the train platform into OKC, but the city had been thoroughly transformed. Its population had nearly doubled, from just under one hundred thousand to nearly two hundred thousand, and some predicted that it would double again in the next decade. Tulsa was no longer a threat. The biggest threat now was Oklahoma City's own growth. The Land Run was not scalable. Planning became more urgent than ever.

Before Draper, the growth of Oklahoma City had been willy-nilly. After Draper, it was calculated, coordinated, deliberate, channeled. In 1930, the city released its first-ever master plan. In place of the torn-up railroad tracks, OKC built grand civic buildings—paid for entirely with federal funds. Draper brought in the Army Corps of Engineers to tame the flood-prone river. He planned huge reservoirs to help the city's water supply keep up with its booming population. He built roads everywhere, including a highway that connected—for no particularly good reason—El Paso to Niagara Falls via Oklahoma City. (Draper knew highway officials in El Paso and Buffalo, and he wanted an excuse to route a major traffic artery through OKC.)

The future of civic power, Draper knew, was aviation, and some of his wiliest moves secured OKC's place in that new world. In the 1940s, when the United States laid out its national skyway—essentially a highway for commercial airplanes—Draper saw, to his horror, that Oklahoma City had been excluded. He used his D.C. influence to pause the process and redraw the lines himself, and—after getting buy-ins from twenty-five hundred other chambers whose towns had also been excluded—he forced the whole thing to be redone. Flights from Alaska to South America were now suddenly routed through OKC. When airmail was new, and OKC was having trouble generating enough volume to justify itself as a stop, Draper personally wrapped and sent bricks to people across the country—no note, no explanation, just a brick. During World War II, when the big civic money was in war contracts, Draper shocked Wichita by outmaneuvering it for an air force base: at the last minute he used a shell company to buy land, secretly, around OKC's little airport, and he granted the military crazy incentives to make that airport the most appealing landing spot in all of the vast flat middle. When a visiting officer disgraced himself (public drunkenness, disorderly conduct) Draper sprang him from jail, put him on a plane home, and had the only copy of his arrest report hand-delivered to him in Washington, D.C. OKC won the contract from Wichita. To this day, Tinker Air Force Base remains a major economic engine in the region.

Thus were things Draperized. This pattern was repeated any number of times, on any number of projects. After a while, Draper could afford to be quite explicit about his power. As he put it, in a widely admired speech: "The properly organized Chamber of Commerce is the best compromise possible between the principles of democracy and those of a benevolent aristocracy." Its leaders, Draper said, were exempt from "the disorderly and violent processes of our elections." The chamber's proper zone of control, he suggested, was basically infinite: "everything which makes life more livable." The true purpose of a chamber of commerce, Draper said, was as "the custodian . . . of the community's 'will to live.'" When the city councilmen complained that Draper was running the city illegally, that he was a quasi-fascist tyrant, he managed to placate them by inviting them to sit in on the chamber's weekly meetings. He liked to say of his critics, "It seems like they're catching on."

Under Draper's command, Oklahoma City progressed from a frontier town still shockingly dependent on booms and busts to one of the solidly established middle-American places, its future existence assured. It was one of the country's major oil producers, a hub for nationwide travel networks, both on the ground and in the air, and its water supply was ready for another hundred years of booms. It had vanquished Tulsa as a serious rival. It was a paradise for cars. You couldn't enter or leave the city without Stanley Draper's help: he had arranged the freeways, the trains, the airports. He had linked this provincial backwater to everywhere else. Oklahoma City was no longer a novelty, a mirage on the plains: it was a real place. "It is easy to have faith in Oklahoma City now," Angelo Scott wrote in the late 1930s. "But those who can remember the dead years of the middle

Skyline and sky, around 1937.

nineties and the still crude country town of that period, know that faith came high in those depressing days. Oklahoma City is too big to go back now, but there was a time when she was not too big to go back. The great boom had not come, and say what you will, it is booms that make cities."

Toward the end of his life, Angelo Scott was named "Oklahoma City's Most Useful Citizen." That was nice, but it wasn't really true anymore. No one, not even the conscience of the pioneers himself, could compete with Stanley Draper. Scott was essentially democratic, fair-minded, and humanistic. Draper was pure control. Although Scott had founded the chamber of commerce, by now it had clearly outgrown him. He devoted his later years to writing a history of Oklahoma City—a firsthand account of its founding chaos and all the attempts at order that followed. Stanley Draper, meanwhile, was taking history and making it his own. He hadn't been around for the original Land Run, but he had enough power, in the middle of the twentieth century, to make it happen all over again.

One of the weirdest displays of power in Draper's long weird reign was an event he called the "Re-Run." It happened in October 1948. (Only Draper would think to stage a Land Run tribute outside of April.) Early in the morning, on an abandoned farm just west of downtown, thousands of volunteers lined up. Military jets flew over on a simulated bombing run—black powder had been planted, beforehand, to explode out of the soil—and two tanks fired their guns in unison. This was the starting signal. Hundreds of horses raced onto the land, carrying settlers, and a wave of heavy machinery followed: bulldozers, plows, tractors, forklifts. With a speed that would have astonished the 1889ers, the land was sculpted, harrowed, fertilized, and seeded with alfalfa. Irrigation lines were set up. A pond was dug and stocked with fish. At a Red Cross emergency tent, fake settlers were treated for real injuries—splinters from broken wagon tongues, gashes from the two miles of barbed-wire fencing they had erected. An actual house was dragged out onto the land and filled with brand-new electric appliances. All of this happened in one day. An estimated twenty-five thousand people came from all over the region to watch. OKC was in the middle of another drought, and the wind that afternoon was outrageous, so the whole event happened in the midst of a whipping dust storm. Stanley Draper stood in the middle of the hubbub, thoroughly coated in dirt. The final task of the day was cosmetic: the volunteers sprayed 250 gallons of white paint on the property's houses and fences, just to add a layer of freshness, to show that OKC's history was new and bright and shining once again. But it was so windy, the *Oklahoman* reported, that "the job took a beating from the dust," and by the end of the day, everything was the color of "deep chocolate."

KALEIDOSCOPIC SPERM EXPLOSIONS

Sometime after three a.m., as the house party throbbed all around us, Wayne Coyne told us his plan. You know how sometimes you see paint spilled in the middle of a road—just like a big accidental industrial splotch of white? Well, obviously those spills are a mistake, right, yeah yeah, but the thing is, Wayne had always actually kind of *liked* them. He thought they looked cool. So it occurred to him: What if someone were to go out and spill paint all over the streets on purpose, in a bunch of different crazy colors, leaving behind this huge tripped-out rainbow that everyone in the neighborhood could walk on and drive over and meet at and take pictures of? Wouldn't that be a public service? Wouldn't it make life just a little bit cooler? Why do streets have to be gray and shitty and boring? Know what I mean?

The house party was up off Classen Boulevard, not far from where Wayne used to work at Long John Silver's, in a neighborhood of brick houses that lined up in tidy rows. All around us, OKC's hipster bohemian twenty-somethings spilled onto the porch, smoking and eating pizza, drinking liquor out of plastic cups, making an unholy ruckus that all the adjacent dark houses were apparently going to just choose to ignore.

Wayne drank from a red cup, and who knows what else he might have had in his system—these days, it was hard to say. Mostly, though, it seemed like he was high on the presence of all these late-night happy people, their crowded young energy, and also on his wild plan to convert a group of us into rainbow vandals.

Rainbows, in Wayne's private iconography, were sacred. They ranked right up there with eyeballs, fetuses, vaginas, and spaceships—

possibly even higher, because all of those things were made up of colors, and rainbows were color in its purest form. Wayne was hopelessly, fiendishly, voraciously, unapologetically, ragingly addicted to color. He spread color over the world the way others spread education, justice, or fast-food franchises. His fingernails, his house, his guitars—color. His girlfriend—color. Any piece of paper within Wayne's reach became saturated, very quickly, by oozing and flowing waves of doodles: kaleidoscopic sperm explosions, alien eyeballs, melting suns, psychedelic sentient vaginas. I have seen Wayne draw, with colored markers, directly on walls. I have seen him pour many layers of paint on floors. The Flaming Lips, in their fourth decade of existence, were as much an industrial-scale color-delivery system as they were a source of rock 'n' roll—in concert, Wayne stood over the crowd in an iridescent turquoise leather suit, face shimmering, bathed in lasers, and as he sang he would thrust out his fist or raise his palm, and these gestures would summon huge explosions, laser sprays, noise blasts, hurricanes of confetti, crises of light. Again and again, the band and its fans were obliterated by vast blinding nuclear detonations of pure color. (SEIZURE WARNING, read signs on the concert hall doors.) Wayne didn't have children, or any kind of traditional family, and I sometimes thought it was because he chose to have color instead. Color was his entire life plan. He was married to color, the father of color.

Wayne would have been a novelty anywhere, in any city, from San Francisco to Beijing, but he was especially one here in Oklahoma City—a vast kingdom of poured concrete that stretched for hundreds of gray miles, with all its color carefully regulated.

This plan to paint a rainbow on the streets, then, was extremely Wayne Coyne. I nodded along, hypothetically, as one does at a house party. Yes, Wayne, great. Cool. Wayne went on talking. As he did so, it became increasingly clear that his rainbow plan was not, in fact, hypothetical at all. He said he had actually already purchased six cans of house paint, in the classic rainbow spectrum, and everything was ready to go. His proposal was as follows: Six of us would lie in the bed of a pickup truck, side by side, and while someone drove us around, we would pour the paint out, in big fat messy lines, trailing a rainbow that would wake up the sad old shitty city streets. Yesss!! I mean, if society was going to pave over all of the grass and the flowers anyway, and shoot fucking—*fossil smoke*—up into the air, and then spend every day driving right past one another without ever looking or talking—well, at least we could do all that on top of some rainbows, right? Yessssssss!!!! Maybe the cops would put a stop to it, but Wayne didn't think so, because no one ever seemed to get stopped for those industrial white splotches we were always seeing, so obviously cops had more important things to do than chase people who were spilling paint, whether it was contractors doing it accidentally or freaks on purpose trying to make the city cool. YESSSSSSSSS!!!!! Or maybe everyone would go to jail, and that would be interesting too, because Wayne had never been to jail.

The house party continued to thump and surge. Wayne was thirty years older than almost everyone else there, but it didn't seem to bother him. He was, in moments like this, eternal—a pigment spirit floating outside of time.

Suddenly a guy burst out of the kitchen, strode right up to Wayne, and shouted, with the ecstatic clarity of four a.m., "Everything great that's happening in Oklahoma City is happening because of you!"

Well, that was nice. This was something Wayne heard more and more these days. For decades, his neighborhood had been notoriously bleak. He still referred to the area, matter-of-factly, as "the ghetto." More than once, Wayne had found himself facedown on his living-room floor after hearing gunshots in the street. With the recent rise of the Thunder and the renaissance of downtown, however, Wayne's neglected old neighborhood was starting to become cool. It was close enough to downtown to absorb some of that energy but far enough away to avoid the soulless corporate skyscraper vibe. Decades of neglect had left the housing affordable for young artists. The abandoned main drag was begging to be colonized by shops. There was the romanticism of mild danger. It was, in short, ripe for gentrification. And so the "Plaza District" was born—a small patch of Great Plains Brooklyn. Artsy midwesterners trickled in. There was a boom economy of locally designed T-shirts, especially artistic homages to the Thunder, and you could buy stylish refrigerator magnets of the Devon Tower or the milk-bottle building or the Gold Dome.

A new gourmet grilled-cheese-sandwich restaurant was so popular it kept running out of ingredients and closing in the middle of the day. Wayne was often credited as the Great Spirit of this rebirth, and his lifelong loyalty to the area added an extra twist of branding—if you moved to the Plaza District, there was a 100 percent chance that you would see him out and about, setting up crazy Halloween decorations in his front yard, drinking at the local bar, inventing crazy schemes at late-night house parties.

Hence this guy bursting ecstatically out of the kitchen to thank Wayne for everything cool in Oklahoma City. Wayne laughed and waved the praise away. He was no community organizer—that was not his vibe at all. He was, he told his fan, just one guy doing what he thought was cool, trying to make his own life a little less boring. He was just following the color wherever it led. And tonight it had led him here.

The crowd began to thicken. All over town, the gravity of Wayne's fame pulled the people of OKC toward him. When the room got too crowded, he'd move to the next room, and then everyone would assemble around him in there. You got a sense of the origin of the word "star" as a metaphor for celebrity: not just a distant brightness but a microdensity so intense it could move other bodies around. I was talking, in the swirl, to Wayne's new girlfriend, who was very young—early twenties—and, like Wayne, wore plastic jewels stuck to her face and crazy paint on her fingernails. Her eyes were accented by thick, dark makeup, and a long pink feather stuck straight up from the back of her blond hair. This was Katy. She was the one who painted Wayne's fingernails to look like eyeballs and watermelons and tiny skeletons wearing top hats. She struck me as irreducibly mellow. She spoke in a gentle, half-tempo drawl, slightly behind the beat of normal conversation. She had a smile that made other people smile. Everyone seemed to like her.

And yet Katy's presence represented a seismic shift in the life of Wayne. For twenty-five years, he and his wife, Michelle, had been devoted to each other, and they had seemed like a perfect symbiosis. Like Wayne, Michelle was an ambitious working-class Okie, a photographer and painter who was also addicted to color. When the Flaming Lips made their first breakthrough video, for the song "She Don't Use Jelly," Michelle was in it, nonsensically holding a plate of eggs and toast in a bathtub. When Wayne led one thousand torch-bearing skeletons on a Halloween march through the streets of downtown OKC, Michelle published photos of the procession in *Spin* magazine. That was her tongue licking someone's eyeball on the cover of the Flaming Lips' EP *Yeah, I Know It's a Drag . . . but Wastin' Pigs Is Still Radical*. Wayne and Michelle had never been official-wedding-ceremony married, but that didn't matter. They were solid. They were a unit. In the 1990s, when the Flaming Lips starting touring the world, Wayne wore a button onstage that said "I ♥ Michelle."

But now, somehow, it was over.

Michelle had fled Oklahoma City, some months back, and word was she was now living on some kind of art boat floating on the Thames in London. Wayne's loose confederation of remaining associates—bandmates, housemates, partymates, roadies—all still seemed a little shell-shocked by her absence. I heard no one speak of Michelle with anything other than reverence and sorrow. Despite all the colorful adventures, Wayne could sometimes be a hard man to put up with. He was fun and creative and generous and fiercely loyal, but he could also be flaky, scattered, demanding, and prickly. He seemed both profoundly in control and out of control. He pushed his band members hard: long hours, endless practices, constant tours, marathon recording sessions. Conversations with Wayne could get so confrontational that people called them "confronsations." He had driven one drummer to quit and had made the bassist cry. It was easy to understand why a relationship with Wayne might eventually strain to the point of breaking.

Still, Michelle had been as central to Wayne's life as the band itself, and on some level Wayne must have been in mourning—although it was hard to detect it here, at this house party, in the giddy middle of the night. Maybe it would come out later, in his music. In the 1990s, after Wayne's father died, he had channeled that pain into *The Soft Bulletin,* one of the era's great art-rock masterpieces, revered by critics everywhere. The music was both symphonic and sad, bereft and joyful. "Love in our lives," he sang, "is just too valuable to live for even a second without it." Perhaps a similar musical triumph would emerge from Wayne's breakup with Michelle. The band was working on a new album, as well as a whole new stage show to go with it, but no one knew anything about it yet.

For now, Wayne had Katy, and he had the praise of the young people at this house party, and he had his plan to paint a giant rainbow all over the streets of Oklahoma City. Somewhere around four in the morning, with the party still going strong, Wayne set the plan into motion. He didn't want to make the rainbow up here, he said, by the house party—he wanted to do it down in the Plaza District, where he could see it and live with it and admire it every day. Neighborhood rainbow pride. So he grabbed us, six of us, and we all got into our cars and started driving south toward the place that Wayne called home, one human for every color of the rainbow.

KISS

In the third quarter of a Thunder victory over the L.A. Clippers, Kevin Durant scrambled his defender with a crossover dribble and exploded toward the hoop. Before long he ran into trouble: three other defenders swarmed him at the free-throw line, blocking his path. So Durant leaped into the air, cocked one extremely long arm back, and lasered a pass out toward Thabo Sefolosha, who was wide open and waiting to shoot. The pass, however, was a bit obvious, and an opponent managed to tip it, and it flew off-target, out of bounds, and hit a little old white-haired woman sitting on the sideline, right in her delicate forehead—a blow that sent her careening backward, stunned, clutching her hair. Kevin Durant glided straight over to her, all the way across the court, a Boy Scout on a mission, and he bent his director's cut body in half and kissed the woman, and she beamed—a moment of chivalry that would be played and replayed to infinity on sports TV. "She's gonna tell all her friends about this tomorrow," the announcer said, chuckling.

It was November 21, 2012—what would have been Stanley Draper's 123rd birthday. For most of Draper's long reign in Oklahoma City, that kiss would have been unthinkable.

TAPS

During World War I, black soldiers boarding trains to leave Oklahoma City held banners that read, DO NOT LYNCH OUR RELATIVES WHILE WE ARE GONE. This was a reasonable fear. Despite all of Roscoe Dunjee's fighting, the white power structure held its grip. One year after Stanley Draper's arrival, in the summer of 1920, Oklahoma City was rocked by a lynching. A white mob arrived at the county jail, broke in with suspicious ease, and pulled out an eighteen-year-old black prisoner—the lone survivor of a bootlegging raid in which two police officers had been killed. The mob took the young man into the countryside, hanged him from an elm tree, and shot him twice in the forehead. The prisoner never should have been held in Oklahoma City in the first place—he was brought there, illegally, by the county attorney, who feared that a largely black jury in the neighboring county might acquit. The attorney was known to be affiliated with the Ku Klux Klan; he made the prisoner's whereabouts known and left the jail unprotected. In the outrage that followed the lynching, the *Oklahoman* reported rather credulously on the attorney's relationship to the crime: "O. A. Cargill, when asked if he had a statement to make about the abduction of the negro last night, said that he had not, except that he was glad that he was at home and in bed when it happened."

"NEGROES URGED TO STAY HOME," read the paper's front page.

Dunjee's *Black Dispatch,* by contrast, raged. "The most dastardly and hellish crime that has or can ever stain the fair name of the State of Oklahoma was staged at the County Jail," it began, and it proceeded to report on the desperate scramble that night on the East

Side, where a thousand people had gathered on Second Street to try to figure out how to help the abducted prisoner before it was too late. Fifty policemen, along with the mayor himself, came out to the East to monitor and constrain the crowd. The police sent the Deep Deuce search party in the wrong direction, so that by the time they found the abducted prisoner, dumped in the tall grass out in the country, he had already been dead for hours. The *Black Dispatch* did not flinch from describing the "ghastly sight" of his body: "his tongue had been choked out and hung limp over his lower lip. His right eye was wide open while the left was closed." Although the dead man had not lived in OKC, his body was brought back to Second Street, where huge crowds came through to mourn.

Roscoe Dunjee ruthlessly mocked law enforcement's official account of the crime. "Three men overpowered the jailor," he wrote,

> tied him, cut his telephone wires and light, HIS TELEPHONE WIRES, OVER WHICH THE EDITOR OF THIS PAPER HELD A CONVERSATION WITH THAT SAME JAILOR AN HOUR LATER. . . . THINK OF IT, IN five minutes, unknown men can come to the jail, tie the jailor, cut the wires and then find the man whom they seek, from among the many cells, they can do all of this without any information or assistance from the inside. THE PUBLIC IS ASKED TO BELIEVE THIS.
>
> Well, WE DON'T BELIEVE IT.

Thus the story circulated through Oklahoma City, the official version and the alternate, the story and the story underneath—the reality of the East Side versus the reality everywhere else. In the streets of Oklahoma City, children walked around selling these stories, hollering out competing newspapers' headlines in their tiny voices.

In Deep Deuce, one of those voices belonged to Ralph Ellison. He grew up so thoroughly immersed in the world of the *Black Dispatch* that he later recalled selling it when he was "just out of diapers." Long before he had any idea that he would become a writer himself, Ellison would visit Dunjee in his office among the jazz clubs of Second

Street. Ellison's father had died when Ralph was only two—a large block of ice he was delivering slipped and gored him in the stomach, and he was buried in the black section of Fairlawn Cemetery, not far from the graves of William Couch and his Boomers, not far from Red Kelley and Officer Burnett.

Shortly after the infamous lynching, in the spring of 1921, Ellison's mother decided that there was no future for her sons in Oklahoma City. The place was too brutal. She couldn't take them to the zoo or to a decent public park. There was not even a proper library for Ralph, an eager reader who had to make do with the discarded books and magazines his mother managed to scrounge from the houses uptown where she worked as a maid. So she quit her job, sold all the family's furniture, and set off with her boys for Gary, Indiana, where her brother worked in a steel mill. On their way north, the Ellisons stopped to visit a cousin in Tulsa. He lived in a neighborhood called Greenwood, and his OKC visitors would have been impressed by a zone of black life so different from Deep Deuce: solid brick homes and shops, lawyers and doctors, wealth from the city's endless oil booms. Ellison's cousin had luxurious furniture and a baby grand piano. Tulsa was still brutally segregated, but at least its black residents had managed to make something grand in their patch.

Gary, by contrast, turned out to be horrible. The steel industry crashed just after the family arrived, and Ellison's mother couldn't find work; they were reduced to eating actual garbage. Before long, they gave up and decided to head back south. Although Oklahoma City was amazingly, maddeningly flawed, it was still home.

On their return trip, the Ellisons passed once more through Tulsa.

This time, Greenwood was gone.

During the family's brief stay in Indiana, a race riot had raged through their cousin's formerly quiet neighborhood. It had been set off by a mysterious incident in an elevator downtown—an alleged assault on a white girl's innocence—and in response a lynch mob had gathered at the jail, and a counter-mob had gathered to hold them off, and in the chaos somebody fired a shot. The apocalypse ensued. For two days, white mobs went to war on Greenwood, burning everything the Ellisons had admired—its churches, shops, hospitals, and houses. Residents trying to escape were mowed down with machine guns. There were eyewitness reports of airplanes circling and dropping incendiary bombs onto the roofs of buildings, burning them from the top down. In the end, thirty-five city blocks were reduced to smoking rubble. Ten thousand residents were left homeless. Hundreds of people slept in tents in the wreckage. No one could even say for sure how many people had been killed. When the Ellisons passed through in the aftermath, the whole ruined neighborhood smelled like death.

Meanwhile, back in Oklahoma City, the KKK was ascendant. By 1923, the organization had grown so powerful that the governor, Jack Walton, declared literal war against it, imposing martial law and mounting machine guns on the roof of the county courthouse. Stanley Draper disapproved of the conflict, worrying that such visible strife would reflect poorly on OKC's growing national reputation as a business destination. The governor was impeached. A few months later, ostensibly in celebration of George Washington's birthday, the KKK took over downtown. Nearly five thousand Klansmen marched with torches, American flags, and burning crosses. Brass bands played, and an airplane swooped festively overhead. Klanswomen rode along the parade route in one hundred cars. Although it was a cold February day, more than thirty thousand citizens came out to watch the parade circle the segregated downtown. It looped past the nine-story Colcord, a giant in the skyline that Ellison's father had helped build. The *Oklahoman* covered the parade with a lighthearted front-page story—"KROWD 'KNOCKED KOLD' BY KU KLUX"—as well as multiple playful articles describing the festivities. "The faces of youth, fresh with the animation and excitement of the event, appeared beside the faces of age, lined with the kares of many events, stern and steady in their rigid turning toward the kross at the head of the kolumn. . . . Haze of mist and smoke could not hide an almost hysterical woman, who, after watching the passing of the first fiery cross, rushed to the line of marchers, and seizing the nearest klansman, kissed him repeatedly, krying, 'Thank God!' "

Not long after this parade, Ralph Ellison turned ten. O. A. Cargill, the county attorney who had presided over the infamous lynching three years before, was elected mayor. The Ellisons settled back into life in Deep Deuce. As a teenager, Ralph took up the trumpet, and the noise of him practicing out of his open window became part of the soundtrack of the community. Every morning, he played reveille— the quick, peppy notes of the military camp song hopped and echoed between the buildings, waking the neighborhood up. Every evening he played taps, a mournful end to the community's day.

In 1930, when Ralph Ellison was sixteen, Oklahoma City released its first comprehensive plan. It was explicit about black citizens' social position.

> Oklahoma City is primarily a city of native born white Americans. This points to the necessity of developing a city to meet the high standards of American living and working conditions. As in most of the cities of the Central and Southern states, the principal racial problem centers about the Negroes. They are a necessary and useful element in the population and proper provision should be made for their living facilities. While it is an advantage of each race that living areas be segregated, the white race should be much interested in the welfare of the Negroes because of the close contact resulting from the employment of the Negroes as servants in various capacities.

Roscoe Dunjee would have read this, of course, with level-headed rage. In the *Black Dispatch,* he railed against the Klan and called the state's new governor, Alfalfa Bill Murray, a demagogue. As OKC continued to expand under the organizing influence of Stanley Draper, as housing developments spread north along freshly poured highways, a white group called the East Side Civic League mobilized to keep black homeowners in their place. Dunjee fought them in his traditional style, pushing the black frontier methodically forward, block by stubborn block, sending homeowners now all the way up to Eighth Street, bailing them out when they were jailed. Alfalfa Bill Murray, outraged, issued an executive order declaring martial law in the East. But it was too late. Dunjee's new housing case was already in the system, and it climbed the legal ladder all the way to the Oklahoma Supreme Court, where Dunjee himself testified on the stand for more than five hours. The court ruled in his favor. Housing segregation was now, once again, illegal in Oklahoma City. Black developments began to spread farther up the East Side.

Based on such victories, Dunjee became nationally known as a civil rights fighter. But he was realistic about the depths of Oklahoma's problems. He had a theory, for instance, about the Tulsa race riots. It sounded like a conspiracy theory, but it also made perfect sense. The riots weren't simply the result of a racist mob, Dunjee argued. It was deeper than that—more chillingly rational. The destruction of Greenwood had solved a long-standing problem for Tulsa's white city planners. After all the recent oil booms, downtown Tulsa wanted desperately to expand. But that expansion was blocked by Greenwood. The neighborhood could not have been easily cleared, as a slum might have been, in the name of civic improvement. Greenwood was affluent and solid. These were not tenants but homeowners. It was the American dream. The riots might have started with primal racial hatred, Dunjee believed, but they soon turned into something else: an opportunistic, strategic, city-sanctioned campaign to clear the land. When Tulsa's black neighborhood was rebuilt, sure enough, it was farther from the city center. The white downtown was finally able to expand.

Eventually, Ralph Ellison reached the same conclusion his mother once had. A future in Oklahoma City, for someone like him, did not exist. In the summer of 1933, at age nineteen, after graduating from high school, Ralph Ellison left. He snuck into one of OKC's many railyards and hopped a Rock Island train. There was no direct route to where he was going, so he rode north, east, and south, through St. Louis and Alabama. He got beat up viciously by white railroad guards. Eventually he reached the Tuskegee Institute, where he would study music and literature and begin to turn himself into the world's writer. Oklahoma City had already taught Ralph Ellison everything he needed to know about invisibility. Before he could begin to make a name for himself, he was gone.

RAINBOW

In the absolute emptiness of the middle of the night, Wayne Coyne's rainbow party crew arrived, one by one, at the point of rendezvous on Thirteenth Street. The headlights of my rental car washed over the neighborhood, revealing block after bleak block of boarded-up houses, pebbled pavement, torn fences, porches leaning hard. Suddenly, out of nowhere, my lights sent up a burst of glitter. This is how I knew I had arrived at Wayne's place. Three jungle gyms sat on the lawn out front, each with a disco ball dangling from its apex. On the front gate hung a canoe that had been painted to look like an enormous smile.

Wayne, of course, did not live in a normal house. He lived in a place that everyone referred to, simply, as the Compound. It was its own self-contained world in the middle of the city—a sort of hallucinogenic Vatican.

The Compound started modestly, back in 1992, when Wayne managed to scrape together just enough money to win a government auction of a derelict home in the depressed neighborhood he grew up in. It was a funky building, cobbled together during OKC's building boom of the 1930s out of leftover parts: a spiral staircase from an old movie theater, kitchen tile from a drive-in restaurant, stained-glass windows from a church. Wayne fixed it up a little, and the band crashed in it. Over the following decade, as the Flaming Lips rose to national prominence, Wayne expanded his inner-city empire. He bought the house next to the original house, then the house next to that one, and then even more houses—and then he knocked down their fences and bulldozed some buildings and joined everything together into a big sprawling psychedelic wonderland that stretched all the way across the block, back to front, from Thirteenth Street to Fourteenth. You could traverse the block without ever leaving the Compound. Wayne built a recording studio in the middle, and the yard filled up with mushroom lawn ornaments and various sparkly things and adopted dogs and cats and, in the center of it all, actual peacocks roaming and flapping.

I parked my car near the grinning canoe and stepped out. The euphoria of the uptown house party—the shimmering world in which we had all agreed to this ridiculous scheme—now seemed three thousand miles away. Thirteenth Street was dead quiet, and its silence felt like a warning. Chain-link fences sagged next to houses that appeared to be abandoned. Wayne produced the cans of house paint and handed each of us a color. I started having flashbacks to suburban vandalisms of middle school slumber parties—egging houses, TPing front yards. But here we were all adults, perpetrators, in a neighborhood that did not look like it was in any mood to play around. Wayne, however, was cheerful and relaxed, totally at ease. At some point, the plan for Operation Street Rainbow had been modified slightly, so now we would be on foot, side by side, dripping paint in a steady stream, ROYGBIV, leaving a big bright circuit all the way around the Plaza District.

I got purple, the final band of the rainbow. Zac, the Flaming Lips' stage manager, punched holes in my can with a long screwdriver. There was some trial and error involved in finding the proper flow—how many holes, how big, in what configuration?—but eventually flow was achieved, and so it began to happen. Wayne Coyne's magical street rainbow wiggled its way, slowly, from the front of the Compound and into the neighborhood. We walked east along Thirteenth, brightening the pavement, then north up Blackwelder Avenue—a street that shared a name with a man who served on Angelo Scott's citizens' committee and later invoked the ire of Roscoe Dunjee by supporting segregation ordinances, which made it illegal for black residents to live on this very street. We dribbled our rainbow lines up Blackwelder, then took a left at the grilled-cheese-sandwich restaurant, pouring color past the salon where Nick Collison, the Thunder's backup power forward, got his debonair hair cut. We passed the midcentury-modern antiques shop and the indie T-shirt store and the tattoo parlor and the local art collective.

Our rainbow stripes were thin and wiggly, and they did not exactly cohere—they wandered or stayed true according to the personality of the person doing the pouring. My stripe had no courage in it whatsoever. I am not, by nature, a lawbreaker, have never even received a traffic ticket, and I was terrified the entire time, and that terror was obvious in my line. It looked like purple was trying to secede from the color spectrum. I kept swerving away from the group, walking far ahead, then far behind, pretending, absurdly, that I was only out for an innocent stroll, that I had no affiliation with these reckless hippie monsters who were sullying the civic landscape of an otherwise fine city. (What about the paint can in my hand, the paint on my pants, the paint all over the tips of my shoes? Officer, the world is full of mysteries.) I felt like a prairie dog lookout, jerking upright at every little sound or movement. A pit bull barked. A car passed through a distant intersection. I was sure that we were going to be arrested at any moment. I thought about Police Chief Bill Citty, about Mayor Mick, about all of the representatives of the City of Oklahoma City who had been so kind to me on my visits. I thought about my parents. I thought about Sam Presti. Could vandalism possibly be part of the Process?

It was hard to say if what we were doing that night was good or bad or neutral. Nice or not nice. By my calculations, we were pouring paint onto three different places at once, and the meaning of the rainbow was different in each.

One was the City of Oklahoma City—the legal entity, entrusted with maintaining infrastructure, with collecting and allocating tax money, with upholding all of the laws and bylaws and procedures and processes upon which a civilized modern city runs. This was the realm of the city council, of the police, and in this context we were pretty clearly violating the law. Our rainbow was happy vandalism, funny vandalism, but a legal entity is not designed to register the different moods or effects of vandalism.

We were also pouring paint onto a very different place, however, one that I had begun to think of as "OKC": the brand name, the PR creation, the city of the renaissance, of momentum and opportunity, of boosterism, the realm of the chamber of commerce. OKC was infinitely larger than the bureaucratic City of Oklahoma City—it was a fantasy that stretched backward and forward through time, from David Payne's Ewing to whatever metropolis the current city builders imagined in their dreams at night. In the context of OKC, our street rainbow was wonderful. Its legal status was the least important thing about it. The rainbow would add raffish charm to the raffishly charming Plaza District. It would bring more buzz to a neighborhood that was driving the city forward. It would look good in the morning to the young people of OKC, and—just as important—to the potential young people of OKC who were currently living elsewhere but might see the rainbow on Tumblr or Instagram and file it away among the many reasons that Oklahoma City was suddenly cool. To this OKC, our illegal rainbow was a force for public good.

The third entity, and the one I felt the deepest allegiance to, was plain old Oklahoma City itself. This was reality, everything, the historical place, the kingdom of dimetrodons, history, anthropology, geology, bedrock. This Oklahoma City didn't care about our rainbow at all. We were value-neutral, an eyelash in a jet stream.

Everyone in town existed in some combination of these three worlds simultaneously. The City of Oklahoma City, OKC, Oklahoma City. Law, fantasy, history; Process, Boom, and a synthesis of the two. We were pouring our rainbow onto all three of these places at once, and in each of them it meant something different.

Wayne was pouring the red paint, on the opposite end of the rainbow from me, and his line was full of courage. He moved with joy and gusto, expressively, and he actually backtracked, retracing his steps, making sure there were no hiccups in his flow. He would leave no inch of this city's pavement gray. He seemed completely unafraid, happy and free, like he was working on an art project in the privacy of his own home. Wayne didn't even stop when his can stopped dribbling—he actually pried off its lid, then turned the can upside down and walked back over the rainbow, for many blocks, covering the whole territory again, shaking out whatever dollops of paint were left. By then I was back in front of the Compound, cowering near my car, bracing myself for the sound of sirens.

Wayne returned a good ten minutes later, happy and relaxed, exuding the spirit of YESSSSS!!!! He was a little surprised, he said, that the lines weren't fatter—he'd been imagining a big monster rainbow eating the entire neighborhood, and this was more like a baby rainbow, crawling around, babbling out the cutest little colors. Still, it looked cool, yeah yeah. Good job, everyone! Wayne was triumphant. My pants and shoes were covered with paint, and I slept for only a few hours that night, fitfully, and I got up early the next morning and drove, cautiously, out to the Plaza District to see if what I was remembering had actually happened—and yes, it had, the evidence was everywhere: an actual rainbow on the pavement, spreading unbroken for many blocks, the whole color spectrum, from the sad trickle of purple to that joyful smear of red. It made me happy; I thought of Angelo Scott picking wildflowers here back when it was a distant wilderness. The rainbow was a gift from Wayne Coyne to Oklahoma City, a declaration of love, color where it had never been before, color where it had not previously been thought to belong.

IN THAT HAMBURGER, THE WHOLE
ESSENCE OF DEMOCRACY LIES

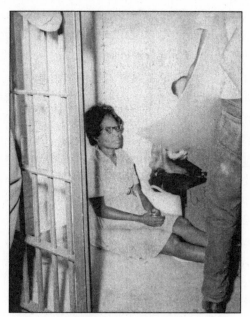

Clara Luper in jail, 1969.
She was arrested twenty-six times.

August 19, 1958, was a Tuesday—a very normal thing for a day to be. The weather was obnoxiously hot, also normal for August in Oklahoma. But that was where the normalcy stopped. That afternoon, Clara Luper and the children drove downtown. They were dressed nicely, as if for church, in dresses and button-up shirts, everything ironed, and the children carried books under their arms. As they got out of their cars, they probably didn't attract any terribly unusual glances, nothing to ripple the pond of the day. This was on Main Street, right in the bustling heart of everything, near the ornate white skyscraper that looked like a Venetian palace and the jogs in the streets and the old juggernaut of the Biltmore Hotel. Clara Luper was thirty-five years old, in her sundress and cat's-eye glasses, purse on her arm. Behind her walked thirteen children, all members of the NAACP Youth Council. They passed the parking meters lining the curb and then under the big neon sign in front of Katz Drug Store— the creepy humanoid cat, whiskers stiff in the Oklahoma wind, grinning and wearing a bow tie. LET'S EAT AT KATZ, the sign said, and this was exactly what Luper and the children had come to do: to sit down and order something like anyone else in the city, to deliberately make themselves a part of that LET'S.

Luper and the children entered the shop. This was allowed. Tuesday carried on.

Then they sat down at the lunch counter.

This was the moment when a switch flipped, when the previously normal Oklahoma City afternoon turned into something else—a day after which no Tuesday, or any other day, would have precisely the same civic texture.

Inside Katz Drug Store, everyone stopped and stared. The place was busy, as usual, with everyday Oklahomans on break from the office or resting their feet after shopping downtown.

"The waitress," Luper remembered later, "suffered a quick psychological stroke."

A manager emerged. Another waitress came over. "What do you want?" she asked, in a tone that suggested she was prepared to give them anything but.

The spokesperson for the children was a fifteen-year-old named Barbara Posey. She put five dollars on the counter.

"Thirteen Cokes, please," she said.

The manager's face went crimson.

The children sat and waited.

This was a test, a deliberate provocation. Luper and her children were continuing Roscoe Dunjee's program of neighborhood expansions, but this time applying that strategy to shared public space. They wanted full participation in the center of the city. They were tired of depending on the small, rare kindnesses of white men like

Angelo Scott. For more than a year, the group had written letters and met with city leaders and asked every institution of power to help. But nothing had come of it, and the children, like children, didn't have the patience to wait. They didn't want to orchestrate legal attacks that would take years to unfold. So they would sit here at Katz until something happened.

Before long, the police showed up—"policemen of all sizes," Luper would write in her memoir, "with all kinds of facial expressions." (Among her many other virtues, Luper was a gifted comic writer.) The media followed: Channel 9, with its big TV cameras, ready to document the disturbance. But the police sent the cameras away. This was, in large part, a war of publicity, and the only way to win was to keep it quiet, to let the scandal blow over. No notice of the sit-in would appear in the next day's issue of the *Oklahoman*.

Clara Luper and the children continued to wait. The five dollars remained on the counter. White Katz patrons swarmed to defend the status quo. They told the children to go away, to show respect for law and order. They used racial slurs. One woman walked over, leaned down, and coughed directly into a child's face. Then she moved down the line, slowly, coughing into each of their faces.

Luper did her best to remain calm. She encouraged the kids to read their books. She had brought a copy of Martin Luther King Jr.'s rules for nonviolent behavior, and she read it to herself over and over.

Somebody knocked one of the little girls off her stool.

Clara Luper began to pray.

An old white woman approached her with a warning.

"If you don't get those little old poor ugly-looking children out of here," she said, "we are going to have a race riot. . . . Don't you know about the Tulsa race riots?"

Luper was a high school history teacher with a graduate degree from the University of Oklahoma. She was a lifelong reader of the *Black Dispatch* and an active member of the NAACP. She could have lectured this woman for five hours about the Tulsa race riots. But Luper stayed calm, and the woman left. Luper explained her intentions, respectfully, to the police, and for several hours the children sat at the lunch counter, keeping their heads down and quietly absorbing the abuse. Finally, Luper and the children got up and walked out and headed back home, away from the city center, back to the East Side.

We don't tend to think of Oklahoma City the way we think of Tuscaloosa or Montgomery or Greensboro or Selma, as a crucial front in the battle for civil rights, and this is largely for very OKC reasons. The PR-conscious local media kept Clara Luper's sit-ins relatively quiet, and the protestors and police managed to work together to avoid any major eruptions of violence. This wasn't the first sit-in movement in the nation—that form of protest had been going on, sporadically, for decades—but it was one of the first sustained movements that would have such a dramatic effect. OKC's sit-in happened a year and a half, for instance, before the much more famous sit-ins in Greensboro. It was a major domino in the line of civil rights victories that would eventually tip across the entire United States.

Luper had benefited directly from the activism of Roscoe Dunjee. She studied at the University of Oklahoma immediately after Dunjee, with the help of Thurgood Marshall, managed to desegregate it, at a time when metal bars still separated the black students from the white. Luper also watched the way Dunjee turned local crises into national victories, the way he and Marshall won case after case in the Supreme Court, the way he eventually rose to take over the whole NAACP.

But again, the sit-in was the kids' idea. Earlier that year, Luper had taken them on a trip to New York City, and after experiencing the integrated East Coast, the children could no longer accept segregated OKC—this sort of half-citizenship, where you could enter shops downtown but not try on a hat, where you could order takeout but not sit down. Soda fountains, in Eisenhower-era America, were like the cafés of 1920s Paris: idealized little nodes of the public sphere. They were long, leisurely, wonderful counters where you could sit and order a sandwich, read the newspaper, gossip, belong. The kids wanted that.

Luper took them seriously. First she took them to the people in charge, appealing to their shared Christian values. But the restaurant owners refused to adapt. Luper finally had nowhere else to go, no higher level of appeal: the men working the levers of power to organize OKC, men such as E. K. Gaylord and Stanley Draper, did not see integration as a priority. "If the business community, led by the lily white Chamber of Commerce, . . . would speak," Luper wrote, "Justice would flow with the speed of an Oklahoma tornado. . . . The Chamber of Commerce's only commitment as I have seen it is to the perpetuation of the system." Finally, at Luper's house, over Kool-Aid, one of the kids just spontaneously said it: "Let's go to Katz." So that's what they did.

After that first ugly day at Katz, Luper and the kids got up the next morning and did it again. No one had expected a miracle, and there was not one. The second day was more or less the same as the first. The children sat down and ordered Cokes, did not receive them, then tried to read their schoolbooks while white customers hovered around them, hurling abuse. The major difference, on day two, was that the protestors were not so badly outnumbered. Instead of just Clara Luper and the original thirteen, the whole community had come out. They filled not only every seat at the soda fountain but much of the rest of the store. In the evening, they all left together and went back to the East, ready to do it again the next day.

Day three, however, turned out to be unnecessary. Katz Drug Store gave in: it announced, officially, that from now on it would serve everyone, black and white, at its lunch counters, not only in Oklahoma City but in all thirty-eight of its stores, in four different states. Luper and the children, from the unheralded center of OKC, had changed the lives of people hundreds of miles away.

They did not stop long to celebrate. Luper and the children began to work their way through the rest of downtown. Every morning they left the shabby streets of the East Side and marched into the signature institutions of the city center. Responses varied widely. At Veazey's drugstore, just down the street from Katz, the owner greeted the activists at the door, said he had been expecting them, welcomed them inside, and announced that he had already changed his policy. Veazey's was integrated, no sit-in required.

But this was the exception. Most restaurants fought. Some chained their doors shut and posted guards outside. Others let Luper and the children in, then poured hot coffee on them. One manager came forward, Luper wrote, "grinning like a grinning champion" because he had removed all of his restaurant's tables and chairs so that *nobody* could sit, black or white. At the Civic Center Grill, behind the courthouse, the owner welcomed the protestors in, then locked the doors behind them, filled the room with smoke, and threatened to douse them with hot grease; someone had to call the police to come and get them out. This kind of thing went on for months. Some restaurant owners told Luper they were keeping a careful tally of all the money they had lost because of her disturbances, and that they would be demanding reparations from the NAACP. On Christmas Day, a restaurant owner spat directly into Clara Luper's face.

Luper, however, was a master of nonviolence. She did not rise to anger. Her rebellion was jubilant. She and the children believed, sincerely, that they were rescuing America from itself. "We love these

White men rally to bar black children
from entering a restaurant.

white people so much that we are going to make them do right," she wrote. "The doctrine of non-violence is rooted in the fundamental truth that whites are human.... We aren't defeating him, we'll be just removing his hostility and insecurities which will prepare him to function as a whole man in a Democratic Society." She wrote open letters to America and signed them, "Your citizen, Clara Luper." She brought a copy of the U.S. Constitution to the segregated Huckins Hotel and dared its proprietors to read it. As she wrote during one sit-in: "Waiting for a hamburger, and in that hamburger, the whole essence of Democracy lies."

Despite the many hours and days and years Luper spent getting assaulted in Oklahoma's public places, she never hardened into a straight-faced paragon of noble justice. She was not grim. She remained cheerful and silly and weird, one of the great personalities in the history of OKC. Under the stress of death threats, in the face of angry mobs, she broke into song and wrote poems:

> If you are superior to me,
> Perform a miracle—
> Command your hamburgers to sing,
> Turn your ice cream into diamonds.

One by one, the restaurants and department stores gave in to Luper's pressure. Up in swanky Nichols Hills, at the venerable Split-T restaurant, white teenagers hurled projectiles and yelled, "Go back to Africa!" Luper responded that Oklahoma actually belonged to the Indians anyway, so the white people should have to leave, too. Bomb threats and hate mail came to Luper's home, and her phone rang constantly with abuse. One day, someone broke in and burned her furniture. On her porch, the KKK left a sack of shotgun shells.

Before it was all over, Luper would be arrested twenty-six times.

The sit-in campaign went on for six years. By the end of that time, no segregated restaurants remained. The history teacher and her students had earned themselves, block by grinding block, a space downtown. By then, however, downtown had become a very different place.

UNIVERSAL CITY

During the second year of Clara Luper's sit-ins, in April 1959, viewers tuning in to the evening news, looking for the latest footage of downtown arrests or escalating spring weather, would have seen, instead, something much more rare: the face of Stanley Draper.

It was like meeting the Wizard of Oz. Over the previous forty years, Draper had revolutionized Oklahoma City, but he was not, in any sense, a public figure. He worked behind the scenes, cajoling donors on his telephone, brokering secret deals in private rooms downtown. But now here he was on everyone's screens, visible to the public whose lives he had invisibly shaped.

The appearance, of course, was strategic. Something important was coming, something that would likely make no sense to most of OKC, and Draper was attempting to rationalize it in advance. It was the civic equivalent of a parent sitting down with a child who was on the brink of puberty: a warning that primal forces were about to be unleashed, explosive growth was on the way, and everyone needed to prepare themselves. The time had come for Oklahoma City to sit down with Stanley Draper for a Very Serious Talk.

The TV channel was E. K. Gaylord's, of course: WKY-TV. The news had produced a segment about the city's rapid growth, both recent and to come. Over the previous twenty years, as Draper had secured new businesses and poured new highways out to new suburbs, Oklahoma City had ballooned from roughly thirty square miles to eighty, with most of that growth coming in a burst of land annexation over the previous six years. This struck critics as excessive. The city government wasn't rich. How could it possibly afford to provide adequate services (fire, police, water) to such a sprawlingly wide area? Weren't there enough problems to address in the city as it already was? How big was big enough?

Draper was on TV to help put everyone's minds at rest. He sat on a couch in a wood-paneled office. He was now sixty-nine years old—no longer the young man who had stepped off the train into the chaotic congestion of a pioneer downtown forty years before. Draper had largely cleaned up that mess. Now his hair was gray, and it stood in a brushy crescent up toward the top of his head, and there were bags under his eyes. As he spoke, a bit of loose skin trembled over the knot of his tie. He was a man from another era, another world. But he still wasn't quite done shaping this one.

On the couch, in front of the camera, Draper seemed uncomfortable. A young reporter sat next to him, holding a microphone to his face, and Draper made very little eye contact. A sheaf of papers rested on his knee. This, he told the microphone, was a federal report, and if you looked at page 32—*riffle riffle*—you would find that Oklahoma City was scheduled to grow to a population of one million by 1975. Draper actually used the word "scheduled," as if seven hundred thousand new residents were going to debark, in an orderly fashion, from some kind of cosmic supertrain, in precisely sixteen years. Draper spoke in the manner of a man who was accustomed to reality obeying his words. After making his majestic projection, he closed the report and paused, looking at the reporter with the satisfaction of a TV lawyer resting his case.

The reporter asked Draper about the recent criticisms of the city's rapid growth—worries that it might be spreading itself too thin, complaints from nearby towns that OKC was threatening to take over the whole region.

"Oh," Draper drawled, in the syrupy cadence of his Carolina youth. "I wouldn't put it that way."

Oklahoma City, Draper explained, was actually doing a favor to the areas it annexed. People in the country were clamoring to join the city—to have access to its services, to be a part of something great—and the city was merely granting their wishes. It was a program of benevolent annexation.

Finally, Draper smiled.

"There's nothing particularly easy," he said, kneading one knee with a large white hand, "about building a city or community. It brings its difficulties. But I do believe this: that the future, the big growth of the future that's gonna come on us so *fast*, and is already on us now"—and at that word, "now," just for a moment, Draper stared directly into the camera, right out of the TV screen, with a look that cut across distance and time—that future, he said, "belongs to those who prepare for it."

A projection of one million people, it should be stressed, was absolutely absurd—a demographic hallucination. As Draper sat on that couch, OKC's population stood at just a shade over three hundred thousand. He was talking about tripling the city in sixteen years— summoning, from nowhere, a Boston's worth of residents.

Then again, Stanley Draper had talked crazy plenty of times before, and reality had generally followed his instructions. In his forty years in power, Draper had already done the impossible: he had guided OKC from a crowded, dusty cow town plagued by a flooding river into a sprawling, orderly, high-speed dream of skyscrapers and airports and industries and highways. He had paved huge stretches of prairie, rendering empty land useful to the modern world. He had seen the city boom, then boom again, and he had tried to find ways to harness those booms, to make them surge and echo into one another, to amplify them into superbooms.

To Draper, a million people must not have seemed outlandish at all. As he neared the end of his career, he was thinking bigger and bigger, beyond the future, to the future's future. Why not prepare for two million, three million, ten million? Why not? The city would need all the space it could find—room for the next Stanley Draper, whoever he might turn out to be, the next visionary who would arrive to transform the city again, on a scale currently beyond imagining.

The biggest threat to OKC's future, Draper believed, was the suburbs. If the settlements ringing the city were allowed to become legitimate cities themselves—to grow and declare independence—OKC would quickly find itself hemmed in. Draper liked to point to Pittsburgh: a great city squeezed into fifty-five square miles, wrapped in a straitjacket of suburbs. All of those outsiders flooded in, every day, to enjoy the benefits of the downtown, draining its resources and tearing up its infrastructure—and then they went home to the suburbs, contributing nothing.

Draper saw one sure way to circumvent this problem: to claim as much land as possible for Oklahoma City. Land meant control. And land was one resource that Oklahoma still had in abundance. It was all just sitting out there, unclaimed, in the great wide-open spaces of the prairie. All you had to do was get there first, before anyone else, and claim it. Once again, Oklahoma City had the chance to make history. Like the settlers of 1889, Draper was not afraid to seize that opportunity, even if it meant doing something completely crazy. And so began the Great Annexation.

The same news segment that featured Stanley Draper also showcased the city's brand-new mayor, Jim Norick. He was thirty-nine years old, the first mayor ever to be born in Oklahoma City, and unlike Draper he was made for TV: handsome and natural, with sculpted hair and a Hollywood smile. Although Norick sounded, in his interview, slightly less sanguine than Draper about the annexation drive—"a calculated risk," he called it—he was still officially on board. "Maybe we're bitin' off a little more than we can chew at the moment," he said. "But give us some time, and I'm sure it'll work out the problems."

But time was about to grab space by the ankles and start doing gyroscopic cartwheels all over the Great Plains. There was no longer any time to be given.

The *Oklahoman* published a handy map showing the surrounding areas that Oklahoma City was preparing to absorb. It looked like an impending military campaign: eight shaded zones on the outskirts of the city, marked for immediate invasion.

At the beginning of May, the Great Annexation began. Oklahoma City officially claimed all of the land on that map, and then it claimed some more. In less than a week, the city grew from 80 square miles to 116. During the following week, it continued to nibble at the territory around it until it reached 128 square miles. A week after that, it was up to 160. The city was inhaling everything in its orbit: clusters of houses that had been previously unincorporated by any town, as well as vast swaths of open country. Distant farmers who had never heard a word from the City of Oklahoma City were suddenly official residents. In three weeks, the city had doubled in size, leaping up the national square-mileage ranks past more populous cities such as Cleveland, Milwaukee, Memphis, Detroit, and Seattle. Philadelphia, which had six times the population of OKC, now occupied only four-fifths of the land. No city had any reason to multiply like this. It was as if Stanley Draper had found a way to reimagine the Land Run on an exponentially larger muncipal scale.

In June, the city's radical growth paused. It was like a snake that had just swallowed a goat. It needed time to digest. People were shocked. "I think this annexation business has gotten completely out of control," said the city councilman from Ward 4. A political bloc was organized to try to restore sanity. Even Mayor Norick, the eager young proponent of growth, agreed that things had gone too far. Growth like this was surely not sustainable.

But Stanley Draper was not done. Not even close. The problem was that he could see the future, and these people could not. A long article appeared in the *Oklahoman* defending the Great Annexation. It was, curiously, unsigned, but it contained all of Draper's favorite talking points, as well as direct quotes from him. "We are going to need industrial sites, lots of them, with integrated housing developments for a city of one million," Draper told the anonymous author. "Cities can't plan ahead except on property inside city limits." Dallas, Draper pointed out, was now more than 300 square miles, and Fort Worth, he claimed, falsely, would soon be expanding to 432. OKC could not afford to fall behind. "The future belongs to those who prepare for it," he said. The article also quoted an anonymous developer, who sounded like a fascist hypnotist: "Everyone needs to understand and accept the belief that what is being done is good."

The Great Annexation was good, of course, for developers and paving companies and car dealerships and oil executives and malls, as well as for consumers who wanted to live in brand-new cul-de-sacs near highways. But it was unclear that it was actually good for Oklahoma City at large.

In the end, however, the critics were powerless. The explosion had begun, and it would not stop until it had found its outer limits. The pause in growth lasted for only one month. On July 1, 1959, OKC started annexing again, feasting on land even farther out, growing from 160 square miles to 217. This city was now, absurdly, nearly as big as Chicago.

Oklahoma City cleared that hurdle the following month. At 265 square miles, it was now knocking on the door of New York City.

Meanwhile, back in the increasingly distant city center, two hundred unhappy citizens from recently annexed areas—the newest members of the OKC family—packed the city council chamber. An angry debate burned on for an hour and a half. The new residents demanded immediate de-annexation. Leave us alone, they begged. One said that his community had received treatment "worse than anything in Poland." Another compared Oklahoma City to a Communist state.

"Now I'll sit here and listen to you until your teeth fall out," the councilman for Ward 3 shot back, "but I'm not going to let you call us communists."

In city hall, planners suddenly ran into an unprecedented logistical problem. The official map of the city would no longer fit on any of the building's walls. Before the Great Annexation, the map had been six feet square. (One inch represented one thousand feet.) Now, six months later, it was fifteen and a half feet tall. The ceilings in city hall were only fourteen feet.

The map was not nearly done growing. The following summer, in August 1960, Oklahoma City metastasized to 392 square miles. The thirty-seventh most populous city in the nation was now larger than New York and rapidly expanding Dallas and even insatiable Houston. Oklahoma City now occupied parts of four different counties. Towns that had once been distant suburbs—Nichols Hills, Bethany, Mustang, Yukon—found themselves completely surrounded. They maintained their independence, but Oklahoma City literally wrapped all the way around them. On the map, they looked like paramecia that had been swallowed by an amoeba, or like islands floating in the ocean of OKC.

Only one city in America, at this point, occupied more land than Oklahoma City: Los Angeles, the palm tree megalopolis, endpoint of every American dream, population 2.5 million.

But OKC was coming for it. In September 1960, the city swelled to 415 square miles. Then it caught its breath and jumped again. In 1961, the City of Oklahoma City spasmed to 476 square miles—becoming not only the largest city in the United States but, reportedly, the largest in the entire world. If someone wanted to know the biggest city on earth, the one that took up the most actual space on the face of the planet, the only honest answer, impossible as it might sound, was Oklahoma City. Its population was 324,000.

Now what? Every rival had been vanquished; all reasonable goals had been surpassed. Every fantasy of the future could now be accommodated. Great networks of new roads were racing farther out into the countryside—roads as fast as workers could pour them, with identical houses stamped down in clusters to absorb all the residents who were no doubt on the way. Still, the Great Annexation continued. The project had taken on its own unstoppable momentum. Rival cities tried lawsuits, but they were only pistols at Godzilla. A state senator tried to pass a law to rein Oklahoma City in, and when it failed he warned Tulsa: "Now they are three miles out on the turnpike and are coming this way."

By the end of 1962, Oklahoma City stretched over 608 square miles. It encroached upon five separate counties. It was nearly forty miles wide and thirty miles tall. The *Oklahoman* announced the final surge with a triumphant map: "City Takes New Areas—71 Square Miles Added." What had begun, in 1889, as a modest rectangle—a postage stamp on the prairie—was now an outrageously sprawling blob, with tendrils of settlement extending east and west from that tiny original core. Oklahoma City looked, on the map, like the silhouette of an extremely fat man, running at a full sprint, arms pumping, legs so fully stretched that he was practically doing the splits.

To mark the end of the Great Annexation, another article appeared on the *Oklahoman*'s editorial page. "The annexation program is not a freakish phenomenon," it insisted, somewhat defensively, and then it quoted urban visionaries predicting that this kind of growth would be the future of human settlements: every city would evolve toward a "universal city," a supermetropolis that would expand, consciously and generously, to absorb all the towns around it, functioning more like a county than a traditional city.

But why stop there? Why couldn't the universal city continue to grow, the author suggested, swallowing larger and larger cities, until it eventually performed the function of a whole state? And why couldn't it grow even farther, absorbing state after state, until the universal city filled the role of a nation? The author cited a nuclear scientist who envisioned the United States, fifty years in the future, as "one gigantic city of a billion population." Once you started thinking along those lines, it was hard to stop. Why couldn't a nation-sized city grow to swallow a continent? And why couldn't it cross the oceans and swallow the entire world?

And why couldn't that universal city be Oklahoma City? Why couldn't it expand to reclaim all of Pangaea? Why not?

Draper's vision, at least for the moment, was slightly more modest. He imagined OKC spreading north to merge with Tulsa, forming what he called a "region-opolis," a megasettlement that would be served by a supersonic airport spread over one hundred square miles. It was only two years later that Draper managed to secure the privilege of hosting Operation Bongo, the series of experimental sonic booms that would rumble down on the people of OKC for six months. Operation Bongo, the chamber believed, would earn Oklahoma City its supersonic airport, and that airport would enable what would inevitably come next: the universal city, infinite boomtown, exploding again and again, until it was bigger than any force that might ever possibly try to slow it down.

PRETTY MUCH CENTRALIZING EVERYTHING

One afternoon, under uninspiring skies, Daniel Orton gave me a driving tour of Oklahoma City. We drifted, for what seemed like forever, along a crowded traffic artery called Northwest Expressway, a six-lane corridor that felt like a vast outdoor museum of America's big box stores and chain hotels and fast-food restaurants. The median landscaping was sponsored by Chesapeake Energy. Orton grew up on and around this road, and he knew it in amazing detail. As we drove, he read it like a fisherman reading a river. The McDonald's had been there since before he was born, he said, but the Burger King hadn't come until he was six. The Chuck E. Cheese's had recently been renovated. The empty shell of a Walmart had been taken over by an Internet-based Christianity franchise called LifeChurch.tv. Orton used to spend so much time driving on this road, exhausted after basketball practices, that he would fall asleep at red lights and wake up to angry honking.

If Orton didn't identify all that closely with Oklahoma City, it must be said in his defense that there wasn't all that much of an Oklahoma City for him to identify with. It's easy now, as an outsider, to show up downtown and fall in love: the restaurants, the coffee shops, the river. The Thunder has turned OKC into a powerful brand, and there is just barely enough of a city to justify it. But Orton grew up without any of that. There was no coherent downtown, no artsy T-shirt shops or food trucks. It was all sprawl. Oklahoma City didn't even occur to Orton as a place to be excited about, because it hardly even really occurred to him as a *place*. The neighborhoods he grew up in were mainly zones of traffic interrupted by malls. Orton was born, in other words, into the territory of the Great Annexation—the bloated universe that Stanley Draper left behind.

Orton drove me to the house where he grew up, in a quiet subdivision out near Lake Hefner. This was where he had slept off his massive adolescent growth spurt—he'd walked into middle school five foot eleven and walked out six foot eight—and where he'd blossomed into a high school superstar, and also where he had rehabbed from his first major knee injury while his mother was sick with lupus. Back on Northwest Expressway, Orton drove me past the cemetery where his mother was buried, and he started to tell me about her cooking— the way she'd fill the house with food on the holidays. I asked him if she had any signature dishes. He made a sound like a punctured parade balloon—"Pssssssshhhhhhhhhssssssssssshhhhhhhh"—and started listing them: fried chicken, greens and ham hocks, three different recipes for macaroni and cheese, raspberry cream cheese sauce to be eaten on Ritz crackers. He told me the whole recipe for cornflake potatoes. Every Christmas morning, Orton said, his mother made monkey bread, a doughy pile of cake that's like the middle of a cinnamon roll extracted and multiplied into infinity. Christmas was her favorite holiday, so it was his, too: monkey bread, his uncle Jack playing with all the kids' toys. I asked him what he did for Christmas now. "Nothing," he said. "Christmas games. I work on holidays. We even play on Thanksgiving."

Everywhere we drove, Orton and I could see the Devon Tower— the disproportionately huge skyscraper that dominated the horizon.

"It's really awkward," he said. "It looks too tall, standing there by itself. They'd have to build at least one more that big before it would start to look normal."

We drove past the building where Orton currently lived: the Founders Tower, twenty stories of glass and concrete that looked like a giant pagoda—an odd relic of the era of the Great Annexation. It was equidistant, Orton said, to all the key landmarks of his life: a fifteen-minute drive from his childhood home, his family's church, the zoo, the Thunder's practice facility, downtown, and his grandparents' house on the East Side.

"I'm pretty much centralizing everything," he said.

We drove east to visit his grandparents, who had lived for fifty years in a small house near the state capitol, in a section of town that Roscoe Dunjee originally opened up to black settlement. If anything anchored Orton to Oklahoma City, it was his family's deep roots in the city's black history. His grandparents had watched OKC explode in size, and the white neighbors flee to the suburbs, and the house values drop, and the neighborhood evolve into what outsiders called "the ghetto." Orton's grandmother studied high school history with Clara Luper herself, as did Orton's mother, who was delivered by Oklahoma City's first black physician. Growing up, Orton read Luper's memoir, *Behold the Walls*, multiple times, and he once actually got to shake her hand at the Oklahoma State Fair, where Luper ran a stand that sold catfish and fried green tomatoes. Orton still referred to her, with polite reverence, as "Miss Luper."

Despite this history, Orton told me that he had always felt awkwardly pinned between the black and white worlds of Oklahoma City. He grew up in a world he describes as a "bubble": the middle-class suburbs, way up north, in an area dominated by white professionals. Although he played a sport that, even in a predominately white city, was dominated by black players, he played that sport for a white high school.

Orton went to the same high school his brother did: Bishop McGuinness, a private Catholic school known for excellence in sports. Orton's brother won three state basketball championships there, so naturally Orton was determined to win four. His first chance came during his freshman year, in 2006, when Bishop McGuinness met Douglass in the championship. The matchup was sociologically loaded. Douglass was the most important school in the history of Oklahoma City's East Side; it was as much a community headquarters as a traditional school. Ralph Ellison played running back for the Douglass football team and trumpet for the Douglass marching band—at halftime, he would scramble out of one uniform and into the other. The jazz legend Charlie Christian built experimental guitars out of cigar boxes on the desks of Douglass classrooms, then played them at night in Deep Deuce.

Bishop McGuinness, by contrast, was a rich private Catholic school whose student body, Orton said, was "ninety-eight percent white, if not ninety-nine." I asked him how that affected him, as a young black man who hadn't grown up on the East Side. "If you go to Bishop McGuinness," he said, "you're considered white, basically."

The 2006 championship game was held on the state fairgrounds, in a place that everyone called the Big House but was officially the Jim Norick Arena. Douglass and McGuinness were evenly matched, and the game went back and forth, then to overtime, and then back and forth in overtime. In the last few seconds, McGuinness found itself trailing by one. Orton got the ball and drove toward the hoop.

This is when the trouble began.

Before Orton could score, the Douglass defense hammered him. Foul. He would have to decide the season with free throws—the weakest part of his game. Orton insists, to this day, that he would have made both shots, but no one else in the arena could have shared that confidence. The point, however, is moot. As Orton walked toward the foul line, it was pointed out that his leg was bleeding. The rules on this were clear: Orton would have to leave the game, immediately, and remain on the sidelines until the bleeding could be stopped. It was a reprieve.

His coach replaced him with a player who happened to be the opposite of Orton in every obvious way: a short, white, sparingly used free-throw expert. He came in and made both of Orton's free throws, putting Bishop McGuinness up by one with seven seconds left. Orton's bleeding, meanwhile, had been stopped, so the coach pulled the free-throw expert out and put Orton back in. Douglass ran a play for its best shooter, who got free and rose for what would have been the championship-winning shot—until Orton flew over, stretched out to his full length, and got his fingertips on the ball. Block. Time expired. Bishop McGuinness won.

It was Orton's eighth block of the game, a play no one else on the floor could have made, certainly not the small white free-throw expert. The McGuinness crowd exploded in ecstasy. The Douglass crowd exploded in rage. There were accusations of chicanery, questions of procedure, controversy over whether or not a formerly bleeding player can legally reenter a game before any time has elapsed from the game clock. Injustice. Racial opportunism. Someone threw a bottle at Orton out on the floor. Orton's team walked to the bus escorted by police officers. For the rest of Orton's high school career, he said, Douglass fans went to his games and rooted against him.

GAME 16: CIVIL WAR

James Harden returned to Oklahoma City, in an enemy uniform, almost exactly one month after he had left: November 28, 2012. This happened to be the 128th anniversary of the death of David Payne, leader of the Boomers, when he collapsed into his breakfast after giving the greatest speech of his life. (Yet another historical anniversary that was not officially acknowledged in the arena.) Harden's performance, during his month away, had been a recurrent waking nightmare for Thunder fans. He had morphed, instantly, from a bench player into a superstar, winning Western Conference Player of the Week after the season's first few games. The debate over whether Harden deserved a max contract—hotly contested, in many circles, only a month before—now seemed ridiculous. He was destroying, day by day, all of the arguments Thunder fans had used to talk themselves into the trade. Apparently, Harden had been sacrificing more talent in OKC than anyone realized. Plenty of subtleties had gone into the decision to trade him, of course—need, chemistry, taxes, the future—but none of that made up for this sickening central fact: the Thunder had had this player on their team, they'd had a way to keep him, and they had chosen to let him go. Sam Presti's Process demanded patience, a long-term perspective. But that was hard to muster, day by day by day by day, as Harden poured in points and stole all the highlight reels and made mediocre Houston look like a rising power.

This was the state of things, at the end of November, when James Harden came back to Oklahoma City.

The only redeeming fact for the Thunder was that they, too, were playing well—in some ways, better than they had with Harden. Despite that last-second loss to the Spurs on opening night, the team was now 11–4. They were beginning to look like the imminent champions everyone had expected before the trade. Two nights before Harden's return, OKC had demoralized the lowly Charlotte Bobcats, winning by forty-five points. The superstars were dominating, as usual, in their very different styles—wild Westbrook and precise Durant—and the role players were filling their roles admirably.

No one knew how the Oklahoma City crowd would respond to Harden's return. Even the individual fans walking into the arena couldn't know how they would act in the aggregate. What was the appropriate response? Applause for the good times, boos for the betrayal, something in between? Should they shower the floor with fake beards—limp, shaggy emblems of the city's ruined innocence? Should they chant, in unison, sarcastically, Harden's old media quotes about brotherhood and sacrifice and the coming Thunder dynasty? Should everyone just bury their heads in their hands and weep? How resilient was Oklahoma City? How far did its niceness extend?

Fans entered the arena carrying anti-Harden signs. "SPEAR THE BEARD." "Hey Harden you may have your $80 ml BUT I BET YOU'LL NEVER WIN A RING!" The Thunder's most colorful regular fan was a rotund twenty-five-year-old who went by the alter ego "Thundor": he stood shirtless in the crowd, just behind the basket, wearing suspenders and a Mexican wrestling mask, shaking his naked belly and shouting at opponents through a megaphone. That night, he had painted an eighty-million-dollar bill on his stomach, in reference to Harden's Rockets salary. (Eighty-million-dollar bills do not exist except on the belly of Thundor.) He held a sign that said "FEAR THE GREED, NOT THE BEARD."

Before the game, Harden was introduced by the arena's announcer with a complete lack of ceremony. His voice was quick and flat, his words blurred together:

"Starting at guard six-five from Arizona State number 13 James Harden."

It was as if he were trying to sneak the announcement past eighteen thousand people. But the crowd had already come to its feet. This was the official moment of response. A warm cheer blew through the arena. There were a few boos, here and there, but these were swept away by the ovation: louder and longer applause than anyone had any right to expect. After Harden's abandonment of Oklahoma, after his success in (of all places) Texas, Oklahoma City was still—despite the mocking homemade signs and the jiggling belly of Thundor—still, in the aggregate, nice. The doubters all were stunned.

Then there was a professional basketball game.

Both teams had spent the previous two days downplaying this game to the media. It was just another game, they insisted, one of eighty-two, nobody cared, nothing special, no grudges. Why were people even talking about it? It was a game, not a civil war.

When the ball went up for tip-off, however, what followed looked exactly like a civil war. The Thunder came out to destroy James Harden—not only to beat him but to embarrass him. Serge Ibaka blocked the Rockets' first shot, then dunked the Thunder's first basket. A minute later, he blocked another shot, then dunked again. When Harden slithered through the defense for a layup, Serge Ibaka rose and swatted it away.

This was how the entire night went. Everyone on the Thunder took turns stealing the ball from Harden and blocking his shots. Whenever Harden thought he had an opening, a Thunder player would invariably come sprinting from behind to spike the ball out of bounds. Even Hasheem Thabeet, the awkward backup center, blocked two Harden layups on a single play. In the third quarter, Harden stared across the court at Kevin Martin, the player who had taken his place in OKC, and seemed to fall into a reverie—*How did that guy end up in my place? Is he going to be better at that role than I was? Did I make a mistake?*—while Martin passed the ball to Kevin Durant, the man Harden was supposed to be guarding, who was now wide open at the three-point line. Harden realized what was happening too late, lunging out just in time to slap at Durant's arm after he had already released the ball. Durant made both the three-pointer and the ensuing free throw.

It was, in short, a nightmare for Harden. At one point, he stole the ball from Westbrook and raced down the floor to drop in a fast break layup over Durant, but Ibaka came sprinting from behind and swatted it to the floor. Then Ibaka blocked one of Harden's teammates' dunks and made a jump shot of his own. Harden couldn't make a shot, and Ibaka couldn't miss. Late in the game, Ibaka even made a three-pointer. He was playing like the perfect third star, supplementing the other two without getting in the way, freeing them up to do what they did best. He was doing what Harden had refused to stay and do.

The Oklahoma City crowd fused into one solid joy-throb. This game was exactly the affirmation they needed. Their team was legitimately great, even in the absence of Harden, and Harden—despite the recent month of evidence—wasn't actually so great after all, not against a team like this. Sam Presti was still a genius. In fact, he had probably somehow engineered all of this as a test for the people of OKC, and although maybe they had doubted him a little, now they would never doubt him again. It was only one game, yes, but what was a season but a bunch of individual games? What was glory but a constellation of individual glories?

Harden, the NBA's leading scorer, did not make a single field goal in the first half. His first successful shot came on a layup in the third quarter that the reporter Sam Amick suggested might actually have been a gift from Ibaka, who looked like he could have blocked it but perhaps felt sorry for his old teammate and didn't. At the end of the night, Ibaka blocked Harden's final attempt at a layup. He had made three shots and missed thirteen. He had three assists but also three turnovers. It was the definition of inefficiency. Durant, meanwhile, finished with thirty-seven points, and Harden's replacement, Kevin Martin, added an extremely efficient seventeen. Ibaka was absurdly effective, with six blocks and eleven baskets in only thirteen attempts. The loss gave the Rockets a losing record. The Thunder improved to 12–4 and were in the midst of what would become a twelve-game winning streak. It was, by far, Harden's worst game of the season.

BLACK FRIDAY

By the end of his career, Stanley Draper had achieved almost all of his grandest goals for Oklahoma City. He had streamlined downtown and radically expanded the city's borders. He had lured industries that would secure the region's future and solved longstanding water problems. And yet there was one great dream that he had yet to realize. Stanley Draper wanted to build a mountain in downtown Oklahoma City.

A mountain, if you thought about it, just made sense. It was really the only thing missing. It would give Oklahoma City, retroactively, a geological reason to exist. All over the world, great cities clustered around and on top of mountains. Here in the Great Plains, however, the earth had clearly made a mistake, and now Draper was going to fix it—to do the work that deep time had neglected. And the best part was that you wouldn't have to wait for a volcano to erupt or tectonic plates to crash: this would be an instant mountain, scraped into existence with gas-powered tractors, the same kind of heavy machinery Draper had used for his Re-Run decades before. The mountain would be three or four hundred feet tall, nearly as tall as the city's tallest skyscrapers. It would rise right next to the freeway. The road to the top would be lined with azaleas, because Stanley Draper loved azaleas.

That Draper did not get to build his outlandish mountain is a mark of the decline of his influence near the end of his career. That he conceived of it at all, however, is a mark of how absolute his power had been at its height.

In the 1960s, in gratitude for all he had done, Oklahoma City showered Draper with honors. The reservoir fifteen miles south of the city—enough water for all the new residents he had made room for—was named Lake Stanley Draper. The Oklahoma House of Representatives passed a resolution officially granting Draper the title "Mr. Oklahoma City." A bronze statue of Draper was unveiled next to city hall. It stood nine feet tall and depicted him wearing a trench coat, pointing to the sky, holding a half-rolled map of the city. The statue's pedestal was etched with a stanza of free-verse booster beat poetry:

> HE DREAMED IMPOSSIBLE DREAMS . . . THEN INSPIRED AND
> UNITED ALL WHO COULD MAKE THEM PROBABLE.
> HE STRENGTHENED OUR STAKES, LENGTHENED OUR
> CORDS . . . AND THE DREAMS SOARED TO REALITY.
> HIS WAS THE SPIRIT OF OKLAHOMA CITY.
> LOOK AROUND YOU! WHAT YOU SEE TODAY WAS HIS
> TOMORROW . . . YESTERDAY.

On the seventy-eighth anniversary of the Land Run—April 22, 1967—650 people showed up to honor Stanley Draper at a black-tie gala in the Persian Room of the Skirvin Hotel. An oil painting was unveiled, and Draper was presented with a sterling silver statue of the Goddess of Achievement. The governor called him "the 'OK' in Oklahoma." The symphony orchestra played, and at one point Draper took the baton and conducted it himself. There were multiple standing ovations. Draper had spent so many years bullying these people, and yet now he wept. The business community had pooled its money for a retirement fund that would allow the Drapers to live comfortably for the rest of their lives. No gift was too great for the man who had harnessed OKC's essential chaos and turned it into a proper city.

The most fitting tribute to Stanley Draper, however, was physical: a new road. The Stanley Draper Expressway was an elevated highway that rose right over the center of downtown—a marvel of engineering, fifty feet high and nearly two miles long, the longest bridge in the state. It cost $13 million. Although the Stanley Draper Expressway had required the nearly complete destruction of Sandtown, the city's oldest black neighborhood, it seemed worth it to the city planners.

Oklahoma City was now linked to Interstate 40, a brand-new torrent of cars that flowed clear across the country, from North Carolina to California, from the Atlantic to the Pacific. The road was the perfect symbol of Draper's career, the ultimate victory over downtown congestion. It would carry sixty thousand vehicles a day—a perpetual gray roar, like an automotive wind. All the compromises and inefficiencies and confusions of the Land Run could now be avoided on this monument to the man who had made modern OKC possible. At the dedication ceremony, Draper planted a tree, and then he led a motorcade of antique cars and fire trucks up onto his namesake highway.

The Stanley Draper Expressway, freshly poured
through the heart of OKC.

Not everyone was sad to see Stanley Draper retire. Mayor Norick, then in his second term, was quietly relieved. Draper had been allowed to wield far too much power, for far too long, and his ideas had become increasingly eccentric. "I say this with no discredit to

Mr. Draper," Norick said, clearly intending discredit, "but I think he needs to rest."

Besides, Norick had bigger problems. In 1969, the city's garbage workers went on strike, and—to Norick's annoyance—it had become an issue of race. Norick had a history of strike-busting; the Norick and Gaylord families had once bonded by working together to break a printers' strike. But now the garbage workers had brought in, as their representative, Clara Luper.

As Stanley Draper's influence had declined throughout the 1960s, Clara Luper's had increased. After the integration of the city's restaurants in 1964, she did not stop organizing. The next year, she led a march against the Oklahoma City police chief, and then a march of three hundred people through freezing wind up to "white town," in the northwest, right to Mayor Norick's house, followed by a series of night marches through other privileged neighborhoods: Nichols Hills, the Village, Capitol Hill, downtown. Luper once led a hundred-mile march from Oklahoma City to Lawton, during which marchers slept on rocks in the Wichita Mountains and on the ground at a gas station, harassed by stray dogs.

Garbage collection got right to the heart of the city's institutional racism. It was one of the few jobs the city would hire its black citizens to do—85 percent of OKC's sanitation workers were black—and yet, for decades, promotions and pay raises went almost exclusively to whites. Asking nicely had changed nothing. And so the workers came to Luper and—after she took some useless meetings with officials and got into a shouting match with the city manager—they decided to take action.

The strike began on August 19, 1969—the eleven-year aniversary of the first sit-in at Katz, and exactly fifty years, to the day, since Stanley Draper arrived in Oklahoma City. Luper and the workers marched to city hall, then to the police station. With Norick's support, the city manager, Robert Oldland, fired all of them. Garbage began to pile up in huge mounds on the sunny streets. It was so hot that the newspaper's weather map showed only a little man sweating, mopping his brow with a handkerchief. The city started to stink. Violence simmered in the background: Martin Luther King Jr., Clara

Luper's hero, had been killed the previous spring during a garbage strike in Memphis. When Oklahoma City hired scab workers to drive its trucks, Luper and the strikers lay down on the road in front of them.

The garbage strike culminated on Halloween, with a demonstration that everyone referred to as Black Friday. Norick had warned Luper not to do it, threatening to block off downtown and arrest anyone who approached—to which Luper responded, characteristically: "No little short, bow-tie wearing mayor is going to destroy

Black Friday protestors march out of the East
toward a confrontation with police downtown.

the U.S. Constitution." At noon, a crowd of either fifteen hundred (according to the police) or ten thousand (according to Luper) assembled on the East Side and began to march toward city hall. They carried signs: "BLACK & PROUD," "NORICK AND OLDLAND CAN'T JAIL US ALL," and simply "BLACK FRIDAY." Downtown went on lockdown. All the stores closed ahead of the advancing crowd. Armed police officers stood on the tops of buildings, and hundreds more stood in the streets wearing riot helmets, with shotguns, clubs, and tear gas. Norick waited on Main Street with a blockade of state troopers.

As the marchers approached, they were greeted by a loudspeaker: "Anybody who doesn't want to be arrested, stay back."

It is hard to say, for sure, what happened next.

The *Oklahoman*'s account was blunt: "Police met the marchers and after a brief hesitation, they were allowed to continue to City Hall."

The version in Clara Luper's memoir is, naturally, much more colorful, and although it is absurd, it has the ring of truth.

Stopped by the blockade and ordered to return to the East Side, Luper responded with improvisational nonsense.

"Umbo umbo umbo umber," she said. "Quis umbo umbo umbo umber. Ochee Ocheo Ocku okro okmu. Sho owon hu chkon chun. Mung ming oh umbo umbo!"

The policemen were stunned. The blockade parted. The march was allowed to continue.

"You have just seen a miracle!" shouted the Reverend W. K. Jackson, in his mighty frog voice, and the marchers all sang "We Shall Overcome," and soon they reached city hall, where—as city council members peeked out the windows—Luper gave a triumphant speech. Not long after this, the city worked out a deal with the sanitation workers, and the strike came to an end. This was a disappointment to Stanley Draper, who had hoped that the city might be able to use all of the many tons of uncollected garbage to begin to build his artificial mountain.

PART FOUR

DISTANCE

All the sacrifices that have helped bring the city into
existence come to nothing if the life that the city makes
possible is not its own reward.

—LEWIS MUMFORD, *The City in History*

Started from the bottom now we're here.
Started from the bottom now my whole
team fucking here.

—DRAKE

Terror is truth and truth is terror and it never ends.

—JOHN EDGAR WIDEMAN, *Writing to Save a Life*

THE GRANDEST STREET THIS
GENERATION HAS EVER SEEN

By 2012, local drivers were terrified of the Stanley Draper Expressway. It was visibly crumbling. Large pieces of the road's surface—"coffee table–sized chunks of concrete," as the *Oklahoman* evocatively put it—routinely fell right out of it, leaving holes that stopped traffic. Nearly fifty years of constant punishment had reduced its surface to a quilt of patches. The sections were loosely joined, and water leaked through, and you could see rust on the exposed rebar. The bridge's support beams were a disaster waiting to happen—the same outmoded design had caused a deadly bridge collapse, not long before, in Minneapolis. And yet Stanley Draper's elevated highway continued to carry its full load of cars. In fact, it carried twice the daily load it had been designed for. Even the grandest projections of the 1960s planners could not keep up with the vehicular firehose of modern American traffic. Oklahoma's state government was, by this point, unbelievably dysfunctional, and the state's infrastructure was the worst in the nation, and roads and bridges were crumbling everywhere. But the Stanley Draper Expressway was a particularly embarrassing example: an eyesore that ran right past the basketball arena and Bricktown—a torn-up welcome mat at the city's front door. For such a self-conscious city, the once-grand road now made a peculiarly bad first impression.

And so the Stanley Draper Expressway was being torn down. Interstate 40 had already been relocated five blocks south, at a cost of nearly $700 million—a tab picked up, naturally, by the federal government. (OKC continued to rely heavily, as it had since the moment of its conception, on federal favors and funds.) The old elevated highway's access ramps were blocked off to traffic, and for the first time in nearly fifty years, since the day when Draper himself had ridden at the head of the ceremonial opening procession, the road went quiet. It was the end of an era. It's silly to get sentimental about a road, probably, but people did. Before the demolition began, the city opened the Stanley Draper Expressway, one last time, for pedestrians to come and pay their respects. People came from all over the city to stand and admire the skyline, to eat lunch on the patchy asphalt, to jog and ride bikes. They left with souvenir chunks of concrete.

Then the destruction began. The road was huge, so the process took many months. All around it, everyone went about their regular business as, day by day, little by little, the town's central monolith came down. Eventually, only the expressway's support pillars remained, looking majestic and forlorn, like the ruins of an ancient temple.

The death of the old was, of course, the birth of the new—an opportunity for another of Oklahoma City's grand plans. For the first time in generations, downtown was no longer bisected by an elevated highway. The core of the city could be fundamentally reimagined. What would rush in to fill that void? What could possibly replace Stanley Draper's namesake road?

The answer was a new road, a better road, a road of the future: the Oklahoma City Boulevard. Officials described it as "a new front door to the city." "We intend to make it," Mayor Mick said, "the grandest street this generation has ever seen." Residents began to imagine something sophisticated and elegant, a sort of middle-American Champs-Élysées, with shops and restaurants and bikes and pedestrians and trees. Perhaps there would be street performers, elaborate fountains, Segway lanes, fruit carts. Times had changed, and the boulevard would reflect that. The new road would be the opposite of the Stanley Draper Expressway—a thriving channel of true public life downtown, a habitat for actual humans instead of cars, a destination, not just a high-speed suburban escape route. And the boulevard would lead, appropriately, right to the new civic temple at the center of OKC: the basketball arena.

GAME 31: KD IS NOT NICE

On New Year's Eve 2012, in the second quarter of a game against the lowly Phoenix Suns, Russell Westbrook went flying wildly to the basket, into a crowd of enemy hands and elbows, and collapsed. Blood came gushing from his face. Was it serious? It looked serious. Durant said later that there was so much blood he thought one of the defenders must have had a knife hidden in his jersey. Westbrook rolled around and slapped the floor and cursed, and Thunder trainers escorted their hemorrhaging point guard off to the locker room. It seemed possible that Westbrook might, for the first time in his whole reckless life, actually be injured. Oklahoma City had never really known basketball without the central chaos of Westbrook. What would rush in to fill that void? How would Durant respond? Might a lack of Westbrook actually bring stability? Was Russell Westbrook, strictly speaking, necessary?

All of these questions would remain hypothetical, because minutes later, Westbrook came charging back out of the locker room, up the tunnel and onto the floor, riding a frenzy of maniacal anger, with eight stitches next to his eye. In only a few minutes he managed to pour in a full night's worth of points, turning the game in the Thunder's favor. OKC walked off with an easy win. Once again, the gods of destruction had been unable to take Russell Westbrook down. It seemed more likely that someday, in the end, he would find a way to take them down instead.

This is how 2012 ended. The Thunder entered the new year with the best record in the NBA, 24–6, having won fifteen of their previous seventeen games. They were blowing teams out, often without even appearing to try. Their biggest alleged rivals in the West, the star-studded Lakers, were imploding under the stresses of injuries and arguments. The Thunder's path back to the Finals seemed clear. The new year, 2013, sounded like the future: odd and angular, not quite real. And that future would belong to Oklahoma City.

The first game of the New Year came at home, where the Thunder were particularly dominant. They had won twelve straight in front of their invariably sold-out crowd. The visitors were the mediocre Brooklyn Nets. There was no reason to doubt that this would be consecutive home win number thirteen.

Instead, right from the start, the game was a disaster. The Nets, somehow, looked like a pack of full-moon Teen Wolves, and the OKC crowd was shocked into silence. At halftime, the Thunder were losing by twenty-three.

"God, we're getting our asses destroyed by the Brooklyn Nets," wrote a commenter on *Daily Thunder*. Another added that it was the worst half of the season, and another escalated even further to say that it was the worst game since 2009, and although those statements were harsh, they might actually have been true.

What was the problem? Well, there were several. Although the Thunder were very good, they were still imperfect, and this Nets game was exposing the team's flaws to an almost comic degree. Westbrook was a tumbleweed in a hurricane—forcing shots, blowing defensive rotations, missing layups, and occasionally dribbling the ball directly into his defender's arms. Although Kevin Martin was, in many ways, an effective Harden replacement, he lacked Harden's funky creative skills, and sometimes the whole offense suffered for it. The centers were slow, with hands made of lunch meat. The coaching staff did not seem imaginative enough to compensate for these deficiencies.

The team's most confounding problem, however, and one the commenters were allowing themselves to harp on more and more these days, was the curious passivity of Kevin Durant. It was that old familiar curse-blessing: KD was nice. Nearly halfway through the season, he was still conducting his strange experiment in altruistic ball sharing. He had even taken to dribbling up the court himself, initiating the offense, acting like a de facto point guard—an odd and often ineffective strategy. It was hard to be mad at Durant, of course, the superstar with the heart of gold, and yet it was also frustrating. Durant had this problem where he liked to throw hypothetically good passes, regardless of real-world conditions—they were an *idea* of a good pass instead of the thing itself. They were superego passes, and most fans just wanted to see him score with his id. During that disastrous first half against the Nets, as the game slipped away, Durant hardly shot at all. At halftime, a *Daily Thunder* commenter clacked a tender wish out of his keyboard into the universe. "I want to see KD rage in the 2nd half," he wrote. "I rarely ever see him rage."

This wish, improbably, was about to come true—although almost certainly not in the way the commenter had intended.

In the second half, the Thunder started to chip away at the Nets' huge lead, and the crowd unmuted itself and urged them on. In the middle of the fourth quarter, Kevin Martin took a pass from Thabo Sefolosha and hit a deep three-pointer, tying the game, sending the fans into relieved jubilations. To come back and win this game, after such a shameful first half, would be like a resurrection—the kind of miracle a championship team pulled off.

In that moment, everybody looked to Kevin Durant. The end of a tied game, momentum seized, home fans euphoric—this was the natural habitat of an NBA scoring champion. But KD, for whatever reason, could not take over that night. He missed a three. He fumbled the ball away. He committed a foul. He missed another shot, committed another foul, missed a layup. The game fell apart. The whole team followed Durant's lead, turning into a sloppy, inaccurate, fouling mess. Almost in spite of themselves, the lowly Nets ran away with the game.

Finally, Kevin Durant couldn't take it anymore. With two minutes left and the game out of reach, after all those saintly years of peace, he allowed the people to see him rage. The referee called an offensive foul—obvious and accurate—on Kendrick Perkins. This set Durant off. He shouted something at the ref and flung one of his exorbitantly long arms.

The referee blew his whistle: technical foul.

This meant another free throw for the Nets, which would put the game even further out of reach. But Durant still wasn't done. He continued to yell, now with such foul-mouthed venom that the referee blew his whistle again: a second technical. Automatic ejection.

The people were stunned. This was brand-new territory, the first ejection of Durant's career. It was like seeing the statue at the Lincoln Memorial stand up from its chair and start pushing schoolchildren down the front steps.

Even then, Durant wasn't done. As he walked off the court, scowling, exiled, as the TV cameras zoomed in, as the viewers at home stared in disbelief, Kevin Durant turned to the referee and said, with an unholy sneer, "Fuck you."

There was no mistaking it. His lips practically read themselves.

Online, the commenters went bananas. Someone posted the word "LOL" approximately four hundred times in a row. "Baby Kevin has grown up," they said.

"I feel so proud right now," wrote someone else.

Inside Chesapeake arena, the crowd produced a thick tide of boos—an unusual, almost unprecedented sound from Thunder fans. Many stayed, even after the game was over, to boo the referees off the floor.

In the locker room, a reporter asked Durant what he had said to the referee.

"I said it was a bad call," Durant told him.

But we had seen what he had said, and that was not it.

A few nights before Durant's ejection, I'd happened to be roaming the outskirts of Bricktown when I saw a billboard that stopped me cold. It was way out next to the route of the newly relocated I-40, where the image would presumably harvest the most possible vehicular eyes, and I walked into a dark, scrubby field and stared up at it for a long time. The billboard featured a picture of Durant, twenty feet tall, larger even than his largeness in life. He was wearing his Thunder uniform and unleashing a primal scream. The caption, adorned with a Nike swoosh, said, KD IS NOT NICE.

Alone in the field, I laughed out loud. This was a bold piece of counterprogramming. The campaign would soon go nationwide, appearing on T-shirts and in TV commercials, in magazine spreads and Foot Locker window displays. "Leading the league in scoring three years straight is not nice," the ads said. "Making defenders famous in all the wrong ways is not nice. Dropping 30 points before anyone realizes what's hit them is not nice. Nailing three-pointers from way beyond the arc is not nice." Durant's entourage started wearing KD IS NOT NICE shirts around town.

Nike's muddying of the moral waters was a naked commercial ploy, but it also seemed to reflect something brewing deep in the psyche of the man himself. Anyone watching Durant that season would have already noticed small signs of strain. His first ejection did not come out of nowhere. The Thunder's Finals appearance the previous summer had launched Durant to a whole new level of superstardom, and he seemed to be struggling a bit with the extra attention. The Thunder's PR handlers were spending much of their time keeping people away from their superstar, denying interview requests, trying to maintain some small bubble of normalcy. Even they were shocked by the degree of attention.

Durant's two technical fouls against the Nets gave him five on a season that was not even halfway over—a far higher rate of misbehavior than he'd ever shown before. He was one of the league leaders now, up there with such notorious hotheads as DeMarcus Cousins, Larry Sanders, and Russell Westbrook himself.

As January dragged on, not-niceness seemed to spread through the Thunder like ink in water. Local radio reported that Eric Maynor, the backup to the backup point guard, had instigated a blowout argument over playing time with, of all people, Sam Presti. Kendrick Perkins's wife, Vanity, got into an altercation with a nail technician at an Oklahoma City salon—an incident that might not have been terribly newsworthy except that Kendrick himself rumbled up in his SUV to defend her, cursing out the nail tech and spiking a Gatorade bottle off the shop's front window. Security footage, along with interviews of the salon's employees, played on the evening news. None of this, of course, was part of Presti's Process. In the middle of a game in Denver, Russell Westbrook, absurdly, made a villain of himself by leaping up and swatting away, at the very last second, a backward half-court shot by the Nuggets' mascot, Rocky—a shot that would have won the entire crowd a prize. Nuggets fans booed, and Westbrook paced the floor and muttered at them like a madman, and later in the game he did it again, catching the mascot's shot just before it fell through the hoop, and this time he actually flung the ball out into the crowd, and he didn't smile or laugh, not even slightly.

Two weeks after Kevin Durant's first-ever ejection, the TV cameras caught him cursing again. His grandmother sent him a text. "Kev kev stop cussing so much," she wrote, "they be showing u when u do." It was unclear if Durant's grandmother was upset that he was swearing or that the cameras were capturing it—if the problem was one of essence or of perception.

"Haha sorry grandma," Durant wrote back. "I be so emotional, I love u . . ."

Before games, as the players warmed up, a new song started to play in heavy rotation on the Chesapeake Energy Arena sound system, an anthem of the defiant underdog called "Started from the Bottom." The players listened to it constantly on their headphones, and they seemed to have taken on its spirit: "Fuck a fake friend, where your real friends at?" The curse words were bleeped out in public, of course, but it was impossible not to infer them. The attitude of the Thunder seemed to be shifting from universally beloved Pollyanna sunshine overachievers to something else—heavy favorites, kings of the hill, struggling against the pressure of expectations.

BLESSED ARE THE PLACEMAKERS

After many months of civic anticipation, as work crews continued to hack away at the remnants of the Stanley Draper Expressway, OKC finally unveiled the details of its plan for the Oklahoma City Boulevard. "Unveiled," actually, is overstating it. The plan came out casually, almost as an afterthought, at a subcommittee meeting about streetcars. Word, however, spread. The grandest street this generation would ever see, it turned out, was not going to be very grand at all. The Oklahoma City Boulevard would not be the charming, cosmopolitan thoroughfare that residents had been encouraged to imagine. In fact, the new road would be a lot like the old road.

The engineers' vision was blunt and unromantic: an auxiliary freeway. The boulevard would be six lanes wide, designed to carry as many cars as possible, as quickly as possible, between downtown and the new route of Interstate 40. Since traffic would be heavy, the engineers posited, there was no reason to let it mingle with the rest of the traffic downtown. It would need to rise up over the city streets. Which is to say: the city planned to replace the old elevated highway with a new elevated highway. Stanley Draper would have been proud.

But Stanley Draper had been dead, by then, for thirty-five years, and Oklahoma City was no longer his. The spirit of the place had changed. Powerful men in smoky rooms could no longer plunk freeways down through the center of town. The public had started paying attention. People cared about downtown again. An advocacy group was formed: Friends for a Better Boulevard. Rallies were held. "Don't replace a highway with a highway!" said the former planning director of Vancouver to the people of OKC.

A PR battle kicked off in the papers and online. The boulevard became a potent metaphor for all that was at stake in modern Oklahoma City. As always, the traffic engineers simply wanted to move traffic. The younger generations, however, wanted something new: a real downtown to live in, a place worth building a collective identity around, not just a bunch of corporate headquarters with parking garages. They wanted to live in a version of Brooklyn: a constellation of funky neighborhoods, each an end in itself, with trees and pedestrians and shops and restaurants. They wanted to walk to grocery stores and sit in parks. In fact, they wanted something closer to the downtown that Stanley Draper had originally stepped into, back in 1919. They wanted some of that vital congestion. Similar dynamics were in play in Charlotte and Des Moines and Durham and Indianapolis—the attempt to redeem downtowns from the city-planning sins of the twentieth century. There were strong echoes of Jane Jacobs versus Robert Moses. In Oklahoma City, signs of young energy were beginning to pop up frequently: a monthly street festival featuring craft beer and gourmet snow cones, a food truck that sold handmade waffles, excellent coffee shops at which twenty-somethings with tattoo sleeves and chunky glasses sat together to collaborate on websites about bike lanes. A buzzword began to circulate in the planning community downtown: "placemaking."

In early 2013, a conference called "Placemaking" drew more than a thousand people to the University of Oklahoma to listen to experts speak about crosswalks and historic preservation incentives and how to reclaim abandoned suburban malls. The crowd included not only young activists but many of OKC's established power players—architects and former mayors and city council members. From the stage, multiple speakers remarked that they'd never seen, in any other city, such a hunger for this discussion. It was, perhaps, a sign of how radically far OKC had gone, under Draper and his allies, in exactly the opposite direction.

The boulevard fight seemed to encapsulate this. After the city's plan got around town, four hundred citizens showed up at a public meeting to object. But officials told them it was too late: promises had already been made; huge stacks of complex paperwork had been filed. The process had begun. Their hands were tied. Citizens couldn't expect to just waltz in at the last minute, with their unofficial emotions, and demand an infrastructure revolution. The engineers showed maps and animations demonstrating traffic inefficiencies. Look at all the cars, they said. What would happen when an accident inevitably shut down I-40? The boulevard would have to be able to handle the overflow. The traffic of the entire continent depended, in a way, on this new road in the middle of Oklahoma City.

The placemakers rejected all of this. Many suggested that the city would be better off with nothing in place of the Stanley Draper Expressway. Downtown should revert to its original street grid, they said. Rewind history, start again. Young people didn't want to organize their lives, as their parents had, around cars, freeways, malls, suburbs, distance. If a new boulevard was truly necessary, they argued, it should be narrow and slow. Stop designing the city around peak traffic volume, which was only two hours every weekday. Think of all the other parts of life.

The city council, however, sided with the engineers. The boulevard, they insisted, had to be wide, high, fast, and open no later than 2014. The new I-40 didn't have enough exits, because it had been designed with the expectation of an elevated boulevard to supplement it, and downtown drivers were already suffering from the lack of them. Further discussion was just a waste of everyone's time.

And so in January 2013, five days after Kevin Durant's first career ejection, the city council voted 7–2 to send the boulevard design to the state for implementation. The Oklahoma City Boulevard would be an elevated pseudo-freeway. As a concession to the placemakers, it would be slightly shorter than it had originally been drawn up, but that was it. After the vote, the council congratulated itself on its flexibility. It was, one member said, "the beginning of new politics and new policymaking" in OKC.

Still, the people would not quiet down.

———

A city manager holds a strange position in American civic life: he or she is an unelected, quasi-governmental official often referred to as "the CEO of the city." The city manager's job is to get things done. While the mayor handles "vision" and the city council processes legislation, the city manager takes care of logistics: traffic patterns, construction schedules, tax revenues. The position was created, in the early twentieth century, as an attempt to extract the nuts and bolts of a functioning city from the hurly-burly of politics.

The City of Oklahoma City's city manager was a no-nonsense engineer named Jim Couch. By 2013, when the boulevard issue was simmering toward a rolling boil, Couch had held the position for thirteen years. This made him a force of unprecedented stability. In the seventy-three years preceding Couch, OKC had run through thirty-four city managers, with one lasting only two days. Couch was a professional's professional, able to get even the most complex projects done on schedule and on budget. He was a Process man, and he'd been instrumental in the downtown renaissance, helping to enable not only the acquisition of the Seattle SuperSonics but the reawakening of the once-dry river and the eight-hundred-foot skyscraper that rose out of an old parking lot. Couch had presided over the revivals of Bricktown, Midtown, the Plaza District, and Automobile Alley. He understood, on a deep level, what made the City of Oklahoma City run. He knew how to work all the levers and cranks and valves back in the engine room. Although he was not nearly as well known as the mayor, Jim Couch was arguably more influential.

One afternoon, in the midst of the boulevard controversy, I went to speak with Couch in his office in city hall. I arrived to find him upset. The *Wall Street Journal* had just published an article, Couch told me, about Aubrey McClendon, one of OKC's most powerful citizens—the Thunder co-owner and fracking legend who had recently been forced to resign from Chesapeake Energy after getting caught in some shady land deals. The article, Couch said, was an obvious hit piece. But he seemed to be most fixated on a small detail in it that had nothing to do with McClendon at all. The reporter, Couch said, had come to his office just like me—in fact, he'd sat on the very same couch that I was sitting on now—and then he had had the gall to publish the following sentence: "A framed team jersey, autographed by the players, hangs on the wood paneling of his office." Couch was furious about this mention of his wood paneling. What *relevance,* he asked me, could that detail possibly have had to a story about Aubrey McClendon? How was the wood paneling in his office in any way *germane?*

I spoke up, on behalf of journalism, to say that sometimes it's important to set the scene, and small details help us do that, and the prominence of that basketball jersey on the office wall spoke to Couch's close relationship to the Thunder—and therefore, by extension, the entire city's relationship to the team.

Couch waved this explanation away. "I just don't see how it was *germane* to the subject," he said. "'Wood paneling.'"

As we talked, I could not help noticing that Couch was standing in precisely the scene the *Wall Street Journal* reporter had described. A Thunder jersey, framed and signed, hung on a wall that was—beyond any possibility of debate—wood-paneled. Couch was complaining about the description of his wood-paneled wall directly in front of his wood-paneled wall. I looked back and forth, from him to it, feeling slightly confused. The description struck me as not controversial in the least. Couch, however, wouldn't let it go. "I just don't see how it was *germane,*" he said.

I had come to talk to Couch not about wood paneling but about city planning—the placemakers, the pros and cons of the various proposed boulevard designs, the controversy, the challenges and opportunities of running a city with an increasingly engaged, increasingly progressive, increasingly planning-conscious young citizenry.

"I've heard a lot of talk about this boulevard issue," I began.

"Really?" Couch answered. He seemed stunned, as if I had told him that everyone around the nation was talking about his favorite flavor of toothpaste.

"Yeah," I said.

"To me, that's kind of a non-issue," Couch said.

"Really?" I said. Now I was surprised.

"Yeah," he said.

"Well, some people got pretty upset about it, it seemed like," I said.

"Yeah," he said.

"Yeah," I said.

"It's kind of a non-issue," he said.

"Really?" I said.

"Yeah," he said.

That was how the conversation went.

Couch walked me over to a big map on his wall. The utopian fantasy of the boulevard, he explained, was based on a complete misunderstanding. The old elevated highway—he stabbed at the map with his finger—had been pulled down and moved south. This was great, because it meant there was no longer an elevated highway running right through the middle of downtown. But its absence created a problem too, because now it was inconvenient for highway drivers to get downtown. This, in Couch's view, was the main difficulty the boulevard had to solve. The project was huge and complicated, he explained, with five separate phases, and people were getting fixated, for no good reason, on this one tiny piece: phase 3. He pointed to the spot on the map where some streets intersected. "This is a disaster right here," he said. "It's a disaster. The highway department in the original plan said: 'We're just going to go over the top of all that stuff. We won't touch it, we'll just go over the top of it, and have a bridge over there.' People said: 'Well, wait a minute, you just took that bridge down. How come you're building a new bridge?' Well, because we've got a horrendous traffic problem over here. You don't want to put lights all the way through here and have it to grade. The boulevard won't be functional. You won't be able to get people in and out of downtown to the interstate."

Couch seemed genuinely proud of Oklahoma City's ability to move cars. "We don't have traffic problems," he said. He was a Thunder superfan, a season ticket holder, and he often thought about downtown planning in terms of how easily he could drive himself from the arena back to his suburban home after a game. Just the night before, Couch said, he had watched the Thunder destroy the Golden State Warriors. (I was there too; at halftime, I had watched Aubrey McClendon dancing, courtside, with wild enthusiasm, to an East Side high school marching band.)

"I live twelve miles north of here," Couch said, getting excited. "I stayed at the Thunder game until the final buzzer, and I was home by nine forty-five. I'm talking about getting out of the arena, leaving the parking garage, getting into the downtown traffic, whatever I had to do to get on the interstate, and getting up to my house, which is twelve miles away. I think the buzzer was around nine twenty-five. It took me twenty minutes. It's pretty sweet."

The purpose of the boulevard, in Couch's view, was to safeguard the sweetness of that deal, both for him and the other drivers of OKC.

But what about all the opposition? I asked.

Couch minimized it.

"It was controversial for a few weeks," he said. "It was really an issue hijacked by a few people on a website. Some social media." And then he shook his head. "That's the generation we're in today."

I asked him about the activists' hopes that the boulevard might create a new neighborhood on the western edge of downtown.

Couch scoffed.

"That's the McDonald's and the City Rescue Mission down there," he said. "The homeless shelter. We're *really* concerned about the development potential in that area? My planner will tell you that it will be generations before downtown will expand into that area."

"Who's your planner?" I asked.

"My planner?" Couch said. "The city planner is Russell Claus."

I met Russell Claus in the old Colcord Building, one of OKC's rare historic skyscrapers to survive into the twenty-first-century—the tower that Ralph Ellison's father had helped build just after statehood, and that the KKK had marched past when Ralph was nine. The restaurant inside was newly renovated; Claus and I sat next to a futuristic-looking gas fireplace, and at one point the waiter brought us complimentary oatmeal cookies with a list of ingredients that went on for about thirty seconds. We spoke for several hours, and later Claus took me for a driving tour of OKC, and at every point in our time together I marveled that Jim Couch would ever send anyone to speak with Russell Claus about anything at all—let alone the boulevard or anything even tangentially related to city planning. To say that the two men did not see eye to eye hardly begins to describe it. The two men did not have the same organs of sight. They were like a bumblebee and a squid looking at the same cloud.

Russell Claus was an outsider. He came from Australia. A series of unfortunate events had brought him to Oklahoma nearly twenty years before, and he had helped to rebuild the empty downtown, and he seemed perpetually astonished to find himself still there. Claus was an outspoken cosmopolitan atheist progressive rabble-rouser in a place that disapproved, vehemently, of all of those things. As we drove, he pointed out, with particular relish, the many planning failures that still plagued downtown: parking garages plunked into the middle of previously vital neighborhoods, empty lots that once held magnificent skyscrapers, neglected alleys, defunct streetcar tracks, a lack of residential buildings bordering the park.

Director of planning in Oklahoma City was a uniquely frustrating job. The city was born, of course, in the spirit of Boom—a crime against the very notion of planning—and that spirit was still very much alive. For most of its history, OKC's planning decisions had been ad hoc, disorganized, and myopic. When they were directed from above, it was usually in secret, by powerful men such as Stanley Draper. Public interest and corporate interests were frequently deemed to be one and the same. Even today, the most basic fundamentals of planning—zoning, for instance—were considered a form of communism. Claus said that one city council member actually referred to him, habitually, as "Comrade."

"The state is full of lunatics," Claus told me. "It's kind of an embarrassment." His planning meetings, he said, were often hijacked by "complete tinfoil-hat guys"—extreme anti-government activists. "I say: 'Well, how did you get here? On a road. How did that road get built?' That kind of logic is lost on them. I say: 'You don't want taxes, you don't want government—there are some great examples of that around the world. Somalia, Libya, Sudan, Eritrea. That's what you want? In your quest for personal property rights and freedom from the government?' Those places don't even have as many guns as we do."

Claus was aligned, in general, with the placemakers. He abhorred the American worship of automobiles and all of the urban diseases it spawned: sprawl, malls, big box stores, interstates amputating historic neighborhoods. He believed in walkable streets, strong public transportation, mixed-use neighborhoods, a thriving downtown. In the planning world, all of this was perfectly orthodox. Among the old guard in OKC, however, it was a scandal. Claus was not allowed to cite, as models, progressive cities such as Vancouver, Portland, or Boulder, because those places were considered too liberal. When he proposed a new idea, he had to show that it had already been implemented in a conservative peer city such as Nashville or Fort Worth. Claus told me he had good, senior-level planning jobs open, but he couldn't convince anyone to come to Oklahoma City to take them.

"The engineers are in charge," he told me. "They're not broad-thinking people. In their mind, their job is only to move traffic. They'll have cars running from one end of the country to the other, and they'll just drop them off in the Atlantic or the Pacific Ocean. It really wouldn't matter to them. In my world, there are connections all over the place—multiple different factors that all influence each other—and you try to guide them, as much as you possibly can, in a way that incubates the good and suppresses the bad. But it's not a perfect science. There are principles that have been proven to work pretty well, but there's always flexibility. For engineers, it's much more black and white: get the big projects done on time and on budget. There's not a lot of thought about *why* we're doing them. They're afraid of things that they can't get a formula for. These are community and economic development projects, but they're all being managed as construction projects."

In the case of the Oklahoma City Boulevard, Claus said, planners had not been part of the discussion. The design was fifteen years old, and the engineers didn't particularly care that downtown had changed drastically in the interim. The plan was the plan.

Claus said that this was largely a product of the city manager's devotion to doing things, no matter what, according to the approved script.

"If you have a process, in his view, that just deals with everything," Claus said of Jim Couch. "It covers his ass with the politicians—because he had a process. They thought the process with the boulevard was great. And I'm saying: Well, it wasn't an outcome-based process. It was a process to have a process. Transportation engineers are classic at running a public process to say: 'Here's what we're doing, thank you for your input, and now we're gonna do whatever the hell we wanted to do anyway.'"

Because of this, Claus said, the fight to meaningfully change the boulevard was doomed.

"It might happen in fifty years," he said. "I think we make a lot of mistakes that can be corrected. But it has to be in fifty years."

As we drove around town, Claus often spoke in these terms. He would point to what had once been Main Street, now cut in half—a one-hundred-year mistake, he said. He would point to a parking garage—a twenty-five-year mistake. The Stanley Draper Expressway, Claus said, was a fifty-year mistake, and now its time was over. But its replacement, the Oklahoma City Boulevard, looked like it would be another fifty-year mistake. This kind of thing would continue, Claus said, as long as Oklahoma City stuck to its old top-down power structure, allowing the important decisions to be made in private, by a handful of rich, white, conservative men.

"The original ones all died off," Claus told me, "so there was a little bit of a vacuum. Now you've got this new elite coming up: the Aubrey McClendons and Clay Bennetts of the world. They have grand visions. Generally, I'd say it's been quite positive. There's a lot of philanthropy. But there has never been that understanding, as you get in European and Canadian and Australian cities, of how to address the entire community's needs. It's more: 'Let's do these big projects and everything will trickle down.'"

This had largely worked, of course, in the case of the Thunder—a grand vision driven by the money and obsession of rich white businessmen, including McClendon and Bennett. I asked Claus if he was a fan of the team.

He was not. Although Claus conceded that the Thunder had been "a large part of the city feeling good about itself," and he insisted that this effect was real and powerful, he mostly resented it as a distraction from real, urgent, grown-up business. "The Thunder is like another religion," he said. "And here we were already dealing with church six nights a week. When it's NBA season, that's all people talk about. It bottlenecks things. 'Oh, we can't work on that tonight because there's a Thunder game on.' You know, the rest of the world couldn't give a fuck about this."

Claus turned wistful. Once upon a time, he said, in the first half of the twentieth century, before men like Stanley Draper cranked the gears of sprawl, Oklahoma City had actually been a sophisticated urban place. Downtown was full of elegant buildings and popular shops and pedestrians. The streetcar system was world-class.

"This was a *real* city," he insisted. "If it had continued to develop at that same rate, I mean, today it would be Seattle."

"What is it now?" I asked.

He thought for a second. His voice became sad.

"Oklahoma City," he said.

I asked Claus if that glorious future might be salvageable—if, in fifty years, Oklahoma City could be another Portland or Vancouver or Seattle or Denver.

"Could be," he said. "There's no reason it can't still be the shining city on the plains."

What are the odds? I asked.

He thought again, then said, "One in a hundred?"

CONTROLLED PROGRESSIVE COLLAPSE

All at once, on a Sunday afternoon in 1977, the people of OKC came back to the center of the city. A crowd of thirty thousand gathered and jostled for position. They had come to witness a public execution: the final death of the old downtown.

BLASTING AREA, said a sign.

SITE OF UNIQUE MYRIAD GARDENS, said another.

The crowd massed around one of the city's signature skyscrapers: the Biltmore Hotel, an ancient giant of the skyline, twenty-eight stories tall, nearly three hundred feet, its upper floors stepped stylishly back like a ziggurat, with enormous letters on the roof—HOTEL BILTMORE. The story of the Biltmore was, in many ways, the story of downtown. It towered up from the intersection of Grand and Harvey, exactly where, in the days of the Land Run, angry crowds had gathered in the dust and grass to argue over the shape of the city. In fact, the Biltmore sat right on one of OKC's infamous jogs, where the street grid hitched suddenly over Grand. The building went up during the Great Depression—it was one of a burst of new skyscrapers that proved, as the world's economy crashed, that Oklahoma City was special, chosen, charmed. The city, at the time, was still riding its original oil boom. The Biltmore Hotel had 619 rooms, green stone floors, seven elevators, and an enormous rug in the lobby woven with idealized scenes from the history of OKC: a tepee, a covered wagon, an oil well, and an image of the Biltmore itself. Amelia Earhart stayed there; Hollywood stars danced to live orchestras in its ballrooms. At age thirteen, Bobby Fischer played his first major chess tournament at the Biltmore. For decades, many thousands of dollars were wagered every night in secret games in the hotel's back rooms—including, on Christmas Eve 1945, a single legendary roll of the dice in which a local institution, Cattlemen's Steakhouse, changed hands. The Biltmore made OKC seem big-time. Tourists sent postcards of it back home. Within a block of the hotel, you could get your hair cut, pick up flowers, buy a necklace, see a movie, or shop at a specialty store that sold only vacuum cleaners. Katz was right around the corner. Sears was directly across the street. The Biltmore stood at the center of a whole thriving world.

By 1977, however, downtown was something very different. No one came there for fun anymore. All of those shops had moved out. The streetcar lines had been torn up and replaced by buses. Although the economy was once again booming with oil, and new construction was going up everywhere, very little of that energy was finding its way downtown.

On October 16, 1977, however, the people were suddenly back. They thronged around the Biltmore, huddling shoulder to shoulder, looking for the best angles. Some stood on the roofs of nearby buildings. Police worked to maintain a safe perimeter. All normal business in the area, or what was left of it, had been temporarily discontinued. Streets were closed to traffic. For twenty years, downtown had been starved for exactly this kind of energy, this kind of crowd. But this was the sad irony of the day: the only reason to come downtown anymore was to watch downtown come down.

The forces that changed the city had been too strong to hold off. After World War II, Oklahoma City found itself subjected to a set of pressures that were operating nationwide. A generation of young white veterans, now heavily subsidized by the federal government, were attending college, buying homes, and starting families. A million suburban developments bloomed, fed by the interstate highways. It was an era of TV and AC. Cities sprawled. Public life began to recede. Malls rose up to service the suburbs, and shops that had anchored central business districts for decades began to close or relocate. All over the country, from Seattle to Minneapolis to El Paso to Niagara Falls, planners were forced to reckon with a difficult question: What was the role of the old downtown in this newly dispersed city? Formerly bustling streets grew quiet. Display windows sat empty, and when they cracked, owners often replaced them with boards instead of glass.

Oklahoma City, of course, was even more radically dispersed than other cities. By 1960, it was nine times larger than it had been before World War II. Concentric horseshoes of identical houses began to sprout at the end of every freeway, and the booming middle classes poured out into them. When Clara Luper was orchestrating her sit-ins downtown, developers opened the Penn Square Mall five swift miles northwest, and the spacious new stores and restaurants drew off many of Katz's former customers. The balance of the city had swung.

Stanley Draper could see, looking out his office window, that downtown was in decline. Blocks that had once been solid with shops were beginning to show patches of vacancy. Foot traffic had thinned. The energy was draining away.

Fortunately, Draper was also aware of a solution. In 1950, Pittsburgh had started a pioneering program of urban renewal, and Draper tracked it with interest. The old city bulldozed dilapidated blocks and replaced them with modern structures: convention centers, highways, parking garages, office towers. All through the 1950s, this trend spread across America. In Norfolk and Baltimore and San Francisco and Cleveland, old wood and brick and stone structures gave way to glass and poured concrete. It was the phoenix principle of city planning: rebirth through destruction. Boston was mowing down some of the oldest neighborhoods on the continent. A new generation now drove the economy, and it had no interest in its grandparents' crowded downtown streets and specialty shops and soda fountains. To survive, downtown would have to reinvent itself.

Oklahoma City, clearly, was not Boston or Pittsburgh. Its oldest major downtown buildings were hardly even fifty years old. And yet Stanley Draper and the other major powers loved the idea of urban renewal beyond all reason or restraint. The Land Run had left the city center frozen in disarray. Its lots were tiny, owned by many different people, impossible to coordinate. The street grid was fundamentally warped. Decades of organizing from on high had not been able to fix it. Urban renewal provided the opportunity. It was, finally, a force of order powerful enough to counteract the initial chaos of the Land Run—a Process strong enough to answer the city's original Boom. It would allow planners to get down to civic bedrock and start over. If the pioneers had created an entire city in a single day, why couldn't modern engineers, with their superior technology, completely destroy that city and remake it in a matter of years?

In the mid-1950s, Draper, Gaylord, and a small group of business leaders took a private plane to study urban renewal in eastern cities. They also went to Washington, D.C., to lobby for federal funds to start a program in OKC. Urban renewal, these men had decided, was the only possible future for downtown.

Naturally, back home, there was resistance. In 1959, the Democratic candidate for mayor issued a laundry list of warnings about urban renewal. Among other things, he told voters, it "destroys homes, creates new slums, increases juvenile delinquency . . . and casts a cloud on the title to every piece of property." But that candidate lost the race to Jim Norick, the telegenic young proponent of modernity and growth. Under Draper's influence, Oklahoma's governor signed a new law that allowed cities to eliminate "slums, blight and deterioration"—wonderfully fluid categories for the men doing the eliminating. Critics filed a lawsuit charging that it was unconstitutional for a city to seize property, willy-nilly. This challenge was enough to put the bulldozers on hold as the case wound its way through the courts.

The delay drove Stanley Draper crazy. Oklahoma City, he felt, was already falling behind. Downtown was getting visibly worse. This was a civic emergency—if OKC hesitated, all of the gains it had worked so desperately for, all of that leaping up the national rankings, would be lost. Draper sprang into action. He deployed the full power of the chamber of commerce, marshaling the city's bankers and energy titans, pooling their money to form a new nonprofit entity he called the Urban Action Foundation. The UAF acted immediately and aggressively to do what the official government could not: to start urban renewal, now, in Oklahoma City.

First, the Urban Action Foundation imported the men responsible for Cleveland's urban renewal program. This included a visionary young architect named I. M. Pei—a rising star, educated at MIT and Harvard, whose Erieview Plan had called for a near-total reset of Cleveland's declining downtown. Draper's UAF paid Pei $200,000—the equivalent of nearly $2 million today—to come up with something similar for Oklahoma City.

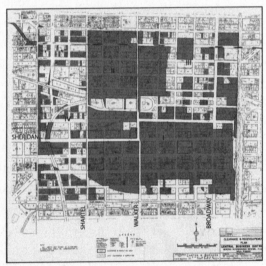

A map of the Pei Plan. Shaded areas represent
buildings set to be destroyed.

On December 10, 1964, OKC got all it had paid for and more. In the Persian Room of the Skirvin Hotel, in front of six hundred people, I. M. Pei unveiled the Pei Plan: a program of downtown annihilation that dwarfed even what was being done in Cleveland. It was breathtakingly extreme. On the map of the plan, cross-hatched lines marked the buildings set for demolition, and there were so many it looked like a map of bomb damage in post-Blitz London. In Cleveland, urban renewal had wiped out most of 163 acres. In Oklahoma City, it would destroy most of 528. Plenty of cities, by 1964, were clearing downtown land, but almost no one was going this far.

In the Skirvin, Pei showed off a large model of the future down-town, ten feet by twelve feet, roped off like a museum exhibit. It was so detailed, there were tiny cars winding between the buildings. The people of OKC gathered around to admire their future. What they saw was a modernist utopian fantasy, a triumph of pure geometry. Residents would live and work in glass towers. Visitors would stay in glass hotels. A state-of-the-art convention center would sit next to an enormous park. Public transportation, Pei believed, was essentially dead, so a network of superhighways and one-way streets would fun-nel cars into downtown parking garages. OKC's tiny blocks would expand into unified superblocks. Main Street itself—a quaint notion in this evolving world—would be torn up to make room for a giant downtown mall. The plan would not be fully complete, Pei said, until 1989. This happened to be an important year: the centenary of the Land Run. Finally, on its one hundredth birthday, Oklahoma City would be the world-class, cutting-edge metropolis its original found-ers had dreamed of.

"You may ask yourself if you cannot afford it," Pei told city lead-ers. "We think you have no choice: you have a wonderful bargain to get more for your money than any city in the country in this plan."

Stanley Draper was delighted. He and Pei spoke constantly about

I. M. Pei shows off his vision of OKC's glorious future.

the city's transformation. OKC's grand new central park was going to be modeled on Copenhagen's Tivoli Gardens, so Draper and the rest of the Urban Action Foundation actually flew to Denmark to inspect the real thing. Draper, according to his traveling companions, walked around Copenhagen like he owned it, as if it were just an unusually distant neighborhood of Oklahoma City.

To sell Pei's vision to the rest of the city, the chamber of commerce and the Urban Action Foundation unleashed a PR offensive. Draper promised the business community $100 million in new construction, plus nationwide accolades for the boldness of their vision. Propaganda films were produced. One showed the Pei Model—"filmed with a special periscopic lens"—contrasted with shabby footage of OKC's actual downtown. Just before Christmas, readers of the Sunday *Oklahoman* found a lavish twelve-page color insert illustrating the glories of urban renewal. "Nothing less than major surgery can save downtown Oklahoma City," it claimed. "If the patient dies, the remainder of the city will be disastrously affected."

There was a moment, before the destruction actually began, in late 1966 or early 1967, when the Pei Plan could have been stopped. Critics tried, pointing out the already clear failures of urban renewal in other cities—in downtown Cleveland, for instance, where Pei's Erieview District now sat idle and undeveloped, destroyed but not rebuilt, a swath of empty land that locals referred to as "Hiroshima Flats." Momentum, however, was on the side of change. Downtown was actually getting worse. All this talk of urban renewal had created a feedback loop, exacerbating the problem it was supposed to fix. Downtown landlords had stopped renovating because they didn't know if their buildings would survive, and the lack of repairs caused more businesses to flee to the suburbs. Main Street was beginning to look deserted. Meanwhile, after a long review process, the federal funding for urban renewal came pouring in—more than $30 million to help carry out Pei's plan. OKC could not possibly turn that down. Wichita, New Orleans, Minneapolis, Kansas City, St. Louis, Dallas, and Houston—all of these competitors had already built themselves new convention centers. How could Oklahoma City afford to wait any longer?

It didn't. In 1967, the bulldozers were finally set loose. They would swarm over downtown for the next several years, demolishing decades of the city's history. As the Great Annexation drove the edges of the city outward, urban renewal ravaged its interior. Even the Urban Renewal Authority's office, on Park Avenue, was destroyed by urban renewal. The authority had to take refuge in the stately Colcord, one of the few historic skyscrapers left intact.

Some of the ruins were filled in, in the early 1970s, by a wave of construction largely paid for with federal funds: the Liberty Tower, a five-hundred-foot-tall pin-striped rectangle of dark glass; the McGee Tower, a thirty-story headquarters for the local energy giant Kerr-McGee; the new convention center. Past all the construction ran a new six-lane thoroughfare lined with parking garages, a road that would eventually be named in honor of E. K. Gaylord—and which connected, naturally, to the Stanley Draper Expressway.

By 1973, the city was ready to move on to the crucial second phase of Pei's plan: the construction of the supermall and the superpark. By this time, however, urban renewal had fallen out of favor nationwide. After twenty years, its failures were impossible to ignore. Countless downtowns had been ruined instead of renewed. In Oklahoma City, demolitions now frequently drew protestors, some of whom marched in symbolic funeral processions. Federal funding was beginning to dry up.

In downtown OKC, the destruction was horrifying. Architectural showpieces had come down everywhere. The eight-story Mercantile Building, tidy and white. The Warner Theatre, once home to the grandest stage in the city, where Sarah Bernhardt and other legends had performed. The Terminal Building, where the streetcars used to turn around. The Criterion Theater, whose fancy columns made it look vaguely Parisian. The Baum Building, modeled on the Doge's Palace in Venice—elegant white exterior, ornate spiraling cupolas, windows upon windows upon windows. "These are not merely huge buildings," Angelo Scott had written about OKC's new skyline in the 1930s, "they are artistic structures within and without, worthy to stand in any city." By the mid-1970s, that skyline was ruined. Downtown was desolate. It would be as if New York City had decided to raze not only the old Penn Station but the Empire State Building and the Chrysler Building too, plus Macy's and Grand Central Terminal. In 1974, John A. Brown's, the department store that had anchored downtown OKC for nearly sixty years, finally gave up and left. A wrecking ball rolled in and blew away the building, whose stately arches had occupied nearly an entire block of Main Street. Grass and weeds, sensing an opportunity, began to emerge downtown. Oklahoma City seemed to be reverting to its early days, scraping the civilization right off of itself, lot by lot. Given enough bulldozers and time, it might have turned entirely back into prairie.

Further destruction seemed pointless, reckless—destruction for destruction's sake. No new buildings were sprouting from the ruins. Members of the city council suggested that perhaps the city didn't need to follow through with the rest of Pei's plan. Perhaps some of Main Street might be preserved as an "Old Town," a touch of quirky charm among all the new glass boxes. Merchants took out radio ads to criticize urban renewal. The planners, however, were drunk on their plans. The Urban Renewal Authority had grown into a monster, with 125 employees and $60 million in assets. It moved in such secrecy that even the city council often had no idea what it was up to. The destruction rolled forward as scheduled.

In the midst of all this, I. M. Pei came back to check on Oklahoma City. "I'm coming in like Rip Van Winkle," he said, with his trademark charm. He told city leaders that he was excited by the progress he saw—the convention center, the glass towers—but he also had a serious concern. The remaining projects, he warned, must be started immediately. The stalled mall and the raw park could not be allowed to fail. Delay too long, Pei said, and the public would lose confidence. Finish the job. "It is a very difficult thing to do," he said. "But you have to do it." Perhaps, Pei suggested, city leaders should hold a groundbreaking ceremony, just to improve the people's mood.

And then he flew away.

The Pei Plan, curiously, did not call for the destruction of the Biltmore Hotel. That was an icon of downtown, and Pei had made it clear that it should be left standing on the northern edge of the giant park—an envoy of the old world presiding over the new. Oklahoma City's hysteria for urban renewal, however, had already exceeded the Pei Plan. Officials were beginning to freelance, destroying buildings that were not on his list. Some deep psychological impulse had taken over: destruction, domination, the total conquest of space-time.

By 1977, the citizens of OKC were used to seeing buildings come down. It was all part of the process, they had been told, of civic self-improvement. They tried to accept that. These were people who did not like to complain. But the destruction of the Biltmore felt different. The building was shabby and empty, yes—the hotel had closed back in 1973—but it *was* downtown. It was tall enough that you could see it from great distances, as you drove on the freeway out to the suburbs—a monument to remind you that, even if you never went there anymore, the city center did still exist.

In those days, however, the Biltmore was like a ghost of the previous city. It stood alone in an alien landscape, no longer surrounded by cafés, cleaners, banks, theaters, and every kind of clothing store. Now there were drug addicts, homeless camps, prostitutes. For the average middle-class citizen, downtown was a place to drive through, if absolutely necessary, but not a place to stop. The Biltmore's luxurious interior had been stripped and sold off to pay old debts. When workers from Southwestern Bell went through the hotel, room by room, to remove the old phones, they had to kick down doors that had been locked by the squatters living inside. In 1977, the Biltmore's abandoned shell stood decrepit on the horizon, still visible from across the city, only now a symbol not of the center's vitality but of its failure.

And so, on October 16, the morning of the demolition, the masses gathered. TV crews set up to broadcast the destruction nationwide. The Stanley Draper Expressway, now ten years old, rose slightly south of the Biltmore, and drivers on it pulled over, got out of their cars, and stood on the freeway to watch. Draper had died the year before, in 1976—an event memorialized by nearly the entire front page of the *Oklahoman*—and this demolition seemed like another fitting tribute: one more spectacular blow in his lifelong mission to make the city great. The Biltmore Hotel was about to become the tallest building in America ever brought down by explosives.

Some spectators cried. This felt like the death of the Oklahoma City they had grown up in. There was some buzz, in the crowd, about something moving in one of the hotel's windows: a blanket, it looked like, or a curtain. People whispered that maybe someone was in there. But the building had been checked and found to be empty.

The Biltmore's skeleton was steel, which made it unusually strong, so eight hundred pounds of explosives had been distributed from the basement to the fourteenth floor. The city had hired, for the job, a pioneer in the field of architectural destruction, a company from Maryland called Controlled Demolition, Incorporated, and the firm called this technique "controlled progressive collapse."

A warning siren sounded. The crowd counted down.

There was a series of faint pops, like the crackling of fireworks, and then a deep rumble, and the Biltmore Hotel basically turned to smoke: its outline fuzzed, and then it lay down, almost gently, right onto its own footprint. The head of the demolition company told a reporter that the collapse had been "perfect—better than we expected. We asked God for wisdom and the good Lord turned on his gravity a little harder."

All around the building, people nearly choked on the dust. When the smoke cleared, it was revealed that the first two floors had failed to fall. The nub of the Biltmore, including its grand old lobby, still stood there, stubbornly rooted to the old downtown, refusing to be renewed. A demolition crew had to go in later and knock it down the old-fashioned way, with bulldozers. In the meantime, the crowd surged forward into the rubble, grabbing bricks and venetian blinds and other wreckage as relics of a vanished world.

The chamber of commerce took its own souvenir—a large piece of marble from the Biltmore's lobby. This was carried, immediately, several blocks away, where it was added to a strange sort of outdoor museum. Directly next to the chamber's offices, in a tiny concrete plaza tucked into the middle of one of I. M. Pei's huge new parking garages, curious pedestrians could visit a new memorial to the old

The destruction of the Biltmore Hotel.

downtown. It consisted entirely of pieces of the buildings destroyed by urban renewal. There was a stone lion's head from the old Terminal Building and finials from the Criterion Theater. There was a grand white spire and a cupola from the Baum Building. Each object was labeled with an explanatory plaque. It was hard to read the tone of this parking-garage museum, to tell if it was intended as reverential, regretful, triumphant, or mocking. It was tempting to think of it in medieval terms—a victorious army displaying the decapitated heads of its enemies, on pikes, just outside the city gates. Now, to this bounty, the chamber added its authentic piece of the Biltmore Hotel.

Years later, when the chamber moved its offices, these artifacts were left behind, in the plaza in the middle of the old garage, where the pieces of the missing buildings weathered and cracked, forgotten and unloved. Sometimes people used them as ashtrays, and many of them were eventually broken or stolen. All over downtown, the spots these buildings had once occupied remained empty. The destruction of the Biltmore Hotel would be remembered, for decades, as a turning point in the history of the city. Where that turn led, however, was not at all where the planners had planned.

GAME 46: THE NEUTRALITY OF THABO SEFOLOSHA

On January 31, the Memphis Grizzlies came to town. No one was particularly excited. It was a Thursday night, Game 46 out of eighty-two,
right in the teeth of the mid-season grind, when the adrenaline of the
early months has worn off and the inhumanity of the NBA schedule
is becoming hard to ignore: fatigue, injuries, boredom. Teams knew
what they had and what they lacked. The Thunder had been on the
road for most of January, including the previous six games in a row—
nearly two solid weeks of enforced togetherness, during which time
they'd won and lost, won and lost, won and lost, a frustrating pattern
for a championship contender. Not-niceness continued to bloom.
Small irritations flared into grievances. There were rumors in the
press about a rift between Kevin Durant and Serge Ibaka. It was some
relief, then, to finally be back home, where the team rarely lost, where
everyone could get away from one another and find their own space.

Outside, the Oklahoma wind was an ice harpy shrieking through
the streets, punishing all humans for the crime of having skin. Thunder fans fought through it and filed into the arena, turning themselves from many small individuals into one big sold-out crowd—the
customary 18,203. On the floor, the players warmed up. Kendrick
Perkins crab-walked all over the court with a giant rubber band attached to his waist. Nick Collison missed a baseline dunk. Durant
was lofting up silly shots, moonballs from the left elbow—he missed
three in a row, then made his fourth and immediately turned and
walked off the court. A game like this was all willpower and professionalism, the ability to force your body and mind to move in

directions they didn't naturally want to move. A referee stood at the edge of the floor by himself, practicing jump-ball tosses. It was Process time in the NBA.

This made it the Grizzlies' kind of game. Their slogan was "Grit 'n' Grind." They were big, tough, and unglamorous at every position, and they basically beat the shit out of you. They were stagnation incarnate. These two teams knew each other uncomfortably well. In the play-offs two years before, the Grizzlies had stagnated all over the Thunder for seven games and three overtimes. The Thunder had eventually won the series but then lost to Dallas, in the following round, possibly out of sheer exhaustion. Memphis's defense was designed to put constant stress on an offense—to find whatever hairline cracks already existed and then press them into full-blown fractures. In the case of the Thunder, that pressure would fall on the cracks between self-interest and the collective good: between Westbrook's freelancing and Durant's efficiency, between the gaudy talent of the superstars and the mere competence of the role players.

From the opening tip, the energy of the game felt off. There was a disturbance in the force. This was likely coming from the Grizzlies, who just the day before had traded away their leading scorer, Rudy Gay, but had yet to receive any new players in return. Gay's remaining teammates seemed to be in mourning; the starting lineup was a patchwork.

The Thunder opened the game by running an isolation play not for Westbrook or Durant but for their starting shooting guard, Thabo Sefolosha. Sefolosha had many things going for him: his name was a perfect Euro-burble (*Lost Ogle*: "Every time I say Sefolosha, I imagine that I have a mouth full of Jell-O and I'm just squishing it out through my teeth"), he had the smooth good looks of an R&B singer or a designer scarf model, and he was a first-rate perimeter defender who often hounded opposing stars into embarrassing nights. But he was not a scorer. The Grizzlies were guarding him with Mike Conley, their tiny point guard, who was a whole head shorter—basically daring Sefolosha to shoot. The Thunder accepted the challenge. Sefolosha backed Conley down near the hoop, pump-faked, spun toward the rim, and—as soon as a second defender came over to help—passed to his now wide-open teammate Serge Ibaka, who made the jump shot. It was Teamwork 101. The basketball gods were pleased, clearly, because the Thunder went on to make their first nine shots of the game, an improbable feat against the Grizzlies' defense, trade or no trade. By the middle of the first quarter, the game was already beginning to feel like a blowout. The home crowd was burbling toward rapture.

And yet, still, there was something naggingly off. For one thing, Russell Westbrook looked disturbingly Westbrookian. He threw a beautiful pass for an Ibaka dunk, then a terrible pass directly to an opponent. He charged down the court and hurtled himself into a pull-up jumper—*swish*—and then Durant found him for a three— *boom*—and then he flung his body into another pull-up jumper: *swish*. Westbrook was hot, but in a way that was slightly troubling. I kept writing "uh-oh" in my notebook. He had that "Why not?" look about him.

Because of the trade, the Grizzlies had been forced to start a bench player named Jerryd Bayless, and Bayless and Westbrook had a history. Both had been drafted in 2008; both were explosive, reckless, emotional not-quite point guards. Some analysts had argued before the draft that Bayless would be the better NBA player. But this was not how it had turned out, and now it was as if Westbrook were playing against a suboptimal version of himself—an alternate-reality version, in which he hadn't panned out—and he clearly wanted to destroy the imposter. To make things worse, in the first quarter, Bayless was just as hot as Westbrook, mirroring him on the other end: three-pointer, flying jumper, pull-up jumper, reckless layup, pull-up jumper. He was making "Why not?" shots, too, and Westbrook was taking it personally. Team basketball was turning into one-on-one. Westbrook isolated on Bayless and banked in another pull-up jumper. Again, in my notebook, I scribbled "uh-oh." Near the end of the first quarter, when Westbrook sat down, he had eleven points, two assists, and three turnovers—an impressive but terrifying stat line for eleven minutes of work. Bayless finished the quarter with twelve points, two assists, and no turnovers. It was an unsustainable pace. At halftime, the Thunder led by twenty-four. But "Why not?" would eventually get its answer.

Whenever I saw Thabo Sefolosha, I always ended up staring at his tattoo. It was one of the great body-art masterpieces in the entire NBA. On his left shoulder, in the position of prime visibility, there was a picture of a basketball wearing a crown, and the image was surrounded by the words "The Game Chose Me"—a short text of almost biblical richness. Read one way, the tattoo was a swaggering statement of destiny: *I am so perfectly suited to this sport that the game itself was forced to recruit ME in order to fully express its true nature, much like Excalibur chose King Arthur.* Read another way, however, Sefolosha's tattoo was passive, almost apologetic—an existentialist shrug: *Don't blame me. I did not choose this game. I play basketball as the gravedigger digs or the louse sucks blood. What are any of us but driftwood on the great tides of history, thrown this way or that until we are inexorably ground into dust against the cruel rocks of fate?* This duality made Sefolosha's tattoo the perfect slogan for his talent. When he harassed LeBron into a turnover or hit a crucial open three, I read "The Game Chose Me" and thought: Good job, game. When he dribbled off his foot or threw the ball into the crowd or mangled a fast break with an awkward spin move, I thought: This is not Thabo's fault; he never asked for this responsibility—he was just standing on a street corner one day, smoking a cigarette, when the spirit of basketball snatched him up and flung him into a gym.

Sefolosha was from Switzerland—the first Swiss player ever drafted into the NBA. As the Thunder rose, in its first few years, from terrible to dominant, Sefolosha played a key role. He was the anti-Harden. He was important to the team, paradoxically, not in spite of his offensive limitations but because of them. He didn't need the ball. In fact, everyone preferred for him not to have the ball, or at least to have it only for the fraction of a second it took him to catch and shoot a wide-open three—a skill he had steadily improved. This allowed him to focus on his defense, as well as to act as a buffer in the offense between Westbrook and Durant, a small absence between two massive presences, a little zone of silence between two walls of noise. Even in 2011, when James Harden emerged as an offensive wizard,

Sefolosha held the starting spot. His presence became a signature of the Thunder's offense: the acid of Westbrook, the base of Durant, the neutrality of Thabo Sefolosha.

In the third quarter of the Grizzlies game, all of the hovering pent-up energy finally broke loose. It came pouring out, naturally, through Russell Westbrook, and it was directed, unfairly, at Sefolosha. The Thunder had come out of halftime still dominating. Their defense was long-armed and swarming. Their offense, funneled through Westbrook and Durant, was overwhelming. The Grizzlies looked dejected and tired. Westbrook was still going after their point guards, especially in the post, down low, where he loves nothing more than publicly humiliating smaller players: turning his back and grinding them into little piles of futility. This game was a full-on Westbrook post-up party. He victimized Mike Conley with another bank shot, drawing another foul. And now he had Bayless on him again, and Westbrook clearly had the exact same thing in mind.

This was when everything went wrong.

Westbrook dribbled up the court, incandescent with confidence. Kendrick Perkins was wide open on the baseline, and he put his hands up to call for the ball—but Westbrook waved him off, and Perkins shuffled dejectedly away. Westbrook now had the entire left half of the floor to himself. He would have preferred, probably, for all of his teammates to actually leave the building, but the rules didn't allow for that, and he didn't have enough time to arrange the logistics, so he got to work in imperfect conditions. He turned his back and started banging Bayless toward the hoop. Dribble, bang, dribble, bang, dribble, dribble, dribble, bang. Bayless, however, wasn't giving an inch, so Westbrook turned toward the middle of the floor to look for space. But another defender was waiting there to help. So Westbrook turned back toward the baseline—bang, dribble, dribble, bang, bang, dribble—only Bayless still wasn't giving him any room. Westbrook turned back to the middle again. Now there was a different defender waiting there to help. Dribble, dribble. Westbrook, the indomitable, the quicksilver, found himself bottled up. What happens to a dream deferred? Where have all the flowers gone? Where are the snows of yesteryear?

The whistle blew: turnover.

The officials had called Westbrook for an obscure and rarely enforced basketball crime: Rule 10, Section 16 of the NBA rule book. ("An offensive player in his frontcourt below the free throw line extended shall not be permitted to dribble with his back or side to the basket for more than five seconds.") It was a relatively new rule, intended to encourage team play, and it was never called, but you couldn't blame the officials. They were doing God's work. Westbrook was in clear violation of everything true and beautiful about basketball. He had plunged off the cliff of self-interest. He had dribbled ten times during that possession, and not one dribble had given him even a split-second advantage. Every problem he'd encountered had represented an opportunity for somebody else—that's how basketball works—but this had never seemed to occur to him. From roughly the third dribble through the sixth, Kevin Durant had been wide open at the three-point line, holding his hands out in shooting position, actually shouting "Hey!" But Westbrook, in these situations, has the peripheral vision of a cyclops looking through a paper-towel tube, so Durant put his hands back down. Around the eighth dribble, Sefolosha came sprinting through the lane, trying to give Westbrook a target to pass to. He was open for half a second—little Mike Conley, Sefolosha's defender, seemed to have been hypnotized by Westbrook's dribbling, along with everyone else in the arena. Sefolosha had scored on a similar play, on a pass from Durant, only a minute before. But Westbrook didn't see the cut. All he knew was that Sefolosha's defender had come over and ruined his opportunity, bottling him up. That was when the whistle came.

The referee's whistle set off a feverish melodrama out on the floor. Every single one of Westbrook's teammates immediately threw his hands up in disgust—not at the call, but at Westbrook. Scott Brooks, sitting on the bench, looked like he'd been hit in the back of the neck with a tranquilizer dart. He stared blankly, paralyzed with wonder. Westbrook, meanwhile, was incensed. He felt, somehow, that he had been wronged. This injustice would not stand. He spiked the ball on the court, hard, twice—even Westbrook's rage was expressed through overdribbling—and in that moment his anger latched onto Thabo Sefolosha.

Right there in public, in the middle of 18,203 fans, in front of a national TV audience, Russell Westbrook screamed at his Swiss teammate, the very model of NBA mildness. Sefolosha, out near the three-point line, stood his ground and tried to explain himself, using his hands to mime the nature of the game as it actually existed outside of the sealed chamber of Westbrook's furious mind. (In the optimistic early days of Sefolosha's career, he had once described basketball as a paragon of democracy: "When you're on the basketball court, everybody's the same," he said. "Everybody's got two legs, two arms.") Durant and Perkins were yelling at Westbrook to stop yelling at Sefolosha. "Come on, Russ!" they shouted. Meanwhile, as the Thunder conducted its Socratic dialogue about the true nature of basketball (DURANTUS: "Surely you saw that I was open?" WESTBRUS: "But can anyone be more open than a man who already possesses the ball?"), the Grizzlies had inbounded and were charging up the court to score. Bayless drove toward the hoop and, instead of forcing his own shot in traffic, passed out to Marc Gasol for a wide-open jump shot. *Swish.* Teamwork 101. Easy. Bayless, Westbrook's inferior nemesis, suddenly looked like the most sensible point guard on the floor.

This was more than Westbrook was willing to endure. He took the inbounds pass, charged down the floor, leaped into two Grizzlies, and fired off one of the wildest shots you are ever likely to see in a professional contest of any kind—a leaning, flying fling that had zero chance of going in. If he was trying to prove something, he had succeeded in proving its opposite. This was the second Thunder possession in a row that Westbrook had wildcatted into smithereens, the second time in a row that none of his teammates had touched the ball. To make things worse, Westbrook's shot missed so badly that it jump-started a Grizzlies fast break, which ended in the worst possible way: with Bayless flying past Westbrook for a dunk.

Scott Brooks roused himself from the depths of a million slumbers and called a time-out. He pulled Westbrook from the game. Westbrook went to the bench, but he was far too furious to sit, too betrayed by humanity and probability and physics and time, so instead he stomped over to the last chair in the row—Daniel Orton's chair—and he threw it over. Orton, standing there, considered saying something, but in the face of Westbrook's wrath he kept quiet, and he watched his point guard go charging off down the tunnel toward the locker room. Mo Cheeks, Westbrook's mentor, hurried after him. Unless a player was injured, leaving the floor in the middle of the game was taboo. In the tunnel, Westbrook was beside himself. He couldn't understand why everyone was yelling at him.

In the minutes following the incident, the Grizzlies cut the Thunder lead from twenty-five down to ten. Westbrook's tantrum had turned the blowout back into a real game.

I LOVE CAPITALISM

On the evening news, on August 5, 1979—the tail end of a momentous decade in OKC—a helicopter circled downtown. This was Sky 5, trusted local source of wide-angle traffic shots and wildfire panoramas and updates on looming weather. Now, however, the helicopter's camera had zoomed in on a building: the Tivoli Inn, which stood alone at the intersection of Main and Robinson. Downtown, in this aerial view, was almost scary in its emptiness. For most of its life, the Tivoli Inn had stood directly next to the Biltmore Hotel, enjoying the same teeming wealth of shops and tourists and restaurants. By now, all of that life had been scraped away. The helicopter showed a landscape that could be described, quite reasonably, as postapocalyptic. There were no shoppers. The streets were barren. Nothing moved. Although something big was about to happen, no crowd had gathered to watch. The helicopter hovered, recording the blankness—until, suddenly, the Tivoli Inn exploded. The building turned to smoke, just as the Biltmore had two years before, and collapsed into nothing. The void at the center of the city expanded. The vastness became more vast.

"Only empty land now," said the news anchor, "but soon the Oklahoma City of the eighties will rise from the dust."

It was still possible, just barely, to believe this.

By the end of the 1970s, the Pei Plan looked like a disaster. The phoenix of urban renewal had, as planned, reduced the city center to ash, but almost nothing new rose out of it. No one lived downtown anymore, and no outsider went there on purpose.

What hope for rebirth was left came from deep beneath the

ground. A new oil reserve had been tapped in the Anadarko Basin, and OKC's energy companies were swarming all over it, sucking up the wealth. As a result, in the late 1970s, the city's economy was booming harder than it had ever boomed. Construction sites were opening everywhere. Oklahoma City's infinite roads filled with Cadillacs. Oilmen flew around the region on private jets the way kids ride bicycles. Helicopters whisked people off for quick lunches in Dallas. From all over the world, fortune hunters streamed to Oklahoma City.

Pouring fuel onto this explosion was an odd local bank that, almost overnight, managed to turn itself into a major player in the U.S. economy. The bank was a novelty, in many ways. For one thing, it was located at the Penn Square Mall. Also, it had a drive-thru window. Most important, though, it operated less as a bank than as a geyser of money, gushing loans toward anyone who happened to glance in its direction—private or corporate, rich or poor, qualified or not. There were red flags everywhere, but it was money, and it was available, and the rewards were too urgent to allow time to worry about the risks. Penn Square Bank was, in other words, the perfect boom bank. In order to maximize profits, it aggressively ignored most of the safeguards set up to keep financial institutions from failing. It sold shares of its loans to other banks all over the country, multiplying the risk exponentially. In only five years, the bank's assets grew from $62 million to $520 million. It was the Great Annexation of lending. It was hard to tell where true wealth stopped and wild speculation began. The bank's reckless generosity allowed total bumblers to become lavish players in the energy game. Gary England, then in his thirties, was just successful enough as a weatherman to afford a new house out in the suburbs. When he went to Penn Square Bank to get a loan for the down payment, the loan officer looked at him like he was crazy. Only $4,000? Why not $10,000? Why not enough to pay off the whole house? Why not an even bigger house? Why not?

By 1980, OKC seemed to have reached its ultimate goal: an everlasting bonanza. Everyone was suddenly investing in everyone else's investments. Everyone ran their very own company, and sometimes two or three. Wayne Coyne's father started a business that distributed office furniture, which kept teenage Wayne and his long-haired brothers busy hauling desks and chairs and cubicle partitions into and out of the headquarters of these booming businesses all over town.

Capitalism had blessed Oklahoma City, and the city wanted to express its thanks. At the height of the boom, local businessmen pooled their money to create a brand-new attraction that, even by the very special standards of Oklahoma City, was spectacularly strange. It was an interactive museum, a kind of secular shrine to free enterprise, designed to help local children appreciate the sanctity of capitalism. It was called Enterprise Square, USA. Fund-raising was led by E. K. Gaylord's son, E. L., who managed to scrape together $15 million. The museum would become, for generations of Oklahoma schoolchildren, a staple on the field trip circuit. Kids rode up a glass elevator, in which they were showered with encouraging messages—"Spend! Save! Buy!" Then they walked through the Hall of Giants, among effigies of the great heroes of capitalism: Alexander Graham Bell, Henry Ford, Sam Walton. They cowered beneath the Talking Face of Government, a creepy giant head covered with flashing TV screens, which taught the children about the dangers of taxation and regulation. Next to the world's largest cash register, four enormous paper bills hung on the wall, and their giant Founding Father heads sang a barbershop quartet about freedom, the animatronic faces jerking

Children learn to love capitalism at Enterprise Square, USA.

around like figures in a Chuck E. Cheese band. Futuristic touch-screen games allowed kids to compete for profits as ranchers or bankers or oil magnates. Many of the exhibits were sponsored by local corporations—dairies, energy companies—and nakedly designed to promote their products. At the gift shop, you could buy bumper stickers that said I LOVE CAPITALISM.

When Enterprise Square, USA, opened, in November 1982, Ronald Reagan himself sent a statement to be read aloud. On its editorial page, the *Oklahoman* published a touching cartoon in which a man labeled "John Q. USA" realizes, with a smile, that "American free enterprise is a *good* thing!!"

The celebration, however, was not quite the full-throated triumph its organizers might have expected. The capitalism museum launched four months too late. Although it was built at the height of the boom, Enterprise Square, USA, opened in the depths of a bust. In July 1982, Penn Square Bank's towering house of cards finally collapsed. When oil prices started to decline, the strain on all those precarious loans was more than the bank could stand. Customers came to withdraw their money, and soon they were waiting outside by the hundreds. The money, insofar as it had ever existed, was gone. The failure of OKC's drive-thru bank set off bank failures across the United States, starting in Seattle, and finally the federal government had to step in with a multi-billion-dollar bailout to keep the blight from destroying the national economy. All over Oklahoma City, companies crashed and folded. CEOs had their Cadillacs seized and auctioned off. Gary England knew an oil executive who was suddenly mowing lawns.

During the boom, it had been easy to imagine Oklahoma City's blasted downtown rallying and rebuilding. The bust destroyed that hope. It was no longer possible to see the ruined core as a landscape in transition. It was, simply, what it was: a self-inflicted wasteland, a nothing where there used to be something. By now, it was clear that the city's grandest plans had failed. Instead of creating a "universal city," the Great Annexation had left a placeless sprawl. Instead of invigorating a declining downtown, the Pei Plan had killed it off. Russell Claus told me that it was as if Oklahoma City felt so bad about what the United States did to Germany in World War II that it decided to do it to itself.

It was a dead decade. In 1984, the National Finals Rodeo—a sort of Super Bowl for cowboys that Oklahoma City had hosted for twenty lucrative years—left for Las Vegas. The luxurious Skirvin Hotel, where Pei first presented his Pei model, had managed to survive urban renewal, but it could not survive the 1980s. It kept changing owners, then went into foreclosure, and finally it was abandoned. Pigeons moved in. In all of downtown, there was only one functional hotel. "Downtown is dead," said a city council member in 1988, "and we helped kill it. There is no major retail, no major attraction, and no place to eat."

At Enterprise Square, USA, the touchscreens and talking robots soon became obsolete, and over the years they broke down, and capitalism provided no money for repairs. The museum grew shabby and sad. The field trips continued, although at this point the children were probably learning different lessons than the ones the founders had intended. All over OKC's deteriorating roads, cars sported a new bumper sticker: PLEASE GOD JUST ONE MORE BOOM. I PROMISE NOT TO PISS IT AWAY THIS TIME.

On I. M. Pei's final trip to Oklahoma, in addition to his advice about finishing the job of urban renewal, he had also offered a few words of wisdom about demographics.

"Bring the young people back," he had said. "Young people are like salt and pepper. They cause trouble, yes, but they also bring excitement."

Young people, however, are not spices that sit around waiting on racks. They are not folding chairs. They are sentient and unruly, and they tend to be drawn to specific stimuli: change, danger, glory, and—above all—other young people. All of those things were now absent from Oklahoma City.

Wayne Coyne, of course, stayed. He lived in the city center, and he worked at Long John Silver's, frying fish bits, on what had become a sketchy stretch of Classen Boulevard. He was such a faithful worker, for so many years, that the restaurant tried, multiple times, to promote him. But Wayne refused, choosing to remain a third mate. The neighborhood grew increasingly bleak, and one day, the Long John Silver's was robbed. Wayne and his co-workers were forced, at gunpoint, to lie facedown on the dirty kitchen floor. Everyone was sure they were going to die. But the robbers eventually left, and everyone was okay, and Wayne and his co-workers leaped around together, next to the deep fryers, hugging and crying and laughing about the glorious miracle of life.

As Wayne put it to an interviewer years later: "The things I used to worry about just didn't matter to me anymore. That I would look like a fool. That I would do something and people would think I'm an idiot. I just didn't give a shit anymore. I was like, I'm gonna do my thing, and if people think I'm an idiot, fuck them. And that's *freedom*." He founded the Flaming Lips shortly thereafter.

In 1989, Oklahoma City celebrated its one hundredth birthday. This was supposed to have been the grand payoff. Back when the Pei Plan had been proposed, in the optimistic days of 1964, city leaders imagined that the centenary would be an orgiastic celebration of OKC's greatness. The city, they fantasized, would host the World's Fair. The new downtown malls would be overflowing with shoppers, the huge new roads surging with cars. The Pei model, by then, was supposed to have come to life in the real world.

Instead, Oklahoma City in 1989 looked only like a ruined version of Oklahoma City. The crowning glory of urban renewal, Pei's grand Galleria mall, was never built. Those six dense urban blocks had been destroyed for absolutely no reason. The area became a vast parking lot. I. M. Pei, in 1989, was off in Paris, presiding over the opening of his celebrated renovation of the Louvre. In Oklahoma City, the roof of the convention center leaked so badly that dinner guests had to hold umbrellas. Even if OKC had managed to win a bid for the World's Fair, it wouldn't have been able to afford to host it. Instead, in 1989 OKC hosted the Olympic Festival, an off-year pseudo-Olympics hosted by minor American cities such as Colorado Springs and Syracuse and Baton Rouge. The festival was directed by Clay Bennett, then only twenty-nine years old. Its motto was "Winning a Place in the World."

In a touch of civic poetry, the mayor in 1989 was Ron Norick, the son of Jim Norick—the mayor who had presided over the Great Annexation and urban renewal. Norick the Younger would have to find a way to rescue the city from the failed grand plans of his father's regime. In 1989, he tried, but failed, to land a new American Airlines maintenance center for OKC. (The company chose the sexier destination of Fort Worth.) The following year, Norick went after United Airlines, which was planning to build a repair facility that promised $1 billion in construction, eight thousand jobs, and $700 million in annual revenue. For that kind of economic stability, OKC would have traded in two generations of its young people. Nearly a hundred American cities lined up to compete, but few of them could muster the raw desperate hunger of Oklahoma City. Legislators called emergency sessions to concoct outrageous corporate incentives. OKC's citizens even agreed to tax themselves to raise $120 million more—a measure that passed, amazingly, with 72 percent of the vote.

One by one, civic competitors fell away—Cincinnati, Dulles, Fort Worth—until OKC found itself in United's final ten. Then it was in the final four, and then—after Denver yielded—in the final three.

Louisville folded.

After nearly a year of wooing, United's decision came down to Oklahoma City and Indianapolis. Outside United's headquarters in Chicago, in full daily view of all the decision makers, a new billboard went up: "Come Fly the Friendly Skies of Oklahoma City."

United chose Indianapolis. The company's CEO told Norick that OKC's proposal had been, by a large margin, "the best prepared, well organized, the most professional, the most courteous, the most responsive." OKC, essentially, had won. But it had lost, and because of one problem: United could not imagine making its employees live there. Indianapolis had NBA basketball, NFL football, public transportation, a downtown canal, and renovated old buildings with shops and restaurants and hotels. Oklahoma City had a dry riverbed and a blasted vacant downtown and empty restaurants that served chicken-fried steak.

This rejection was a new civic low point. Revenue was zero, the infrastructure was wrecked, the population was unnaturally dispersed, and the young people had—quite sensibly—left. Oil companies were beginning to sneak off to Houston. Everything the city tried only seemed to make everything worse. Oklahoma City's grandiose self-image bore less resemblance to reality than it ever had. The place was, as Mayor Norick put it, "a blank." "You could shoot a cannon down the street," he said, "and it wasn't going to hurt anybody." The chamber of commerce polled OKC's citizens and found that 65 percent did not think it was a good place to live. The chamber responded, naturally, with a PR campaign, disseminated on the radio and in print, called "It's a Wonderful Life (in Oklahoma City)." But it wasn't, not in most of the important ways. No more booms were on the way. The city had no more dice left to throw.

GAME 70: WESTBROOK, WESTBROOK, WESTBROOK, WESTBROOK, WESTBROOK

On the basketball court, all through the spring of 2013, the Process held. After KD's cursing and Westbrook's storming, the squabbles quieted. Tempers cooled. Wins mounted. Heading toward the end of the season, there was exactly the lack of drama you would want in a serious title run. The team looked like heavy contenders—more dangerous, even, than they had been the year before. They were 50–19, the best record in the West, and they were outscoring opponents by an average of more than nine points a game—a margin that put them right up there with some of the best teams in basketball history: Bill Russell's Celtics, Magic Johnson's Lakers. A rematch with Miami in the Finals seemed like a virtual certainty, and this time the Thunder would go into it better than the year before. They were efficient, long, fast, mean, professional, and wildly athletic, with two legitimate superstars. Looking this good, after sacrificing a talent as magnificent as James Harden, was already a front-office victory. But of course what counted, at this point, was success in the play-offs.

In the last few weeks of the regular season, Kevin Durant found himself in a virtual statistical tie with the Knicks' Carmelo Anthony for the league lead in scoring. A little push, a few extra shots here and there, would bring him his fourth scoring title in a row. Instead, Durant let it go. He shot infrequently and sat during blowouts, watching his average decrease. It was as if he were doing Anthony a favor, or perhaps proving a point. Over the final ten games of the season, as Anthony hoisted twenty or thirty shots a game, Durant held himself to a modest ten or fifteen. He was done, it seemed, with individual accolades. All he wanted was a championship.

The Thunder were so dominant toward the end of the year that even Daniel Orton started to get real playing time. Over one two-week span, he played in five games, including nearly half of a game against Sacramento, during which he looked like an all-star: he flew around the rim, tipping in multiple Russell Westbrook misses, and threw down one dunk so hard that the ball came popping back up off the floor like a champagne cork. Even the visiting announcing crew was impressed. His career, perhaps, was beginning to find its feet.

On March 22, the seventieth game of the season, the Thunder went to Orlando. For Orton, it was a kind of homecoming. This was his first NBA team; he still had a house in the city. These were the fans who had clamored to see him play when he'd first entered the league, when he'd been a first-round pick full of promise.

The game turned out to be a fairly comfortable Oklahoma City win, but Orton didn't play. Afterward, a crowd of fans stood waiting near the Thunder's bus to get a glimpse of the players. When Orton walked out, a cheer went up, screams of recognition.

People started to chant.

West-BROOK!

West-BROOK!

West-BROOK!

West-BROOK!

Orton kept walking and got on the bus.

THE EAST

As I explored Oklahoma City, I got into the habit of asking the people I met—architects, journalists, historians, policemen, athletes, planners—to show me around *their* OKC. It's such a big and disconnected place; eventually, I figured, I'd be able to overlay all these different maps, to start to understand how the many worlds inside of the city related to one another. Early on, I drove around the city with a rapper and activist named Jabee Williams. He was polite but also bluntly honest, acknowledging the city's failures while declaring, almost in spite of himself, his love for it. He had moved constantly as a kid, so he knew the whole city, and to drive with him was to see an entirely different OKC from the one I'd been shown on my official city-sanctioned tours. It was like seeing the place under an ultraviolet light. He pointed out neighborhoods that were excluded from all the tourist maps, places I'd passed by hundreds of times without even thinking to look. We drove through the North Highlands, right next to the super-rich enclave of Nichols Hills, and although it looked to me like any other suburb, Jabee said it was one of the poorest places in the city, gang territory, and as we drove he kept pointing out red cars, which he said meant allegiance to the Bloods. We passed apartment complexes that had recently been fixed up and given fancy names like "Heritage Pointe," but Jabee said not to be fooled. Those places were bad—so bad that you wouldn't go in unless you had family there. Every thriving section of OKC seemed to have some secret pocket of misfortune attached to it, one or two blocks off, places that were immune to booms and somehow extra vulnerable to busts. We drove through Deep Deuce and an area called Parker Estates. We drove past farms, woods, empty lots, abandoned strip malls, and vast stretches that looked like untouched prairie. Jabee knew it all.

"What's this neighborhood called?" I asked at one point, in what seemed like the middle of nowhere.

"I don't think this really has a name," Jabee said. "We would probably just call it the East Side."

But the East Side seemed to be everywhere. "There's a lot of East," I said.

"Exactly," he said.

The city's white neighborhoods had, in recent years, been lovingly divided into distinct microhoods. You couldn't go three blocks without encountering a sign: Automobile Alley, Midtown, Heritage Hills, Mesta Park, the Plaza District, the Paseo. And yet large portions of the East Side, which dwarfed all of these neighborhoods geographically, remained untrendy and unlabeled. Even to those who knew it best, much of it was simply the East Side.

Mayor Jim Norick's urban renewal board was, naturally, entirely white. When challenged on this point, he was defensive. "There are people on this board who can represent the Negroes on the eastside as well as anyone," he insisted.

Unfortunately, the evidence did not bear this out. James Baldwin once said that urban renewal meant "Negro removal," and this was certainly true in Oklahoma City. On the East Side, the city's urban renewal vision revolved around a huge new medical complex that would require bulldozing large swaths of houses. Some influential leaders of the black community, however, agreed to support it. Their thinking was that urban renewal was an anti-poverty program, and the East could use some anti-poverty. City planners promised that dilapidated buildings would be knocked down, but that homes worth saving would be fixed, and that the area's terrible infrastructure would finally be improved. Local civil rights leader Jimmy Stewart, a disciple of Roscoe Dunjee's, agreed to participate as an adviser.

Things did not work out as he had hoped. In true OKC style, the plan quickly grew out of control. In 1965, the city's leaders visited Texas, where they saw that Houston's new medical center was practically a city unto itself. They came home inspired. In Oklahoma City's original plan, the medical complex took up fifty acres. Now it would occupy more than two hundred. This would mean, of course, the destruction of more of the black community—not just dilapidated tenements but solid middle-class homes. Stewart eventually pulled his support and started fighting urban renewal, but by then it was too late. Neighborhoods were cleared. The medical center was built. New freeways, with their gigantic cloverleaf ramps, were stamped on top of more bulldozed black homes. The fractions of neighborhoods that survived were suddenly islands, cut off from the rest of the city not only by the freeways and the medical center but, eventually, by large new government buildings with parking lots the size of city blocks. What would once have been a pleasant walk down to Deep Deuce was now basically impossible.

Toward the end of my drive with Jabee, he steered me over toward the medical center. Medical *centers,* actually, plural, because over the decades, they just kept coming, stamping out more and more houses in the East. The poor neighborhoods got smaller and poorer. Jabee drove me to one of the tiny remaining pockets, where his aunt still lived in a house that had been in the family for generations. Traffic roared nearby on the freeway. Next door, an abandoned house had recently burned down. Not far from there, we passed the Governor's Mansion, and then the Oklahoma History Center, a shining glass temple to the preservation of the past. Jabee waved his hand at it. "All this used to be houses," he said. "I had homeys living in these houses. All this was houses. All this was houses." Where did they go? I asked. "They went further East," he said.

GAME 83: FIVE AGAINST ONE

The NBA play-offs started on a Sunday: April 21, 2013. This was what all of Oklahoma City had been waiting for. The regular season was fine, it was a blessing, it had its moments, but this was where the glory was. All year, the time had been streaming by like wind, streaming toward this, and now the great low-pressure swirl of eternity was beginning to gather itself up, thickening, condensing into a single moment that everyone could inhabit and savor and remember forever. It was all beginning to happen. The previous year's loss in the Finals, the self-doubt after the Harden trade, OKC's many decades as a national nonentity, a site of only tragedy or disappointment, a non-place—all of this could change now. A non-place did not win an NBA championship.

That morning, like most of the rest of Oklahoma City, I went to church. I did so at the urging of Wayne Coyne. This was a crucial aspect of the culture, Wayne said, something most residents built their lives around, and I would never fully understand the place if I neglected it. And, of course, that was true. Angelo Scott had helped found First Presbyterian, Clara Luper had gathered her sit-in demonstrators at Calvary Baptist, Stanley Draper had been a superintendent at St. Luke's. (He'd always left precisely on time, and if his family wasn't in the car, he drove off without them.) There were many hundreds of churches to choose from, but Wayne recommended, as a perfect distillation of the current culture of OKC, a new one called LifeChurch.tv. This was a rapidly expanding franchise. Its reputation was young, hip, modern, suburban, and light—church for young pro-

fessional families, convenient to the freeway, without all the boring ceremony or historical baggage of the older churches downtown. If you couldn't make it to your local branch of LifeChurch.tv in person, you were invited to watch on the Internet, following along in your e-Bible, with no shame or judgment attached.

And so, very early in the morning, I found myself merging onto the freeway to drive up the Centennial Expressway, north, along the border of the East Side, next to the route of the original railroad tracks, all the way out to suburban Edmond, to the flagship campus of LifeChurch.tv. I slid into the enormous parking lot and entered the capacious lobby. I passed the children's play area, which was bright and extravagant and fully staffed, like a displaced pocket of Disney World. An usher handed me a pamphlet. I entered the sanctuary, which was vast and dramatic in the style of a TV game show set, complete with dramatic miniature spotlights pointing every which way and exposed steel beams all over the ceiling and live music from a rippingly professional Christian rock band. If a Starbucks drin[k] could be a church, it would be LifeChurch.tv.

I settled into a pew.

The pastor strolled the stage in jeans, and after some introducto[ry] remarks he directed our attention to a large screen on which anot[her] man in jeans, with rolled-up sleeves and the hint of a goatee, sp[oke] enthusiastically about the Lord. "Oh, snap!" he said. "Check this[.] Jesus had a problem." He referenced Twitter and Facebook and "YouVersion Bible app." The day's pamphlet had a series of fi[ll-] the-blank questions, and the speaker prompted us frequently [for] the answers. "Let's bring this down to street level," he said. "Jesu[s is] really serious about this deal."

When the e-sermon was done, the screen went dark. Ou[r] emcee stepped back onstage. It happened to be the Sunday aft[er a ter]rorist attack at the Boston Marathon, an incident that, for hi[storical] reasons, had special resonance in OKC. Our LifeChurch.tv [pastor] offered the congregation guidance. "Here's what we do," he s[aid. "We] shine brightly. That's what we do. We let the light of Jesus[, in] us, shine as brightly as it can, because there is no darknes[s

no terror, there is no hatred or evil that could even come close to competing with the light of Jesus Christ. The light of God eradicates it and illuminates it, all day long."

As the offering plates came around, the minister told us that anything we could spare would help the church spread the gospel, via the Internet, "primarily in Muslim countries."

"Do you realize that?" he said. "You are lighting the world when you give."

Before sending us back out onto OKC's freeways, the LifeChurch .tv emcee mentioned one last thing. The NBA play-offs were beginning that night, he said, and this prompted a theological question. Did God prefer one team over the others? The crowd laughed knowingly. As a man of God, the minister said, all he could do was consult scripture. He opened his Bible and read us Psalm 29. "The voice of the Lord is over the waters," he said. "And the God of glory"— he paused to look out meaningfully at the crowd—"thunders." The sanctuary exploded.

The play-offs could begin, now with God's blessing.

The Thunder's first-round opponent did, in fact, seem divinely chosen. It was the Houston Rockets, which meant that OKC's title run would have to begin with the destruction of James Harden, the first impurity in the Thunder fairy tale, the cause of so much trouble and wounded love and civic self-doubt. During Game 1, I sat next to Royce Young, proprietor of the *Daily Thunder* blog, who drew my attention before tip-off to the teams' official programs. The cover of the Rockets' featured Harden, by himself, screaming ecstatically while popping his jersey in triumph; the cover of the Thunder's featured a photo of the entire team, all twelve of them, from Kevin Durant to Daniel Orton, looking serious and professional and determined. It was the perfect statement of the two different organizational philosophies, and at least part of the reason Harden had wanted out of OKC. The Thunder, with two of the brightest superstars in the game, refused to promote any individual over the group. Their portrait was

defiantly, boringly corporate. Orton was, at least on paper, as important as his miniature doppelgänger Westbrook. It was pure Sam Presti.

Game 1 was a sustained on-court demonstration of these competing philosophies. While the Rockets relied almost exclusively on Harden, the Thunder were cohesive and overpowering. It was an almost instant blowout. The Thunder dunked and swatted away layups, the Rockets missed their first nine shots, and OKC led at halftime by thirteen, and in the fourth quarter by thirty-five. Harden was swarmed and harassed, reduced to nearly impossible shots—stepback jumpers and twisting layups—and the crowd cheered each of his many misses as if they were apologies. The game was one long civic party. The fans whipped towels around while full-throatedly singing the title song from *Oklahoma!* Whenever a Thunder player missed a free throw, the crowd gave him a huge ovation to encourage him for the next one. It was a whole new level of ecstasy, beyond anything I'd seen in the regular season. During a break in play, when a fan made a half-court shot to earn $20,000, the cheering was so loud it felt like a solid block of noise on the floor. At one point I shouted at Royce, who was sitting two feet away, about how loud it was. He shouted back that this was nothing—during previous play-off runs, he said, we wouldn't have been able to hear one another even if we'd been screaming directly into each other's ears. So OKC was holding something back. It had been to the first round plenty of times before, had begun to expect the glory. In the fourth quarter, after the blowout was secure, Scott Brooks pulled all the starters, and OKC fans started to leave the arena with six minutes left to play. That, it seemed, was that.

Westbrook and Durant appeared at the postgame media table together. Durant wore a leather jacket over a paisley button-up shirt. "There's nobody like this guy," he said of his point guard, who wore large translucent glasses along with a thick gold chain over a sleeveless black sweatshirt.

Later, Harden slouched over the same table, his beard tucked against his chest, murmuring sadly. He complained that every possession felt like he'd been going one-on-five—an analysis that was essentially correct. But then that's what he'd signed up for when he'd left Oklahoma City, and it was clearly not going to be enough to win, at least not this year, not against this team. Game 1 felt, somehow, like a single-game series sweep. Game 2 was coming, and a couple of more games after that, but Thunder fans were already allowing themselves to begin to think ahead, not just to the second game but to the second round, and then the third, and then the Finals, and then the championship parade on Reno Avenue, and then further championship parades in the years to follow. James Harden was now no longer part of the story of the destiny of OKC, and that seemed just fine. It was his loss. Two superstars would to be more than enough.

WE WHO HAVE LONG BEEN DUST SALUTE YOU

Children reenact the Land Run at school.

At midnight, while the city was still basking in the afterglow of Game 1, the calendar clicked over to an extremely important date in Oklahoma City: April 22, Land Run Day—the anniversary of the chaotic beginning of it all.

OKC loves to celebrate the insanity of its origin, so April 22 has always been a low-grade secular holiday. In the city's early years, there were downtown parades featuring the 1889ers themselves, who would ride in wearing the same gear they'd rode in with on that first afternoon. As the decades passed and the pioneers died off, young Oklahomans learned to carry on that tradition. Land Run Day became part of the elementary school curriculum. Every April 22, a new generation of OKC kids was taught to re-create the historic event in miniature out on the playground. They'd dress up in cowboy hats and bonnets, unite into temporary families, form strategic alliances, load up little red wagons with supplies, and then—at noon—they'd race off to stake claims next to the monkey bars or the curly slide or the baseball diamond or the tetherball poles. Jabee, the rapper, told me that his mother refused to let him participate—she said the Land Run was not for black people, and anyway, the land had been stolen from the native tribes, so her son would not be playacting any kind of tribute. His teacher let him sit out while the other kids ran.

April 22, 2013, was an even more special Land Run Day than usual. The people of Oklahoma City had been waiting for it, in fact, for exactly one hundred years. The day had arrived, finally, to open the Century Chest—the time capsule buried by Angelo Scott and the other leading citizens of 1913.

Around 9:00 a.m., people started to file into the wooden pews of the First Lutheran Church. The governor and the mayor came, as did bankers and oil barons, chamber of commerce members, city council representatives—all the people you would have seen at the play-off game the night before. So many ordinary citizens showed up that the crowd overflowed the church itself and spilled into an auxiliary tent out back, where a screen had been set up to show the ceremony via live stream. This added an appropriately 1889 vibe: under a cloudless April sky, a throng of citizens crowded into a tent. History seemed ready to burst out into the present.

And history did. A crew of workers, solemn as pallbearers, carried the Century Chest into the church. It even looked like a crude coffin: a battered metal box big enough to hold a man. The mood in the room was subdued exhilaration—a crowd trying hard not to be as excited as we all actually were. Time capsules are notoriously disappointing. They are supposed to be magic existential wormholes to a lost reality, but instead they are almost always empty, damaged, full of junk—further depressing evidence (as if we needed any) of the absolute tyranny of time. Oklahoma, in fact, had recently experienced one of the most notorious time capsule disappointments in history. In 2007, the citizens of Tulsa had gathered to see a 1957 Plymouth sports car, fresh from the factory, brought up out of a concrete bunker that had allegedly been strong enough to withstand a nuclear bomb. After fifty years underground, however, the car looked less like a cherry antique than like an ancient shipwreck, a car-shaped film of rust, and everything inside it had dissolved, and one of the organizers actually cried.

The Century Chest had been entombed, beneath five feet of concrete, since the year before the breakout of World War I. It sat, now, in front of us in the church. We silenced our cell phones and fidgeted in our pews. Politicians made prefatory remarks. Finally, the chest was opened. There was a moment of suspense before the historians, with their white gloves, began to remove the items, one by one. As soon as they did, it became clear that the Century Chest was not going to be disappointing at all. The Ladies Aid Society had sealed the box perfectly. We were about to experience something that felt like time travel: the world of 1913 right there in the room with us, in all of its fresh urgency.

The historians held up item after item for the crowd. A little boy's dress suit, from one of the old downtown shops, still folded neatly and looking brand-new. A wooden Choctaw bow. A 1913 phone book, plus a clunky old-timey phone to make calls with. A judge's gavel. A glass container of wheat. Newspapers from the day the Century Chest was sealed, hot off the presses, tucked into the chest moments before the lid went on. A black pair of ladies' shoes, retail price five dollars, still gleaming with a visible shine.

It was an overwhelming abundance. The documents were all marvelously dry, and the colors were so bright that, more than once, the crowd in the church gasped. This was the Platonic ideal of a time capsule—no mold, no rust, no death, no decay. There were photographs of Geronimo, of David Payne, and of OKC in all of its early phases: one hour before the Land Run, nine days later, six weeks later. There was a Kodak camera full of undeveloped film. There were hotel restaurant menus and high school yearbooks and reference works about the science of chiropracty. There was a Choctaw hymnal and an Osage translation of the Lord's Prayer. There were personal letters addressed "to my children's children," "to the Modern Woodmen of America," "to the Art Museum," "to the Worshipful Master, Wardens and Brethren of Oklahoma City Lodge No. 36, A.F. & A.M. and its Masonic Posterity of the Year 2013." The blind citizens of 1913 had included a letter, in Braille, to the blind citizens of 2013. It was an effort of the past to reach out and touch the present.

The historians took out wax cylinders, which contained—almost unbelievably—audio recordings of the early citizens singing and speaking. The chest even contained a machine to play the cylinders on. One cylinder held the voice of Angelo Scott himself—he had recorded it, on this very spot, inside the First Lutheran Church, exactly one hundred years before, at the original Century Chest ceremony. Scott read, aloud, the letter he had written to us, the people of the future. He was an orator, trained in the grand old nineteenth-century style, and on the wax cylinder his voice sounds echoey, a little stilted. But what he said gave me chills. "We are consciously making ancestors of ourselves today," Angelo Scott told us. "We who have long been dust . . . salute you."

One hundred years was suddenly nothing. Our now began to blend with the now of the Oklahoma City that was gone. Time circulated freely, we inhaled and exhaled it, we twisted with its twisting. We felt the fullness of these absent people's lives and, by extension, the fullness of our own future absence. It was disorienting, uncanny, thrilling, scary.

The Century Chest organizers had commissioned the leading citizens of 1913 to write predictions about life in 2013. A physician predicted that we would all have evolved to be physically short, weak, and nearsighted, with giant heads, but also that we would by now have eradicated cancer and houseflies. An Episcopal bishop predicted that all the world's religious sects would have merged into Christianity. "The newspaper of one hundred years hence," the editor of the *Oklahoman* wrote, "ought to be, and will be, I believe, a veritable paragon of accuracy, terseness and comprehensiveness." A lawyer predicted the liberation of women. "Where now women amuse themselves with bridge whist and pink teas at their social functions," he wrote, "then they will pass the time discussing affairs of state, and the betterment of their fellow beings." Anton Classen, the father of the streetcar system, prognosticated that transportation in 2013 would run on compressed air. The president of the American National Bank seemed to predict e-mail.

The 1913 manager of the Huckins Hotel wrote a letter to the hotel's current manager, summarizing the building's history and financial prospects, as well as sharing strangely personal details: "The writer is about 5 feet 11 ½ inches tall, and weighs 231 pounds, with redish [*sic*] hair, and slight [*sic*] bald." It ended on a note of optimism: "Wishing you success, and trusting the property is still a handsome money maker." The Huckins Hotel had been demolished in 1971, however, as part of urban renewal.

The inventory of the Century Chest was admirably precise. It accounted for every single object but one. There was, somehow, an inexplicable glass marble. It was loose, unwrapped, unlabeled, rolling freely around in the chest. The historians were flummoxed. Their best guess was that a child might have popped it in there at the last second, while none of the adults were looking—perhaps while they were praying. And that of course was the perfect OKC touch: one speck of uncertainty, a single atom of chaos, had been rattling around, for one hundred years, in the midst of all the order.

ALL YOUR BAD DAYS WILL END

Sitting in my Century Chest pew, in that tangle of Oklahoma City time, I started to feel existentially confused. Everything in OKC seemed to be coming together: its founding and its future, its basketball and its civics. The place seemed, against all the odds, right on the verge of realizing its founders' most grandiose visions. The Spirit of the Land Run was alive, galloping around, firing its pistols into the air, and—to my surprise—it was alive in me, too. For many months I had been reading about Oklahomans, talking with Oklahomans, dancing with Oklahomans, gossiping with Oklahomans, interviewing living Oklahomans about dead Oklahomans, thinking about what made Oklahomans Oklahoman, trying to distill their Oklahoma-ness. The vanished people and their vanished places had begun to seem alive again. I had come to believe in Oklahoma City as a radical experiment in something—an expression of American democracy or American foolishness—and I felt a stake in its well-being. I wanted its public tax programs to remain wise and generous, wanted its boulevard to be well-designed, wanted the black and white communities to know and respect and love one another. I wanted its remaining interesting buildings to be saved. I wanted honesty and openness to prevail over secrecy. I wanted its actual history to be acknowledged, regardless of how ugly. I wanted Kevin Durant and Russell Westbrook to coexist, wanted the loss of Harden to be survivable, wanted Presti's Process to be vindicated and celebrated, wanted the city to abandon its booms and busts and embrace something more sustainable. I wanted Daniel Orton to play himself into the rotation and get meaningful minutes during the play-offs, to somehow find himself on the court in Game 7 of the Finals, where he would block LeBron James's game-winning dunk attempt as time expired and become the hero who brought a championship to his hometown. I wanted Wayne Coyne's love to come into full equilibrium with the external world. I wanted tragedies to stop busting out of the Oklahoma sky, for no good reason, on otherwise clear spring days. Irrationally, at this point, I felt almost Oklahoman myself. I felt that I existed in all the different versions of Oklahoma City at once. I felt like I wanted to make the Land Run.

A little before noon, I got up from my church pew and left the Century Chest ceremony. I walked out to my rental car and drove away from downtown—it was so easy to leave, so fast and smooth— and I merged onto the Centennial Expressway heading north, and then onto Stanley Draper's Highway 62 heading east, and soon the City of Oklahoma City receded behind me until all that was left was the Devon Tower on the horizon, and soon even that was gone, and the city turned into the country, and I felt like I was driving backward in time, rewinding the founding. The prairie began to reassert itself, the wide sky to spread out wider. I drove out into the vast non-human expanse, past the borders even of the Great Annexation. The towns that had tried to take purchase here, over the years, had never amounted to much. This was land that still belonged stubbornly to the land.

I drove as near as I could to the eastern border of the Unassigned Lands, what the settlers of 1889 called the "Pott Line," because the territory on the other side belonged to the Potawatomi Indians. It was the closest point of entry to the spot that would become Oklahoma City, and—best of all for the settlers—it was unsupervised. On April 22, the morning itself, something like a thousand people gathered there, at a ranch house right near the border, which belonged to William McClure, who would become (thanks to his relay of fresh horses set along the trail) the first legal settler of Oklahoma City. In the absence of soldiers, the Pott Line settlers had to signal the start of the Land Run themselves. At noon, or something like it, a man tied three handkerchiefs to a pole and swung it down. Everyone charged off into the future.

I arrived from that future, exactly 124 years too late. Today the Pott Line is nothing. It runs, unmarked, through a small country town called Choctaw, which sits just outside the reach of modern Oklahoma City's massive gravitational pull. I drove down Choctaw's abbreviated Main Street and parked behind a Baptist church. I tried to imagine what the scene would have looked like 124 years earlier. There would have been no church, of course, no asphalt. A ranch. The primordial trees uncut. Prairie grass up to my knees. I would have stood jockeying for starting position in the middle of a thousand competitors—men on horses, on wagons, on foot. "Oklahoma or Bust," some of the settlers would have scrawled on their wagons, ignoring the fact that those options were not mutually exclusive. We would have smelled terrible, waiting there, like many lifetimes of non-showers, and we would have exuded the unsettling buzz of mass desperation—that very Oklahoman, very American feeling that everything was right about to change forever, for the better. Most of us would have been wrong.

On this day, in 2013, the Pott Line was quiet. At noon, I fired a mental starting gun and began to walk west toward Oklahoma City.

I walked down the middle of a residential street. A military jet made a shredding noise overhead; a rottweiler in someone's yard strained murderously against its chain. Everything else was quiet. It was as if the population of Choctaw had been vacuumed out, as if they had scattered in another Land Run a few minutes before I arrived. Only the wind remained, stroking the trees. The weather was sunny and warm, with cotton-puff clouds, completely unthreatening, exactly as it had been in 1889. The sky, the wind—they hadn't changed at all. What had changed were things on the ground.

On the edge of Choctaw, I passed through a failed shopping center. An abandoned Blockbuster Video was wrapped in yellow crime-scene tape; a 99-cent superstore had handwritten CLOSING SALE signs taped to its dark windows. What looked like an abandoned construction site—a huge field of bright red dirt covered in concrete tubes—had a sign in the middle that said CHOCTAW TOWN SQUARE.

I kept walking. One advantage I had over the 1889ers was that

I was able to follow a straight and steady road. This was a gift from Stanley Draper: Highway 62, four lanes of traffic that extended, for no good reason, from El Paso to Niagara Falls via OKC. There were no sidewalks, so I walked through the dry, scrubby grass on the shoulder. Grasshoppers, big and small, hurled themselves away from my feet. Cars passed constantly, at roughly fifty miles per hour, a speed that seemed to belong to a different world. At one point, the driver of a white pickup truck stuck his head out the window and yowled at me—an incoherent animal scream, dopplering off toward the horizon in the direction of Buffalo.

For the next two hours, that yowl was the only human contact I had. Otherwise, it was just me and the signs: speed limits, city limits, and advertisements for stores that looked like they'd been empty for thirty years. Each sign was a little slab of frozen Oklahoman language. Papa's Pawn Shop. WE DO BOAT SEATS. Trailer Trash Treatz: Gourmet Shaved Ice. Don Shawn Drilling. DP's Cutrate Liquor: STACK 'EM HIGH, SELL 'EM LOW. I passed a yard sale that consisted entirely of animal cages, ranging from the size of a deer to the size of a squirrel.

Failed businesses lined the highway like bad metaphors, their billboards speaking empty words to cars. A big red arrow pointed to a beaten yellow shack. EDIE'S CHICKEN, said the sign. Its front door was held shut by a cinder block and labeled with a handwritten note:

> Thief Beware
> Traps have been set.
> Enter at your own Risk.

I kept walking. I passed a dirt field that seemed to have been set aside for dumping dirt on. I passed prefab houses lined up like canned goods. I passed multiple automated ice booths. I passed an old yellow race car, gutted, with solid grass growing up in place of its engine block.

Every once in a while the landscape offered a scrap of pure beauty. A little creek ran off undisturbed into the woods, swooped over by iridescent birds. There were huge grassy sweeps that seemed untouched. I walked over dry Oklahoma dirt, Martian red and cracked, sculpted with occasional ant mounds.

Four miles in, a blister started forming on my left heel, and I could feel the skin on my face getting tight and hot and tender in the sun. Summoning the Spirit of '89, I marched on. I started tallying the roadside garbage: hubcaps, empty rounds of chewing tobacco, soda cans crushed and bleached beyond recognition, a child's old bedroom door covered with Mickey Mouse stickers, a discarded work glove, a blank CD on which someone had written, in cursive letters, "Melissa." I saw something that looked like a grenade but was actually a drink called Buzzballz. At a twenty-four-hour gas station, probably around where William McClure had changed horses for the first time, I bought two Clif Bars and a toxic-flavored orange sports drink containing protein, which I had seen on the NBA's postgame media tables. This, I felt, was what the pioneers might have bought. A killdeer sprinted across a field, faking a broken wing, trying to lure me away from its nest.

I'm not sure what I had expected to find on my walk, but it was something slightly less shitty than this. All cities are rimmed by some form of non-city: wilderness, emptiness, suburbs. But this was uncommonly bleak. The outskirts of OKC had not been buoyed, through the global economic meltdown, by fracking money or public taxes. Beige vinyl siding reigned supreme. It made me think about OKC's obsessive quest, for its entire history, to turn itself into a real city—to build as majestic a downtown as possible and annex all of this inhuman prairie scrub and fill it with homes. OKC was more than just a city; it was an existential crusade, an attempt to assert the primacy of consciousness, of human life, in this endless sea of nothing. It had to keep booming, because whenever it stopped to rest, the prairie rose up and tried to swallow it. The promise of 1889 had turned out to be, for almost everyone involved, a fantasy. The route of the Land Run was filled with failure—ancient, recent, present, and imminent. Oklahoma's various busts had run on through the decades, mutating and growing, all the way to now. This countryside felt impossibly far from the downtown renaissance, the placemakers, the international glory of the Thunder.

After four and a half miles, the land rose gently and I thought I could see something in the distance: a vertical line bisecting the horizon, the tiniest hint of the Oklahoma City skyline. I couldn't tell if it was the Devon Tower or the capitol dome, business or civics, but it seemed like an outpost of civilization, so I kept walking. My sunburn was getting worse, and so was the blister on my heel, and as the landscape gently dipped and rose, that shadowy vertical line appeared and disappeared, over and over, and I started to wonder, after a while, if it was a mirage. Maybe the pioneers had seen it, too. A mile or so later, just past Boss Hog Automotive, I recognized what I was looking at: it was the Devon Tower, far ahead and hazy, off to the left—but also, straight ahead of me, on Twenty-third, the dome of the capitol. Business and civics, both of them. I kept walking, past wasted wheelless cars sitting up on blocks, past a place called Anointed Hands Salon, "Where We're Not Just a Salon But a Ministry Experience."

Two hours into my Land Run walk, I reached a cluster of big box stores. My legs, at this point, were tired. I was breathing hard. The skin on my face was now officially burned. My blister was a problem. I bought sunscreen at Walgreens. On the counter was a stack of newspapers called *Just Busted,* the cover of which promised "METH & MURDER PAGES INSIDE!!!" I asked the woman at the counter who would ever buy such a thing, and she said people bought them all the time. I bought one. It was a grid of mug shots, page after page, people looking dopey, vicious, angry, or blank—a fold-out gallery of desperation, defiance, befuddlement, shame. It occurred to me, for the first time, that I might not be entirely safe on my Land Run walk. Outside the Walgreens, I took my shoes off and put multiple Band-Aids on my heel, and the wind lifted the wrappers and scattered them across the parking lot.

I walked again on Highway 62. Soon I passed over a concrete bridge. A sign said, CRUTCHO CREEK. My heart leaped. This creek, in 1889, had hosted a notorious nest of Sooners, camping out illegally to wait for the Run. Occasionally, in the weeks before April 22, troops would come here to drive them all away, and the Sooners would scatter and hide in the woods. In the 1890s, Roscoe Dunjee crossed Crutcho Creek all the time, hauling fresh tomatoes from his father's farm to sell in OKC. I stopped and looked over the edge of the bridge. There was hardly any water, and the creek bed was loaded with old tires.

I passed a green hill leaping out of a lake, and I wondered if this was perhaps the site of Ewing, David Payne's great early city in the wilderness in the middle of the Unassigned Lands—and I could see exactly why he would have chosen it, because it was epic and lovely and just the place. But then I saw big industrial trucks driving all over it, and a booming sound filled the landscape, and a thick bad smell took over the road, and I realized that this was a landfill, a mountain of garbage.

I kept walking.

An oil pump worked in a field directly across the road from a group of rough-looking men sitting outside the Oklahoma County Social Services building.

Finally, after nearly three hours of walking the Land Run route, I reached the outer edge of Oklahoma City. This was marked by the North Canadian River, which at this point was shallow and wandering, with sand humped into irregular patterns by the wind and water—not at all the brimming canal it had been turned into downtown. The dirt here was deep red. Green grass waved on the banks. Birds flew everywhere. It was sunny and easy. In the distance, in the sand next to the river, a man on an ATV took a turn too fast and rolled over.

WELCOME TO OKLAHOMA CITY, a sign said, under an outdated drawing of the skyline.

Here, then, was the place the settlers had gone to so much trouble to create—all of that death and risk and lying. But few of the 1889ers would have stopped all the way out here. This was Great Annexation territory—it would have been aimless prairie then—so I kept walking, too.

Eventually, civilization started to thicken. I passed an old religious complex that had been abandoned and a new religious complex that had never been finished—both casualties of the economic crash. Inside the city limits, Highway 62 turns into Twenty-Third Street, the old commercial spine of the East. This threshold was marked, for me, by two things: the arrival of a sidewalk—the first I'd seen in nearly twelve miles of walking—and a bad smell so sudden and strong that I almost vomited. It took me a few seconds to find its source. It was a dead pit bull, its back half crushed and rotting into pulp. A used condom sat near it on the grass.

I thought of Wayne Coyne, who was always texting me pictures of dead dogs from his neighborhood. Wayne had been in my head anyway, because a Flaming Lips song was stuck in there, looping over and over to the rhythm of my footsteps, for hours. It was a song from the early 1990s called "Bad Days," and its chorus went: "All your bad days will end. All your bad days will end. You have to sleep late when you can. And all your bad days will end." Involuntarily, this had become the soundtrack of my Land Run walk. What struck me about it, somewhere in the third hour, was the sly double meaning of those words, optimistic and pessimistic at once: all your bad days will end.

I was getting now into the meat of OKC. BEAUTIFUL AND HISTORIC NORTHEAST 23RD STREET, a sign said, and I walked over a freeway overpass, and another sign peeked out from the trees: CLARA LUPER CORRIDOR. Cars roared beneath me. This struck me as an insanely insufficient memorial to one of America's great unheralded civil rights leaders, but that was it and there it was. I walked on. I passed the entrance to a residential neighborhood whose sign was missing so many letters—NOR H CRE ON H LI S—that it took me a while to realize it was North Creston Hills, one of the subdivisions created during the 1928 oil boom by John James Harden, the "asphalt czar" who made his fortune, in Draper's era, paving the city's exploding network of roads. Harden had pitched Creston Hills as a fail-safe investment for homeowners—whites only, of course—but it soon crashed because of the Depression, and by 1960 it was, like most of the East Side, predominantly black, and its sign had fallen into illegibility. NOR H CRE ON H LI S.

I walked on, past long rows of boarded-up strip malls. This was a place Jabee had told me about: empty parking lots where kids from the East used to congregate every Sunday night, by the hundreds, to hang out and party—the Strip, they called it—until the police decided to shut the gatherings down. As I walked, multiple cars honked at me. Two different drivers slowed down and yelled out the window in a way that struck me as unfriendly. Outside the dollar store, a woman approached me and asked for a dollar. Then she asked if I was walking to the mountain, and I wasn't sure how to respond, since the nearest mountain was a hundred miles away.

I reached the fourteen-mile mark. I had been walking now, in almost total isolation, for four hours. Near the state capitol, the sidewalks suddenly disappeared, and I had to sprint across a freeway on-ramp, then through a concrete tunnel full of traffic. I passed the fancy new government complexes built on top of obliterated black neighborhoods. I stopped at a Burger King and drank cup after cup of ice water until my head felt like it belonged on my neck again.

I passed under the elevated portion of Interstate 235, the Centennial Expressway, where a homeless community seemed to be living near some bronze statues of buffalo. I passed the Blue Note, the dingy club where the Flaming Lips had played their first show ever, during the bust of the early 1980s, and nearby there were boarded-up houses and ads for gun shows and a payday loan company with an ominous sign on its door: "Attention Customers: For your protection and ours, you will be asked to remove any hoods or face coverings before you are allowed entrance!" I passed the former site of El Charrito, the Mexican restaurant where Gary England ate on his honeymoon and where, right around the same time, Clara Luper led sit-ins.

After five hours, for the first time on my Land Run walk, I turned. I took a left on Robinson Avenue, toward the city center. It was almost instantly a different world: white upper-middle-class OKC, with its picturesque cottages set back from the road—neat brick, fresh paint, elegant windows, ample lawns. I had come a long way from the beige vinyl siding of Choctaw and the chain-link fences of the East. The sidewalks here were smooth, the greenery manicured. Everything seemed intentional. I passed Angelo Scott's old house, where the cows used to moo, and the lavish mansions of Heritage Hills, and then I passed the grand facades of the churches on Church Row, including

First Lutheran, where I had been sitting nearly six hours earlier for the Century Chest ceremony. There were joggers jogging around, and a young woman walking a puppy, and a bespectacled hipster wearing a white fedora and a pin-striped salmon blazer, carrying an iPad. From the Towers Apartments, a man missing multiple teeth trotted over to tell me that he'd run out of gas, and could I please give him a dollar. I gave him a five.

Eighth Street, Seventh Street, Sixth Street, Fifth. I reached the bombing memorial, the heart of OKC terror, where everything had gone undeniably wrong—not just business failure or urban renewal but absolute cataclysm: death, amputation, psychological trauma that continued to spread through generations. I looked through the memorial's gates of time—9:01, 9:03—and thought about everything that happened at 9:02, how much time and life got compressed into that single minute.

I kept moving south. I was almost done. I stepped over a rust-colored manhole cover featuring a map of downtown bordered by the words OKLAHOMA CITY—A LAND RUN CITY. Everything started moving fast. I passed through I. M. Pei's OKC—cold glass towers, empty streets, the convention center—and through the construction zones of the current renaissance, the Thunder bonanza, and I made my way over to the corner of Main and Broadway, where Angelo Scott led the mass meetings that saved the city from civil war. On a Monday, at 6:30 p.m., no one was there. In a bank window stood a life-sized portrait of Russell Westbrook, fake smile on his face, holding his arm around the silhouette of a normal-sized human. Fans were supposed to stand there and take their picture next to him.

I did not. I kept walking south, past the Devon Tower, on the site of I. M. Pei's unbuilt supermall, where a stone bench now bore the motto "Leave things better than you found them." I paused in the absent shadow of the absent Biltmore Hotel, and then I kept walking south until I reached, finally, the place I had been walking to all along: Chesapeake Energy Arena, right at the base of downtown. From out front, I could still see the destroyed remnants of the Stanley Draper Expressway. The arena was empty, but it would soon be full again for Game 2. The energy that used to be expressed through Angelo

Scott's mass meetings, that occasionally spilled out into the streets in the form of gunfights or marches—the wild frenzy of civic self-creation—now got funneled, most often, into this building. It was as a basketball crowd that the city, these days, felt itself most powerfully as a community. Game 2 would take place two nights later—the next chance for Oklahoma City to explode into collective ecstasy.

TEAM IS ONE, a huge marquee said on the outside of the arena. OKC EST. 2008.

THE TERROR

Early in 2013, Warner Bros. Records sent out a press release announcing a new Flaming Lips album later that spring. It would be the band's thirteenth, and it would, according to the release, "reflect a darker-hued spectrum than previous works." To this, Wayne Coyne added his own statement: "If we have love, give love and know love, we are truly alive and if there is no love, there would be no life." That was classic Wayne: the whole universe orbiting a pulsing core of YESSS!!! But he continued. "*The Terror* is, we know now, that even without love, life goes on . . . we just go on . . . there is no mercy killing."

Well, that was a bummer. And it did not sound like Wayne at all. It made me both curious and afraid to hear the new album. In the intervening months, however, I forgot about it, because every time I saw Wayne he was his usual colorful self. He sat at his kitchen table, surrounded by coffee cans stuffed full of colored markers—more markers than I had ever seen outside of an art store—doodling a comic book in which the sun gets sick but then is healed by sentient brains, and a blind princess urinates rainbows and whatnot. I continued to get texts from Wayne at all hours, usually bright photos of landscapes taken out of airplane windows or of our street rainbow still wiggling around his neighborhood pavement. He appeared on TV commercials for Verizon and Hyundai, the latter of which aired during the Super Bowl. He was, in other words, good old Wayne: avatar of wacky fun.

Flaming Lips music, I had found, made a good soundtrack for jogging around OKC—its bouncy noise paired nicely with the streetscape. I figured that, when *The Terror* finally came out in April, I would add it to my playlist.

But then *The Terror* came out, and I listened to it, and it made me feel like I would never jog again.

The Terror lived up to its name. Wayne's lyrics were unrelentingly dark and sad. All hints of bounce were now absent from the band's sound. The goofy sing-along rainbow pop had been replaced by scrapes, screeches, crashes, and fuzz. It was desolation. Wayne sang as if he were buried under something heavy—as *Pitchfork* put it, "like someone who's strapped to a hospital bed." He moaned inscrutable philosophical questions:

> Did God make pain so we can know the high that nothing is?

> Is love a God that we control to try to trust the pain?

> How can we find arms to hold the days?

Song after song, the album hammered pessimism into its listener's ears:

> Always there, in our hearts, destroying everything we know
> Always there, in our hearts, not forgiving those who are
>   weak
> Always there, in our hearts, shame that we are all powerless

This was a bleakness much more extreme than "all your bad days will end." *The Terror* was what was left when all your bad days had already ended, in the worst possible way, and now here you still were, standing, surveying the wreckage. And then what? Nothing good. You weren't even afforded the simple grace of being gone. The album was an elegy for things that had already been lost, plus a portent of more loss to come.

Like all of Wayne's music, *The Terror* was obsessed with love. And love had always been complicated for Wayne: it was colorful and powerful and happy, yes, but it was also dangerous, because it could bind you to things that might hurt you. Sometimes love could be messy and gross. At the Compound, Wayne had a housecat that he liked to say was the pure embodiment of love, because it attached itself to visitors' necks and then drooled all over them unstoppably.

In *The Terror*, however, love was not just complicated—it was futile:

> Love is always something
> Something you should fear
> When you really listen
> Fear is all you hear

To promote *The Terror*, the Flaming Lips unveiled a new stage show. The old days of colorful characters zanily dancing, the DIY psychedelic rainbow orgasm, Wayne shooting lasers out the palms of a giant artificial hand—all of that was gone. In the new stage show, Wayne stood alone, elevated on a platform, surrounded by weird mounds of mirrored domes. He looked like the nerve center of the stage; into his body flowed dozens of glowing white tentacles, heaps and heaps of electro-spaghetti that pulsed in patterns of light. It looked like the religious shrine of an alien civilization that worshipped intestines. There were no balloons. The confetti was entirely black.

Wayne Coyne, surrounded by tentacles, holds his fake baby.

The creepiest part of *The Terror* stage show was the baby. Wayne held it while he sang. It was only a doll—no one would have given Wayne a real baby—but it was the best simulation that money could buy. The doll was disturbingly realistic, with solid weight and wispy golden hair, because it had been designed to be used as a therapy baby by mothers who had lost a child. It was a tool for mourning. Onstage, Wayne cradled the baby in his arms as he sang. He kissed it between lyrics. He put its small hand tenderly to his mouth as the lights flashed in the strands around him. The whole thing was extremely creepy and depressing, and no one quite understood the point of it. Zac Cox, the band's stage manager, told me he had a theory about what the baby meant, but he refused to share it. The obvious reading, I thought, was that the baby stood in for Wayne's failed marriage: the death of his twenty-five-year relationship to Michelle. He was mourning the loss of his anchoring domesticity. The most beautiful song on *The Terror*, a ballad called "Try to Explain," seemed to chronicle the breakup directly. Wayne sings about "a love that explodes," then launches into a slow, wounded chorus, his voice cracking into falsetto. "Try to explain why you've changed. I don't think I'll understand. Try to explain why you're leaving. I don't think I'll understand." For someone like Wayne—someone who stayed, who prized loyalty and steadiness over everything else—this was the ultimate trauma: to leave, to change. And what came next? I remembered his album statement: "*The Terror* is, we know now, that even without love, life goes on . . . we just go on . . . there is no mercy killing." This album was the sound of someone stepping into the abyss.

PART FIVE

MOTION

Like Rain it sounded till it curved
And then I knew 'twas Wind.
—EMILY DICKINSON

Where does true power lie? Can it be found in life's
tornadoes or does it happen in the quietness of one's soul?
—CLARA LUPER, *Behold the Walls*

You cannot stir things apart.
—TOM STOPPARD, *Arcadia*

BUFFALO

The Buffalo Bills were the best. This was in 1990, 1991, 1992, and 1993—for four whole years, they crushed the other football teams. Total domination. The Bills didn't lose a single play-off game at home for six seasons. Even on their very worst days, when their star quarterback was injured and they fell behind 35–3, the Buffalo Bills found a way to come back and win. They had stars all over the field—quarterback, running back, wide receiver, defense—and they tormented opponents with an innovative quick-strike no-huddle offense that produced highlight after highlight after highlight: boom, boom, boom, boom, boom. The Bills not only won, they changed the whole time signature of football; they made the notoriously slow game flow. Defenses could hardly get set before the Bills were scoring all over them. It was one of the great charmed runs in the history of American sports, and the best part was that it was all happening in snow-buried, Rust Belt, shitty old Buffalo—a paragon of uncool, edge-of-the-map, glamourless American suffering, where the old industrial jobs had long ago dried up and tourists had absolutely zero reason ever to visit. Buffalo's winter wind was so strong that it tipped the stadium's goalposts to one side; fans came to games dressed for polar expeditions.

Before this, for decades, the Bills had been terrible. Back in the early 1970s, things got so bleak that the owner had very nearly moved the team to Seattle—Seattle, of all the distant goddamn places—but the fans had risen up and the Bills had stayed in Buffalo, and now, as they flat-out embarrassed all of the traditional big-city powers (New

York, Dallas, Los Angeles), the team had become a source of inde-
scribable spiritual joy and civic pride to the long-suffering people of
the city. The star players populated national TV ads. Buffalo, if only
in this one single way, was glamorous. It seemed not like a question
of *if* the Bills would win the Super Bowl, only of how many times.

Their first chance came in the winter of 1991. The Bills stormed
through the play-offs, beating their archrivals—the decadent, tropi-
cal Miami Dolphins—after which the home fans rushed the field and
tore down the goalposts. Then the Bills destroyed the L.A. Raiders
51–3 and entered the Super Bowl as heavy favorites. Their opponents
were the New York Giants, media darlings of the megalopolis to the
south, which meant that this was an opportunity to work out some
major civic anxiety in front of the whole world. And it actually *was*
the whole world: this was the first Super Bowl in history to be broadcast globally. It took place in January 1991, right near the peak of the
Gulf War, and was therefore an extremely American affair. Whitney
Houston sang the national anthem with such glorious patriotic vigor
that the recording went on to become a charting pop single; as her
last note died away, four F-16s ripped over the stadium in tight formation. The halftime show was emceed by Mickey Mouse, dressed in
stars and stripes, and featured perhaps the most American sentence
ever amplified through a stadium: "And now, to honor our armed
forces' children, Coca-Cola proudly presents the New Kids on the
Block." It was a vortex of Americana, and somehow Buffalo was at
the center of it.

Unfortunately, agonizingly, the Bills lost. The Giants bullied Buffalo's famous offense, ate up the clock, and as time expired, the Bills'
kicker missed a tragic field goal, just wide right. ("He can fire the shot
heard 'round the world now," the game announcer said just before
the miss.) It was the narrowest loss in Super Bowl history: a single
point. Grown men wept. The citizens of Buffalo would have to wait
one more year for glory.

The following year, the Bills overcame some injuries to win thirteen games and reach the Super Bowl again. This time they played
the Washington Redskins—America's team. It was a clash of the two
best offenses in the NFL, but, inexplicably, for the second year in a

row, the Bills' offense didn't show up. Their superstar quarterback threw four interceptions, their superstar running back ran for only thirteen yards, and Buffalo lost by thirteen points—their second consecutive Super Bowl failure. It was, for a force as powerful as the Bills, a crushingly bad run of luck. The people of Buffalo were left waiting, exasperated, once again.

Great teams, however, are built to persevere, and the Bills were clearly a great team. In 1993, the road was a little harder—everyone seemed to get injured, and they had to pull off the most improbable comeback in football history—but still they clawed their way into the Super Bowl. Things were beginning to take on the weight of destiny. Even the backup quarterback was playing like a star. Only one other team in NFL history had reached three Super Bowls in a row, the great Miami Dolphins of the 1970s, and they had won two of those. It seemed inconceivable that any team could *lose* three in a row. It made no sense: to be dominant enough to get there back-to-back-to-back but not dominant enough to win even once. Every individual game, of course, has to be taken on its own merits, and yet given the weight of narrative probability, this game seemed basically impossible to lose. Things had reached a level of likelihood that bordered on the absolute. This had to be the Bills' year.

Given all of this, it is easy to imagine how a twenty-four-year-old Buffalonian, a young man who felt like his life was falling apart, whose ties to the social contract had been severed, who had recently suffered a nervous breakdown and seriously considered suicide, who was almost certainly suffering from undiagnosed PTSD, who—although he was a decorated veteran of the recent Gulf War—was now working as a poorly paid security guard on the graveyard shift at the Buffalo Zoo, with side gigs as a rent-a-cop at local pro wrestling matches and monster truck rallies, who was therefore so short on money that he didn't even have phone service, who spent his free time nursing conspiracy theories about the U.S. government and writing ominous letters to the editor of his local paper—it is easy to imagine how this young man might have been lured into making a bad decision: into betting all of the very little money he had, and then some, on a victory for the Buffalo Bills in Super Bowl XXVII.

The young man was Timothy McVeigh. He was a Buffalo Bills superfan. McVeigh grew up in a rural town called Lockport, just on the
edge of Buffalo—the fringe of the American fringe—and Bills football was a sort of religion for him. He was a bright but scrawny kid
("Noodle McVeigh," bullies called him) raised mostly by his father,
who worked at a radiator factory. During McVeigh's adolescence, his
mother took his sisters and moved to Florida. But McVeigh chose to
stay behind, with his dad, with the Bills. Before he left for Iraq, he
had actually been there in the stadium, in Buffalo, to watch the Bills'
first run to the Super Bowl; he was part of the jubilant Buffalonian
mob that rushed the field to tear down the goalposts. Immediately afterward, McVeigh went off to the Gulf, where he established himself
as a rising star of a soldier—an acer of all the tests, an unbelievably
accurate shot, a meticulous cleaner of guns and uniforms and of the
Bradley armored vehicle in which he was the gunner. In 1991, when
the Bills were losing their first Super Bowl, McVeigh was busy overseas, preparing to take part in Operation Desert Storm. He would be
at the crest of that overwhelming military wave: tanks from horizon
to horizon, rolling forward to stomp out the terrible despot holding
the world's oil fields hostage.

Like many young soldiers, McVeigh shipped out as an idealist and
came home a cynic. The mighty Iraqi army he had trained so hard to
fight turned out to be nothing more than a sparse, disorganized, un-
derequipped handful of soldiers straggling across the desert, begging
to be allowed to surrender. McVeigh saw abandoned corpses being
eaten by dogs. He listened to the U.S. military lie about murdering
civilians. And he became, himself, a killer. In the midst of all the
chaos of smoke and sand, to the amazement of everyone around him,
McVeigh took out an Iraqi soldier in a bunker with a miraculous shot
from something like a mile away. He watched, through his scope,
the man's head and body burst. McVeigh hated all of this. He did not
feel like a hero. The war, for all intents and purposes, was over in less
than a week, and McVeigh was awarded five medals.

Now it was two years later, 1993, and Timothy McVeigh was back
home in Buffalo, and his life—his exceptional mind, his rising military career—had gone to shit. After Iraq, McVeigh went to try out

for the Special Forces but, broken by the war, performed poorly and dropped out. At age twenty-four, he was a washed-up war hero with nothing going for him, no community or connections, no meaning-ful way forward. So McVeigh called his bookie and wagered $1,000 on the Super Bowl. There was simply no way the Bills were going to lose again, not for a third consecutive time. That would be a world in which nothing made sense, in which an entire community had been unjustly worked up into a fever of false hope. Now was his chance, McVeigh figured, to make everything instantly a little bit better.

He settled in to watch the game.

The national anthem at this Super Bowl was performed by Garth Brooks, perhaps the world's most famous Oklahoman; he grew up in Yukon, right on the edge of Oklahoma City. This fact probably didn't mean much, at the time, to McVeigh, who had never even been to Oklahoma and was hopped up with anxiety for kickoff.

The beginning of the game would have pleased him. The Bills sti-fled the Cowboys' opening drive, blocked their subsequent punt, and scored a quick touchdown. They stuffed the Cowboys' second pos-session, too. Finally, everything in a Super Bowl was going Buffalo's way. McVeigh had always been a dramatic TV watcher, yelling and cursing and throwing objects at the screen when things went wrong, and at this point he must have been practically doing backflips.

Then, suddenly, everything fell apart. The Bills made a careless throw. The Cowboys intercepted it, returned it thirteen yards, and scored moments later. The Bills fumbled. The Cowboys recovered and scored again. The Bills' star quarterback threw an interception in the end zone and then, to make things worse, reinjured his balky knee. At halftime, despite that wonderful start, the Cowboys led 28–10. They had scored a pair of touchdowns only fifteen seconds apart, and then a *second* pair of touchdowns eighteen seconds apart—a new speed record in Super Bowl history.

At halftime, Timothy McVeigh had to sit there and wait, ponder-ing his increasingly long odds, while Michael Jackson sang "We Are the World" with thirty-five hundred children.

The second half was, if anything, worse: more interceptions, more fumbles, and—another Super Bowl first—twenty-one unanswered points in the fourth quarter. The Bills lost 52–17. It was not only their third consecutive Super Bowl loss, it was, by far, the worst of them all.

It was at this point in his life that Timothy McVeigh gave up on any kind of a normal future. He paid off his gambling debt with a cash advance from a credit card—a debt he fully intended never to repay. The future was no longer relevant to him, no longer something to be planned for. McVeigh left New York State, his only real home, a few days later. From that moment on, he would live unmoored from any particular place in America, adrift in a nomadic life of gun shows and spiraling extremism.

Just four weeks after that disastrous Super Bowl loss, McVeigh found and latched onto the cause that would define the rest of his life. A group of citizens in Waco, Texas—a religious cult called the Branch Davidians—had refused to surrender its weapons to the federal government. A standoff ensued, and McVeigh became obsessed. He read and watched everything he could, then loaded his car with anti-government pamphlets and bumper stickers (WHEN GUNS ARE OUTLAWED, I WILL BECOME AN OUTLAW) and drove down to see the action firsthand. He sold his paraphernalia to other militants and gave interviews to the news media in support of the persecuted. When, some weeks later, the Waco situation went terribly wrong— the FBI set fire to the compound, killing almost everyone inside— McVeigh watched the news footage and wept. That injustice became the core of his case against the United States government. Revenge became his new life's mission.

I am not saying that Timothy McVeigh bombed Oklahoma City in 1995 because the Buffalo Bills lost four Super Bowls in a row. (They made it back in 1994 and—incredibly—lost that one too, cementing their reputation as the greatest losers in NFL history.) Such a claim would be absurd. Human motives are incalculably complex. But that Buffalo heartbreak was one of the many shadows that fell across McVeigh's life between his unstable childhood and his perpetration of mass murder in Oklahoma City. The almost unbelievable failure of the Bills, and the civic pain it caused, amplified his native pain. After McVeigh returned from the Gulf War, his Bills fandom was one of the few positive social networks he was able to plug back into, one of the most powerful, stable, visceral communities to which he unquestionably belonged. Its failure was devastating, to him and to everyone else in the area. To this day, even well-adjusted Buffalonians walk around imagining alternate lives in which their team actually won four Super Bowls in a row, becoming arguably the greatest team in NFL history, putting the city on the map in a way it otherwise never could have dreamed of. Or at least won *one* Super Bowl, securing a happy little foothold in history. Instead, that 1990s Bills team is remembered as a tragic joke. It's easy to pretend that sports doesn't matter in real life, but for many millions of people, it does. It matters profoundly, every day. After Super Bowl XXVII, Timothy McVeigh went looking for somewhere else to be, something else to do—something bigger, more meaningful, more real. Reality had failed him, in so many ways, so he went off to pursue his own fantasy of justice, very far from Buffalo.

OUR LIFELINE IS CONCRETE

The Alfred P. Murrah Federal Building
freshly poured, windows shining.

The Alfred P. Murrah Federal Building opened, in downtown Oklahoma City, in March 1977. This was before urban renewal had been fully abandoned, when the economy was booming and workers were streaming in from all over the world and the demand for office space was insatiable. If you squinted, you could still just barely see the potential of I. M. Pei's vision of the city: all of those stylish glass malls and modernist towers springing up out of the wreckage, drawing life back downtown.

The new federal building was exactly such a structure. It was one of urban renewal's cut-glass jewels. It rose, the *Oklahoman* wrote, "like a 20th century castle near the center of downtown." Over the course of two years, citizens watched the new building take over a shabby block at Fifth and Robinson, a former wasteland of weedy lots, failed hotels, and vacant pseudo-civic buildings (a Shriners' temple, a Catholic charity's offices). History was scraped away, and a huge foundation pit was dug. The federal building was not so much built as it was poured, day by day, into existence: a slow-motion flood of wet gray sludge that hardened into walls, floors, ceilings, and support pillars. The biggest threat to its existence came when local concrete workers went on strike, temporarily crippling the entire project. "Our lifeline is concrete," the project manager said.

The finished building was nine stories tall, sleek and clean and powerful, a $13 million showpiece of concrete and tinted glass that looked, from the north, like a one-hundred-foot-tall solar panel: a shining grid of dark windows. Its corners were rounded to help it withstand the constant Oklahoma wind. In classic OKC style, two-thirds of the block was devoted to parking. There was an enormous underground garage, three levels deep, on top of which sat a parklike plaza complete with trees and a fountain and a state-of-the-art robotic flagpole. By the summer of 1977, people were driving through the federal building's parking garage so recklessly, for fun, that the United States attorney had to step in. (Some employees, the *Oklahoman* reported, "wondered if they hadn't taken a wrong turn onto an interstate highway.") The complex was connected to the rest of downtown by an underground network of concrete tunnels that allowed citizens to walk, regardless of the weather, in carpeted, climate-controlled comfort.

The function of the federal building was extremely literal. It allowed eighteen different U.S. government departments, formerly strewn around the sprawling city, to consolidate under one roof. The Secret Service, U.S. Geological Survey, Federal Energy Administration, Civil Service Commission, Social Security, and a whole tumble of very serious acronyms—HUD, HEW, ATF, FHA, FDIC, APHIS—were now centralized downtown. This is where bureaucracy lived, where forms got filled out in triplicate, where watermarked documents were issued, where meeting minutes were coded and filed, where spreadsheet cells were painstakingly populated with official government data. If you needed to change your name or purchase a savings bond or find out about death benefits for your grandmother, you would head downtown to the federal building. Every day, more than five hundred people congregated to work there.

The Alfred P. Murrah Federal Building was, in other words, a candidate for the most boring place on earth: 180,000 square feet of logistics and errands. And yet it was essential to Oklahoma City. It would be hard to find a place more dependent on the federal government—a city that was created, on someone else's land, by federal fiat and then bailed out and subsidized more or less constantly to ensure its survival and flourishing. The U.S. government had saved the people of Oklahoma City from starvation and bank failures. Even the renegade capitalists of the oil and gas industry, the source of the modern city's booms and busts, prospered largely through the generosity of huge federal tax breaks. It seemed appropriate that Oklahoma City's new federal building sat right at the base of Church Row, directly between two churches, because it was its own kind of temple—a shrine to civil society and professionalism and the endless daily grind of maintaining a functioning democracy. The building's employees came to work every morning to keep the country going. They were responsible for translating, form by mimeographed form, the great shining ideal of America's Founding Fathers into modern reality. The Murrah Building was, in short, a sanctuary of the American Process. All of those hundreds of citizen employees, and the citizen customers they served, formed a community within the community of larger OKC—a little core of common purpose at the heart of a city that had become so radically dispersed after the Great Annexation.

In the beginning, the new building had only a generic name: the federal building. While it was under construction, however, a more human, more perfect name presented itself—Alfred P. Murrah. Murrah was a local legend and an unlikely Oklahoma success story: an orphaned country boy who, inspired by the biography of Abraham Lincoln, turned himself into a legal prodigy. He built his career practicing law in the rowdy Oklahoma boomtowns of the late 1920s, defending prostitutes and oil workers, and his firm became so profitable that he was able to move it into downtown Oklahoma City itself at the height of its first oil boom, onto the fourteenth floor of one of downtown's brand-new skyscrapers. He became the youngest federal judge in American history, appointed at age thirty-two by FDR, and over the next three decades he came to be seen as the human embodiment of the rule of law. Toward the end of his career, Murrah was deemed such a shining example of the judicial mind that he moved to Washington, D.C., into an office across the lawn from the White House, to train other federal judges how to properly do the job. When Murrah died, in 1975, the flags in Oklahoma hung at half-staff for three days. It seemed only right that the new federal building, still being poured into place, would be named in his honor and conducted in his spirit.

On October 14, 1977, the Alfred P. Murrah Federal Building was officially dedicated. The ceremony was delayed, ominously, when a bomb threat forced the sudden evacuation of all of the federal buildings downtown, old and new. In the end, however, it turned out to be nothing, and the dedication ceremony went forward as planned, and all of the government workers went back to work. Two days later, in the last great blast of urban renewal, Oklahoma City blew up the Biltmore Hotel. In with the new, out with the old. The demolition drew thirty thousand people downtown for a single afternoon, then helped usher in the decades of emptiness that followed. During which, as always, the hundreds of people who worked at the federal building went to work and did their jobs.

Window washers on the Alfred P. Murrah Building, 1977.

GAME 84: THE AWFUL HAZARD

George Burton of Deadwood, South Dakota, did what many outlaws in Deadwood did: he killed a man during a poker game. Then he left town. He ended up, naturally, nine hundred miles south, in the wild young town of Oklahoma City, where he established himself very quickly as one of the place's leading misanthropic ruffians. On February 13, 1903—about a year before the infamous Red Kelley incident—someone at the Two Johns Saloon made the mistake of stepping on George Burton's foot. Burton got his revenge by chasing the man up Broadway, clubbing him with a pistol on the back of the head, and shooting him from behind. Even for Oklahoma City, this was a bit much. But justice was slow, and it took another six years before Burton got what was coming to him. On June 10, 1909, he was heading to a different saloon on the very important errand of killing its owner—but the owner had been tipped off in advance, and so he managed to turn the tables and kill George Burton instead. Whereupon the preacher, at Burton's funeral, offered the following words of wisdom to the people of Oklahoma City.

"The life of the gambler," he preached, "is one of intense excitement. The chances and hazards, the skill of one man against another, the uncertain and exciting moments until the stakes are won has a deadly fascination for many a man, until too often, the soul and eternity are the stakes for which men make the awful hazard."

Plenty of OKC's early residents needed to hear this warning—the saloons were stuffed full of them—but then of course they had already heard it many times before. It was exactly the kind of message that would never get through. A true gambler believes that he can't lose—not seriously, not permanently—and that whatever losses he does suffer will be nothing, in the end, compared to all of those glorious improbable wins. To believe otherwise would contradict the very spirit in which Oklahoma City was founded. And yet the preacher, on the occasion of Burton's death, tried to make the people understand that an invisible tab is always mounting, even during winning streaks, and eventually the gambler, in one form or another, will have to pay. The house always wins. George Burton, the preacher was telling everyone, had been killed by the spirit of Boom. He must have known that his message would be almost universally ignored. But maybe this time he would get lucky. Maybe, against all the odds, the preacher's sermon would save one other solitary soul before the tide of luck inevitably shifted.

Game 2, Rockets versus Thunder, promised to be exactly like Game 1: an Oklahoma City blowout. The Rockets were clearly overmatched. James Harden had not managed to find any help in the intervening two days, and as impressive as he was, he wasn't nearly good enough to beat the Thunder by himself. No one on the roster could defend Westbrook or Durant, let alone both of them at the same time. The series had become a formality, a friendly tune-up for the Thunder's deeper play-off run.

Inspired, perhaps, by these long odds, the Rockets' coach, Kevin McHale, decided to try something new. For the first time ever, he inserted into his starting lineup a deeply unheralded point guard named Patrick Beverley. This seemed less a strategic decision than a cry for help. Beverley was an unknown quantity—not at all the sort of player you suddenly see featured in the play-offs. Game 2, in fact, was the very first start of his NBA career. He was twenty-four years old, ancient for a rookie, and had played in portions of only forty-two games, or roughly half of one regular season. He was undersized, an unreliable shooter, and an erratic decision maker. His career, up to that point, had taken place literally off the map of U.S. basketball. Although Beverley was American, formerly a Top 100 high school recruit, he had run into academic trouble in college and been forced to cobble together a pro career overseas: Russia, Greece, Ukraine. At the beginning of the year, playing in front of small crowds in St. Petersburg, Beverley was far less likely to make an impact on an NBA team than, say, Daniel Orton. And yet here he was, the smallest and least famous player on either roster, starting at point guard in a play-off game.

Beverley wasn't on the floor for his shooting or passing or dribbling. He had only one job in the game, and it was simple but impossible: to stop Russell Westbrook.

Westbrook, of course, took Beverley's presence on the court as he took many things in life: as a cataclysmic insult. He loved to overpower smaller guards, and this went double in a play-off game against a smaller guard who had no pedigree or reputation or obvious skills. From the opening tip, Westbrook seemed determined not only to take advantage of Beverley but to embarrass him, to send him scampering back to whatever substandard, unobserved Euro-gym he had managed to claw his way out of.

Instead, something amazing happened: Westbrook couldn't. Beverley turned out to be the rare player who was every bit as hungry and unreasonably aggressive as Westbrook himself. He looked completely unintimidated. He stayed in front of Westbrook, pestered him, frustrated him, baited him into offensive fouls—all of which, naturally, only made Westbrook even more furious. His anger began to feed on his anger. He spent the whole first quarter forcing shots over Beverley, missing many of them badly, and in the second quarter, even when Westbrook did manage to turn things around—when he flew through the air to seize one of his signature stratospheric rebounds and charged down the floor to hit one of his signature pull-up jumpers—the Thunder couldn't shake the Rockets off. The OKC crowd seemed uneasy, ready to explode but without any good reason to do so. In the middle of the second quarter, Houston scored a couple of easy baskets and—the ultimate insult—actually took the lead.

The crowd went moodily quiet.

Scott Brooks signaled for a time-out.

This was when it happened.

It's tempting to imagine all the ways the next moment could have gone differently. Beverley could have never made the NBA. He could have made the NBA but stayed rooted to the bench. He could have made it onto the floor but behaved like a normal player—meaning he would have turned around, when the referee blew his whistle, and walked back toward his own time-out huddle.

Or the Thunder could have played more like themselves in the first half, so they would never have surrendered their lead and, therefore, never been forced to call a panicked time-out. Or Durant could have been dribbling the ball instead of Westbrook. Or Westbrook could have been a little less intense, a little more normal, the kind of player who didn't whip opponents up into ultracompetitive antagonistic frenzies. Or Westbrook could have seen the hit coming and braced himself.

But none of that is how things went down. What happened, instead, is a moment that everyone in the arena would think about for the rest of their lives.

Scott Brooks signaled for a time-out. Westbrook dribbled casually toward the sideline, as is customary, preparing to hand the ball to the referee. That was it. Just as the referee blew his whistle to officially stop play, just as all of the players on the court started to walk off toward their respective benches, just as Scott Brooks stepped out onto the floor to organize his huddle, right on the threshold between game and non-game—Patrick Beverley, the no-name nonentity, suddenly lunged for the ball.

Technically, Beverley was trying for a steal, but mostly he was just being a pest. He was reminding Westbrook that there was no pocket of space-time, no matter how tiny, in which he should allow himself to feel safe. It was a silly gamble. The odds were maybe one in three hundred that anything good would come of that lunge—that the referee would be slow to blow his whistle, that Westbrook would be careless with his final dribble, that Beverley would surprise him and poke the ball away and then race off to the other end of the court for a layup. It was the kind of play that only a hyperaggressive maniacal risk-taker would ever think to expend the energy on. It was, in other words, a Russell Westbrook kind of play. And it did, against all the odds, have a major effect: it changed the series, and the Thunder's season, and NBA history, and possibly the whole civic trajectory of Oklahoma City.

Beverley's lunge knocked Russell Westbrook down.

Westbrook fell hard to the floor. He sprang up, angrily, and hopped on one leg to the scorer's table, which he leaned over and—BOOM—slammed with his fist, not lightly, in casual frustration, but with all the strength he could summon in his arm, a strike of total outraged vengeance.

BOOM.

The sound exploded through the arena. There were those on the Thunder's bench who thought nothing of the incident until they heard that sound—a concussion so loud, so unreasonably violent, that it was clear that something important had just happened—that some plan had just been wrenched off track.

Westbrook doubled over in pain. He stood back up. Clearly, something was wrong. And yet, at the same time, it couldn't be. Russell Westbrook was indestructible. He had never been injured in his whole reckless life, at any level of basketball: he'd played in every single game since grade school, including every game in the history of the Thunder franchise. But here we all were, watching him, and now it looked like something was wrong with his knee. He doubled over in pain again, then turned and limped not toward his own time-out huddle but toward the Rockets' bench, breathing terror, staring a bolt of pure hostility at Beverley. Hasheem Thabeet, all seven foot three of him, held Westbrook back, and eventually Westbrook turned away and—after doubling over once more in pain—managed to limp back to his own bench.

It's amazing, in light of what we would learn the following day, that Westbrook did not leave the floor. He didn't even check out of the game. More amazing still is that he actually played well. After the time-out, he was right back in the action, assisting a Sefolosha three-pointer, then stealing the ball and racing the full length of the court for a layup. Something, however, was subtly wrong. Westbrook was still moving extremely fast, but he was moving at the speed of a fast professional athlete, not at the hypervelocity of the regular Russell Westbrook. It looked, from the stands, like he was running with a tiny hitch. Patrick Beverley, meanwhile, refused to back off: he kept lunging, grabbing the ball, bothering Westbrook's shot, even occasionally scoring on the other end. He was deep under Westbrook's skin. On one play, Beverley knocked Westbrook over and then reached out to help him up—at which point Westbrook looked at him in disbelief, with double-barreled horror, and slapped his hand away. Every time Beverley touched the ball, the Oklahoma City crowd booed him as if he were a wrestling villain. In the fourth quarter, he rose up and blocked Westbrook's pull-up jumper—a thing I had never seen anyone do and had not thought was even possible. Either something was terribly wrong with Westbrook or Beverley was better than anyone thought. Perhaps both were true.

Westbrook played the entire second half. The game wasn't safe until time expired, and in the end the Rockets missed some makeable shots and the Thunder escaped with a three-point win. This gave them a 2–0 lead in the series. But it felt more like luck than merit.

The postgame media session should have been fascinating, but somehow, even then, blandness prevailed. Scott Brooks practiced his tautologies. (How had the Rockets adjusted to play so much better tonight? he was asked. "That was their major adjustment," he said. "They played much better tonight.") As always, Westbrook and Durant came to the media table together. Westbrook wore a skintight black leather button-up shirt that made him look like the leader of a twenty-third-century motorcycle gang; Durant wore a gray hoodie. The reporters asked them about Harden, rebounding, and the flow of the game, and as the players made mouth noises in response I kept waiting for someone to ask about Westbrook's knee. No one did. It occurred to me that maybe *I* should be the one to ask, but some powerful force kept me silent. Perhaps it was just a fear of looking silly. Westbrook, after all, had played every second of the second half, so how serious an injury could it be? But I think what stopped me was something else, something deeper, a collective holding of the breath.

A fear now hung over the city like weather. The sound of Westbrook's fist on the scorer's table still echoed in everyone's minds. We were terrified of acknowledging what we all might have just seen. Terrified that something was actually wrong. So we would live without naming it for a few more charmed hours.

Westbrook probably would have dismissed any question about his knee anyway, because—although it was sore—he believed as much as anyone else in his own invincibility. The true gravity of things wouldn't strike him until later that night when, after the media session, the Thunder slid him into an MRI tube. Good news, he knew, did not come out of those tubes.

And good news did not. Russell Westbrook's scan revealed a lateral tear in the meniscus of his right knee. His season was over, all because of an unknown player's impulsive lunge in a trivial moment. It hardly seemed fair. All of that work wasted, all of that time gone. Westbrook, the ultimate gambler, was being forced to pay for another gambler's gamble.

Under the blaring headline "NOW WHAT?," next to an anatomical diagram of the human knee, the *Oklahoman* referred to the revelation of the injury as "Black Friday."

The Thunder, *Sports Illustrated* wrote, were now "in a unique and terrifying space."

"It feels like the day the Thunder traded James Harden," wrote Royce Young. "It's shocking, it's landscape-changing, it's unbelievable."

Online, the mood ranged from despondent ("We are done." "Guess he was vincible after all") to guardedly hopeful: "Some sick part of me is excited to see KD go into hero mode."

At least one Twitter user managed to bring Westbrook's injury back to Sam Presti, bellowing: "Westbrook is done now!? Wow, there u go Miami!? Free championship? SHOULD'VE KEPT HARDEN. Harden/Durant >>> Westbrook/Durant!"

In Las Vegas, Oklahoma City's odds to win the championship dropped precipitously overnight. The team had been the favorite to win the Western Conference but was now suddenly only a co-favorite, as well as a heavy underdog to Miami in the Finals, and those odds would continue to fall. Gamblers scrambled to abandon the Thunder.

Sam Presti issued a press release: "Russell's health and well being are obviously our number one priority through this process and today's procedure helped solidify our belief that Russell will have many productive years of basketball in his future." In a conference call, a reporter asked how Oklahoma City could recover from such a loss. "I don't think we have to rally in any sense," Presti said. "The mentality of the group is in place."

For four solid years, fans and columnists and TV talking heads had been debating this question in the abstract: How much did this juggernaut of a team, and the city it stood for, depend on the most individualistic individual in the group? Suddenly it was no longer hypothetical. It would be tested in the actual world. Was Russell Westbrook necessary? We were all about to find out.

ARE TORNADOES NECESSARY?

The first photograph of a tornado, May 12, 1896.

Despite all the ways Oklahoma City had changed throughout its history—from grass to tents to skyscrapers to rubble to renaissance—the sky remained the same. The same wind flowed over every resident who ever lived there, from the prehistoric Mound Builders to Roscoe Dunjee to Wayne Coyne. Every spring, the same storms formed, and tornadoes dropped out of them like monsters. On May 12, 1896, when Oklahoma City was suffering through its fourth consecutive year of drought, three separate funnels passed near the town. A photographer managed to capture one on film—the world's earliest known photo of a tornado. It looks essentially modern: an agitation in the upper clouds, with one of them narrowing into a needle of wind, swooping almost elegantly down to probe the houses and power lines. Dark dirt billows up from the ground, like an explosion, at the point of contact. Similar tornadoes had touched down for centuries before that one, of course, and many thousands have touched down since. But this was the first image that outlasted the storm—the first time people who hadn't been there could see it. It was the beginning of the tornado as media spectacle—the birth, in a way, of Gary England. The walls of England's office were covered with such photos, and they all looked almost exactly like the first.

Long before that image was taken, the Plains Indians knew tornadoes well. A Kiowa legend tells that these storms are the result of a beast in the sky, a horse with the tail of a fish. It was born of hubris, when an ancient clay sculpture of a horse suddenly came to life. "Well, the horse began to be," writes N. Scott Momaday. "But it was a terrible, terrible thing. It began to writhe, slowly at first, then faster and faster until there was a great commotion everywhere. The wind grew up and carried everything away; great trees were uprooted, and even the buffalo were thrown up into the sky."

To this day, the Arapaho people go outside during a tornado to put a specially blessed knife into the ground in its path. This splits the storm, they believe, and sends it safely around their territory. The Cheyenne, similarly, have sacred rituals that allow them to communicate with a tornado—the funnel speaks to them, in their own language, in a voice that sounds like fire. It tells them how big it will be and where it is going. Sometimes they can convince it to turn away from their land.

I once asked Gary England why modern meteorology hasn't figured out a way to stop tornadoes. Why can't we build some kind of barrier, a massive artificial windbreak, out near the border of where they usually form—a fake mountain, perhaps, that would shred any large sheet of wind before it could get itself organized? Why can't we shoot missiles or giant tennis balls into the clouds before they start to spin? Surely professional meteorologists, with their encyclopedic knowledge of the ingredients of storms, should be able to come up with a way to tweak conditions to disrupt the worst of them.

"They're just so friggin' strong," England said. "They can have multiple times the energy of a nuclear bomb. A whole thunderstorm is miles and miles and miles across, and it's rotating, and it has its own fuel supply coming into it—this inflow of warm air. How do you stop that? It's going to blow down anything you put in front of it. Someday maybe some brilliant engineer will come up with a metal that can't be bent—but even then, it would have to be awfully tall, because those storms go from the surface to forty or fifty thousand feet."

The most interesting answer is not just that we can't stop tornadoes but that we shouldn't. This was the answer I got from Greg Carbin, one of the wind geniuses at the Storm Prediction Center in Norman.

"Why can't we stop tornadoes?" I asked.

"Well, what is the purpose of a tornado?" he responded.

It had never occurred to me that a storm had anything as grand as a purpose.

Consider a hurricane, Carbin said. It acts as a kind of air conditioner for the planet, pushing excess heat from the equator off toward the poles. Similarly, he said, a tornado releases pent-up instability. "In the process of that turning," Carbin told me, "there's something that the atmosphere is releasing, or relaxing. So if you could eliminate tornadoes, what does that mean? How does the atmosphere react to the fact that you've now suppressed this natural phenomenon? It's going to manifest itself in some other way."

On this, the Plains Indians and the meteorologists agreed.

I spoke with a Cheyenne chief named Gordon Yellowman, who told me that a tornado is not some evil predatory force, nor is it a random assault from a cruel universe with no concern for human life. Every tornado has a job. "He keeps us in balance," Yellowman said. "He can become very angry when certain things aren't done respect-

SOLO

Timothy McVeigh loaded the truck himself. There were thirteen barrels—eight white, four black, one blue—and he planned to arrange them in the back of the truck in roughly the shape of the letter T, a formation he had settled on after mapping it out, on a kitchen floor, with soup cans. It was grueling work. He and Terry Nichols, his old anti-government army buddy, had stockpiled more than one hundred bags of fertilizer, and they were heavy, and then there were the three big drums of liquid nitromethane, four hundred pounds each—a combination that, along with some other odds and ends, would make a weapon violent enough to put the U.S. federal government on notice, possibly even to take it down. McVeigh's fantasy was to kick off a second American Revolution. He was, in his ever-narrowing mind, like a hero in an action movie, and this would be revenge for Waco and all the other injustices he had become increasingly obsessed with as he moved from gun show to gun show, with no real community or psychological help, studying conspiracy theories from the books advertised in the back pages of his gun magazines.

McVeigh loaded the truck in Kansas, at a storage facility, all alone, because everyone else had failed him. Terry Nichols was flaking out, right at the crucial moment, refusing to show up. McVeigh had tried to lure Michael Fortier, one of his other conspirators, with a sports metaphor: "You're like the person who sits on a bench in a basketball game: somebody comes out of the game, and you come in." But Fortier refused.

McVeigh was preparing to cross the threshold that separates paranoid delusion from real-world action. But now others were refusing fully or in harmony. It's his job to remind us, because we take things for granted. We forget about the power of the forces of nature. Every time he comes, he reminds us of that power. He brings perspective."

In times that are particularly agitated, Yellowman said, the storms will only get stronger.

"We need to be paying attention now," he said. "Things are getting more unbalanced and uneven. When we see mass destruction, we'd better be paying attention. We need to learn from one another instead of fighting. Learn."

Everyone seemed to agree that the atmosphere, on some level, *needs* its worst storms. What looks like chaos is, from another perspective, only a return to equilibrium. That is the process: balance, imbalance, destruction; balance, imbalance, destruction. Instability is inevitable. There is no point in suppressing or avoiding it. The best a meteorologist can hope to do is to warn people—to figure out, as precisely as possible, when and where a potentially deadly atmospheric strike might occur, then tell as much of the public as possible. And then everyone just has to help one another.

By April, when the NBA play-offs were in full swing and OKC was celebrating the Land Run, Gary England and every other meteorologist knew the storms were coming. No one could do anything to stop them. All anyone could do was focus and rally and work together to survive whatever eventually arrived.

to join him. McVeigh just kept going. He was used to being alone. He had convinced himself that it was American to be alone.

McVeigh and Nichols got along, to the extent that they did, because they were both obsessed with what they saw as the decline of individual rights in America. They had systematically detached themselves from every community that might have absorbed them—school, work, friends, family, the army. Terry Nichols was a serial loser who deliberately ran up credit card debt without any intention of paying it off. When the bank finally came after him, he sent it a homemade "Certificate of Credit," which he argued was just as valuable as the government's bogus paper money; when the bank took him to court, he refused to recognize the judge's authority over him because he had already renounced his American citizenship. Together, McVeigh and Nichols represented a logical end of radical individualism. What they hated, what they were determined to attack, was not just the U.S. federal government but the very notion of *federation*: all of the complications, compromises, and sacrifices required by togetherness, the inevitable mess that came along with being a human among other humans. They were adolescents trapped in adulthood. Their mission was to assert the glory of the heroic individual against the disgrace of collective life. It shouldn't be too surprising that, in the end, they worked so poorly together.

But it was hard loading the truck alone. Finally, Nichols showed up and, after McVeigh chewed him out for a while, they worked together to finish loading. By the end of the day, the truck was a rolling bomb. McVeigh could have driven it right then to Oklahoma City, but it wasn't quite the time yet. He was a strong believer in numbers and dates, anniversaries: those magic moments when the big plates of history overlap and bring together radically different temporal worlds. History would align in Oklahoma City. McVeigh would force it into alignment.

TOGETHER

Ron Norick seemed, somehow, like a fitting mayor for Oklahoma City in the early 1990s. He was not glamorous in any way. He was not photogenic like his father. He didn't have the sculpted hair and the charming smile. He was bald and round. And, of course, he was not leading a rapidly expanding city in the middle of a postwar boom. He was not struggling to harness the energy of wild growth. Mayor Norick the Younger presided over a city that was in a very sorry state. Downtown was ruined. The economy had not recovered from its bust ten years earlier, and United Airlines had just rejected a staggering package of incentives in order to avoid making its employees suffer the indignity of living in OKC.

Somehow, Mayor Norick's career was not dragged down by the city's misfortune. He was given a chance to make it better. He had good political instincts. After decades of neglect, Oklahoma City's infrastructure was crumbling, and the city could raise no public funds, so Norick announced a program called "Adopt-a-Pothole." For ten dollars, you could sponsor one of the many cavities that plagued the local streets, and the city would fill it. It was the perfect blend of sad and funny, despondent and determined, private and public. The program was picked up in the national news, and people from all over the country sent money to fix OKC's streets. Eventually, in the wake of this success, Norick was able to convince voters to do what a normal city would have done in the first place—to approve bond money to fix the city's infrastructure. Public money for the public good. It hadn't been done in Oklahoma City since the 1970s.

In 1991, Norick won reelection with 81 percent of the vote, and he decided to use this overwhelming political capital to do something grandiose. The city, he knew, couldn't go on this way. It needed something big. But what kind of dramatic vision would also bring sustainable success? How could OKC improve itself without simply chasing another boom? What was the alternative to the grand gamble?

Mayor Norick decided to wager his political future on a truly radical idea, an approach completely foreign to the Boom mentality. It was not fast or exciting. It was as boring as a field of grass. It went against everything OKC had learned to believe about itself, all the swashbuckling stories of heroic daring and sudden triumph.

Norick's solution to Oklahoma City's problems was, sacrilegiously, a public tax. He proposed a voluntary one-cent sales tax, spread over five years, that would fund a program called Metro Area Projects. MAPS would thoroughly rebuild downtown, infusing much of the energy that urban renewal and the Great Annexation had removed. It would build hotels, sports stadiums, a library, a canal. The dried-up river would be refilled. Culture would be tentatively reintroduced. Downtown would become a real place again, a destination. The mistakes of the previous forty years would be reversed. "We are trying to create mass," Norick said. "We need to have mass—everything dealing with tourism and sports in one location."

Like a Stanley Draper scheme, MAPS was crazily ambitious. Unlike a Draper scheme, however, it would be initiated through official government channels and approved by a formal public vote. The chamber of commerce pitched in, funding a PR campaign that urged the people to "Believe in Our Future!" "Do we compete with other cities," a flyer asked, ". . . or do we just stop trying?"

MAPS would require, from the people, a leap of faith. The citizens were not naturally inclined to trust the city, for very solid historical reasons. So many grand plans had failed so spectacularly. So much potential had been squandered. OKC, in the early 1990s, was not really a "togetherness" place. Its residents were dispersed. Its culture was suburban, individualistic. And even in the best of times, Oklahomans were notoriously anti-tax. Over the previous decade, multiple attempts to impose temporary sales taxes to improve the city had failed. When the people *had* allowed themselves to be talked into taxes, to help lure the airlines, the airlines had rejected them.

In this environment, MAPS was a civic moon shot. Early polls showed 32 percent support. The Gaylords opposed it, as did the NAACP. Advisers tried to convince Norick to abandon the project, or at least to delay the vote.

Mayor Norick said that he would actually prefer not to be mayor than to preside over a place that wouldn't work together to improve itself. He went all over town, speaking to every group he could gather, telling them that he understood that his plan was extravagant, that it was unusual, that its deferred payoff might be frustrating. But to reject it, he argued, would be to give up on OKC's future residents, everyone's children and grandchildren. MAPS was a grown-up thing to do. It was the Process.

Norick's great strategic gamble was to bundle all nine major MAPS projects together into a single up-or-down vote. If you wanted a new library, you had to approve a new minor league baseball stadium. If you wanted water in the river, you had to vote for the new sports arena and the art museum and the hotel. "We've got to roll the dice," Norick said. "We've got to do it all as one. . . . It's all or none, folks."

In December 1993, as the date of the vote approached, the city held a downtown rally at the dilapidated convention center. Barry Switzer, longtime football coach at the University of Oklahoma and therefore a local deity, pumped everyone up for MAPS. "The ball is on the one-yard line!" he shouted. "Let's put it in the end zone . . . and then we will be number one in the twenty-first century!"

The MAPS vote came on a Tuesday—December 14, 1993.

An hour into the voting, returns showed the new tax trailing 54–46.

Over the course of the day, however, those percentages began to crawl closer and closer together—and then they actually flipped. MAPS won with 54 percent of the vote. Norick was exultant. "Oklahoma City," he shouted at the watch party in Bricktown, "welcome to the big leagues!" Everyone stood together and cheered. Outside those doors, the city was still bleak and abandoned. Nothing on the ground had actually changed. But now there was hope, flung forward in time—hope that in five or ten or fifteen years, Oklahoma City might be a real place again. Its citizens had agreed, just barely, to sacrifice their immediate interest for the long-term collective good. They would succeed or fail, slowly, together.

GAME 85: STORMS

In the early days of the Thunder, when the team was new, when citizens gathered in the boxy MAPS-funded arena only to witness loss after loss after loss, when Sam Presti's Process was grinding through its frustrating opening phases, OKC fans believed that bad weather was a good omen. The Thunder seemed to play a little better when it stormed. People would check the season schedule against the weather forecast and watch Gary England and cheer for dark clouds. Over the years, as the team improved, as the gears of the Process cranked irreversibly toward glory, this superstition faded. The Thunder were so good that they would blow you out on a perfectly clear afternoon or in the middle of a hurricane or during a hailstorm or when the city was caressed by sweet, gentle breezes. It didn't matter. The Thunder were their own self-contained weather system. So it was fine that, in recent years, the weather in OKC had been relatively mild, that major storms had been sparse.

Now, however, there was a basketball emergency. For the first time in the history of the franchise, Russell Westbrook was absent. He would watch the game in civilian clothes, on crutches. What the Thunder would look like without his wild motion, no one could say. They were already down James Harden: a self-inflicted blow. Surely the team couldn't survive this second blow, too. There was a minority opinion that the Thunder might actually function more efficiently without Westbrook—that the remaining players might have to work a little more traditionally, with more sanity and patience, with more respect for the community at large. Durant, in particular, might flourish in this environment. But there was a strain of wishful thinking to such talk. Maybe it was time to renew the old superstition. The team would need luck from somewhere, so why not from the sky? Perhaps the weather gods would speak, once again, just in time, in OKC's favor.

As if in solidarity, dark clouds began to gather before Game 3. The series had moved to Houston and, all day, the sky hammered the city with storms. Ropes of lightning whipped down. The rain gushed in sideways, shutting down neighborhoods, forcing drivers to abandon stalled cars on the freeway. Hailstones shattered windows. The roofs of buildings collapsed. An entire hospital had to be evacuated.

And indeed, back on the basketball court, the chaotic skies did seem to tilt things the Thunder's way. Kevin Durant started Game 3 on fire, stepping back for unguardable threes, punishing defenders with screaming dunks. It was as if he were not only himself but Westbrook, too. By halftime, he already had twenty-seven points, and OKC held a commanding lead.

Then the Rockets came back. Durant went cold. Harden went off. He skittered through defenders, threw bullet passes to teammates, calmly stroked in threes himself. He waggled his arms to pump up the crowd. Westbrook watched motionless, with his crutches, as Houston erased a twenty-point deficit. All through the fourth quarter, the game went back and forth. With less than a minute left, the Rockets took the lead.

This was exactly the sort of situation in which Westbrook would have charged forward, with his maniacal lack of fear, to do something astonishing—either good or bad or, more likely, impossible to categorize in traditional human terms. Instead, for the first time ever, with the future on the line, there was only Kevin Durant.

Durant dribbled left, far behind the three-point line, probing the defense. Suddenly, impulsively, still hounded by his defender, he rose up to shoot. This was an objectively bad shot—a long, contested three-pointer, precisely the sort of selfish heave that Westbrook was always launching, the kind of thing the media was always criticizing him for.

Sure enough, Kevin Durant missed. The ball caromed hard off the back of the rim.

But this was the moment when the old sky magic, the good charm of the bad weather, really kicked in. Durant's shot hit the back of the rim and bounced straight up into the stratosphere, a good twenty-five feet over the court. It seemed to pause at its apex, then fell back down like a stone, hard and straight, and on its way to the ground it happened to clip the front of the rim. This sent the ball ricocheting to the back of the rim, which popped it up off the glass, which sent it back to the back of the rim—and then, after this whole ridiculous Rube Goldberg routine, the ball fell softly through the net.

The missed shot became, miraculously, a made shot. It was the most circuitous three points of Durant's entire career, way beyond anything that might reasonably be called a shooter's roll.

With that gust of luck, the Thunder regained the lead in the game, and—after Harden threw the ball away on the final possession—they managed to hang on and win. This put them up 3–0 in the series, right on the brink of a sweep. It was a dominant advantage, a lead no team had ever lost before, but it was not at all a dominant feeling. OKC had survived one more night. In the meantime the atmosphere seemed to have worked out whatever instability it had built up over the previous days. But surely the weather would change.

9:02

April 19, 1995. Wednesday. An unusually busy morning downtown. Just after 6:00 a.m., before the sun was even up, nearly thirteen hundred of Oklahoma City's power players were already on the move, driving down to meet at I. M. Pei's convention center, which was now so run down that people worried its roof might collapse. Drivers with their radios on might have heard Gary England, the official voice of the Oklahoma sky, pop in with his morning forecast: cool day, clear skies, chance of a big evening storm. City officials, chamber of commerce members, oil executives, media personnel—everyone parked as close to the convention center as they could, which wasn't hard, because downtown was almost entirely parking. The mayor's annual prayer breakfast started at 6:45. It was an opportunity for city leaders to ponder all of the many ways in which a close relationship with God could power OKC's civic and corporate good. The special speaker that morning was a Ford executive named Dick Fenstermacher—a curious last name, German for "window maker."

For the first time in a long time, the feeling downtown was optimistic. The city had been collecting the special MAPS sales tax by then for nearly a year, and the various projects were being planned. The front page of that morning's newspaper carried a story about the different bids being considered for the minor league baseball stadium to be built in Bricktown, the once-empty warehouse district. All this growth was still distant and theoretical, and downtown was still stagnant, but at least now it seemed like things wouldn't get any worse. The process had begun.

The mayor's prayer breakfast ended at 8:30 a.m.—just in time for everyone to head off, with supercharged faith, to take on the workday.

And so the leaders of Oklahoma City scattered throughout downtown, radiating out from the convention center, past the intersection of Broadway and Main, where Angelo Scott once stood on a box to lead his mass meetings, past the jogs in the streets, past the old site of the Biltmore Hotel, past the huge empty lot that was supposed to have been Pei's grand mall, past the formerly booming blocks where shoppers had stepped out of streetcars for sandwiches at what used to be Katz Drug Store and John A. Brown's.

As the city leaders scattered into those vacancies, a white van would have been passing through downtown. Inside it was the Orton family, out on its morning routine. Daniel was four years old and headed for preschool. The van stopped, first, right in the heart of everything, on Broadway, between the convention center and the Murrah Building. Orton's mother worked for the phone company, in a grand old skyscraper on Third Street—a product of the city's original oil boom that had survived urban renewal and was now nearly seventy years old. Orton's mother said good-bye and got out of the van. The remaining Ortons drove north, past the Murrah Building, and stopped on Tenth Street. This was Daniel's favorite part of the day: Brown's Bakery, where he always ordered a strawberry doughnut and milk before his dad dropped him off at school.

McVeigh's yellow Ryder truck, meanwhile, was heading south. If he had the radio on, he might have heard Gary England too, back on the air with his 8:00 weather report. Cool and clear, possible storms in the evening. McVeigh drove more or less on the route of the Land Run, on roads planned and executed by Stanley Draper, toward the outskirts of the Great Annexation. He drove with extra caution, paying special attention to the speed limit, avoiding unnecessary attention.

A few blocks from Brown's Bakery, Wayne Coyne was inside the Compound, sleeping a deep, working-class, middle-American rockstar sleep. The Flaming Lips had just flown back from Australia, where they had played a couple of shows with Nine Inch Nails, and Wayne felt completely displaced in time. They were at the exhausting tail end of a long, grueling, acrimonious process of recording their seventh album, *Clouds Taste Metallic*: sixteen hours at a time holed up in a run-down studio on the bleak edge of downtown, across the street from the city's sewage treatment facility—two solid months of late nights, bad food, cigarettes, arguments. The lead guitarist was on the brink of quitting the band. The drummer's heroin habit was growing. Wayne was trying to hold it all together long enough to record the album, which would contain such sing-along classic choruses as "All your bad days will end." But for now, finally, Wayne was sleeping.

The yellow Ryder truck kept coming south, at precisely the legal speed limit—a secret pocket of destruction tucked into the usual traffic. At some point on the freeway, a police car pulled up behind it, inexplicably, and followed it for several miles. After five minutes or so, however, the policeman sped off somewhere else, and the plot continued rolling forward.

Gary England sat up in bed and blinked. He put his headphones back on and got his mike set up. His habit, for these early-morning radio spots, was to call in to the station, read out the forecast, then fall backward into bed and go immediately back to sleep until it was time for the next forecast, an hour later. Now it was time for the 9:00 a.m. crowd. He called into the station and said hello to the producer again. He waited for his colleagues to get everything set up, for his introduction. He half-listened to them doing the news, blinking, waiting for his cue. Clear skies, cool morning. Storms coming in the afternoon and evening. Chance of high winds, heavy rain.

The scene at the Murrah Building, that morning, was completely mundane. It was Wednesday. Capable people were dealing competently with tasks. The workers there at that time would have been the punctual ones, the ones who came a little early to make sure everything was in proper working order. The customers they were serving would have been similarly eager: the kind of people who ran errands as soon as the office opened in order to avoid the lines. They said good morning to one another, asked if anything was new. "You have a good day." "Thanks, you too." All the normal small kindnesses.

Out in the middle of nowhere, in the vast northern stretches of the

Great Annexation, the Ryder truck officially entered Oklahoma City. As it kept coming south, at precisely the speed limit, it passed near Gary England's house on 122nd Street. Minutes later, it was driving down the East Side, past Daniel Orton's grandparents' house, past Clara Luper's Freedom Center, past the medical centers and government buildings that had been built on cleared neighborhoods, past Douglass High School and Deep Deuce.

When Timothy McVeigh reached downtown, there would have been no traffic to speak of.

At the first stoplight he hit, McVeigh put in a pair of green foam earplugs. He drove a little farther, then pulled over and, using a cigarette lighter, started the five-minute fuse. This produced so much unexpected smoke that McVeigh had to crack the windows, but no one was around to notice. He kept driving. At precisely 8:56:53, a security camera in the lobby of an apartment building captured an image of the truck passing. McVeigh looked like anyone moving into a new apartment, like any guy coming into OKC to take a job in an office somewhere. Shortly afterward, at another stoplight, McVeigh lit the two-minute fuse.

Daniel Orton, at this point, was playing outside. After the doughnuts, his father had dropped him off, as always, at preschool at Villa Teresa, where Carmelite nuns watched over the children. Daniel was out on the playground.

McVeigh cruised east on Fifth Street, through the heart of the downtown grid, earplugs in, smoke pouring out the cracked windows. Empty lots, parking garages, bail bond offices, payday loan shops, empty lots. Finally he reached the Murrah Building, still rising like a twentieth-century castle in the middle of downtown, its north wall a tall sheet of glass. There was a little drop-off zone directly out front, a recess in the curb for trucks making deliveries. McVeigh pulled in and cut the engine. The Ryder truck was now parked under the building's shimmering wall of glass. Directly on the other side, on the second floor, was America's Kids, a day-care center, where twenty-one children were settling in for Bible time.

The Ryder truck's fuses continued to smoke. McVeigh got out. He started to walk away from the truck and the building, doing his best to seem normal, to walk unremarkably, to not get caught. He could have been anybody: windbreaker, baseball cap, jeans.

McVeigh crossed Fifth Street, heading north, not looking back.

At Sixth Street he passed a police car, parked, with someone inside it, but he kept moving. He reached an alley and broke into a jog.

Right about then, in an office just across the street from the Murrah Building, the Oklahoma Water Resources Board sat down to start its morning meeting. It had a case to settle: the permit request of a local family that wanted to bottle and sell its groundwater. There was a tape recorder running. "This is Wednesday," a woman said, "April the nineteenth, 1995."

McVeigh was approaching the getaway car when it occurred to him that the explosion probably should have happened already. He considered turning back, striding right up to the truck, pulling out his Glock, shooting the bomb directly to make sure it went off—but some force, cowardice or confidence or inertia, kept him jogging down the alley.

"This is a hearing for protest of groundwater application number 94501," said the woman running the Water Resources Board meeting. "Basically, there are four elements that I have to uh, uh . . . receive information regarding."

That was exactly when it happened.

At this point in its history, Oklahoma City was familiar with just about every possible kind of explosion. This one, however, was unidentifiable. It was on a whole different scale. All across the spread-out city, people heard the noise and struggled to make sense of it. They thought it was everything except what it was: a gas line exploding, a train rumbling by, a Dumpster being dropped, a sonic boom, thunder, a tornado. Wayne Coyne's family had a business downtown, and all of its windows blew out, and their first thought was that an airplane must have crashed outside in the alley. Daniel Orton's grandfather was sitting at his dining room table reading the newspaper when his house started to shake. He thought it was an earthquake, something he'd never felt before. Clara Luper's son, Calvin, figured a jet pilot had come in too hard at Tinker Air Force Base, causing the whole city to boom. So many hundreds of other causes were more likely than what it was.

At the Water Resources Board hearing, in the building across the street from the Murrah, the woman speaking about groundwater application number 94501 was interrupted by a thick rumbling roar so deep and loud that it overwhelmed the tape recorder's little microphone. It sounds, on the old tape, like a thousand thunderstorms exploding inside of one another. All of Oklahoma City was filled with that noise.

In the meeting, the woman's calm voice turned loud.

"Everybody!" she screamed. "Let's get out of here—now! WATCH THE ELECTRICITY LINE! Out the main door! All the way to your right!"

Up at the Compound, Wayne Coyne sat up in bed. Recently, some houses had blown up in his neighborhood—hot water tanks, unmaintained for years. This, he figured, must have been another of those. He listened for a few seconds, then went back to sleep.

Out on the playground of his preschool, a mile north of the Murrah Building, four-year-old Daniel Orton was running around when, out of nowhere, the ground shook violently underneath him. All the windows suddenly blew out of his school building, sending glass flying everywhere, kids screaming, everyone sprinting back into the school, to shelter, but Orton went the other way—toward the noise, all the way to the playground's fence. He stared downtown. His mother was down there. Smoke was starting to come up from the center of the city.

Gary England, at his home fifteen miles north, heard the explosion in double—in his headphones once, and then again in real life. He was still on the line with the radio, waiting to do the 9:00 a.m. forecast. His whole house shook. The producer told him that something bad had just happened, and England ran downstairs, out the front door, to look up at the sky—a habit he'd picked up from many years of reporting the weather. But he couldn't see anything. So he went back inside and turned on the TV.

What came out of Timothy McVeigh's yellow Ryder truck that morning was a huge, scorching wind. This wind, more than the fire, was what did most of the damage. It poured out at seven thousand miles per hour, far faster than any wind ever naturally created by the atmosphere of the earth, more than twenty times faster than wind inside even the fastest tornado. This burning wind slammed instantaneously into the front of the Alfred P. Murrah Building, and many of those who died did so in that first blast, in an unimaginably small fraction of time: one two-hundredths of a second.

In only half a second, the wind was gone, replaced by a vacuum, which sucked everything violently back out.

These forces were much more than the structure could take. The Murrah Building's strength came entirely from its concrete, and the hot wind ripped right through it, turning it to dust. Several crucial supports failed. The floors were jolted violently upward by the bomb, then slammed back down by gravity, and in that motion they broke and fell: nine stories popping down on top of one another, heavier and heavier with each floor. Where the Ryder truck had parked was now a thirty-foot crater into which people and rubble were falling.

Inside the building, there was no time to process anything. Normal life became, without warning or transition or explanation, apocalyptic. Workers were at their desks clicking into the system or calling spouses on the phone; they were walking to the coffee machine or just sitting down to take a computer class. Two customers had brought their four-year-old granddaughter to run an errand at the bank on the third floor. A pregnant woman who worked at the DEA was showing co-workers a picture of her recent sonogram. Meetings were being called to order. People were waiting for elevators. It was a normal office building—attacked, without warning, as if it were a military target. People had no way to prepare, and survival was random. In that first moment of chaos, multiple government workers thought that their computers had suddenly blown up in their faces, or that they had fallen asleep at their desks and were only having a

nightmare. On the fourth floor, a man was sitting in his chair when he saw a woman across the room suddenly put her arms straight up in the air, and he wondered why anyone would do that, and then he realized it was because the floor was gone and they were both falling, and when he stopped he was sitting not on his chair anymore but on a three-story pile of rubble. One woman who worked at the bank had just taken out a can of air freshener—someone with bad body odor had walked by—and the moment she pushed the button, the entire building exploded. She was in a coma for five weeks and woke up with this memory.

I got to know people in Oklahoma City who would tell me everything about their lives, every inch of the deep history of the city, but they could not talk to me about anything they saw on April 19, 1995.

The bomb shattered the Murrah Building's windows into a storm of broken glass. It filled the atmosphere, shredding everything, driving itself into the walls of neighboring buildings. Glass filled people's shoes. The scope of the damage, the horror of it, is hard to describe. Every vulnerable body part, every soft tissue, was pierced. Everything horrible you can imagine being inflicted on a person happened almost instantaneously. It was one of those disasters where clothing ceases to have meaning. People's shoes were blown off their feet. To this day, some survivors still have slivers of glass embedded in their bodies.

The blast was felt thirty miles away. It damaged every single building within sixteen blocks, some of them beyond repair. The noise was so huge that, for a few seconds afterward, everything went silent. The first rescuers on the scene heard birdsong. Then the noises of emergency filled the space: yelling, screaming, muffled cries for help. Car parts burned in the tops of trees and on the roofs of nearby buildings. There was a large parking lot across the street, and now it was full of burning cars, their alarms blaring in insistent loops, and soon the burning cars began to explode, sending a huge column of black smoke into the air. Clear over on the East Side, at Calvary Baptist Church, where Clara Luper had started so many of her sit-ins, all the stained-glass windows blew out. Five blocks west of the Murrah Building, at police headquarters, the tile shook so hard, and so many

windows broke, that a policeman named Bill Citty, sitting in his office, assumed a bomb had gone off in his own building. But papers were raining down all around him—forms, memos, schedules—and Citty grabbed some out of the air and saw that every single one had come from the federal building. That was how he knew. He got there as fast as he could.

In and around the Murrah Building, it was almost impossible to breathe. The formerly clear air suddenly contained all of that pulverized concrete. Survivors emerged from the rubble so covered in dust that you couldn't tell if they were male or female, black or white. Even children had gray hair.

Gary England stood in his living room, frozen, watching the TV as the first image of the damage was broadcast. A local news helicopter, out scanning traffic, had been diverted to the Murrah Building. At precisely 9:13, it turned the corner to see the front of the building, where McVeigh had parked his truck. Everyone knew, at that moment, the full extent of things. The north side of the building was gone, and what had survived was shredded, sagging, on the verge of collapse.

"Car bomb," England said out loud. It looked exactly like images of terror attacks he had seen broadcast from Lebanon. He stood watching the footage of emergency responders rushing into the building, survivors staggering out covered with dust. England had been down there recently—right there, at the Water Resources Board—talking to its employees about how to survive a tornado. And now he was looking at the whole area destroyed on his TV. At one point, as everyone was still processing what was going on, there came news of the threat of *another* bomb inside the building, and the ruins of the Murrah Building had to be evacuated, and England saw something he would never forget: Randy Renner, one of his very first storm chasers, a friend and colleague, as affable an Oklahoman as you were ever likely to meet—good old good-natured Randy Renner suddenly came sprinting out of the Murrah Building in obvious terror. England had seen Renner driving toward tornadoes, right into the danger, but now he was running for his life, along with a whole crowd of other people, everyone bracing themselves for the sound of another explosion behind them. In that alien landscape, among the rubble and the chaos, to suddenly see a familiar face—it jarred England, and that image of Randy racing out of the ruined building would pop into his mind again and again, for the rest of his life.

Even as time moved on, it remained 9:02 downtown. The bomb had frozen wristwatches and wall clocks. Rescuers rushed to the Murrah Building from all over Oklahoma City. A nurse named Rebecca Anderson came from ten miles away to help victims, only to be struck in the head by falling debris and become a victim herself. (She collapsed on the scene and died in the hospital four days later.) National disaster technicians mobilized to assess the damage. The ruined building was complex and unstable—a whole new horrible landscape—and rescuers had to figure out how to get in and save whatever lives they could. First responders looked for voids: spaces in the rubble, angles of concrete in which people might have survived. They reinforced these cavities with steel braces and wooden beams, listened for muffled voices, and went in again and again. Live electrical wires hung down everywhere; cold water rose in every depression. Almost immediately, rescuers started to map and name the different zones of the wreckage: the Pit, the Pile, the Forest. From the top of the building hung precarious slabs of concrete, dangling from bent rebar or stretched wires. One huge block was nicknamed the Mother: thirty-two thousand pounds, with rebar sticking out in every direction. Rescuers were constantly aware of it as they worked.

Office chairs were used as gurneys. The injured sat or lay, in long lines, on the sidewalk outside, and medics tagged them according to severity. It was a war zone, the very definition of a triage situation, and some victims were so badly hurt they had to be allowed to die. Some survivors passed their jackets to others, and people kneeled together to shelter each other from the wind.

Timothy McVeigh's bomb hit the day-care center directly, killing fifteen of the twenty-one children. One boy survived because he had been lingering in the bathroom, playing with the water, and the extra infrastructure was just strong enough to hold.

The rescuers put themselves in grave danger and saw unimaginable things. One woman was pinned so tightly in the rubble that a doctor had to climb on top of her and, with his left hand, laboriously amputate her leg at the knee. Rescuers looking up at the crushed floors saw blood dripping through the cracks, as if the building itself were bleeding. A firefighter, Chris Fields, arrived minutes after the bombing and was working through triage cases when a policeman approached to say that he had found a baby. Fields took the baby in his arms; he could see, immediately, that she was dead, and the thought passed through his mind that somebody's whole world was about to fall apart, and just at that moment a photographer took his photo. That image became the symbol of the bombing, published on the front pages of newspapers and magazines all over the world.

The Oklahoma City federal building, previously unknown outside the city itself, was instantly the talk of the globe. Its image broke into scheduled programming everywhere. Local stations started to broadcast from the scene without commercial interruption. The big networks' celebrity anchors mobilized to OKC. A hundred TV crews took up semipermanent residence at a nearby intersection, with so many trucks that the spot became known as Satellite City.

One of the happiest memories of Daniel Orton's life remains the moment, sometime after the noise, when his mother and father, both of them, walked through the door of his preschool to pick him up.

Wayne Coyne woke up properly later that morning, when the phone rang, and it was Michelle's mother, who worked in a building downtown—things were blowing up, she said, and no one was being allowed to leave. At the Compound they turned on the TV, and Wayne stood there watching the images of the center of the city burning—the most familiar place in the world, the landscape of his whole life, looking suddenly foreign. It felt surreal, and then it occurred to him that he was actually only a few minutes away from the reality of it, so he got on his bike and rode south, through the nameless neighborhoods of his childhood, the places where nothing ever happened, until after a few minutes he reached the actual place, in person, that he had just been watching on TV. The scene looked strangely familiar, like things he had seen all his life: neighborhoods turned inside out by tornadoes, skyscrapers knocked down by wrecking crews. Wayne felt terrible for all the people involved, but he did not feel involved himself. It felt strangely personal but also far away. He was suddenly right in the center of the world but also removed from what was happening. He watched for a while, and then he rode back home.

It was spring in Oklahoma, and the weather didn't stop. Gary England's morning forecast turned out to be correct. That afternoon, as the rescue crews worked to extract survivors, serious thunderstorms formed in the sky, and as evening fell they erupted, drenching everything, soaking everyone, gusting wind so hard that the ruins started to rock, threatening to collapse. The hanging concrete blocks, including the Mother, swung back and forth on their strands of rebar. A tornado watch went into effect. Lightning flashed. Eventually, rescuers knocked holes in the back wall of the ruins to try to let the wind pass through.

In the midst of all this, the sun set. Rescue work went on by spotlight. That evening, rescuers heard a faint cry, deep in the rubble, right under a cluster of hanging concrete chunks. They called for quiet. It was a girl's voice, emanating from underneath four feet of rubble, calling out that she couldn't breathe. A doctor was able to reach down and hold her hand while firefighters dug, for hours, until they found her, still alive. She was fifteen years old. She had been at the Social Security office. No one knew it then, but she would be the final survivor.

After that, no more voices came from the building. The task became mainly to remove those who had died. Emergency crews searched the rubble systematically, with fiber-optic cameras and acoustic listening devices, using a technique called checkerboarding: clearing and searching fourteen-foot squares. What they found was so terrible that some workers had Vietnam flashbacks. Even the rescue dogs became visibly depressed.

The search went on for more than two weeks, until every accessible inch of the Alfred P. Murrah Federal Building had been analyzed. On May 4, just before midnight, the rescue operation officially stopped. In the final accounting, 168 people had died. Two hundred nineteen children had lost a parent; 30 were orphaned completely.

More than 500 people were injured, many severely, in ways that would never fully heal.

Clara Luper's radio show, three days after the bombing, felt like a church service. She expressed her grief out loud, in public. She wept. She repeated, over and over, a rhythmic refrain: "It happened in the heartland of America." She asked the people of the East to bring food and supplies to the Freedom Center—canned goods, diapers, dog food, safety glasses, baby food, deodorant, raincoats, soap, flashlights, lotion—anything that might help the rescue workers. She lauded the nobility of the dead and injured, "these hard-working people that went to work on time." One of Calvin Luper's old fraternity brothers, Clarence Wilson, had been an attorney at HUD, on the Murrah Building's eighth floor. During Black History Month, Clara Luper had gone there to speak to all the employees, and the memory of it now drove her to despair.

"I *knew* those people," she said. "Those were my—my *friends*. But now Clarence is gone!"

"No, Mama," said Calvin. "He—"

Calvin was still trying to believe that Clarence might only be missing, or might still be alive in the rubble.

"*Oh,* my God," Clara went on. "Not only Clarence, all of those workers. And those little children. How could anybody do it?

"Oh, it's an emptiness," she moaned. "An emptiness! What is it like? It's like looking up to the sky—and there's no sky. It's like looking at the fields—and there's no grass."

At the end of the show, she signed off, simply, with "This is Clara Luper saying, I love you."

JUSTICE

Every time a new player joins the Oklahoma City Thunder, before he ever plays a game, he is required to go downtown and take a tour of the bombing memorial. He sees the twisted axle of Timothy McVeigh's demolished Ryder truck, still labeled with evidence tags from the investigation. He sees stopped clocks and broken coffee mugs. He walks among the 168 bronze-and-glass chairs, arranged in neat rows inside the footprint of the missing building, each chair inscribed with a name of one of the dead. He walks around the reflecting pool, on the space that was once Fifth Street, and along the chain-link fence outside, where people still come from all over the world to leave photos, poems, and stuffed animals. He sees the Survivor Tree, a gnarled elm that somehow lived through the blast. The memorial visit is official team policy, required without exception. Daniel Orton told the team that, since he had actually experienced the bombing in person, since his mom had been right down near it, since his uncles were firefighters who helped at the scene, since he had been to the memorial a million times, he didn't feel he needed to take the official tour. But the Thunder made him go anyway. It was part of the Process.

The connection between basketball and the bombing may seem like a stretch. Regardless of how much energy we pour into it, sports is not life or death. Nick Collison, the Thunder's longest-tenured player, once told me that he was cautious on this point. "It's just basketball," he said. "I would hate to have someone who lost family members in the bombing hear some player say, 'We're here now, we're winning, so it makes it better.' They're totally different things. I do think the

Thunder has been positive for the city, and the city has really gotten behind us. But I'm not gonna say we've made up for anything. I'll let people who live here say that, if they believe it."

Many people do, indeed, believe it. From my very first day in Oklahoma City, I heard it frequently: the arrival of the Thunder had helped heal the wound created by the bombing. McVeigh's attack was front-page news for months and years. Tragedy became Oklahoma City's national brand. For a city so invested in its place in the world, a place always stung by a civic inferiority complex, this shift in its reputation, at such a low moment, was not trivial: it deepened all of the other sadnesses. It made a full recovery seem, at times, impossible. The Thunder's arrival, thirteen years after the bombing, and its nearly immediate excellence, was not so much about sports glory as it was about identity. People were coming to Oklahoma City, celebrating Oklahoma City, reading about Oklahoma City, for reasons that had nothing to do with tragedy. When the Thunder made the Finals in the spring of 2012, it was as if the city had been reborn—bonded again in collective joy.

Perhaps the most articulate proponent of this belief is Justice Steven Taylor of the Oklahoma Supreme Court. He makes the connection between basketball and the bombing explicitly, without hesitation, in long enthusiastic paragraphs that pour amiably out of his mouth.

"My interest in the Thunder is about more than just basketball," he told me one day in his chambers. "It is about what that organization has done spiritually, economically, demographically—all the social sciences—for this community. Basketball has been the vehicle. When I go into that arena, I know there will be nineteen thousand citizens in the stands. I purposefully use the word 'citizens.' Most of them would tell you that, five years ago, they could barely spell the word 'basketball.' They had no interest in the NBA. They're there as *citizens*. They're there because that's Oklahoma's team. Chesapeake arena is a community gathering place. I've been to every home game for five years. I've had the same seat, and I've gotten to know the people around me. They're from all different walks of life: blue-collar, white-collar, professional, retired. They're there as *citizens*. That's why I'm so enthusiastic. It's not that I'm some big basketball nut. It's because I love this community and I love this state."

Justice Taylor was uniquely qualified to speak on this subject. He was not only a Thunder superfan but also the judge who sentenced Terry Nichols, in 2004, to 161 consecutive life sentences. You can find Justice Taylor at every OKC home game, in section 120, right at the top of the lower bowl, on the aisle—a seat he chose because it backs up against a concrete wall, which means he can stand throughout the game without bothering other fans.

By the time Terry Nichols entered Justice Taylor's courtroom, he had already been convicted in federal court. He was already going to spend the rest of his life in prison. But Oklahomans wanted local justice. They wanted Nichols held responsible for everyone who'd died—not just the eight officers covered by the federal case, but the 160 civilians, too. So there was a state trial. It couldn't be held in Oklahoma City, because every judge in the county had recused himself. Instead, the trial was held in McAlester, Oklahoma, a small town out in Choctaw Nation, a couple hours' drive to the southeast. This was how Justice Taylor came into things. He knew that everyone was watching, and he became obsessed, above all, with due process.

"I told Terry Nichols, eyeball to eyeball in the courtroom, with everybody listening and all the press, I said to him: 'I'm going to make you one promise, Mr. Nichols, and that is that you're going to get a fair trial. I know you think this is some kangaroo court. But you are either going to get a fair trial or there's going to be no trial at all.' I turned to the prosecutor and said: 'I mean that. If we cannot have a fair trial, then I'll dismiss this and we're done.' So we had a fair trial."

It was the largest murder trial in the history of the United States. When Justice Taylor announced his ruling—161 consecutive life sentences, no parole—he pointed his finger at Nichols and lectured him. "Mr. Nichols," he said, "it is quite ironic that the government that you hate so much is big enough and strong enough and good enough to give you a fair trial. You need to think about that."

Justice Taylor said he still thinks about the Nichols trial every day. And he thinks of Oklahoma City's current renaissance, and especially the Thunder, as a direct rebuke to the terrorists of 1995.

"The bombing brought Oklahoma City to its knees," Taylor told me. "At that point, this community had two choices. One was to go down and stay down. The other was to get up and prove that civics and citizenship and the rule of law will overcome and prevail. We are so strong and resilient that we are actually going to be *better*. That's what we did. The Thunder is Exhibit A that this community recovered, was resilient, and is actually better than it was before McVeigh and Nichols tried to strike a blow to its heart. The downtown growth, the buildings—those are physical signs. The Thunder is more than physical. It's not a building; it's a feeling, it's a spirit."

Next to Taylor's desk was a row of tiny photos mounted on cardboard: every school picture of his son, Wilson, from kindergarten through high school. Wilson Taylor was now in his twenties and worked for the Thunder as manager of team operations. He restocked the practice facility's mini-fridges, kept track of the players' shoes, sat on the baseline during games, and gathered dirty laundry in the locker room afterward. This is how Oklahoma City works: the son of the judge who tried Terry Nichols was the one who made sure that Kevin Durant had the proper shoes in the middle of an East Coast road trip. This is what residents mean when they call the place the biggest small town in America. The interconnectedness can sometimes be overwhelming.

McVeigh wasn't snagged in some dramatic nationwide manhunt. He was pulled over on a routine traffic stop, up near the Kansas line, by a police officer determined to keep doing his job by the book, even after all hell had broken loose to his south: Charlie "the Hangman" Hanger, so named because of his harshness over minor infractions. This was ninety minutes after the bomb, on I-35, eighty miles north of Oklahoma City. He had no idea who McVeigh was or why he was driving north. Earlier that morning, just after the bombing, Hanger had actually gone speeding south toward OKC to help out, like everyone else, but he had been called off because there were plenty of police officers there already.

Hanger saw an old yellow car without a license plate. He sped up and pulled alongside it. The driver was a young guy, slim, crew cut. They exchanged a look. The officer nodded. The driver nodded back. The officer dropped back and put his lights on. McVeigh later told people that he had considered drawing his weapon, but he'd decided he didn't want to kill another person and risk hurting the mighty justice of his cause. Until the end, he still basically thought of himself as the hero of an action movie.

McVeigh was booked into the Noble County Jail, on misdemeanor charges, in the minuscule town of Perry, Oklahoma, about an hour north of OKC. He spent two days there as an ordinary prisoner, watching the bombing coverage on the jail's TV like everyone else, listening to the national media whip itself into a frenzy about Arab terrorists. No one at the jail suspected that McVeigh had anything to do with the bombing. In fact, he was almost released. The judge hearing the case had to delay it twice, once because another trial ran long and then because his son missed the bus to school. This allowed investigators just enough time. McVeigh was actually in the courtroom, about to be released on bail, when a sheriff walked in and handed the DA a note: *This is the Oklahoma City bomber.*

The criminal investigation had begun the moment the bomb went off. Even as the rescuers worked through the rubble, the police were gathering clues. Investigators suspected immediately that this was a gun-rights extremist, probably ex-military. April 19 was the second anniversary of Waco, the 220th anniversary of the beginning of the American Revolution at the Battles of Lexington and Concord. They smelled ammonium nitrate. They marked a twenty-block perimeter with yellow tape. Officers took photos of every car in the area, inspected every piece of debris. The Ryder truck was found, in pieces, shredded and scattered over five square blocks. Its rear axle had flown a block and a half and crushed the front of a red Ford Festiva parked near the Regency Towers Apartments. The VIN number on that axle led police to the shop that had rented it to McVeigh, which revealed his alias (Robert Kling, born on April 19) and produced a police sketch and led to the Dreamland Motel in Junction City, Kansas, where McVeigh had stayed just before the bombing.

McVeigh was found guilty just over two years later, on June 2, 1997—"He looks like such a nice boy," someone in the courtroom said out loud—and he got the death penalty two weeks later, on Friday the 13th. As McVeigh left the courtroom, he flashed the jury a peace sign. He ended up on death row in Indiana, obsessively watching cartoons and movies on a thirteen-inch black-and-white TV. He was killed by lethal injection on June 11, 2001. At the moment the drugs were administered, McVeigh stared directly into a TV camera, on the other end of which more than two hundred people were watching the execution live via closed-circuit television in Oklahoma City—survivors, city officials, families of the victims. The people of Oklahoma City were together, and he was alone. They would go on, and he would not.

Just over a month after the attack, the remains of the Alfred P. Murrah Federal Building were blown up, on purpose, by the city. In fact, city officials hired the same company that had demolished the Biltmore Hotel almost twenty years earlier. It took 150 pounds of nitroglycerine—more than they'd expected, the company said, because the ruined structure had been so thoroughly shored up during the rescue, which had made it surprisingly strong. The remainder of the Murrah Building collapsed in just 7.75 seconds.

GAME 93: THAT ARM BECAME A HEAVY ARM

Without Westbrook, the Thunder did manage to finish off the Rockets in the first round. But it wasn't easy, fast, or convincing. Kevin Durant now sat next to two empty lockers, and that turned out to be one too many. During the rest of the series, James Harden showed everyone the full scope of the talent the Thunder had traded away. He jittered and danced, set up teammates, sliced through space for layups, and calmly stroked three-pointers. He was, at his best, like a combination of Westbrook and Durant—the perfect blend of selfishness and benevolence. It was impossible to watch Harden and not imagine how much he would have helped the Thunder at precisely this moment.

Durant's very lucky shot in Houston had put the Thunder on the brink of a sweep. But then they managed to lose the next two games. In Oklahoma City in Game 5, Westbrook was in the arena with his crutches, looking helpless, wearing the same oversized blue T-shirt as all the other home fans, watching while James Harden went incandescent, making nine of his first eleven shots. In response, the Thunder melted down. OKC missed thirteen three-pointers in a row, Kevin Martin shot one for ten, and Durant—perpetually lost in crowds of defenders—failed to score at all in the fourth quarter, for the first time in his entire play-off career.

After the game, Durant complained about the Rockets defense loading up on him. "They don't really care about anyone else on the team," he said.

"That arm became a heavy arm," Scott Brooks said about his lone superstar.

After that game, with the Thunder now ahead in the series 3–2, people began to wonder if OKC might become the first NBA team ever to surrender a 3–0 series lead. Going into Game 6, Vegas odds-makers actually favored Houston to win—unheard of for a No. 1 seed against a No. 8 seed.

"The Thunder-Rockets series is proving two things," wrote Berry Tramel in the *Oklahoman*. "How good Kevin Durant is. And how good Russell Westbrook is."

"We did not know how important Russell Westbrook was," wrote the *Daily Thunder*. "We had absolutely no clue. We knew he mattered, yes, but not this much. . . . With Westbrook on the floor, it was always guaranteed that, no matter what, we had one person that was going to be going as hard as he could possibly go until the world finally rested around him, then he'd take it up seven more notches while everyone slept. He was the lifeblood, the conductor. The one that let the crowd know it was okay to turn the volume up. Without Russell, sometimes it looks like we're shopping for beds."

Game 6 was back in Houston. Over the first five minutes, the Rockets scored fifteen points in a row—Harden assist, Harden three, Harden assist—and the crowd, sensing a historic Game 7 against a wounded team, got raucously Texan. The Thunder, however, came back. Kevin Martin, Harden's replacement, finally got hot, launching his weird-looking flings from all over the court. The game went back and forth, and the Thunder finally pulled away at the end, silencing Houston and advancing to the next round. Things were still, technically, on script. But it had been a scrappy, contentious, ominous, unsatisfying series. OKC no longer had the look of a contender steamrolling its way to the Finals. It was limping ahead.

I don't want to say that the second round of the 2013 play-offs didn't happen. It did. The schedule shows that games occurred. There are numbers, photos, video footage. A few of the games were even close. But it may as well not have happened. Everyone watching could tell.

In the second round, the Thunder faced their old nemesis, the enormous and brawny and violent Memphis Grizzlies. Durant was eternally swarmed and harassed, and despite it all he was magnificent.

Without Westbrook, however, the team looked stagnant and unsure. They could keep games close but never boost ahead. Kevin Martin established himself as a bona fide non-star. In Game 5 at home—in front of the mayor, the police chief, the city council, Justice Taylor, and the naked belly of Thundor—Durant had an open shot to tie the game and extend the series, right near the free-throw line, a shot that he does not miss. But he missed. That arm was a heavy arm. The season was over, and the glory-starved crowd went home to sit and think about the distance between potential and reality, process and results.

After the game, Durant sat at the media table alone, sneaking glances at the box score. "Sometimes you've got to ride out the storm to get to the sunshine," he said. "We've got to continue to keep believing in each other and believe in this process and we'll be all right."

Daniel Orton, the hometown kid, Russell Westbrook's gigantic simulacrum, did not play a single minute in the play-offs. He sat behind the bench in his suit, stone-faced through the drama, watching helplessly like everyone else. There is an advanced statistic called VORP—value over replacement player—which measures an actual player's performance against a hypothetical average. Ratings can be positive or negative. Durant's VORP that season was 7.6; Westbrook's was 5.1; the rookie Perry Jones's was –0.5. Orton's rating was exactly 0.0. He was perfectly neutral, remarkably unremarkable—anonymous even as a statistic. For OKC's native son, the great revelation never came. The fairy tale was over.

THE AIR SMELLED ALMOST LIKE FISH

After the bombing, being a citizen in Oklahoma City meant something new. The civic weave was tighter. The formerly dispersed people had been brought back together by trauma. In the weeks and months following the tragedy, after the memorial services had been performed and the ruins of the Murrah Building had been demolished, as the legal cases against McVeigh and Nichols mounted, the people of OKC remembered that they had MAPS. In the time before the apocalypse, they had all somehow been persuaded to approve this public tax program to remake the center of the city. That program now took on new existential weight. In the wake of such devastating destruction, the idea of building things seemed even more transformative—and not just building anything but building new public spaces, places of congregation, in the shared space of downtown. By 1995, OKC needed MAPS more than it ever had.

The projects, however, were slow.

That was the nature of the beast. MAPS was not the Land Run. It was not Stanley Draper raising millions of dollars over lunch for one of his secret initiatives. MAPS was a hugely complex tax program run by the city government. This meant red tape everywhere, multiple meetings to discuss every little step, competing bids on every project, the laborious acquisition of land, and infinite other bureaucratic details. There was an official twenty-one-member Citizens Oversight Board. That was the cost of doing public work properly. As Mayor Norick put it: "We know the key to doing MAPS right will be planning, planning, planning."

The people were not used to this, and they didn't like it. As everything fell behind schedule, as construction budgets grew, as designs were exposed to be flawed, as sites turned out to be hard to procure, as it was unclear that the river would hold water, the citizens of Oklahoma City began to complain. A groundbreaking ceremony was held for the minor league baseball stadium, in Bricktown, long before designs were even ready, just to create the illusion of movement. But the people were not fooled.

In 1997, when the NHL officially rejected OKC's bid for a pro hockey team, many in town argued that the city shouldn't even bother building the new MAPS sports arena. It would be a waste, they said. Just use that money to cover cost overruns elsewhere.

Finally, in the summer of 1998, something positive happened. In front of a crowd of thirteen thousand, Ron Norick threw out the first pitch in the new minor league baseball stadium in Bricktown. Many of the spectators had not actually been downtown in years, and everyone was amazed. There was construction all over. The Bricktown Canal was beginning to wind through the previously empty streets, among all the old warehouses. The stadium was better than it had to be—some said the best minor league park in the nation.

There was a new mood in the city. In the spring of 1999, OKC celebrated the completion of the steel frame of a new fifteen-story hotel downtown. Norick was there for a tree-raising ceremony. He talked about the long-awaited return of hotels, the future visitors they would attract. Slowly, but for real this time, downtown was being reborn.

The weather report in the *Oklahoman* on the morning of Monday, May 3, 1999, promised quiet skies. "Partly cloudy today and breezy," it read. "Storms will develop on Tuesday." But Gary England felt that this was not true. As he left the house, he told his wife not to expect him back for dinner. The air smelled almost like fish. This meant moisture drifting up from the Gulf of Mexico: fuel in the atmosphere. He would be proven disastrously right. By early afternoon, the storms gathering out west started to look dangerous. Just before 5:00 p.m., England interrupted his station's regular programming to warn the public about tornadoes dropping out of the sky. The storm chasers had footage: low, wet clouds, funnels reaching down, looking almost delicate from a distance but actually heaving trees and barns into the air. The funnels kept forming and coming, drifting east, and England warned people street by street, road by road.

Right around 6:00, a hook echo appeared on England's radar—a little curl at the back of a storm, all by itself. This was often the most dangerous part of a system, because it was isolated, and it could monopolize all the atmosphere's remaining fuel. The storm drifted toward Oklahoma City, rotating slowly, organizing itself. And then, sure enough, it dropped a tornado. This was not a small, probing funnel but the biggest Gary England had ever seen: a thick, dark wedge, more than a mile wide, pressed to the ground, churning and churning. Winds inside the wedge exceeded three hundred miles per hour, the fastest ever recorded, and it was heading toward the southern edge of Oklahoma City, where several suburban communities— Moore, Bridge Creek, Midwest City—mingle with the fringes of the Great Annexation. Val Castor, the network's leading storm chaser, said the tornado was so big he couldn't even fit a shot of it on the screen.

Finally, it zeroed in on Moore.

"You need to be below ground to survive this storm," England told his viewers. "Do not try to ride this storm out in your home unless you are trapped. Get in the center part of your house, a closet or a bathroom. Cover up with pillows and blankets. Lots of blankets. Get in the bathtub, put the kids in the bathtub, get in on top of the kids."

Block after block, the tornado wiped Moore clean of structures. It threw cars all over the freeway, uprooted huge trees, and snapped bridges. The damage was elemental. What was left looked like a world beyond the possibility of humans.

"If you're listening to me, get off the road, even if you have to break through a fence," England said. "Don't mess with it. Don't go outside and look at it. It'll kill you."

England stayed on the air until late that night—one of the longest stretches of live weather coverage in history. His eyes burned, his feet ached, his mouth went dry. But he couldn't stop. That day, more than seventy tornadoes dropped out of the sky. The storms killed more than forty people and injured nearly seven hundred. They caused more than $1 billion in damage. "It was the Oklahoma City bombing all over again," one resident told the *Oklahoman*. By the end of the night, England was so exhausted that his wife drove to the studio to pick him up. As they headed home in the dark, England considered quitting—the pressure and trauma and responsibility were overwhelming. But he stayed on. It was a day that divided Gary England's life. Before it, tornadoes had been exciting, invigorating. After, they were only horrible. His tone changed. This was the storm that turned him from a leading local weatherman into an Oklahoma legend, a cult figure, an international celebrity. BBC camera crews came to interview him. Survivors wrote to the station and said that the harshness of England's warning, his urgency, had saved their lives. He went and visited survivors in the hospital. It took him years before he could talk about the storm without crying.

Tornado damage in Moore, May 3, 1999.

THE LOWERINGS

On May 19, 2013, Oklahoma City should have been hosting the Western Conference Finals, beating San Antonio on the way to a rematch with Miami. Instead, the Thunder's players had all scattered off to their homes, in the cities they were actually from, to try to relax and live as normal humans again. The exception was Russell Westbrook, who stayed in OKC to rehabilitate his knee; characteristically, he got so deeply immersed in the process that he bought high-tech rehab equipment to keep at his own house, so he would never have to stop. In Game 1 of the Western Conference Finals, the Memphis Grizzlies stood in for the Thunder, and the Spurs walloped them by twenty-two points. San Antonio would go on to sweep Memphis and reach the Finals in OKC's place.

Few in Oklahoma City, however, would have been watching that series, and not just because of resentment. Once again, Gary England had taken over the city's TV screens. He was showing everyone radar imagery: a psychedelic cluster of red, yellow, and orange blobs that were merging south of the city. "That's a big-time supercell tornadic thunderstorm," England said.

Three years of relatively light storm seasons were about to come to an end. Dangerous conditions were churning in the atmosphere. Systems were crawling overhead, gathering strength, beginning to rotate, attempting to organize themselves. Late in the afternoon, two storms succeeded, and in the areas surrounding OKC they started dropping tornadoes, one after another.

"Gary! Gary! Gary! Take our stream! Take our stream!" shouted David Payne.

During severe weather coverage, England did not work alone. He presided over a large team of meteorologists, both in the studio and out in the field. England was like the emcee, and while he spoke to the public, activity buzzed all around him: meteorologists sifting data, reading maps, posting social media alerts, taking phone calls. Occasionally a colleague would lean onscreen to tell England something urgent: that the wind had just changed direction, or that the National Weather Service had issued one of its official warnings. All the beeping and blinking and rushing around made the studio feel like a hospital emergency room during a time of crisis.

Outside the studio, prowling back roads in search of good angles, were the storm chasers. Every network had its own team, spread across the region in SUVs, competing ruthlessly for the best footage. Whatever network got the clearest shot of a major tornado would almost always win the ratings war that night. This made storm chasing an uncomfortable mixture of science, thrill seeking, self-aggrandizement, and sensationalism. But storm chasers also added a crucial layer of insight. Radar data, like starlight, is information about the past: it tells you about the distant object it bounced off seconds or minutes before. This can tell you a lot—that conditions are perfect for a big storm, that *something* is in the air—but it can't actually look at the storm for you. For that, you still need people. Storm chasers provided the stations with what they call "ground truth."

England had a complicated relationship with his chasers. He relied on them, but they also drove him crazy. He wanted his chasers to stay calm, to act as a neutral set of eyes in the field, to inform the public—no shouting, no exclamations, no orgasmic savoring of destruction. He hated when chasers took unnecessary risks to get spectacular shots.

This, however, was a losing battle. Even the calmest storm chaser, in the face of two-hundred-mile-per-hour winds, found it hard to remain low-key. During severe weather, England toggled constantly between maps and graphics and live footage, deciding which was most valuable for the viewer to see at any given moment. Inevitably the voices of the chasers would break in to fight for his attention.

"Take my stream! Take my stream!" Viewers could hear much of this, and a large part of England's job was to try to keep things calm and focused—to prevent the chaos of the storm from infecting the coverage.

This year, Channel 9 had a new storm chaser: David Payne, England's replacement-in-waiting. As the star chaser at Channel 4, Payne had become famous for his white-knuckle pursuit of tornadoes and his occasional narrow escapes. He sometimes described the churning of a major storm as if he were watching his coolest friend do amazing snowboarding tricks. Now, Payne would be the eyes on the ground for Gary England. It seemed like a less than ideal pairing.

On May 19, 2013, the sky was dropping tornadoes everywhere. One was nearly a mile wide. Another lifted a semitruck and threw it off of I-40. In Edmond, a tornado passed right near LifeChurch.tv. A whole subdivision was destroyed.

"Big tornado, Gary, big tornado!" shouted Payne. "Look at the violent tornado, look at it here!"

England put Payne's video stream on the screen."It's a half mile wide, Gary! It's an EF4, maybe an EF5! Look at the formation! Ah, it's turning into a wedge, Gary. It's probably a half a mile wide. Big tornado, big tornado, Gary."

"Yeah, we see it," said England flatly, and he started explaining the radar images to his viewers, pointing out the storm's projected path.

"It's become stationary!" Payne shouted over him. "It's diggin' a hole!"

England ignored him and kept warning towns.

"Wowwww!" shouted Payne. "Oh! This thing is on the ground, it's right—"

Payne's video stream was fritzing out, breaking up, and soon another chaser started shouting over him.

"Guys," England said, in the tone of a school bus driver at the end of a very long day.

"Do you have our stream?!" Payne shouted.

"Guys, I'm gonna talk here just for a second," England said.

One viewer called the station to say that the chasers were scaring her children.

The following day, people who had lost their homes were still in Red Cross shelters, recovering, when everything got even worse. It was May 20. Once again, Gary England cut into the regular programming. The elements in the sky were lining up more dangerously than the day before, and by the middle of the afternoon, the radar images looked fantastical—like the blobs had all somehow set themselves on fire. To England, the storm seemed to be almost self-sustaining, creating itself out of nothing, building exactly the environment it needed to thrive. He started having flashbacks to May 3, 1999.

"It's gonna get ugly," said David Payne, "and it's gonna do so quickly."

Payne was right. At precisely 2:40, the National Weather Service issued its strongest possible warning: a Tornado Emergency. The funnel touched down sixteen minutes later. Gary England didn't even have time to take off his jacket.

"It's a big fat cone!" shouted Payne. "Here it comes! Here it comes!"

On the screen you could actually see the tornado begin: a thick shaft dropping through a band of bright sky, snuffling the ground with its funnel, like a creature searching for something.

"Take your immediate tornado precautions," England said.

"Take our stream!" shouted David Payne. "Wow, Gary, it's a destructive tornado. If you take our stream, you'll see it!"

"We got it," England responded. The storm was near the southern edge of Oklahoma City, and he narrated its progress street by street: Southwest 149th and Portland, Southwest 156th, Southwest 160th.

On the screen, the tornado grew. "Humongous," said Jim Gardner from the helicopter. "It is getting bigger by the minute." The funnel fattened and lost its shape. It became blurry and dark—a thick, ragged cloud pressed hard against the ground. The winds flowing into the storm, feeding it, were moving more than one hundred miles per hour. You could see the tornado mowing right toward neat rows of suburban houses. That, once again, was the city of Moore.

"My God," England said, almost to himself, and his voice took on a new quality: focused and efficient, calm to a degree that suggested not a natural response but a learned skill. "Get below ground, if at all possible," he told the people of Moore. "If you don't have that, you get in a well-constructed building. You get in the center part of your house. Closet or bathroom. Put as many walls between yourself and the tornado as possible." England started naming streets and projected times of arrival.

"This is a *huge* tornado, Gary," said Val Castor from his car. "Every bit as big as May third."

"Val, we can *see* the tornado," England said. "We just need where you're looking, where it's heading, that sort of thing."

The tornado, still pressed against the ground, entered Moore. It was now an EF5—the meteorologists' strongest designation. The bottom of the funnel was generating its own dark cloud of debris: people's houses, cars, furniture, lives. Every few seconds, the whole mess lit up from within: power lines snapping, transformers exploding. There was so much debris in the air that even the helicopter, from a distance, was having trouble seeing anything.

England's voice turned sad. "Houses and trees in the air, unfortunately," he said. "Make sure you call your friends, you tweet 'em, you Facebook 'em, whatever you want to do."

"GARY!" yelled Payne. "I'm at Southwest 134th and Penn! It's doing total destruction to every house down here! I'm seeing homes completely leveled! Houses are disappearing right in front of us! . . . There goes another house!"

"Gary, I see boards, I see roofs of houses, I see tin," added Val Castor. "Gary, there's houses in the air here."

"I know," England said. "I know."

"This is May 3, 1999, all over again," Payne said. "It's almost going down the same street."

It was true. It was fourteen years later, but the paths were uncannily similar. England had the feeling of living, for a second time, through the worst day of his life. Meanwhile, everyone was waiting for the tornado to weaken, or at least to lift off the ground, but it wouldn't. It was now completely wrapped in rain and debris—a black, smoky fuzz heading in the direction of Lake Stanley Draper.

"Goodness gracious," England said. "It made a jog there. I think the schools are in there."

A few minutes later, the news anchors came on to say that, indeed, Briarwood Elementary School had been hit.

Of Oklahoma City's more than one thousand police officers, Sergeant John Blumenthal was one of only eight who were federally certified in urban search and rescue. This meant he had completed a rigorous program that trained first responders in how to pull victims out of extreme situations—floods, fires, collapsed buildings. This storm season, Blumenthal's services would be much in demand. Just the previous day, after the May 19 rash of tornadoes, he had been called out to survey the rural towns of Shawnee and Little Axe. It had been dark, and he'd moved cautiously through the area with a headlamp and his gun, searching the woods for damaged houses and for trailers that had been blown off their concrete pads. Some of the property owners, suspecting looters, came out with guns drawn, but he managed to make sure things didn't escalate. Blumenthal got home sometime after 6:00 a.m.

Now, on almost no sleep, he was up and outside again, monitoring this new tornado. He stood on the edge of a storm shelter, inside of which his girlfriend and youngest son were huddled. The door was open so Blumenthal could dive in if he needed to. His three older children were at a school nearby. The sound of the tornado filled the landscape. It sounded nothing at all like wind; it was an overwhelming roar, like a machine. Blumenthal was watching the funnel, radioing its position to the department, when it passed a mile from his house. Debris started falling all around him. As soon as he was sure it had missed his kids' school, he left the shelter and drove toward Moore.

Before long, Blumenthal had to abandon his car. The debris was so thick that there were no streets left to drive on. Over the radio, he heard that Briarwood Elementary School had been devastated, and that kids were trapped inside. He felt a lack of emotion, only an urgent need to get there—this was part of the training. Blumenthal couldn't see the school, because there was nothing left of it to see, so he started running toward its absence. He knew that the neighborhood had four main streets, and that he'd entered on the eastern one, so he kept trying to weave his way west.

The tornado, at this point, was still churning a few hundred yards away from him—a dark column that sounded now like a train, chewing up metal, spitting fresh debris. As Blumenthal ran, he passed people emerging from the rubble of their houses, bleeding, running, collapsing. He ignored them, as he was trained to do. He made his way to what used to be the front door of the school. People were staggering around everywhere, screaming. Things were still falling out of the sky. The survivors shouted something about trapped and dead children, something about the second grade. Blumenthal's son had gone to kindergarten and first grade at Briarwood, so he knew its layout. He went to where the second-grade classroom should have been and he found, in its place, a pile. A tanker truck, parked nearly a mile away, had flown over and crushed it. He shouted, "Search and rescue," heard a scream in response, and looked down to see a woman's foot, wearing a flip-flop, sticking out of the debris. The children started screaming, too. Blumenthal crawled under a steel beam and managed to clear a narrow path, about eighteen inches wide, into which—although he's a big man—he was able to crawl. The foot, he found, belonged to a teacher's aide, who told Blumenthal that two adults and eighteen kids were trapped in the pile. He stayed with her, talking, while other officers cleared a path from the back side—a path eventually big enough for all of the kids, and their teacher, to file out. Miraculously, everyone was alive and more or less unharmed. The teacher's aide, however, was stuck: she had been impaled through the calf by a metal table leg. Blumenthal got a pocketknife, and working together, they managed to unscrew the table leg from the table. He and the other officers widened the path and pulled her out. They loaded her, the metal spear still stuck through her leg, into the back of a 4x4 pickup truck, which rumbled over debris to the hospital.

Once the tornado had passed, once everyone could look around, it was clear that Moore had ceased to be a town. Even people who lived there, after they managed to crawl out from storm shelters buried under piles of rubble, didn't understand what they were looking at. The tornado had churned an entire middle-class suburban neighborhood, as well as the rural areas around it, into an indistinguishable hash. Street signs and landmarks—everything you might use, consciously or unconsciously, to navigate—had been carried off. The streets themselves, as well as the driveways and sidewalks, were so thick with debris you couldn't even see them. It was a wilderness; everyone was lost and confused. The tops of trees were gone or twisted. Cows and horses had been impaled by flying boards and shards of scrap metal. Huge electrical poles had been bent in half, their power lines whipped around so hard that they'd unbraided into thin metal strands. Major roads were impassible. Minor roads had disappeared. It was pouring rain. First responders struggled to get over branches and live electrical wires, past hazards big and small: nails, broken glass, scattered pesticides, open gas lines, ruined transformers that sent arcs of electricity back and forth across the roads. Survivors were crawling out of the rubble and going straight next door to help their neighbors crawl out of the rubble. Families had to be dug out of storm shelters. Late into the night, shotgun blasts rang out: people killing injured horses.

After clearing the school, Blumenthal helped clear the rest of the neighborhood. His team dug people out of storm shelters, searched and marked houses, probed the piles with audio sensors, and sent in rescue dogs. He finished, again, at five or six in the morning.

The next day, he was part of the team that cleared Plaza Towers, the other elementary school the tornado had hit. Nine children had died. Their bodies had already been removed, but Blumenthal's team was told there might be another child inside, so they took the building completely apart: stripped everything down to the concrete, pulled carpets off, took walls down. After sixteen or seventeen hours, they were confident the building was clear. Blumenthal went home, slept a little, and then worked twelve-hour shifts for the next nine days in a row.

Kevin Durant was out of town—he was in off-season mode, recovering from the play-off loss—but he called the Thunder immediately to tell them that he was going to donate, unprompted, $1 million to the Red Cross. The Thunder matched that money, as did Nike. Russell Westbrook called the team shortly after the storm to say that he wanted to be out there with the people. The day after, still in a wheelchair from his knee surgery, Westbrook rolled around a children's hospital meeting survivors.

"It's not fun anymore," England told me. This was one week later, and he was leaning back in his chair, drinking a warm Sprite Zero. We were in his office, which is basically a private museum of tornado culture. There are framed pictures everywhere: old news teams, a portrait of England sitting at one of his early radar displays, a caricature of him as the Wizard of Oz ("We're off to see the Doppler"). There is a blown-up ticket to the Oklahoma City premiere of *Twister* and an image of the gloriously 1970s cover of his first book, *Oklahoma Weather*. Most of all, there are photos of major tornadoes: dozens of funnels that looked, to me, more or less the same, but which England knew individually, like children or prize farm animals. He walked me around the room, introducing me to them. Many were from May 3, 1999.

These days, England said, he still loved the process of preparing for a storm: studying the maps and the data, trying to predict what would happen, deciding how his team should handle it. But he would have been perfectly happy to live the rest of his life without seeing another tornado.

This, however, would not be possible. In fact, more tornadoes were already on the way. The computer models predicted, exactly as they had the week before, a three-day crescendo of severe storms, with the third day another possible historic disaster—another May 3 or May 20. As we sat in England's office, the storms were already brewing. His phone kept beeping, loud and shrill, to alert him that the National Weather Service was issuing severe thunderstorm warnings. He ignored it. Outside his office, meteorologists were gasping about radar images and storm chaser footage: power lines flashing, clouds lowering. England shook his head and chuckled. "The young ones," he said. Despite all the gasps and alarms, despite the rain outside that was coming in sideways, England was sure that this afternoon's storm was nothing to worry about. He was right. Despite some tense moments, the atmosphere never managed to get itself organized enough to do major damage. Although the next day was more worrisome—"I wouldn't bet a plug nickel on what's going to happen," England said at one point, an idiom that mystified his younger colleagues—that day, too, passed without lasting trauma. Which brought us to May 31.

When he left for work that morning, Gary England told his wife, Mary, that she should stay home. It was day three of the three-day crescendo, and the data did not look good at all. The National Weather Service had issued a Particularly Dangerous Situation watch, a distinction it gives to fewer than 3 percent of potential tornadoes. Even May 20 hadn't merited a PDS. The skies, for now, were idyllically blue, with fluffy clouds, but the data was clear: it was coming. If Oklahoma City took a direct hit, England told Mary, he would come back out to the house and get her.

Storms were already forming out west. Chasers all over the region were setting up, staking out positions. Many of them had hardly slept for a week. They were all watching the edges of the clouds, looking for clues, monitoring a drama that takes place silently at tens of thousands of feet: waiting for the storm to break through the cap. Unstable weather, like champagne in a bottle, wants desperately to rise. The cap is the atmosphere's cork: a layer of warm air, high up, that prevents storms from exploding through. Being held back only

makes violent storms more agitated. They test the cap constantly—probing, punching, slapping against it—creating a state of suspense that meteorologists call "explosive potential." These attempts show up as small green blips on the radar. Clouds that try but fail to break through the cap lose their crisp edges; they look like someone has run a paintbrush over them. If the cap manages to hold, things will remain relatively calm. (If there is no cap at all, the clouds shoot straight up and just make normal summer storms.) If the cap holds out for a long time, however, allowing miles and miles of increasingly unstable air to build up underneath it, and *then* it suddenly breaks— that's when the tragedies happen.

Today, the edges of the clouds stayed sharp for a very long time. "This whole area is percolating," David Payne told Gary England on the air. "They're firm, they're crisp. They look like big blobs of cauliflower out here."

Inside the Channel 9 Weather Center, there was a sense that history was preparing to erupt from the sky. The morning meteorologist, Jed Castles, strapped his iPhone to a banister to live-stream behind-the-scenes footage. A young meteorologist named Nick Bender was standing inside a hallway of screens, tensely directing the storm chasers. People were paying particular attention to the fixed-layer Significant Tornado Parameter, an index that helps predict destructive tornadoes. Serious tornadoes tend to occur when the number is higher than 1. People really start to worry when it gets up to 3. On May 20, when Moore was destroyed, the number went as high as 8. Today it was 11. There was so much moisture hanging in the air that you could see it on the radar. It was everything a tornado could ever want.

Gary England's bad feeling was getting steadily worse. Three clear storms were beginning to emerge, feasting on the moisture, moving through it, growing stronger. They were starting to organize themselves, to focus their energies and rotate, turning from normal thunderstorms into supercells. On the edge of the horizon, in front of a small strip of blue sky, one low cloud had such an unnaturally sharp edge it looked like it had been shaped by a tool. "Days when I see stuff like that are days when we see bad things happening," Payne said.

All over Oklahoma City, businesses had closed early, and people were trying to get to safety. Even at Channel 9, some employees had already been sent home. Across the city, the normally free-flowing traffic was locked. A fifteen-minute drive now took nearly an hour.

When England appeared on camera, he wore no jacket. His mood was grave. He seemed to have transcended TV news altogether—the nonsense of it, the showmanship. He struggled for a few seconds to find the right graphic to pull up on-screen, got irritated, and gave up. "Why don't you find it for me?" he said to a young meteorologist. "We've only got about seven hundred graphics there." He seemed to resent anything that stood between him and the storm.

Finally, invisibly, high above us, the cap broke. The storms gushed through. Clouds surged up, higher and higher, bubbling with new energy, and on satellite images it looked like all of Oklahoma was slowly beginning to explode.

"This is happening," Bender said.

"As serious as can be," Castles said.

"Bad things happening, simply put," said one of the chasers on the air.

"Holy moly!" screamed another, who said debris was falling around him.

Up in the helicopter, Jim Gardner's camera showed low, dark clouds massing west of Oklahoma City. They filled the screen. Gardner said he could see dirt being sucked up off the fields into the storm—it looked like a staircase, he said, rising from the earth into the sky.

A huge cloud heaved itself away from the group and hung low over I-40. A horizontal band of peach-colored light stretched between two masses of darkness. The radar screen looked like a medical scan: a terrible bright malignance, multiplying out of control. For viewers, England drew arrows to show the storm's most likely path, east and northeast. That's how tornadoes almost always moved: east and northeast. The track England traced was right along I-40, directly through the city of El Reno, and from there into OKC. El Reno was almost certainly about to be obliterated. England emitted a sad sigh. "That's an ugly wall cloud," he said, scrutinizing the helicopter footage. When he asked viewers to take tornado precautions, it sounded like he was begging them for a personal favor.

Storms rose everywhere, rotating hugely. The radar looked like an open wound. The lowerings began. The chasers started screaming.

"Gary!"

"It's touching down again!"

"Gary, a large tornado!"

"Right in the middle of my shot."

"A large tornado! Take my feed!"

"Guys," England responded, in a tone of almost disbelief at their behavior. "One at a time. One at a time."

On the radar screen, the biggest storm went purple. It was now pounding El Reno with baseball-sized hail, and it had yet to even fully reach the city. The storm chasers were all beginning to get stuck in traffic. Bender's voice trembled as he directed them. All around the storm, vast currents of air were whipping fuel back up into it at seventy-five miles per hour. The storm was sucking up even its own rain and hail. It was hard for anyone to see, firsthand, what was going on. The sky was a charcoal smear, as dark as the meteorologists' screens were bright. Although radar indicated the presence of a huge tornado, it was so rain-wrapped that no one could confirm it. The storm had lowered. It was turning.

"This thing is going to be an animal," England said. "You need to be below ground."

"GARY!" shouted David Payne, somewhere near El Reno. "GARY! Hey, this is Payne, listen! There's a new mesocyclone developing south of I-40 now! It's gonna produce a tornado! It's gonna do it here in just a minute! Oh my gosh! Look at the speed! Tornado is imminent! Tornado is imminent!"

Against a backdrop of white sky, a huge, dark wedge lowered.

Bender, directing the storm chasers, had two phones pressed to his ears at once, like a cartoon of a frantic person.

On the radar, the velocity couplet, which in a normal tornado is green and red, went purple and blue. Someone emitted a weird laugh.

"I wish you guys could see this!" Payne shouted. "This thing is *really* impressive!"

On Highway 81, traffic was bumper to bumper.

Over I-40, a funnel tried to form, but it was able to make it only halfway to the ground.

"This thing is gonna blow away anything it hits," England said.

Many of the chasers had posted themselves, by now, around the El Reno tornado. Most of them sat in the pocket of safety just to the south and the west. They crawled closer and closer, getting as near as they could, streaming footage back to the networks.

England looked at his chasers' feeds, then looked at their icons on his map, and finally he couldn't take it anymore. On the air, in front of the whole world, he scolded his two lead storm chasers.

"David and Val," he said, "you're *not* in a good position. You guys listen to me. You're not in a good position. This thing is very, very close to you. You don't need to get that close. You're in the circulation, I'm telling you." Payne responded with a hint of defiance: "It's *not moving* though. This thing is stationary."

"Let me tell you," England said. "You may think it's not moving, but it is moving. We can see it on radar."

"I'm going," Payne said, sounding sulky.

Around this time, just outside El Reno, Gordon Yellowman and the other Cheyenne elders were performing their ancient tornado ritual. Their land was directly in the storm's path. They spoke to the tornado in their language, and it answered them in a voice that sounded like fire. It told them its size: huge. The elders asked it, with respect, to turn away from their land.

This was when something unbelievable happened. The gigantic tornado, which until this point had been moving normally, north and east, toward El Reno, suddenly lurched off course.

It turned, inexplicably, south, away from El Reno.

The storm chasers watching from their pocket of safety were suddenly in the storm's path. It came straight at them. The wind grabbed Channel 4's eight-thousand-pound tornado tank, the Dominator, and ripped off its hood. It lifted a Weather Channel car and threw it clear off the road, killing all three passengers. It broke the windows of a state trooper's vehicle. As the chasers fled south, toward what they thought was safety, the tornado seemed to chase them. Emily

Sutton of Channel 4 thought she was safe, but then all around her the landscape went surging forward, shattering her car's back windshield, pelting her with debris, and her camera went dead, and everyone watching assumed the worst.

England stared at his radar screen. When he spoke, he sounded genuinely surprised.

"It's turned," he said. "A little to the south."

By this point, the storm was beyond huge. It was everything. There were funnels all over—inside the rain, outside the rain—and England was seeing velocities on the Doppler that he almost couldn't believe. The main tornado was dragging a debris ball more than a mile wide.

"The whole sky is just sitting on the ground," said the chaser Hank Brown.

"The motion is so big and so wide that it doesn't even look like a tornado," said Payne, who had managed to escape.

The mood in the studio had turned to awe. The tornado was now more than 2.6 miles wide—the widest in recorded history. There was bumper-to-bumper traffic everywhere, and England was telling people to get off the roads. "This thing is absolutely horrendous and is a threat to your life," he said. "You can't outrun it."

And yet everyone seemed to be trying. Strings of headlights spread in every direction, from Oklahoma City out into the plains. All the roads were clogged.

"It's titanic in size," England said. He seemed overwhelmed. This was worse, he thought, than May 20. Maybe even worse than May 3, 1999. He'd never seen anything this big acting this wild. How could you predict a storm that randomly changed direction? There were too many people to warn, too many roads and intersections and towns to list. At one point on the air, England said "Kingfisher" when he meant Canadian County.

Off camera, someone interrupted him: "It's looped back north."

"That's what they're saying?" England asked. He looked at the radar in disbelief. "It is moving northeast. Yeah, it is."

The tornado had turned again, this time back to its original course. England stared at the radar. He frowned. "It's oscillating along," he said, quizzically. "Kind of like a hurricane does, along the center line. In a few minutes it may drop back to the south."

But the tornado seemed to have made up its mind. After veering out of its way to miss El Reno, it was back to normal.

It was coming to OKC. Outside, the air turned green. It was as if the atmosphere were trying to become its own radar image. Huge, warm raindrops started to fall. On the map, Oklahoma City lit up purple and orange. The storm was coming. The tornado crossed I-40.

"Mother of God," Bender said. "I've never seen this in my life."

"This thing needs to just die already," said someone else.

Gary England turned and looked into the camera. "Let me talk to any kids that are home alone," he said. He spoke seriously but gently, like a children's TV host raising a very important subject. If you can't get underground, he said, put on a football helmet, long sleeves, wrap up in blankets, get in the bathtub.

Multiple cars, by now, had flipped on the interstate. The helicopter footage showed the storm's dense front edge plowing forward toward OKC—and then the city's lights went out, and darkness poured over darkness. England spoke to anyone on I-35 who might have been listening to their car radio. He told them to get out of there, get in a building or even just a ditch.

The funnel passed over I-35. It was so shrouded in rain that no one could see what was happening. It was hard to know anything about the storm at all, except that it was coming. Even at Channel 9, there was talk of taking shelter in the women's bathroom. On the radar, a debris ball showed up at the state fairgrounds. Part of the roof was ripped off the airport. A red wolf escaped from its enclosure at the zoo.

Finally, just before it reached the heart of OKC, the tornado lifted. The city was spared the very worst. But this was when the floods began. The air in Oklahoma City turned to water. An ocean seemed to be falling down, dumping itself into the streets, surging over the sidewalks, bending streetlamps in half. The wind snapped trees. Roads became rivers. Drivers were forced to climb onto the roofs of their stranded cars. Houses and businesses overflowed. The water, now, was its own deadly threat, rising to fill the places in which people were hiding from tornadoes—the ditches and culverts and basements. Through it all, England continued to talk to the people of Oklahoma City, pointing them toward safety, narrating the floods.

By midnight, although the rain continued, the tornado threats had passed. The storm had made itself fully understood. Gary England staggered out of his command module of screens. He looked depleted. He had just guided the city through the largest tornado in recorded history, plus months of rain compressed into only a few hours. I asked him what on earth he was going to do next. England looked at me for a second, with glassy detachment, as if I had just spoken to him in a foreign language. Then he said he was going to do what he always did: go home, drink a glass of wine, and eat a big plate of nachos. But he spoke without enthusiasm. "I've been eating too many nachos lately," he said. With that, Gary England walked out to the station's garage, toward the most hail-damaged vehicle I have ever seen in my life. Inside was Mary, his wife, who had come to pick him up. She had seen him on TV and could tell he wasn't fit to drive. England climbed into the passenger seat. "That's it," he told Mary. "No more." The sky had outlasted him. The young ones could have it. Without saying good-bye, Gary England drove off, through a wall of rain, into the flood.

THE SPEED OF SHADOWS

In the middle of the storm, Classen Ten Penn went dark. The sky hammered at Wayne Coyne's neighborhood until well after 4:00 a.m., toppling streetlights and trees, knocking down the Compound's front gate, sending the grinning canoe floating out into the yard. At some point in the chaos, a house down the street exploded—rumors swirled that it had been a meth lab. One of Wayne's giant foam laser hands, sitting on a disco ball in the grass, was suddenly whipped away by the wind, never to be seen again. Water surged into the recording studio, flooding drum kits and keyboards. It gushed into the main house, soaking the skull chair, overflowing the space-pod bathtub, ruining paintings that sat propped on the floor. Water filled the basement. Thor, the Chihuahua, was driven upstairs into the Compound's library, where he waited out the storm on an antique green sofa, shaking.

The next morning, Wayne and his crew gathered to assess the damage. May 21 was beautiful, calm and warm, as if the sky were apologizing. Wayne wore orange pants and tall red moonboots, and a big clump of keys jangled from his belt; he seemed cheerful and eager to work. Everyone was particularly relieved that the peacocks had survived unharmed.

Load by load, Wayne and the crew emptied the Compound's flooded basement. Everything was soaked. Out on the lawn, they unpacked it all and spread it—delicately, slowly—in the sunshine to dry. It looked like the world's least practical yard sale. There were Santa hats and severed heads piled next to the most feather boas I have ever seen in one place. There were microphone stands and drum kits and tangled cords and guitars and amps and tambourines. There were plastic bins loaded with mysterious objects that looked like giant worms and ostrich eggs. There were multicolored haystacks of tinsel. There was a pirate sword. The stuff stretched out and took over the whole yard. It looked like Wayne's entire subconscious had been vomited out into the world.

At some point during all this, a pit bull puppy wandered in through the Compound's broken gate. It was lost and ragged-looking, with no collar or tag. Wayne Coyne picked it up and bounced it in his arms, appraisingly. Storm Dog, he called it. Just like that, the Compound had another member.

Later that day, I met Wayne at the Red Cup, a hipster vegetarian restaurant right around the corner from the old Long John Silver's where he had once survived a stickup. I found him on the patio, talking, surrounded by the next generation of OKC's freaks: young people with shaved heads and ripped clothing and heavy boots and piercings—all the classic signals that they were not interested in working in the energy industry or at insurance companies, as their parents probably had. Unlike previous such generations, however, these kids were going to stay and rebel in Oklahoma City. The sun was extremely bright—the sky was continuing to act like nothing at all had happened the day before—and the restaurant's awning cast a sharp line of shadow on the pavement next to us. Wayne challenged everyone to a little parlor game. He put a stick down in the sunlight, a few inches from the edge of the shadow.

"How long will it take the shadow to reach the stick?" he asked.

For some reason everyone looked at me. I had no idea.

"Thirty minutes," I guessed.

Wayne laughed, and everyone else joined in. I didn't know if my guess was too short or too long. I'd never really thought about the speed of shadows.

"Five minutes," Wayne said.

We stared at the stick, watching the darkness glide toward it. The shadow was moving so fast that you could almost, but not quite, see it moving. It was hypnotic, suspenseful. Finally, the rim of blackness overtook the stick. Five minutes exactly.

Then Wayne stood up and said he had to get going, had to head back to the Compound, where all of his gear was still spread out on the lawn, because it was probably dry by now—yeah yeah—so he was going to pack it all away and put it back where it belonged, underground, dry until the next flood.

THREE EPILOGUES

The whole calculus of probability was discovered by
mathematicians whose real interest was the
rationalization of gambling.
—ABRAHAM FLEXNER, *The Usefulness of Useless Knowledge*

There are some enterprises in which a careful
disorderliness is the true method.
—HERMAN MELVILLE, *Moby-Dick*

BUT STILL

The Oklahoma City Thunder, the young dynasty with every success in front of it, never made it back to the NBA Finals. I'm sorry, but that's how this story ends. If, at some point in the wide Oklahoma future, the Thunder ever does make it back, it will be as a different team, with different major players, and the sparkle of youth will be in nobody's eyes. You get only one beginning, one first time, and this was theirs, and it ended in failure. Russell Westbrook's knee, after the 2013 play-offs, took a very long time to properly heal. His next season was pocked with follow-up surgeries and rehab stints. In Westbrook's absence, Kevin Durant was forced to go solo, to embrace Westbrook-style id-ball. Durant did this spectacularly well, of course, because that was the nature of his talent, even if it was not the nature of his soul. He faced a degree of difficulty that seemed almost cruel, and yet he dominated, and he was named league MVP, and his acceptance speech made all of America cry. ("You the real MVP," he said to his mother.)

For the first time in Thunder history, however, the team's regular-season record declined. It was only one win—fifty-nine instead of the previous year's sixty. But the smallest numerical difference can carry massive symbolic weight. The extra loss meant that Oklahoma City's momentum had, after those five charmed early years, measurably turned. Westbrook came back for the play-offs, but then Serge Ibaka tore his calf. Things fell apart. It was the second play-off run in a row cut short by a major injury.

Still: the following year, everyone was back and healthy. This, then, had to be the Thunder's year.

Instead, Kevin Durant broke his foot. His whole 2014–15 season was a nightmare. Surgery, rehab, return, relapse, surgery, rehab, return, relapse. A screw from one of the surgeries, it was eventually determined, had been rubbing against a bone near his ankle.

Whispers began to circulate, doubts about the competence of Oklahoma City's medical staff, doubts about the wisdom of Sam Presti and his advisers. Maybe they had been rash, people started to say, in bringing Durant back so quickly. Maybe Westbrook's lingering knee problems the year before had been the result of that rashness, too. Maybe the injury plague was karmic retribution sent, at the speed of sound, all the way from the city of Seattle. Or it was karmic retribution for the hubris of trading Harden. Perhaps the Process was a sham—maybe the Thunder had actually only been gambling all along, just like everyone else, and now they had hit their inevitable cold streak. Perhaps this bad luck was more telling than the earlier good luck had been. The years were beginning to pass. The math was adding up. The Thunder seemed to be under a plague.

I thought often, during these sad days, of my first conversation with Sam Presti, as we walked around the bombing memorial. That was at the height of the Thunder's good fortune, when the mantra all over town was "In Presti we trust" and the team had just been voted the No. 1 organization in all of professional sports, and everyone assumed it would be taking up permanent residence in the NBA Finals for the following decade. Even then, at the height of the boom, Presti had predicted that this day would come. He had stressed to me the team's incredible luck, which he'd refused to take any credit for, and said that we would see the true strength of the organization when all of that luck wore off, when the injuries and losses started to mount. At the time, standing under the wide, sunny sky vectors of October 2012, next to the bombing memorial's reflecting pool, in the center of a city that was overflowing with cheerful insanity about the Thunder and its future, this negative scenario seemed almost laughable, entirely hypothetical, impossible to imagine. But it started to happen almost immediately afterward. Presti had called it. This, too, was part of the Process.

As in a Greek myth, the bad luck got worse and worse. Even the team's weak supporting cast began to crumble around Westbrook. Ankles, knees, hands, backs—everyone's everything began to break. The luck of OKC's early years had reversed itself completely. There were games, late in the season, when the team barely had enough professional players to legally take the floor. The Thunder won only forty-five games and, for the first time since their first year, missed the play-offs. Things had been trending downward, but this seemed like the true end of an era: the golden flow of magical ascendance had congealed into khaki sludge. Key players from the triumphant early years were gone. Kevin Martin, the shooting guard who replaced James Harden, who was supposed to have been an even better complement to Westbrook and Durant, left in free agency as soon as his contract was up, after only one season. Thabo Sefolosha, the defensive specialist who kept Harden out of OKC's starting lineup, suffered a season-long shooting slump, fell out of favor with Scott Brooks, and left for the Atlanta Hawks. Kendrick Perkins, the stout veteran who was supposed to push this young team over the top, was finally traded, a few years after his value had peaked. The power of the Process was not, in the end, strong enough to salvage Hasheem Thabeet—the tallest man in the NBA, the former No. 2 pick in the draft, the player who might have solved OKC's size problem. He was dropped from the team and was soon out of the league.

In the end, Daniel Orton's heartwarming hometown NBA career hardly happened. In the summer of 2013, after Westbrook blew out his knee and the team failed to return to the Finals, Orton was cut. OKC's team would move on without its only OKC player. Orton was picked up by the very worst team in the league, the Philadelphia 76ers—a team so bad that it had begun to lose on purpose in order to win high draft picks, a strategy known as "tanking" or, to some, "the Presti method." In fact, Sixers GM Sam Hinkie, in pleading for patience from the fans, liked to use a familiar term: the Process. We have to trust the Process, he would say, over and over, until it became such a mantra in Philadelphia that the home crowd would chant it during games.

In the middle of the season, Orton was cut from the 76ers, and he would go on to travel the world in search of a viable basketball career:

China, the Philippines, Greece, Mexico, Lebanon, Thailand, Japan. It seemed hard to imagine that he would ever live in Oklahoma City again.

As the Thunder fizzled out year after year, talking heads on cable sports shows became very loud on the subject of Oklahoma City's failure. Presti's approach was all about subtlety, nuance, probability, incremental steps, long-term thinking. Now it got reduced to a cartoon sports narrative: he had been sitting on a dynasty, but he blew it by trading Harden. That trade became shorthand for every Thunder failure. Presti's Process, critics argued, had malfunctioned. It had taken too long to make obvious moves (trading Perkins, firing Brooks) and it had moved too quickly where it should have been cautious (trading Harden, bringing Durant and Westbrook back from serious injuries). The Process was supposed to be smarter and better than everyone else's way of thinking. There seemed to be a certain glee, to the critics, in seeing it fail.

Meanwhile, Oklahoma started shaking. A place that was famous for having absolutely no geography to speak of, no tectonics, was suddenly as seismically active as California. At first the quakes were small and infrequent. A novelty. Locals were amused; there were little social media earthquake parties. Over time, however, the tremors became stronger and more common. It began to seem unnatural. By the summer of 2013, larger and larger earthquakes were coming more and more frequently. Before the twenty-first century, earthquakes above a magnitude of 3.0 were basically unheard of in the state. In 2013 alone, there were 109. In 2014, there were 579. In 2015, 903. It was like the Great Annexation of underground destruction.

There was all kinds of speculation about the cause of this strange trend. Perhaps the fluctuating water levels in local lakes and aquifers, the local media reported—all those months of terrible drought followed by severe rain—had put unusual pressure on the earth's innards, forcing it to tremble.

It seemed much more likely, however, that the real cause was less

natural, and less innocent, than any of that. The real cause, sane people agreed, was the oil and gas industry, and particularly fracking.
Nothing else made sense. Part of the process of hydraulic fracturing
is pumping wastewater—all that leftover chemical slurry—deep into
the ground, at extremely high pressure. The effects of this were fairly
well known, although the energy industry wasn't eager to spread
the news, and the Oklahoma City media, as a whole, given its close
relationship with its corporate sponsors, was happy to fully explore
every possible competing theory. Even the state's official geologists
were slow to acknowledge the true cause of the quakes. Finally, after
years of denial, in 2015, Oklahoma acknowledged the truth: that this
unprecedented earthquake swarm was, in fact, self-inflicted. It was
a side effect of high-pressure wastewater disposal wells. The cost of
Oklahoma City's wealth, of its glittering downtown and its low cost
of living, was now, in part, an unstable earth.

The price of oil began to plummet, taking the energy industry
with it. Wayne Coyne became best friends with Miley Cyrus, and
their Instagram feeds became tributes to each other—marijuana,
matching tattoos, collaborative recording sessions. When Miley
hosted Saturday Night Live, the Flaming Lips appeared as her house
band. They toured together all over the world. This did not ease some
locals' concerns that Wayne was now an old rock star desperate for
new relevance. Nor did it help his cause when he was embroiled in
a scandal after posting offensive photos of his friends, along with a
dog, wearing Native American headdresses.

All of which is to say, the OKC renaissance, including the sudden
rise of the Thunder, was beginning to look like exactly what everybody denied it was: yet another boom that would go bust. Downtown's
signature Art Deco skyscraper, the First National Bank building, was
falling apart in the center of the city, and things finally got so bad
(no toilet paper, no air-conditioning) that all of its businesses went
streaming out, and it was abandoned and put into receivership, its future unclear. Another old architectural showpiece, Stage Center, was
bulldozed to make way for an alleged skyscraper, but then—just as
in the old days of urban renewal—it remained an empty lot after the
economy began to collapse. A huge puddle formed there, and people

started calling it Lake Lackmeyer, in ironic honor of the local writer and historian Steve Lackmeyer, a passionate advocate of saving historic buildings. Oklahoma City seemed to be repeating its mistakes. Nothing, apparently, had been learned from its volatile history. The Oklahoma City Boulevard, great hope of the placemakers, stalled out—the plan for it was adjusted and adjusted, and it would sit, for years, half-finished. The new front door to the city was a temporary plywood barrier. Russell Claus, the city planner, would not be there to see it: after two decades, he decided he couldn't take OKC anymore, so he went back home to Australia.

Oklahoma's ultraconservative government, after years of aggressive tax cuts, even during boom years, had bankrupted the state. Social services, mental health programs, public transportation, and infrastructure were all in various stages of collapse. The public education budget was stripped so bare that teachers started flooding out to neighboring states in search of living wages, forcing Oklahoma to patch the gaps by issuing hundreds of emergency teaching licenses and even cutting some schools back to four days a week. It was a radical experiment in anti-government governance, and it was failing miserably. In 2014, Oklahoma botched an execution badly enough to horrify the entire world. The state was becoming what it used to be: a nowhere place that occasionally erupted with very bad news, a kind of grim American joke.

James Harden, in Houston, became an absolute superstar, a perennial MVP candidate, one of the undisputed top five players in the league. The Thunder could not seem to break out of his orbit. His old locker remained empty for years—an apparently permanent monument to his absence. When the team acquired the shooting guard Dion Waiters, he requested the uniform number 13. The Thunder refused. It seemed that the organization, however much it insisted that the trade was justified, could not, in fact, get over Harden.

The Thunder's roster, meanwhile, was treading water. Sam Presti signed the Turkish backup big man Enes Kanter to a contract extension worth $70 million—far more money than Harden had asked for just three years earlier. This deal was roundly mocked. As the sports site Grantland put it: "In other words, one of the biggest mistakes in

NBA history just turned into . . . another big mistake? . . . And if this all ends badly, the 'cheap or stupid?' question of this summer could turn into a legacy for the Thunder management that's closer to cheap *and* stupid." There was very little trust left in the old motto "In Presti we trust." OKC's rise to power looked less like a method than a fluke, an insane run of luck that was now very much over. The Process had failed. Boom, along with its inevitable busts, reigned supreme.

This reached its climax in the shocking news of March 2, 2016. Federal investigators had finally caught up with Aubrey McClendon— co-founder of Chesapeake Energy, co-owner of the Thunder, patron saint of everything OKC, the Russell Westbrook of the energy world, reckless gambler, always on the edge of disaster, the human embodi- ment of Boom, simultaneously one of the richest and poorest men in America, because every bit of wealth he got he would leverage into new wealth, until it was all just basically a ladder of toothpicks reaching to the moon. A grand jury indicted him on charges of rig- ging land deals. The next day, McClendon drove his car up to the distant rural edge of northern OKC, at ninety miles per hour, and crashed—no seat belt, no evidence of braking—into the side of an overpass. His car exploded. He was identified by his teeth.

AND THEN

The Thunder limped through the beginning of 2016, looking disinterested and disorganized, impressing no one. The NBA world was, by then, fully mesmerized by the Golden State Warriors, a charismatic superteam that was on the verge of breaking, with total cohesive joy, Michael Jordan's twenty-year-old record for most wins in a season. The Thunder made the play-offs but weren't expected to go far. They had the air of a team in late middle age, a team that had missed its window. To vex everything even further, Kevin Durant would be a free agent at the end of the season, and every single NBA team was lining up to try to steal him away. The question of whether he would stay or go hung over OKC all year long.

Somehow, in the second round of the 2016 play-offs, the Thunder beat the mighty Spurs—a stronger statement of purpose and power than anyone had any right to expect. Unfortunately, the only thing this won them was a chance to get crushed by the Warriors. Almost no one gave them a real chance of winning. Making it a decent series would be a victory in itself. A good showing would guarantee that Durant would stay, and it would likely help convince another star to come join the Thunder too. That would reenergize the whole franchise, setting it up for a more serious run the following year.

Then the truly incredible happened. The Thunder dominated the invincible Warriors. Out of nowhere, the team looked like its old self—the absolute destroyer that had rolled through the league in 2012 and 2013, before and after the Harden trade, before Westbrook blew out his knee, before the tornadoes descended and the earthquakes started up and Aubrey McClendon's SUV exploded way out on the edge of the endless city. Just like in the old glory days, the Thunder were fast, long, and aggressive—too much to handle, even for a superteam. The Thunder, once again, had surprised everyone. They were now the superteam.

This version of the Thunder, in fact, was even better than the earlier one. Durant and Westbrook were older, more skilled, more mature. Westbrook was slightly more selectively crazy. The bench was better, including Enes Kanter, for whose contract Presti had been so roundly mocked. The X factor was a gigantic New Zealander named Steven Adams, a huge, hairy seven-footer with a ridiculous mustache who was beginning to look like a special player, possibly a future all-star, and the answer to OKC's longstanding lust for size. The best part about Adams, the real narrative cherry on top, was that he had been one of the returns of the Harden trade: the No. 12 pick of the 2013 draft. Once again, it seemed that Presti had found gold where no one else had seen it. Adams was beginning to become a folk hero in the way that Harden had been before he'd left—the subject of T-shirts, street art, and tribute hipster facial hair. It was, for Presti, redemption. The Thunder beat the Warriors in Game 1 largely by bullying them with size. Out of nowhere, if only for one game, OKC appeared to be a championship team.

The Warriors won Game 2, and the series moved to Oklahoma City. The city held its breath. There was no need. In Game 3, the Thunder not only beat the Warriors, they blew them out—destroyed them so thoroughly that the Warriors left the floor looking mystified. OKC, for at least one night, was finally living its greatest dream.

Between Games 3 and 4, I went out for Mexican food with Gary England. He was now settling into his retirement, but everyone still treated him like a star. "We miss you!" the other customers kept saying, to which England always replied, cheerfully, "I miss me, too." The waitress was so starstruck she sat down in the booth and made me take their picture. England and I talked about weather and his grandkids and the history of OKC. We talked about the bombing, and—right there over his enchiladas—England broke down crying. It was strange to see: England had always been professionally composed in the face of the most horrible natural disasters, but suddenly he couldn't speak, and his famous boyish face contorted, and he said that he couldn't get out of his mind that image of Randy Renner, his old storm chaser, suddenly sprinting out of the destroyed Murrah Building in terror because the cops were screaming that there was another bomb.

Outside in the parking lot, I mentioned that I had heard there might be a tornado today. He said not to worry. The air didn't smell almost like fish. And, of course, Gary England was right. The sky remained clear.

At Game 4, the Thunder blew out the Warriors again. The crowd was so loud this time it was almost scary: gladiatorial, ancient. It occurred to me that the meaning of OKC's basketball success had changed radically, for the locals, over the previous few years. It was no longer the inevitable crowning glory of the unstoppable renaissance. It was now a much more desperate thing—after the Harden trade and Westbrook's knee and Durant's broken foot and the energy industry collapse and the loss of momentum. With Durant's impending contract decision looming, it would mean quite a lot more to win a championship now.

The arena's media tables were so crowded that I sat, during the game, at an unofficial folding table back in the tunnel leading to the Warriors' locker room. I could see only about 70 percent of the floor—everything felt like total chaos, the crowd right on top of me. The usher standing next to me, directing traffic in the tunnel and managing the fans in that section, was a woman with a gold tooth named Sandra. She was like a celebrity in this corner of the arena—everyone seemed to know her. She told me she'd been doing this job for eleven years, since the Hornets had come to town after Katrina. She remembered the first time Durant walked into the arena; she looked him up and down and said, with great feeling, "You're TALL." He took to calling her "Mom" and giving her a hug after every game. I asked her where she grew up in OKC. The East, she said. She'd known Clara Luper. In fact, she'd driven Luper's children to their mother's funeral, which was held right at the convention center next to the basketball arena in 2011, just after the Thunder had lost in the Western Conference Finals, the year before they made it all the way to the Finals and the real frenzy began. Sandra was so cheerful and nice and Oklahoman that, after the game, even the few dejected Golden State fans who'd been sitting in the section—venture capitalists who'd paid thousands to fly out there and see their invincible team get crushed—came over and thanked her for being so kind. The Warriors walked down the tunnel right past me, after the game, looking furious, stunned, lost, helpless.

The Thunder now led the series 3–1. After the game, in the bowels of the arena, all of us walked around looking at one another, shaking our heads, saying very cautiously, not even believing we were saying it: This team is going to win the championship, isn't it? After all those lost years, after the Harden trade and the unlucky injuries, this is the team that's actually going to win, isn't it? We couldn't believe it. But the version of the team we had just watched for two games was, without question, a championship team. To conclude anything else would have been silly. It felt like an out-of-body experience—like some kind of magic impossible holiday had been dropped into the calendar to reward OKC for everything it had been through. The Process was finally going to come through, at precisely the moment everyone, myself included, had given up on it.

After the game, in the press room, I happened to run into Randy Renner—the man Gary England had seen sprinting out of the ruined Murrah Building the morning of the bombing. Randy now wrote about the Thunder for NBA.com. I had seen him a billion times over the years, typing up game stories and the insipid quotes the players gave us at the practice facility. He was a total mensch, unpretentious, very Oklahoman, friendly, shaggy white mustache. I had no idea, until England told me, that Randy Renner had been the first reporter into the Murrah Building, and that he'd stayed there for three days with hardly any sleep. I had no idea that he'd almost been killed by tornadoes, either. He's not the kind of guy who would bring that stuff up. Randy and I talked about how crazy all of this was—Shaquille O'Neal walking around Oklahoma City, the team on the brink of going back to the Finals, after all those years, after the optimistic narrative had curdled and everyone had given up on them. The improbability of Westbrook and Durant finally making it work, of the

Harden trade producing Steven Adams at precisely the moment OKC needed him. The eighteen thousand Oklahomans roaring in terrifying unison, stacked hundreds of feet in the air, wearing matching shirts, right in the middle of downtown. Randy said he used to cover downtown when the only reason to go there was "to get a whore." He remembered when the only thing in the state to be proud of was OU football—the joke was that someday, maybe, the college itself would become something the football team could be proud of. He could only shake his head, in disbelief and amazement, at how far things had come.

I told Randy that I'd had lunch the day before with Gary England, his old pal, and that made him happy. Gary, what a guy. Back in the early crazy days of storm chasing, Randy said, Gary used to bribe them with a case of beer for every tornado they got on tape— and suddenly they started seeing many more tornadoes. I mentioned what Gary had told me about the bombing, that he couldn't shake the image of Randy running out of the building, and Randy nodded and told me, very matter-of-factly, in a perfectly Randy way, affable and casual, about his experience that morning: how he got to the building almost immediately because his crazy cameraman was driving over medians after they heard the noise, how it was hard to do your job in the midst of so much confusion. He remembered approaching the Murrah Building from the south, where it looked basically normal, but then turning the corner and seeing the entire north side gone. His producer asked him, over the radio: Do you think anyone is injured? Randy said: I think probably there are hundreds dead. And then Randy, right there in the media room, among all of these local and national writers in their beige cubicles typing game stories and Twitter jokes—Randy Renner started crying. He couldn't speak. He apologized, trying to fight it back. He started to talk again, but only for a second. Then he had to stop.

A few minutes later, I said good-bye and left Chesapeake Energy Arena. Outside, the first thing I saw was the Devon Tower, the disproportionately giant skyscraper that sprouted out of the empty site of I. M. Pei's hypothetical supermall. The building was lit up the side, eight hundred feet in the air, with the words THUNDER UP. I walked north from the arena. It was midnight, and downtown was almost entirely empty. Despite the Thunder, despite all the new restaurants and coffee shops and the bike-share program, downtown OKC still has a particular way of feeling devastatingly barren—something deep in its DNA, the original prairie asserting itself, whispering emptiness through the thin concrete crust of civilization, the wind circulating its absence into every inch of open space. The streets get so wide and quiet, the sky seems so big and dark, that it feels like nothing has ever happened there or will ever happen again.

I walked north through the empty convention center, which had been, in the days of the Land Run, a hodgepodge of dirt alleys and wooden saloons where gunfighters gambled and brawled. I stepped back out onto the streets, past the ghosts of the old beautiful buildings that had been blown up and bulldozed during urban renewal. The Biltmore Hotel, the Huckins Hotel, the Baum Building, the Criterion Theater. I passed what would have been Katz Drug Store, where Clara Luper and the children sat on stools and defiantly ordered thirteen Cokes and were spit on and cursed at in return, but kept sitting, and so eventually desegregated the city. I passed the huge, brand-new headquarters of SandRidge Energy—a headquarters started during the boom and now stalled because the company had been forced to declare bankruptcy, and the building's bottom floor was a lavish fitness gym that no one ever seemed to use, and the company's founder, Tom Ward, was Aubrey McClendon's former partner at Chesapeake, and he was now himself in trouble with federal investigators. I kept walking north until I reached the building where Daniel Orton's mother used to work, in the zone where glass would have rained down for ten solid minutes on the morning of April 19, 1995. There was no traffic, no people. Everyone had gone home, ecstatic, unable to sleep, anticipating Game 5, when the Thunder would have a chance to finish off the Warriors and advance to the Finals for their long-awaited rematch with LeBron. Under all the surface turbulence, the Process had been cranking steadily, unglamorously along. And all your bad days will end.

WHY NOT?

The Thunder did not return to the NBA Finals. They held a 3–1 lead over the Warriors, the most dominant 3–1 lead I have ever personally witnessed in sports, and yet they lost three games in a row and, therefore, they lost the series, and I'm still not quite sure how. I remember a barrage of inexplicable three-pointers from Klay Thompson in Game 6, each less probable than the last, and I remember a peculiarly bad Game 7 from Durant, in which he looked, in the biggest game of his life, almost like he wasn't sure he wanted to be there.

And perhaps he was not. After the play-offs, Durant became a free agent. There were red flags from the beginning. He took his meetings, for instance, not in Oklahoma City, not even in Washington, D.C., but in a mansion in the Hamptons. The Celtics brought Tom Brady to the meeting, which reportedly impressed Durant very much. Oklahoma City brought only the usual suspects: Sam Presti, Clay Bennett, staffers—people Durant had spent his career with. If Durant stayed, the organization was almost certainly going to sign Al Horford, another big prize in that year's free-agency market, which would have made the team even better than the year before, an absolute juggernaut, a threat to the Warriors in every way.

But that, of course, was all contingent on the return of Durant.

Westbrook and Durant went out to dinner. Westbrook reportedly told Durant that he would do whatever it took to make sure Durant came back.

Durant, allegedly, agonized over the choice. He tossed and turned. The night before his decision, he got a crucial piece of advice from his father. This was Wayne Pratt, the same man who had upset the eleven-year-old Durant so deeply, in a game of driveway one-on-one, that he had vowed to ruthlessly control his negative emotions from that moment forward. Now, on the brink of the most important decision of Durant's professional career, his father had one piece of advice: Be selfish. Do something only for yourself.

That, Durant said, is what made up his mind. He did the unthinkable: he left Oklahoma City. He joined, unbelievably, the Golden State Warriors. The superteam added yet another superstar.

Oklahoma City was bereft. Kevin Durant, of course, had always been the one who was going to stay. That was the narrative from the beginning. He was humble and quiet, no-nonsense, rooted to the city of OKC. Westbrook was the peacock, the reckless one-man show. He would inevitably leave in search of glamour and glory elsewhere, probably in Los Angeles, and OKC would be sad to see him go but it would still have Durant, the superstar, the pillar of stability, the nice one. Now people were burning his jersey. And the expectation, then, was that Westbrook would leave, too. The team would not be good. The future no longer looked bright.

Westbrook, however, immediately signed a mini-extension to stay for two more seasons. It was exactly the declaration of commitment the city needed. The Devon Tower lit up, that night, with the message THANK YOU RUSS. Mayor Mick declared an official "Russell Westbrook Day." The Thunder held a re-signing event festooned with banners reading, WHY NOT? The narrative had flipped: Westbrook, all along, was the one everyone thought KD had been. The wild gambler was the pillar of stability. Boom was the Process.

In the absence of Durant, the Thunder unveiled a perfect new slogan, a classic OKC time tangle: "Taking on tomorrow. Today."

No one expected the team to be good, and they were not. Westbrook, however, with the spotlight all to himself, had arguably the greatest individual statistical season in basketball history. He played with what seemed like a jubilant rage and did things no one had ever done. He seemed determined to prove that *he* had been sacrificing every bit as much playing with Durant as Durant had been sacrificing to play with him. In the end, he matched one of the most sacred feats in basketball: averaging a triple-double for an entire season—

something previously done only by Oscar Robertson in 1962. Westbrook beat out James Harden to win league MVP. Durant, meanwhile, got a giant tattoo on each leg—large, detailed portraits of legendary California transplants Tupac Shakur and Rick James—and won his first championship with the Warriors. He was named Finals MVP.

Durant and Westbrook now had a grudge. Westbrook represented the people of OKC, and the people of OKC were angry. Durant, apparently, had not told Westbrook about his free-agency decision face-to-face, or even on the phone—he told him via text, and the two did not talk for many months. There were rumors, in Oklahoma City, of nefarious behavior: that KD had been texting with the Warriors all year long, even during their play-off series. That members of KD's entourage had been house shopping in San Francisco for months. That Draymond Green, after the Warriors' heartbreaking victory over the Thunder in Game 6, actually took an Uber out to KD's house to hang out.

OKC residents no doubt found some twisted comfort in knowing that Durant did not get out of their city totally unscathed. Given the general decline of the local economy, the slowdown of the renaissance, Durant had a terrible time selling his two OKC properties, and he was eventually forced to take huge losses.

But everything, finally, does come to an end, whether it feels like ending or not. In the summer of 2017, when Westbrook won his MVP award, Thunder fans found themselves in a dreadfully familiar position. Like Harden and Durant before him, Westbrook was heading into the final year of his contract. No one knew if he would be willing to commit to the Thunder again, or if he felt that he had already put in his time, that the real glory was waiting for him elsewhere. It would have been easy to argue that Westbrook had done his duty, many times over, to the people of OKC. He'd stayed, voluntarily, after Durant left. He'd helped them survive that period of heartbreak. He'd given them something to celebrate. By now, he had earned the right to go.

The Thunder, of course, offered Westbrook a maximum contract extension. But then it just sat there. He wouldn't sign. The whole summer passed. July, August. This was very bad. Westbrook is epically stubborn. He makes up his mind quickly, defiantly, and then he does what he has decided to do. There was no way he was not signing because he was waffling. That was absurd. The only good explanation was that he had made up his mind to leave. Russell Westbrook, like Harden and Durant, would choose to abandon the Thunder.

Then, suddenly, there was a twist. Toward the very end of September, as the contract situation escalated toward a crisis, Westbrook told the Thunder that he was ready. He would sign the extension. He would commit to playing the remainder of his prime years in Oklahoma City. The team, naturally, was elated. This announcement would breathe life into the city; it would cleanse so much of the bad energy left behind from the previous summer. Oklahoma City had finally been *chosen* by a superstar at his peak—a feeling it had never experienced before. The team would prepare a grand announcement for the weekend, when everyone could really celebrate. But Westbrook said no. The announcement had to happen today. He had been waiting for this day, apparently, all summer. It had to be exactly then. So the Thunder announced it, right away, on September 29. It was Kevin Durant's birthday.

ACKNOWLEDGMENTS

This book, and my entire writing career, would not exist in anything like their current form without the frankly unrealistic patience and support of many people and institutions, only a tiny fraction of which I will be able to name here. I'd like to give special thanks to Donna Uzelac, who helped teach me, many years ago, how to actually sit down and write. That was, and remains, the crucial thing.

I'd like to thank everyone in Oklahoma who took the time to speak with me, openly or in secret. Steve Lackmeyer, human archive of the history of downtown, made crucial introductions, told me what to read and where to go, and gave me a ride back out to Choctaw when my legs were about to fall off. Bob Blackburn and his wonderful team at the Oklahoma History Center—Rachel Mosman, Chad "Century Chest" Williams, Bruce Fisher, et al.—have devoted their lives to keeping the past alive; we should all give them money. Thanks to Anthony McDermid, for the grand hospitality and the long conversations, and for blending accents that otherwise would never have met. Russell Claus, for the honesty and the laughs. Bill Citty and Dexter Nelson, for the tours. Jabee, for showing me the East. Heidi "La La" Rambo-Centralla, for all of the inside baseball. Wayne Coyne, for the color. Elemental Coffee, for being my OKC office, and Café Kacao, for the motuleños. David Holt, Blair Humphreys, Ed Shadid, Patrick from the *Lost Ogle*, Mayor Mick Cornett, Ed Ruscha, Mason Williams, Harper Langston, and far too many others to mention by name. OKC's reputation for kindness is well deserved. Thank you.

On the basketball side, I'd like to thank Matt Tumbleson and his squadron of bad CIA agents, especially Michael "Alfalfa" Ravina and John "Ace Ventura" Read, for forcing everyone to talk to me. Sam Presti, Darnell Mayberry, Randy Renner, Fred Katz, Erik Horne. Justice Steven Taylor and Wilson Taylor. Daniel Orton and his grandparents. Royce and Kari Young—brave, good, funny people.

Thank you to the weather experts: the legendary Gary England and his crew (Susan Ghere, Matt Mahler, Nick Bender, et al.), Greg Carbin and the other geniuses at the Storm Prediction Center, Emily Sutton, Gordon Yellowman.

In the writing world, I'd like to thank my agent, Jay Mandel, who happened to read an issue of *The American Scholar* back in 2004 and has stuck with me ever since. Jim Catano, all the triads are for you. David Samuels was a generous mentor when I was young and very anxious. Hugo Lindgren originally sent me to Oklahoma City and gave me the perfect advice: "Don't depend on quotes from basketball players—make this your own thing." Jake Silverstein, Lauren Kern, Sasha Weiss, Mike Benoist, and a small army of copyeditors and factcheckers helped wrench early versions of some of this material into *The New York Times Magazine*. Mark Vandewalle helped me with research. Kathryn Schulz told me to start with the story of Red Kelley, which was of course correct. Zach Wagman did the brutal work of lugging the unwritten book forward, and Kevin Doughten heaved it over the finish line with spirit, bravado, and a touch of derring-do. For many months, Kevin got so deep into the vortex of my writing process that I feared for his safety—but in the end he emerged, alive, with this book, a feat of bravery for which I will always be grateful. Molly Stern smiled through all the delays. Thanks to Bonnie Thompson, for going above and beyond, and to Craig Adams and Jon Darga and all the rest of Team Crown. Jared Hohlt gave me gently brilliant editorial advice. Ella's Bellas served me quiche. Vassar Library gave me guest privileges.

Thanks to the band Deafheaven, whose album *Sunbather* played on a loop in my headphones for years as I wrote and revised this book.

On a personal note, I'd like to thank my parents, Peter Anderson and Renée Airola, for making me curious and telling me stories. Pat: I can sleep with the light on. Regan: Gonzo's nose knows. Ellen Chandler pulled me out of a deep hole and then wouldn't let me climb back in. David Rees and Jon Kimball texted me constantly. The Reis-Larsons were reliably fantastic. Steve and Pam and Wayne and Deanie and Elma have given me decades of happy support. Chad: I can answer your calls now. Alan Page: V.v.V

And finally, to Sarah, Gretta, and Beckett: look, guys, I finished my book.

NOTES ON SOURCES

The pattern for this project was set when, reading a book on my first flight out to OKC, I stumbled across the following sentence about the origin of Oklahoma's violent weather: "The state is situated in a zone where three climatic regions—humid, sub-humid, and semiarid—meet and mingle." My mind made a little leap; in the margin I wrote, "Westbrook, Harden, Durant." That very basic insight—that OKC was a place where powerful forces came together from great distances, creating crises of equilibrium—led to years of further research, during which I found similar patterns in books, newspapers, magazines, dissertations, old TV footage, blogs, comment threads, and more. I made charts and transhistorical calendars and printed out so many mountains of paper that my daughter finally begged me to stop. The book that set all of this off, on that airplane, was *Oklahoma: A History,* by W. David Baird and Danney Goble—a resource to which I returned many times.

I read the histories of the Land Run with a frequently gaping mouth. Angelo Scott's *The Story of Oklahoma City* is the definitive firsthand account, and a book that admirably reflects its author: clear, balanced, vivid, humane. Bunky's *The First Eight Months of Oklahoma City* is, by contrast, extremely colorful but obviously unreliable—a perfect match for the place itself. The king of the modern Land Run historians is Stan Hoig, whose books *The Oklahoma Land Rush of 1889* and *David L. Payne: The Oklahoma Boomer* were central pillars of this project.

Too often, OKC's history of racial discrimination has been excluded from the city's official narratives. But it is impossible to understand the place without it; you may as well try to ignore the presence of the river. In his article "Oklahoma City's Historic Sandtown Neighborhood," Ronald James Webb explores the city's early black history in revelatory detail. A more comprehensive resource is *Journey Toward Hope: A History of Blacks in Oklahoma,* by Jimmie Lewis Franklin. I owe special thanks to Bruce Fisher for helping me recognize, in the middle of my project, the crucial importance of Roscoe Dunjee—about whom I learned much from Bob Burke and Angela Monson's *Roscoe Dunjee: Champion of Civil Rights,* as well as William Sullins's master's thesis, "Roscoe Dunjee and the Oklahoma City *Black Dispatch.*" Two Ralph Ellison biographies—one by Arnold Rampersad, another by Bob Burke and Denyvetta Davis— were particularly helpful, as was *A Passion for Equality: The Life of Jimmy Stewart,* by Vicki Miles-LaGrange and Bob Burke. (Bob Burke is OKC's Boswell—look into almost any nook of the city's history and you will find him already there, peeking out at you.)

Clara Luper's memoir, *Behold the Walls,* is a characteristically spirited chronicle of the struggle for civil rights. You can get a direct hit of her voice by listening to her weekly radio show, many episodes of which—complete with East Side funeral announcements and enthusiastic ads for Wonder Bread—are available on YouTube courtesy of the Oklahoma Historical Society. No citizen has ever spoken the words "Oklahoma City" with more pride.

Residents of Oklahoma City tend to be so in love with the place that even good histories are boosterish—exercises in OKC evangelism. The only full-length biography of Stanley Draper, for instance, is also a volume of Oklahoma Trackmakers, a series of admiring local histories commissioned by Draper himself. As a result, James Smallwood's *Urban Builder: The Life and Times of Stanley Draper* is at times laughably reverential. ("Apart from his apparent lack of consideration for others, caused by his intense devotion to his job, Stanley had few character flaws or vices.") But it is easy enough to read between the lines. Humans are complex, and we do them no favors by trying to simplify them.

An essential corrective to OKC's booster instinct is Albert McRill's *And Satan Came Also,* a scandalously frank account of the city's seedier side. It is full of yarns that would have horrified the chamber of commerce, including the bloody showdown between Red Kelley and Officer Burnett. McRill's book was out of print for decades—like many people, I first read it as a photocopy of a photocopy. But it has recently been reissued with crucial annotations by the historian Larry Johnson. (Johnson's own book *Historic Photos of Oklahoma City* was another valuable resource.)

Steve Lackmeyer and Jack Money's *OKC: Second Time Around* is the indispensable account of OKC's modern history, from urban renewal to MAPS. On twentieth-century politics, I learned much from *Norick: The Mayors of Oklahoma City,* by Bill and Rick Moore. Jim DeRogatis's *Flaming Lips: Staring at Sound* was an entertainingly thorough guide to the colorful history of Wayne Coyne and his band. I devoured Blair Humphreys's dissertation "The Early Planning and Development of Oklahoma City," as well as the many other readings Blair generously passed my way. Bob Burke's biography *Friday Night in the Big Town* was an excellent overview of Gary England's life and career, as were England's own books, *Oklahoma Weather, Those Terrible Twisters,* and *Weathering the Storm: Tornadoes, Television, and Turmoil.* A key resource on the 1995 bombing was *In Their Name,* edited by Clive Irving. Much of my knowledge of Timothy McVeigh came from *American Terrorist,* by Lou Michel and Dan Herbeck. Mark Singer's *Funny Money* is a colorful and deeply reported breakdown of the 1980s bank bust. Russell Gold's *The Boom* taught me much about Aubrey McClendon and the energy industry. David Holt's *Big League City* is a deep record of the tricky machinations involved in converting the Seattle SuperSonics into the Oklahoma City Thunder.

In a relatively minor city, where global historians do not flock to document all the messy layers of the past, enthusiastic amateur historians play an enormous role. A wonderful example of this in Oklahoma City is Doug Loudenback, whose blog, *Doug Dawgz,* is a model of meticulously researched civic curiosity. His thoroughness is both inspiring and daunting—the equivalent of many books. Loudenback's summaries of key nodes of OKC history (from Deep Deuce to the Great Annexation to urban renewal and beyond) are authoritative and transparently sourced. No matter how much I thought I knew about a given subject, I always found more to learn on *Doug Dawgz*, as well as new research trails to follow.

Those trails led, most often, through the Gateway to Oklahoma History, a digital archive maintained by the Oklahoma Historical Society—a vast collection containing everything from hundred-year-old issues of Dunjee's *Black Dispatch* to a photo archive capturing the human reality of people and places that might otherwise seem only mythological.

Finally, I could not have written this book without the work of journalists at the *Oklahoman*, past and present. The paper has taken its hits over the years, but, in the midst of financial woes and political pressure, its reporters and photographers have continued to do the heroic work of capturing, for posterity, the day-to-day life of this strangely fascinating city. Every chapter of my book has been enriched by reading the *Oklahoman*'s contemporary accounts of events. Without the paper's work, millions of details would have been lost forever. Extrapolate that loss out to every other city in America, big and small, and think of all the life we're losing as we allow our newspapers to fail. I hope that, as our nation continues its struggle to become a better version of itself, we can find a way to continue to support them.

Page 224 Bob Albright, Oklahoma Publishing Company Photography Collection, Courtesy of the Oklahoma Historical Society, 2012.201.B0259.0490

Page 226 Jim Argo, Oklahoma Publishing Company Photography Collection, Courtesy of the Oklahoma Historical Society, 2012.201.B1209.0215

Page 254 Courtesy of (and with shading by) Blair Humphreys

Page 255 Tony Wood, Oklahoma Publishing Company Photography Collection, Courtesy of the Oklahoma Historical Society, 2012.201.B1004.0003

Page 260 Monty Reed, Oklahoma Publishing Company Photography Collection, Courtesy of the Oklahoma Historical Society, 2012.201.B0961.0293

Page 272 Oklahoma Publishing Company Photography Collection, Courtesy of the Oklahoma Historical Society, 2012.201. B0956.0333

Page 288 Joe Miller, Oklahoma Publishing Company Photography Collection, Courtesy of the Oklahoma Historical Society, 2012.201.B0362.0212

Page 306 Bryan C. Parker

Page 318 Courtesy of the Oklahoma Historical Society, 2012.201. B0962.0629

Page 321 Oklahoma Publishing Company Photography Collection, Courtesy of the Oklahoma Historical Society, 2012.201. B0962.0615

Page 330 Thomas Croft, Courtesy of the Oklahoma Historical Society, 23171.1

Page 368 Courtesy of Gary England

PHOTO CREDITS

Page 8   Garrett W. Ellwood, Getty Images, 145860610

Page 23   Courtesy of the Oklahoma Historical Society, 18792

Page 31   National Opinion Research Center, "Community Reactions to Sonic Booms in the Oklahoma City Area," by Paul N. Borsky, 1965

Page 62   Courtesy of the Oklahoma Historical Society, 7287

Page 65   Courtesy of the Oklahoma Historical Society, 15730

Page 77   Courtesy of Gary England

Page 91   Courtesy of the Oklahoma Historical Society, 1974

Page 94   Courtesy of the Oklahoma Historical Society, 9616

Page 95   Garrett W. Ellwood, Getty Images, 159808384

Page 100 Oklahoma Publishing Company Photography Collection, Courtesy of the Oklahoma Historical Society, 20738.N22.A

Page 133 Courtesy of the Oklahoma Historical Society, 19442

Page 140 Oklahoma Publishing Company Photography Collection, Courtesy of the Oklahoma Historical Society, 2012.201. B1156.0332

Page 145 David Thornton

Page 169 Courtesy of the Oklahoma Historical Society, Urban Builder 69

Page 178 Courtesy of the Oklahoma Historical Society, 20533.1.A

Page 198 Associated Press, Oklahoma Publishing Company Photography Collection, Courtesy of the Oklahoma Historical Society, 2012.201.B0366B.0560

Page 203 Courtesy of the Oklahoma Historical Society, 20246.38.83.9

INDEX

ABOUT THE AUTHOR

SAM ANDERSON is a staff writer for *The New York Times Magazine*. Formerly a book critic for *New York* magazine and regular contributor to *Slate*, Anderson has won numerous awards for his journalism and essays, including the National Magazine Award for Essays and Criticism. He lives in New York with his family.